The Big Book of New York Ghost Stories

The Big Book of

New York
Ghost Stories

Cheri Revai

STACKPOLE
BOOKS

Published by
STACKPOLE BOOKS
5067 Ritter Road
Mechanicsburg, PA 17055
www.stackpolebooks.com

Printed in the United States of America

10 9 8 7 6 5 4 3 2 1

FIRST EDITION

Library of Congress Cataloging-in-Publication Data

Revai, Cheri, 1963–
    The big book of New York ghost stories / Cheri Revai. — 1st ed.
      p.   cm.
    Includes bibliographical references (p.).
    ISBN-13: 978-0-8117-0455-7 (hardcover)
    ISBN-10: 0-8117-0455-6 (hardcover)
    1. Ghosts—New York (State) I. Title.
BF1472.U6R473   2009
133.109747—dc22

                                2008044905

Contents

The Adirondacks

Western New York and the Finger Lakes

Syracuse, Central New York, and the Capital District

Hudson Valley and the Catskills

New York City and Long Island

Introduction

*H*istory often comes back to haunt us. The crimes of our past leave an indelible stamp on our surroundings that current and future generations must confront and resolve, at least to the best of our ability. Consider the following examples, for instance.

Manhattan, 1799. A brutal, unavenged murder. Two days before Christmas, a beautiful woman is viciously beaten and thrown into a well at the intersection of Spring and Green Streets—a well that, many years later, would be unearthed in the basement of the Manhattan Bistro at 129 Spring Street. The victim's boyfriend is indicted by a grand jury on suspicion of murder. But his famous defense team convinces the jury that he is as innocent as the victim was suicidal. The battered body pulled from the well and placed on public display for several days tells a far different story. Yet once the chief justice deliberately stresses to the jury that the case against the victim's boyfriend is entirely circumstantial, the jury takes the hint and quickly acquits him. Public outrage forces the killer to flee the city, fearing for his life—but at least he still has a life to fear for. An apparition matching the description of the victim has been seen ever since, flitting about the neighborhood where the crime took place, so often that the Spring Street Ghost even inspired a series of paintings.

Cutchogue, Long Island, 1854. A heinous double homicide. On the evening of June 4, an Irishman named Nicholas Beheenan enters the farmhouse of attorney and retired merchant James Wickham, hell-bent on violating a young servant woman named

Ellen. A fourteen-year-old boy wanders into the hallway, catching the intruder off guard, so Beheenan strikes him in the head, nearly killing him. Mrs. Wickham awakens to the screams and implores the man to stop. Instead, he turns toward her, hitting her so ferociously in the head with his ax that her brains are splayed across the floor. Now bloodthirsty, Beheenan turns on Mr. Wickham, striking him savagely about the head and face as well, until the retired merchant and attorney is maimed beyond recognition and mortally wounded. The servants run screaming from the house, alerting neighbors to the carnage. Several days later, Beheenan is captured, convicted, and sentenced to hang for his crimes. Previous owners of the former Wickham farmhouse reported feeling cold spots; hearing unexplainable sounds, such as footsteps leading to what had been the master bedroom of the Wickhams; and seeing an apparition of a man hovering menacingly over their bed.

Brooklyn, 1897. A calculated, brutal murder. George Stelz, assistant sexton of Brooklyn's Most Holy Trinity Church, is slaughtered in the church vestibule as he descends the stairs after ringing the church bell. The poor boxes have been emptied, and Stelz's engraved watch is missing. Though he had been struck viciously in the head seven times, the cause of death is ultimately determined to be strangulation. Three days before Halloween, police arrest Constantine Steiger for killing a police officer during a botched robbery attempt at another city church. He has in his possession Stelz's watch. Steiger is convicted of murder for killing the police officer but refuses to admit he killed Stelz several months earlier, despite overwhelming evidence suggesting otherwise. As a result, nobody is ever held accountable for killing the sexton. Since then, there have been reports of mysterious footsteps pacing the floors and traversing the stairway of Most Holy Trinity in the middle of the night. The bell in the tower is alleged to have rung for no reason, and bloodstains stubbornly continue to surface occasionally on the wall in the vestibule where the murder occurred so long ago.

In each of these examples, the metaphoric Grim Reaper arrives to collect his harvest at a different time, in a different place, and under different—though invariably brutal—circumstances. Yet each victim dies at the hands of another, his or her last moments of life unspeakably horrifying. Imagine the shock to one's psyche as it is jolted from its familiar physical form and thrust into a purely spiritual realm, where it is reluctantly forced to bear silent witness to the solemn reality of its own death. It sees, in disbelief, its mutilated, lifeless body. It sees the heart-wrenching anguish of its loved ones as they learn of the person's passing. And it sees its killer getting away with murder. In light of such circumstances, how can a soul in such distress be expected to continue merrily on the journey we all must make, when every ounce of its now ethereal form is plagued by shock? Most victims of crime or tragedy may make a smooth transition to heaven, the other side, or whatever one's particular belief system calls it, but it seems that not all do. And these souls need our understanding, rather than our fear.

There may be as many reasons for a spirit to haunt a place as there are ways to die. When a cold-blooded murder occurs, as in the cases described above, a spirit may linger until its killer is brought to justice. But even if the soul does cross over to the other side, it's possible that the energy of its last traumatic moments before death may still imprint on the environment, where it remains indefinitely. Such a residual haunting would not be able to interact with the living, because there is no awareness associated with it. The soul is no longer there, but has left on the environment only a fleeting snapshot or movie clip, if you will, of a moment in its life. This phenomenon is commonly likened to a recording that continues playing long after the individual has moved on into the afterlife. It may be a recording of a mundane, routine moment in which the individual is doing something he or she did regularly while alive. Or it may be a glimpse of a pivotal moment in the deceased's life, an event that somehow had a profound impact. Most such cases seem to be a glimpse of the last seconds of an individual's life, such as the Seneca Hill Ghost running down the road in mortal fear for her life. Another common example is the victim of a fatal fall down the stairs whose residual haunting subsequently shows an apparition descending the stairs, seconds before the fateful event.

In some cases, it could be that the emotional energy expended in those final moments before death was so deeply charged by the heinous nature of the crime, or the severity of the tragedy, that it left an indelible imprint on the environment. Just as victims of unspeakable horror sometimes detach themselves emotionally from the incident, or their personality splits, or they repress their memories—all for their very survival—the psyche may splinter at the moment of a horrendous death so that the soul can adapt and move on. When there has been such an unspeakable death, it often seems to result in either a residual or a traditional haunting. Other explanations for traditional hauntings may include the individual's fondness for a place, object, or person; apparent unawareness of his or her own death; and the proverbial unfinished business.

This book includes stories of both types of hauntings, traditional and residual. Some are old, some are new; some are bold, and others are subtle. In some cases, only one or two incidents occurred at a place, and they happened long ago, but often there have been ongoing incidents that continue to this day in places that have remained actively haunted for a hundred years or more.

New York State has eleven distinct regions, by most accounts. In this book, I've merged them into six: the St. Lawrence Seaway; the Adirondacks; Western New York and the Finger Lakes; Syracuse, Central New York, and the Capital District; the Hudson Valley and the Catskills; and New York City and Long Island. Because this is my seventh book specifically about hauntings around New York State, I tapped into many of the previous places I've written about, rewriting each story to include extensive (and often incredible) additional research and updates, where possible. I've also included many new stories as well. I hope the book instills in you a greater fondness for ghost stories and, perhaps more important, a greater respect for history. Hauntings and history will always remain inherently related. Enjoy the compilation.

St. Lawrence Seaway

Seneca Hill Ghost

The most shocking tragedy in the annals of this county was enacted this morning near Fulton village, twelve miles from here, as the result of which Charles Smedley and his wife were cruelly shot down, and, after failing to kill his wife, William Cooper shot himself to death.

All that can be learned at present is that Cooper returned home from a night of dissipation and engaged in an argument over the farm property, during which he fired a shot at his young wife, which missed. Seizing her two little children, the horror-stricken wife fled to a neighbor's place, and while she lay prostrate on the ground, Cooper completed his work of destruction.

—New York Times, June 25, 1898

In *Haunted New York*, I wrote a story called "Seneca Hill Ghost," about the well-known apparition of a frightened woman, often seen running with a young girl in tow as if fleeing in terror. She has been observed many times in the past hundred years in the vicinity of Seneca Hill near Oswego. At the time of that writing, I was unaware of any documented tragedy or murder involving a young woman and child in that hamlet, and I said that nobody had been able to find a reason for the well-known manifestation. Since then, however, I've been poring over old newspaper articles now available online and discovered that quite the opposite is true. A number of tragedies and murders took place on or near Seneca Hill, including the one described above.

Seneca Hill is a small community on the Oswego River between Oswego and Fulton. The majority of sightings attributed to the so-called Ghost of Seneca Hill occur along Kingdom Road, Dutch Ridge Road, and Routes 481 (along the railroad tracks), 57 (along the shore), and 45 (near Minetto). In other words, either our lady really gets around, or there are several female apparitions haunting the region. The latter seems more plausible, because witnesses describe the ghost in a number of different ways. The most common description is of a young woman running with a little girl, both of them barefoot, terrified, and wearing nightclothes. This would coincide with the probable physical appearance of the individuals involved in the dreadful Cooper crime scene. Cooper returned home late at night and shot at his wife, and the horrified woman grabbed her children and ran out the door, down the road. They were likely barefoot and wearing nightclothes, and they certainly would have appeared to be terrified as they ran to their neighbor's house. They were, after all, running for their lives. Even though the woman and child were not killed at that time, this had to have been the most traumatic event of their lives.

As also reported in the *New York Times*, a young lady named Callista Robinson was killed by lightning on July 14, 1859, in another tragedy near Seneca Hill:

> An eyewitness describes the catastrophe as follows: The house was filled with smoke and the floor covered with plastering from the walls, and the parents almost distracted. I immediately sent for Dr. Place, who arrived in about an hour after the catastrophe. In the meantime, the youngest (aged 6 or 7 years) began to show some signs of life—but the deceased was killed instantly. She was a young lady aged about 16 years, uncommonly active and full of animation. She was struck on the head, badly burning her hair, also the sun bonnet which she was wearing. The lightning tore down the door casing, tearing it off and striking the girls, who had just ran there and clung together through fear of the terrible flashings.

Once again this was a real situation where a young lady and a young girl were reportedly running together in mortal fear of being struck, only in this case by lightning. The young woman died, and the little girl's condition was grave at the time the article appeared in the paper. The similarities between this incident and some versions of the sightings on Seneca Hill are remarkable. First of all, most of the sightings have occurred in July, October, and November. The above incident occurred in July. Second, just as in the majority of the ghost sightings, the terrified young woman was hurriedly pulling a young girl of approximately six years of age along the road, as they tried to get to shelter to avoid being struck by lightning in the severe thunderstorm. Some accounts say that the apparition they saw was wearing a bonnet, and Callista Robinson was said to have been wearing a bonnet when she died. The Robinson sisters may have been barefoot, and they may have been carrying baskets, as some of the ghost sightings have reported, depending on whether that event took place in the daytime or at night. We'll never know. But the Seneca Hill Ghosts are often seen wearing white nightclothes in Civil War–era style, and this particular event occurred just a few years prior to the start of that war, so this would have taken place during the appropriate time period.

One man said he was startled to see what he later learned was the Seneca Hill Ghost run right in front of his car out of the blue, and then into a nearby home. He asked his wife, who was sitting right beside him in the car, whether she had seen it, but she hadn't. What's interesting about this man's account is that he saw an apparent apparition running frantically down the road, then up onto a porch and into a house. And that's exactly what the news articles say occurred in the two cases described above—the horrified wife who fled to a neighbor's house, inadvertently leading her murderous husband right to the doorstep of her neighbors, whom he then killed, and the sixteen- and six-year-old sisters who ran back to the entrance of their house in a futile attempt to escape the deadly lightning.

Other versions of the Seneca Hill apparition have the woman wearing a high-necked dress and racing past them, child in tow. But one individual described the apparition he saw on Kingdom Road as a woman who was walking, not running. She, too, was wearing nineteenth-century clothing. She had pale skin, and her hair was pulled up in a bun, but she didn't have the usual wide-eyed, horrified expression on her face so commonly reported of the Seneca Hill Ghost. This individual saw the apparition around Halloween time, so he assumed it was a person wearing a very authentic costume on her way to a masquerade party. He had never heard of the Seneca Hill Ghost until he mentioned the oddly dressed woman to his friends, who then let him in on the story. Maybe it was Mrs. Warren E. Carpenter, whose husband was accused of murdering her in

1885. According to a *New York Times* article regarding that Oswego incident: "The District Attorney, becoming satisfied that he could not produce sufficient evidence to warrant sending the case to the jury, moved to discharge the prisoner. The court advised the jury to find a verdict of not guilty, which was accordingly done, and Carpenter was discharged. The prosecution was unable to prove that the woman was murdered." Thus in the case of Mrs. Carpenter, it was never proven that her husband had killed her. If he had, he got off free. And if he hadn't murdered her, then who did? These are the kinds of scenarios that are believed to leave a spirit unable to rest in peace.

One woman reported that the apparition she saw on Seneca Hill was wearing Victorian clothing, accessorized by a white bonnet and a basket. She said that by the time she did a double take in her rearview mirror, the strangely dressed woman had completely vanished, out in the middle of nowhere, where there were no houses around for miles. Maybe she had seen Anna Brown, a nineteen-year-old who was killed instantly in 1897 when she was struck by a passenger train as she drove over the railroad tracks a few miles south of Oswego.

A common theory regarding the spirit that roams Seneca Hill is that she is a mother from yesteryear searching for her daughter who drowned in the Oswego River. A mother searching in vain for her child might have left enough residual energy from such raw emotions as shock, horror, fear, and hysteria to continue to manifest a hundred years later, still running down the road trying to find her child. And there have certainly been many drownings in the vicinity of Seneca Hill over the years. One was a thirteen-year-old girl named Pearl Wilson, who drowned on June 18, 1900, along with her brother James in the Oswego River near Fulton. According to the *New York Times*, "The children were rowing across the river with their brother. Becoming frightened, they accidentally capsized the boat, and all three were thrown into the water. The elder brother clung to the upturned boat. The others were drowned."

Over the years, the river at Seneca Hill has claimed many lives. Countless other tragedies and murders that occurred in the area have been lost to time.

Francis Marion Brown Theatre

The homeless old man hunkered down in his secret hiding place in the abandoned building at Fort Ontario Park one cold winter night in the 1930s, unaware of the fate that was about to befall him. The building had no heat, but at least he was out of the biting wind and the elements. His hands were numb, his face was icy, his teeth were chattering. North Country winters are so unforgiving, especially to the indigent. The hobo pulled his knees up tight against his chest and wrapped his shivering arms around them, gathering all of his extremities inward against his torso as if to intuitively protect his vital organs, and he sat there for hours. His swollen, blue-tinged fingers and toes throbbed with unspeakable pain . . . until, after far too long, they relinquished all feeling and simply went numb. Sweet relief. Then the urge to let his heavy eyelids close washed over him. How could anyone think of sleeping in such conditions, we might wonder. But that's just it . . . he wasn't thinking. At least not clearly. His mind had become as numb as his body. For no particular reason, he attempted to stand—perhaps the fight-or-flight reflex—but his movements had become choppy, exaggerated, like someone in the throes of an epileptic fit. He no longer had control of his extremities. They failed him when he tried to stand. But he didn't care as he slumped back down on the mattress . . . his body was slowing down, he could tell. Yet he welcomed the kind embrace of unconsciousness as it swept over him. No more pain. No more pain . . .

The United States Border Patrol and the Art Association building that houses the Francis Marion Brown Theatre, also called the Oswego Players Theatre, replaced an old train station and vacant Army building that once stood there in Fort Ontario Park in Oswego. But apparently someone forgot to tell a former resident or two that the buildings they once inhabited in the flesh are no longer there— and neither are they.

Francis Marion Brown founded the theater group in 1938, and today the organization is one of the oldest continuously running theater companies in the United States. The Oswego Players believe their theater in Fort Ontario Park is haunted, and most agree that the ghost is an old homeless man who froze to death in a crawl space in the basement of what was then the train station—the place he called home. Today the crawl space is located right under the theater's kitchen. On the night the homeless man died, the secret hiding place that had so often sheltered him in his times of need had become as inescapable and inhospitable as a prison in Siberia. According to one member, whose father-in-law had lived in the neighborhood in the 1930s and readily recalled the incident, the old man's body was not discovered until spring, when nearby residents recognized the distinct, unforgettable smell of rotting flesh and followed it straight to the crawl-space hideout in the abandoned, unheated Army building. There they found his body lying on top of a mattress.

Members of the Oswego Players who frequent the building have heard strange voices, unexplained bugle calls, and doors opening and closing. They also have felt the strong presence of some unseen person in the dressing rooms. One lady saw a hanger on the door in the women's changing room swinging rapidly and then abruptly stopping. It couldn't have done that unless someone had grabbed it and held it in place, but nobody else was in the room with her at the time. Members have often reported cold spots in the building, and some have seen a shadow believed to be a ghost. It looked exactly like a person's shadow moving along, but there was no physical body casting the shadow. One member has seen the stage curtains sway as if by a breeze, even though there was no air circulation anywhere in the building. Props have been knocked over, tools have been taken, and so on. One night, as the director was stepping down from the stage to return to her front-row seat, she lurched forward, fell off the stage, and broke her wrist. Witnesses claim they saw a sudden jerk at her midsection just before she fell, as if somebody had pushed her.

It seems as if every old theater has a resident ghost, or maybe it's just that we notice unusual phenomena more when we're in a building where our primary task is to pay attention to the sights and sounds of the performance venue. The Oswego Players have told news media that they like the idea of having a ghost; it doesn't scare them. They say the amount of paranormal phenomena has decreased in recent years, but this doesn't necessarily mean that the ghost of the old hobo is gone. He may simply be lying low, trying not to attract attention toward himself, especially if he thinks people are on to him. If he didn't want to be seen or caught while he was alive, why would he would want to be noticed now?

Kappa Delta Sigma House

There is an enduring, albeit unproven, legend that a woman named Elaine hanged herself in the closet of a second-floor bedroom in the front right corner of the Kappa Delta Sigma House in Canton, and it is said that her spirit now haunts the sorority sisters' house. Though no part of that legend appears to hold any merit, there does seem to be a benevolent *someone* watching over the young women passing through the doors of 53 Park Street.

More than a hundred years ago, this historic house on the corner of Park Street and University Avenue was built and briefly occupied by Heman Matthews, an early contractor who also constructed some of the other historic village homes that have since become St. Lawrence University sorority or fraternity houses. It then began a long stint of ownership by the Hale family, which is prominent to both Canton and the university.

In 1876, Ledyard P. Hale graduated from the university and moved to Wisconsin, where he continued his studies and began a law practice. The year 1879 was a pivotal one for him, as in that year he married Georgettie Bachellor; his father, Canton resident Horace W. Hale, died; and his newly widowed mother, Betsey Russell Hale, joined him and his new wife in Wisconsin. But according to early newspaper articles, the change in climate didn't agree with the elder Mrs. Hale, so in 1881, the three returned to Canton, setting up house at 53 Park Street. Hale became the St. Lawrence County district attorney and county judge, and he and his wife raised two children, Horace C. and Irma, both of whom were born in the house. Horace eventually became a major and practiced law in Canton, and Irma married Carl F. Pfund.

Other than the busy social schedule one would expect of such a prominent family, the lives of the Hales were fairly uneventful during the many decades they occupied the home. There were births, wedding breakfasts, teas, and occasional natural deaths, to be sure, but no scandals or tragedies that would substantiate the legend of Elaine. Nobody named Elaine ever actually died in the home, as far as I could determine, although several Hales did. Matriarch Betsey Russell Hale died there while her son owned the home, in 1907. She was ninety-three years old, and the funeral was held at the house. Ledyard P. Hale also succumbed there in 1926, following a critical illness. Georgettie passed away at the home in 1935, after two months of declining health. The house was then occupied by daughter Irma and her husband.

The house finally left the hands of the Hale family when Irma sold it to St. Lawrence University's Kappa Delta Sigma sorority in 1941, and it continues to be owned by that sorority today. The October 19, 1951, issue of the *Commercial Advertiser* stated that improvements and expansion of the home made it "one of the finest of many fine chapters of university sororities at St. Lawrence." But it was that same remodeling that also may have attracted curious spirits from the past.

It is not clear when the ghost stories regarding Elaine began, but in 2002, the house historian and vice president, Megan Crowley, told me that ghost stories were part of the orientation into the sorority, so it is customary to pass them on to each group of girls who live there. She gave me the rundown of what she and her sisters had experienced, saying that she sometimes scares even herself while recounting the ghost tales.

Many girls have had the phone go dead while talking to guys, so the sisters reason that Elaine must not care for those particular guys. In other words, if Elaine doesn't like him or thinks he's no good for "her" girls, the phone goes dead. Conversely, if the boy *does* somehow find favor with Elaine, she assists in the process of bringing the young couple together. One girl was trying to send an instant message to her friends one day, but the computer screen kept scrolling down to her old boyfriend's name every time she attempted to type. Becoming increasingly frustrated, she finally decided to call her ex, whom she hadn't spoken to in quite some time, and she asked him if he was somehow tampering with her screen on his end. (It should be pointed out that the phone didn't go dead right then as it usually did when a girl was talking to a guy.) He assured her that he wasn't responsible for the computer mystery. What's more, the two decided then and there to give it another shot, getting together again, and today they are happily married. So it seems that Elaine had some divine insight that proved to be correct. Stories such as these tend to keep guys on their best behavior while visiting the house, in an often futile attempt to win the matronly spirit's approval.

Maybe the spirit they call Elaine is actually one of the Hale women watching over the girls. According to her obituary in the July 23, 1907, issue of the *Commercial Advertiser*, Betsey Russell Hale, the family matriarch, was a woman "whose whole life was an example of beautiful Christian womanhood. Hers was always to do and look unselfishly to the interests of those near and dear to her." The sorority sisters would be fortunate to have such a caring soul watching over them. Or could it be Georgettie Bachellor Hale, a woman whose "loyalty to St. Lawrence University never faltered," according to her obituary in the same paper in 1935. Though Georgettie never completed her college experience because of a health condition, she became a charter member and was one of the founders of St. Lawrence University's Kappa Kappa Gamma. Does she now watch over the sorority girls occupying her former abode? If so, the young women in residence today would surely please her by planting flowers outside and keeping fresh flowers indoors. Georgettie was a member of the Canton Garden Club and loved flowers.

The sleeping quarters at the Kappa Delta Sigma house are called the "cold dorm," because the windows are kept cracked open throughout the year to allow ventilation, so there's always a slight chill in the air. But even if the windows were closed tight, there might still be a chill in the air in the form of a cold spot, as the sleeping quarters are believed to be haunted. One of the sisters awakened to the sound of someone quietly sobbing on the bunk closest to the door one night. Talking is forbidden in that room, to ensure that there's always one silent area of the house where the girls can get a good night's sleep, so she didn't ask her distraught sister what was wrong, much as she wanted to. But the next morning, she did. Imagine her surprise when the girl responded that she hadn't even slept at the house that night and had, in fact, just gotten home. So who *was* the woman she heard crying, and whose form she saw under the blankets? The sisters decided it must have been Elaine. But since there doesn't appear to have been an Elaine in the history of the house, could it have been the spirit of Georgettie, crying over the loss of her husband, Ledyard, who died nine years before she did?

While I was there, I experienced some inexplicable phenomena as well. I was using a miniature tape recorder with new batteries and a new cassette to record the ghost stories Megan was recounting. On my way home from the visit, I played the tape and was disappointed to find that when it got to the part where we entered the room where the spirit dubbed Elaine allegedly hanged herself, the tape became very garbled, sounding as though it had been stretched and was ready to break or the batteries were about to die. Thinking that maybe the batteries were faulty, I pulled off the road and tried a couple other new ones, but that portion of the tape remained the only section too garbled to understand.

No matter who may be haunting the Kappa Delta Sigma house, everyone who has experienced something unexplainable there agrees that it's an unusually helpful, if not doting, spirit who always has the girls' best interests at heart. And that, my friends, is an undeniable Hale family trait.

Kendrew Corners

Who haunts the bridge at Kendrew Corners in DeKalb? Could it be a restless spirit from the nearby cemetery? And is this phantom responsible for the countless accidents, near misses, and bizarre sightings at that location?

One fateful, foggy night in 1982, a Riley sports car traveling at about twenty-five miles per hour approached the bridge at Kendrew Corners heading toward Ogdensburg. Suddenly, out of nowhere, a debonair middle-aged man wearing a bow tie, white shirt, and black cape appeared, stepping directly into the path of the slow-moving vehicle. At the moment of impact, he looked the twenty-year-old driver square in the eye, showing no concern, no surprise—nothing. The driver of the Riley, on the other hand, stared in horror as the imminent event unfolded. He braced himself and instinctively raised his forearm to protect his face, expecting a body to fly up onto the hood or windshield of his car. Instead, the man he struck fell straight backward—impossibly straight. Expecting the worst, the young man jumped from his car. But the stranger in the road was gone. After a frantic search of the roadside and surrounding grounds, the young man raced to his father's house. *Was he losing his mind?*

He was white as a ghost when he blurted out to his father that he'd just hit a guy near the bridge but couldn't find him anywhere. In an instant, his father was back in 1955, reliving an identical experience he'd never told his son about. The repressed recollections suddenly fresh in his mind, he asked his son if the man had been wearing a cape and bow tie and looked as though he were coming from a costume ball. The young man was speechless—it was as if his father had been with him and had seen the same thing. This was partly true. His father *had* seen the same thing . . . twenty-seven years earlier. He had been the same age as his son, and at the same exact location, when he and his friends encountered the phantom of Kendrew Corners. And like his son, they were unable to find any trace of the man they hit.

In 1955, the father, then twenty years old, was driving a 1947 Chevy convertible about twenty-five miles per hour, on account of the fog, as it crossed the bridge at Kendrew Corners on Route 812. He and four friends were on their way to a dance in Hermon. Suddenly a man dressed in a ritzy outfit from the 1920s or 1930s appeared out of nowhere in the middle of the road. There was no time to for the driver to react. The five young people in the Chevy stared wide-eyed at the man as he hit the car and fell back, straight as an arrow. They jumped from the car with flashlights, expecting the worst, but the man was gone. There was no sign of him anywhere—no mark on the car, no footprints in the soft earth on the side of the road to indicate the pedestrian had run off into the woods. Just to be sure, they searched the woods too, but still found nothing.

They had all seen him, they agreed. He seemed to purposely step out in front of the car as it approached, before turning to look straight at the youngsters, coolly, as if he'd been waiting for them. They would never forget what he looked like, how strangely he was dressed—and yet, he was gone.

Bewildered, the youngsters analyzed each second of the ordeal. Though they had seen the man hit the car and go down, they never felt or heard the thud of his body against the car. They watched him fall straight backward in complete and utter silence, even though they knew he should have been thrown up onto the car or slumped over the hood, since they were going so slow when he was struck. Then it dawned on them: they must have hit a ghost. Opting not to go to the police, for fear of being mocked, they instead waited several agonizing days to see if anyone was reported missing, injured, or even dead in the area, especially near Kendrew Corners. As they expected, no such report was made. Not in 1955 . . . and not in 1982.

The odds of two members of the same family experiencing the same chilling, unexplained incident at the same age and same place twenty-seven years apart were astronomical. But apparently it happened.

If two generations of the same family saw the phantom, how many others have seen it over the years? One woman who lives in the vicinity told me that when she was a teenager, she saw a man dressed similarly walking down the road past her house on Route 812 in broad daylight. The stranger's appearance was so unusual and out of place that she ran to the barn to get her sister, but when they came back out to look, the man was nowhere in sight.

The bridge at Kendrew Corners, five miles from Heuvelton, has been the scene of countless accidents, some fatal. And we'll never know whether some of the victims swerved to avoid hitting something standing suddenly in front of them at the bridge—like a man who has a habit of disappearing quickly. There was a fatal accident a few years before the 1955 phantom sighting and another tragic accident a year after it. In 1951, a horrific accident claimed the lives of three young men, ages seventeen, eighteen, and twenty-four, when the 1949 Chevy pickup they were driving struck the bridge's concrete abutment. The driver's disappearance from the scene of the crash led to speculation that he had wandered off somewhere, the victim of amnesia. But his body was discovered several miles downstream in the Oswegatchie River four months later, effectively ending that mystery. Five years later, in 1956, a forty-two-year-old former Ogdensburg man struck the guardrail at the Kendrew bridge and died after being thrown from the vehicle.

We may never know who the phantom at Kendrew Corners is, or why he chooses to prey on cars carrying young men on foggy nights. All we can do is slow down as we approach the bridge, so we don't lose control—and pray that a caped man doesn't suddenly appear in front of us before it's too late to stop.

Pine Grove Cemetery

Joan and Blake Szarka were strolling along Pine Grove Cemetery's winding paths one balmy summer evening, when the wind suddenly picked up, and their dog halted and began to whimper. Just as a chill shot through Blake, they heard someone behind them hiss, "Turn around." Without looking back, the frightened couple made haste to the main gate and out onto the safety of Beach Street, more than a little shaken.

At the time of the incident, they had been discussing one particular tombstone—that of a man named Dragon Obretenoff, who was killed in 1949 when a hunter allegedly mistook him for a deer and shot him in the face and chest. The Bulgarian native was a well-known restaurateur who owned Wimpy's Diner and the Pine Grove Restaurant in Massena at the time of his death. He was also a well-known womanizer, a fifty-two-year-old single foreigner with a penchant for the ladies. Now the man who once publicly professed his love of the Massena area is buried in a plot to the left of the mausoleum at the rear of the cemetery on a downhill slope. His modest tombstone simply says, "Dragon Obretenoff, 1897–1949." Joan and Blake had been wondering about him as they walked past his tombstone, knowing that he had been shot and killed, but unaware of the specifics of the incident. They were discussing various theories when they heard the slow, menacing command to turn around, leading them to wonder whether the voice had anything to do with Dragon or his tragic fate.

Pine Grove Cemetery in Massena is a classic garden-style cemetery common to the Victorian era. Built in 1872, it features majestic old pines, winding paths that are paved and wide enough for one-lane traffic, an abundance of trees, and hundreds of gravesites, all incorporated harmoniously into the hilly landscape. There is only one entrance—a tall, wrought-iron arch that many people say they have been relieved to see from the inside of the cemetery, when they were trying to get out in a hurry!

Joan's chilling encounter with something at Pine Grove was the first story I had heard regarding that particular cemetery, and I included a more detailed account in *More Haunted Northern New York*. But around midnight one night a couple years ago, when I was still awake with my daughter Jamie, we saw a car stop in front of our house, and a man got out and walked briskly toward my front door. I went outside and asked if I could help him (a little too trusting, even for me), and it turned out that he was a policeman with an unmarked car. He told me there had been a burglary in the area, and some of the contents from the glove compartment of my car had been strewn about the road, so he wanted to let me know that I could claim my items at the police station after the investigation. But while he had me there, he said, "Hey, aren't you the one who writes the ghost books?" When I admitted I was, he proceeded to tell me about his partner's experiences at Pine Grove Cemetery. So there we were, in the middle of the night, in the middle of the winter, in the middle of my front yard talking about yet another local haunting, as Jamie stood beside me, grinning and shaking her head. She knows too well the life of a local ghost author.

The policeman told me that one night, when his partner was on patrol with another officer, just as they approached the vicinity of the entrance gate to Pine Grove Cemetery, their radio frequency scrolled all the way up and all the way down erratically. It returned to normal as they left the area. When the officers returned to the station that night, they told the others about the anomaly, and everyone down at the station got a good chuckle out of it, not really believing the two until another pair of officers on patrol in the vicinity of the cemetery had the same thing happen to them.

In 2005, the Shadow Chasers, paranormal investigators from the Potsdam area headed by founder Phillip Creighton, made their first of several visits to Pine Grove Cemetery. Phillip and his team set up all of their equipment for a full investigation, and then paired off into two groups that went in different directions. Shortly thereafter, two cops showed up on their routine cemetery patrol. They didn't realize they were walking into a ghost trap of sorts. The paranormal investigators had set up a digital voice recorder (DVR) with the audio amplifier on a tripod toward the rear of the cemetery, where Dragon is buried and most of the activity seems to occur. The contraption allows one to pick up, via earphones from some distance away, any ghostly chatter that might take place near the DVR. But instead of ghostly chatter, they heard the police officers surrounding the device, which looks like a little, transparent satellite dish, asking each other what it was. As they leaned in closer, their faces were practically in the amplifier, so Phillip read them loud and clear and was probably stifling a grin as he made his way back toward the curious cops.

After he explained that they were paranormal investigators, and hence the fancy equipment, one of the police officers said, "You should be here at 3 A.M. if you want to catch something." He then relayed the same story I had heard in my front yard that night not long before. Furthermore, as the officers were leaving, one of them admitted to seeing "shadow people" darting about the cemetery. It wouldn't be long before the investigators witnessed the phenomenon for themselves.

Every member of the Shadow Chasers experienced something unusual that night. The freshly charged batteries on the camcorder died instantly, much to the dismay of the cameraman. Then when two members were joking about the *Ghost Hunters* television series, saying how funny it is to see the cast literally chasing—as in running after—ghosts, all of a sudden they both heard a loud "psst" in their ears. At the same time, Phillip's static monitor made the same sound at full power. Other members of the group heard the sounds of someone running after them, and two members reported becoming nauseated—often a sign of exposure to high electromagnetic fields, which could indicate the presence of spirit energy. All the members of the group, in fact, experienced some degree of nausea, but the investigation went on.

Phillip was looking toward the end of the road at the back of the cemetery, at an area lit by a streetlight on the corner, when his attention was drawn to the street lamp itself. It seemed to be pulsating between bright and dim. As he drew closer, he saw what appeared to be the silhouette or shadow of a person, but there was no actual person anywhere in sight that could cast such a shadow. His shadow person suddenly darted from under the light toward the cemetery, and as it did, the street lamp brightened again. Phillip summoned another member to the area just as the shadow returned. Both watched, transfixed, as the figure darted to the light and away again, as if toying with its audience. Then they noticed that the bulb had obviously been recently replaced, because the bulbs on nearby street lamps were yellowish, while this one was bright white—except when the ghost was under it, at which time it dimmed. Whatever it was made a swishing sound as it darted continually past them. Not only did it appear to be feeding off the electrical energy of the street lamp, but considering the group's nausea, it was quite possibly feeding off each individual's energy as well. In fact, the longer they stood there watching it, the faster it became. It seemed to be what was causing the street lamp to flicker and dim and the investigators to feel sick.

Phillip's group had enough personal experiences at Pine Grove to confidently say it is haunted. They also have audio evidence, as well as some amazing photographs, including one taken right next to Dragon Obretenoff's stone. It shows what appears to be an apparition of a man walking toward the road from the gravestones. The misty anomaly in the photograph reveals what looks like the side angle of a man's upper and lower body. Perhaps it's the elusive Pine Grove shadow person captured by the only means possible— on film. Or maybe it's the spirit of poor Dragon Obretenoff. Whatever it was, at least it didn't dare the investigators, or the local police, to "turn around."

LeRay Mansion

About 155 years ago, a farm manager shot and killed a man lurking in the early-morning mist on the grounds of the James LeRay family farm at Fort Drum. When questioned by the police, he said he was hunting and thought it was a red fox he was shooting at, but it turned out to be an apparent trespasser on the property. The tragedy was deemed an accident, and the farm manager was off the hook. It is thought, however, that in reality, he had encountered an unfamiliar person hanging around the entrance to the mansion and was leery that the stranger intended to break in. Without conscience or even a word of warning, he fired once, killing the man. Thus nobody ever learned why the man had arrived on the estate. At any rate, one would think that the ghost associated with that incident would be that of the murdered man, but instead, they say that it's a phantom *fox* that is seen on foggy November mornings, trotting across the field. There are, however, other spirits haunting the mansion, according to a number of people who wish to remain anonymous.

A security guard told Specialist Travis Burnham of the 27th Public Affairs Attachment that while patrolling the grounds, he had seen mysterious figures in the house, but he has never found an actual person there to explain the phenomenon. Others, according to Burnham's article in the *Fort Drum Blizzard Online*, have heard baffling footsteps and found that furniture had been somehow moved during the night when nobody was in the house. A sudden, overwhelming sense of fear has gripped more than one individual. A woman named Anne who works in the Office of Cultural Resources wrote an article called "The Slightly Haunted LeRay Mansion at Fort Drum," which told of a brief visit to the cellar of the mansion in search of its alleged ghost. Though the visitor didn't find anything definitive to corroborate the ghost legends associated with the mansion, she did admit to having a funny feeling the last two times she was in the basement. And sometimes that is all we get when our sixth sense becomes alert to the possibility that we're in the company of a ghostly visitor.

In the late 1700s, Count James LeRay de Chaumont, whose father was a French nobleman who helped finance the American

Revolution and befriended Benjamin Franklin, purchased more than six hundred thousand acres of land in northern New York to sell in parcels to immigrants, thus ensuring his family's fortune. Construction of the LeRay Mansion at Leraysville (now Fort Drum) began in 1826, after the first LeRay home there burned to the ground.

According to the Cultural Resources Department of Fort Drum, the LeRay property was originally a formal estate combined with a model farm, with much more than what now remains. When construction was completed, in addition to the mansion, the property included servants' and farm manager's quarters, farm buildings, a large barn, chapel, icehouse, park, land office, and French gardens. Today, besides the mansion, only the land office, icehouse, and servants' and farm manager's quarters still stand. It was from the quarters of the farm manager that the shot rang out through the morning long ago, when the man claimed to have mistaken an intruder for a fox.

The only member of the LeRay family buried on the property was James LeRay's granddaughter Sigit, the daughter of Therese de Gouvello. Sigit was just fifteen months old when she died at the estate. The heiress toddler was buried near the formal pond, across the field in the forest, and her tombstone stands alone in the woods of the LeRay property. Although hers are the only remains buried there, she was not the only person to have died naturally on the grounds. The LeRays owned the mansion until 1840, when it was sold to the Jules R. Payen family. Mrs. Julia Phelps, the daughter of Jules Payen and widow of William Phelps, died at the mansion in 1912 at the age of eighty-four. She had been just twelve when her family moved from France to the area and purchased the mansion, so she lived there almost her entire life. Her husband predeceased her around 1882. Their granddaughter Mable Anderson was then the only surviving family member of the Phelps family, and she was still living at the mansion the late 1920s.

By 1935, Leraysville had become Pine Camp at Pine Plains, and the LeRay Mansion was being used as commander's quarters. Today the mansion and the servants' and farm manager's quarters serve as visiting officers' quarters. The Directorate of Community

Activities manages the property and holds formal events and celebrations of a military nature there. The Department of Cultural Resources and Directorate of Community Activities work together to preserve the LeRay Mansion, which was placed on the National Register of Historic Places in 1974.

Murphy Residence

Imagine the shock of going out one weekend night and arriving home to find your yard filled with fire trucks and your house destroyed by fire. As you get out of the car, numb and speechless, a distraught fireman approaches, saying, "We're very sorry. We were not able to save your grandmother." That's what happened to Fred and Diane Murphy of the Baxterville area one night back in 1991. But it's hard to say who was more shocked, the couple or the fireman, when he told them of the grandmother and they replied that there *was* no grandmother living with them. Nobody had been home at all on the night of the fire. Yet the fireman insisted that he and several others had seen an elderly woman in the upstairs window screaming. They saw her so clearly that they could describe her clothing and hairstyle in detail. She had her gray hair in a bun and wore a polka-dotted dress, and she was banging hysterically on the windowpane. Because of that very clear image, the firemen made it their first priority to get to that room and save the woman, but when they got there, she was nowhere to be found. They believed their frantic efforts had been for naught.

I later found out, after mentioning this house in *Haunted Northern New York*, that one of the firemen actually quit after the double shock of first seeing a woman consumed by flames and then learning that it was a ghost. A firefighter's wife told me that when her husband was following another fireman down the stairs after not being able to find the elderly woman, he was stopped in his tracks by something he couldn't see. It was like a force field on the stairway that he couldn't pass. He watched the other firefighter continue on down the stairs, but he had to call out to have the man come back up and help him get past whatever the invisible obstacle was. It was a night the local firefighters would not soon forget; nor would the Murphys.

The ghost in the fire was the talk of the town for a while, especially because it's so rare for a group of people to witness such a startlingly clear apparition at the same time. A few weeks later, a controlled burn was conducted to eliminate what remained of the structure, because the Murphys had decided to rebuild on the property. They took photographs of the second fire and were shocked when one showed an image of a woman in the same window where the firemen had seen the elderly lady. She appeared to be looking sadly down at them, but they hadn't caught even a glimpse of her at the time they took the photograph.

Three months before the fire, Diane had been doing some research on their old, red brick farmhouse on West Hatfield Street. Baxterville is a hamlet of Norfolk, but it is in close proximity to the town line of Massena. Diane found out that the early occupants of the home were notorious womanizers, gamblers, and brawlers. At the time Diane was beginning to think their house was haunted; that might have explained a bizarre phone message she received one day. Their answering machine at the time flashed once for each message received, but that day she returned home from work to find it flashing repeatedly, indicating the message limit had been reached. The machine ordinarily allowed only one minute for each message before cutting off the caller. But when Diane pressed the playback button, she was stunned to find one long, disturbing message taking up the entire memory. It was a confrontation between a couple. At one point, a woman's voice cried, "It's all your fault I'm pregnant!" This was followed by a man snarling at her to shut her mouth and the sound of a loud slap. The sobbing woman said, "I can't take it anymore." Thankfully this was an isolated incident, and the machine never again recorded one message that took up the entire memory. Diane said it was as if someone had been in the room using whatever means they had available as a recording device—perhaps trying to relay a message from beyond.

Diane also learned that there had once been a trapdoor in the basement that led to a first-floor room that was accessible only through the basement, suggesting that it had been put to good use during Prohibition. The Murphys had lived in the old house for nine years and had never seen a secret room, but Diane couldn't get the possibility that one existed out of her mind. In the basement, they noticed a possible trapdoor that had long since been hidden by piping and wires. When Fred was away on business for a few days, Diane resolved to tear down the wall by herself where she thought the room must be. She took a hammer to it, and sure enough, there was a closet-size room that could easily have served as a little whiskey stand. Though no signs remained of what once had transpired in that space, at least Diane knew the room existed, so she was happy.

Fred, however, was not happy about coming home to such a mess, and there was apparently a disgruntled spirit that wasn't very happy with the sudden renovation and discovery either. Diane said that after she tore down the wall, all hell broke loose, meaning that paranormal activity increased decidedly. One day when she went home for lunch, she cleaned up some items the rest of the family hadn't put away before leaving that morning. Someone had left a coffee mug on the counter, so she grabbed it to put it in the dishwasher. But even though nobody had been home for several hours, the mug was too hot to handle, so she set it back down, baffled. Half an hour later, before she went back to work, she again grabbed the mug—which should have had plenty of time to cool off by then—but she found it was still too hot to hold. That night when she got home, the mug was back to room temperature.

After the controlled burn of the house, the basement was filled in with topsoil, and a beautiful modern home was built slightly behind the site of the original house. No trace remains to indicate that the old red house had ever been there, and the Murphys hope the spirit—or spirits—have moved on as well.

Tau Epsilon Phi House

Clarkson University's Tau Epsilon Phi fraternity house sits proudly atop a hill at 209 Sissonville Road in Potsdam. The hundred-year-old white house has aged gracefully. But like many long-standing structures owned by prominent families from an area's past, it has acquired its share of sordid legends—and they *are* just legends—along with the requisite ghost story or two.

Legend: A salesman was found brutally murdered in his guest room, the door to which had been locked on both sides to prevent the visitor from robbing the wealthy Sisson family. The ensuing investigation found footprints believed to be the killer's in the snow leading from the house to the garage, but there was no return set of footprints, so the killer got away.

Legend: A desperate Sisson daughter hanged herself in her wedding gown the night before an arranged marriage was to take place. The story goes that her family had arranged for her to marry her uncle to keep the Sisson wealth in the family, very much against the young woman's wishes.

Legend: A hired hand now dubbed Otis was involved in a tunnel collapse beneath Potsdam. (*Legend within a legend*: Some of Potsdam's most prominent families built tunnels connecting their homes and properties to smuggle alcohol around town during Prohibition.) Knowing that their loyal servant would not live long, the Sissons granted his wish to be allowed to die "like a king" in their master bedroom suite.

Legend: Some of the Sisson children born in the house long ago had varying degrees of birth defects as a result of intermarriage between relatives. The children were shunned by their own family and allowed to roam through the tunnels. To avoid publicity when they died young, they were buried in the family's own graveyard behind the house.

Now here's the real story. A settler from Vermont named Samuel R. Chandler purchased the property in question from Lord Clarkson in 1811. He ran a farm there for many years, and then passed it on to his son John. In 1886, a young schoolteacher named George W. Sisson Jr. purchased the property from John Chandler.

The twenty-five-year-old Sisson married Mary Howes of Gouverneur the following year, and the newlyweds immediately moved onto the property. Eventually they purchased more acreage for their farm, securing some seven hundred acres total. In 1894, they tore down the old farmhouse to make way for the beautiful white Victorian that stands there to this day. The Sissons' estate, Hillview Farm, was famous for its cattle. George Sisson's passion was cattle breeding, and his Jersey cattle, known as the Sisson herd, won awards throughout the eastern United States. More important, each cow yielded four hundred pounds of butter per year—double the typical yield of cattle in New York State at that time. In this way, the Sissons enjoyed great prosperity. Sisson Jr. was also a past president and chairman of the board of the Racquette River Paper Company up until the time of his natural death.

George and his wife had five children, two of whom died young. Their first child, daughter Emma Howes Sisson, died in 1893 at just five years old, and their third child, the first George Wing Sisson III, died when he was only ten months old. The other three children went on to live long, happy lives. Marian Grace Sisson married Frederick B. Weed of Albany, Stanley Sisson eventually moved to Paris, and the second George Wing Sisson III remained in Potsdam, following in his father's footsteps. So the truth is, no family members intermarried, and no Sisson daughter hanged herself in a closet. To drive this point home, the following 1902 article from the *St. Lawrence Herald* gives an idea of the kind of normal existence the Sisson family enjoyed in their years on the Sissonville Road, as opposed to the sordid fictitious picture that has been perpetuated over the years:

> About forty friends of Mr. and Mrs. George W. Sisson, Jr., gathered at their pleasant farm home Tuesday evening for a husking bee. Eighteen went on a load of hay, and the others in private convenances. Antique costumes were in fashion. All enjoyed a pleasant evening, husking corn and cracking jokes, after which a sumptuous farm supper was served, followed by farewells and a jolly ride home. It was a very pleasant affair.

With that said, even though the often-told legends appear to hold no truth, the ghost stories about the fraternity house are taken very seriously. It seems clear that someone has been haunting the Tau Epsilon Phi house. The question is, who? We know that the two young Sisson children died there of maladies common in the late 1800s. They most likely were buried properly, since the Sisson family was an upstanding, law-abiding family. I'm not sure whether anyone else ever died in the home, but I'd need to do further research to determine that. Of the Sisson family, however, I do know that only little Emma and George Wing III died there. Mr. and Mrs. Sisson lived until a ripe old age at Hillview Farm. Mrs. Sisson died in 1953 at the age of eighty-four at the Dunlop Sanatorium in Madrid, where she had been a patient for four years, alongside Mr. Sisson. Services for Mrs. Sisson were held at Hillview Farm, now the Tau Epsilon Phi house. Mr. Sisson passed away at the sanatorium the following year, when he was ninety-two years old.

Four years after their father's death, the three surviving Sisson children sold the house to Alden Fitzgerald, who held cattle auctions in the barn while running the dairy farm. Because of financial problems, Fitzgerald remained there for just three years. In 1966, a Clarkson professor bought the house, but when he was fined for swindling, he was forced to sell the house and move out, according to the fraternity brothers. In 1968, Tau Epsilon Phi purchased the gorgeous old house for $31,500. It was renovated to consist of fourteen bedrooms on the second and third floors and six more bedrooms in the annex, for a total of twenty bedrooms. In a hundred years, it has gone from housing a family of five to a brotherhood of forty-four. With that much renovating, it would not be surprising if the house really is haunted. And like the members of most fraternities and sororities, the brothers of Tau Epsilon Phi love to share the stories they've either experienced firsthand or heard over the years.

The Frying Pan Room, so named because of the heat the east-facing bay window generates on a sunny day, is where a Sisson bride-to-be was said to have tied one end of a rope around the bulb socket in the closet and the other end around her neck, stepped off a chair, and hanged herself right there in the closet. She is called the White Lady. As with the purported murder of a salesman, if such a tragedy had occurred, it would have been reported in the local newspapers, but it wasn't. Nevertheless, for whatever reason, people really do feel an almost suffocating feeling as they stand near the closet door, and they can't help but reach a hand up around the neck as they contemplate the alleged hanging. The brothers say that animals, dogs in particular, are afraid of something at the closet door. They look at it and growl, or run away yelping if forced into the closet. Today the whole gruesome scene of the alleged tragedy is acted out for the annual Halloween Haunted House that the Tau Epsilon Phi brothers hold for charity. (I wouldn't want to be the girl standing on a chair in that closet all night!)

The White Lady has also made an appearance in the Tent Room, a small room with sloped walls. (Each room of the house has a nickname.) One unfortunate brother in the early 1990s awakened to see what he described as a lady in white standing at the foot of his bed, jutting out halfway through the wall. She solemnly told the student what day he would die. Understandably, it disturbed him so much that he immediately packed up and left the house for good. He graduated from Clarkson in 1993 without ever telling another soul what "death date" he had been given. Also in the Tent Room, a child has been heard laughing or playing, especially when a girl is visiting one of the brothers. Could it be the ghost of little five-year-old Emma Sisson?

One night, some of the brothers had drawn a pentagram on the third floor with chalk. They were quickly rewarded with frightening unearthly sounds and took off running down to the Frying Pan Room. It gives new meaning to the phrase "Out of the fire and into the frying pan"! In this room, they again heard loud noises and watched in horror as a Led Zeppelin wall hanging arched out from the wall like a parachute. They claim that books on the bookshelves then began popping out randomly. It seems they had to learn the hard way not to dabble recklessly in the occult, which some believe can attract unwanted negative energy and spirits. And that may explain the paranormal phenomena occurring there better than any rumor about the Sisson family.

The Chancellor's Suite is so-called because it's believed to have been the master bedroom suite of the "leader" of the house, who was once George W. Sisson Jr. (along with Mary). This is the room where it is said Otis asked to die like a king. When television sets throughout the house mysteriously change channels and video-cassettes go flying across the room, everybody blames Otis. After all, if the king doesn't like what's playing, he can have whatever he wants! Otis has also been blamed for haunting the basement, where the sound of someone playing pool has been heard by more than one individual. The brothers who have heard it were surprised to find the lights off and the balls still moving on the pool table when they've gone to investigate.

There was also once a report of an ex-chancellor being awakened by the annoying nudging of a small boy, who looked him squarely in the eyes and asked, "Do you want to play?" Then he vanished into thin air. Another resident in the house alone during winter break heard voices coming from one bedroom, but when he checked, the door was locked, just as it had been left. When the voices continued, he ended up calling the police to search the house and find the source of the voices. They even brought a dog to sniff through the house but came up empty. When the room's occupant returned from break, the door to his room was wide open, even though the brother who had been staying there alone, and the police who had searched the house, left it locked as it was.

Suffice it to say, there seems to be an awful lot of paranormal activity occurring at the house on Sisson Hill. The legends of the Sisson family may have been debunked, but too many people have experienced too many unusual things to dismiss the ghost stories. Based on the experiences of many people, the Tau Epsilon Phi house really does appear to be haunted.

Harison–Morley Grist Mill

Charlie LaShombe had stepped away from the Harison-Morley Grist Mill in Morley for a moment and was just heading back to the work site when he saw his carpenter, Jeff, running breathlessly up the road toward him. He knew something had to be wrong. It was the middle of a nice, sunny day. So why did Jeff look as if he had just seen a ghost?

The Harison-Morley Grist Mill was named after a prominent local landowner, Thomas Ludlow Harison, who had the mill built in 1840. The stone from which the mill was constructed came from Harison's own quarry in Morley. Daniel McKenzie, a native of Scotland, moved from Canada to Morley to do the ironwork on the mill. He eventually settled in the area after being issued his naturalization papers in 1844. The first operator of the mill, handpicked by Harison, was Rufus K. Jackson, who was charged with the daunting task of grinding grain into flour and meal around the clock from late summer through the winter season. Then McKenzie, the Scottish blacksmith, twice married with fourteen kids, took over. Local newspapers of the time called him "an interesting man."

William Newby was next at the helm. In his 1933 obituary, the *Commercial Advertiser* said that Newby had "acquired an interest in the stone feed mill near the bridge with A. J. Bartholomew" in 1903. The partnership ended three years later, leaving Newby the sole owner and operator of the mill for the next sixteen years. In 1919, the sixty-seven-year-old Newby retired, and his son-in-law Leland Freeman briefly took charge of the mill. But Freeman was a teacher by trade, not a mill operator, so in 1922, Earl McFadden took over. McFadden had electricity installed when the dam that originally powered the mill failed. A few years later, in 1927, an article appeared in the paper saying that the mill was being leased by S. S. and D. E. Myers, and that "custom grinding" would "engage their attention." In 1935, the mill was shut down after being in operation for nearly a hundred years.

Many years of neglect and disrepair followed before Michael and Rose Marie Costanzo purchased the old mill in 1980 from Eugene Potter of Madrid. They began what they anticipated would be an extensive restoration process, starting with stabilizing the eroding foundation; they also saw that the mill was added to the National Register of Historic Places in 1982. Today the Heritage Grist Mill Association, a nonprofit preservation group headed by Charles R. LaShombe, controls the mill. With continued community volunteer efforts and public and private financial assistance, the association is in the process of fully restoring the mill to working condition—once again actually grinding grain—so that tourists and especially schoolchildren can experience the atmosphere of an authentic nineteenth-century gristmill. And what could be more authentic than an actual old-time miller haunting the grounds?

Jeff, the hapless carpenter, was first to become aware of the gristmill ghost in 2002, and he was about to make Charlie the second. He explained, as the two men returned together to the mill, that he had heard somebody walking back and forth overhead on the second floor, as if pacing the floor. Yet he had been the only person in the mill at the time, and he hadn't seen anyone come in. Still, he was certain he had heard the very distinct sound of footsteps above. If that were the case, Charlie figured someone must have entered the building when Jeff wasn't paying attention, simply to have a look around. Just then, the two of them heard the footsteps overhead again. It sounded as though someone was walking all the way across the floor above them and then back again. Charlie gallantly raced up the stairs to confront the intruder, but the second floor was clearly empty. Undeterred, he raced up to the third floor in hot pursuit of the prowler, but it too was empty. Only Charlie and Jeff were in the building. Nobody else. Running on pure adrenaline, Charlie bounded back down to the first floor just as Jeff started cautiously up the stairs. One look at his boss's face, and Jeff knew it wasn't good. He found himself once again racing out of the building. Later Charlie and Jeff attempted to replicate the sound with various types of shoes, and they found that only hard-soled shoes, like those worn in days of old, made the same sound.

Not long after that incident, Charlie asked Ghost Seekers of Central New York to come in and investigate the premises. Team members captured video footage of orbs in movement, with some coming up off the floor before disappearing. They also heard the sound of something being dragged across the second floor, where Jeff and Charlie had heard someone walking. Jeff, by the way, is over the ordeal and has given the resident ghost a fitting name, Igor. Whoever is, or was, haunting the mill may simply be a visitor from the past who is curious about its restoration. Charlie's father-in-law, who does not believe in ghosts, told Charlie of a dream he had one night in which he was sitting upstairs at the mill, speaking to

Mr. Harison himself. The presence is not a frightening one in any way, shape, or form. To the contrary. The mill is a very peaceful, historic, wonderful old building that is simply being awakened after a much-needed rest—and maybe that's what's happening with the spirits people have encountered there as well.

Burrville Cider Mill

Cindy Steiner had just propped open the cooler door at the popular family-operated Burrville Cider Mill near Watertown one late-summer day so she could restock it. As she went about her business filling the cooler, she suddenly got the sense that she was being watched, but she hadn't heard anyone come in over the sound of the fans. Still, something told her she wasn't alone, so she jokingly blurted out, "Hello, Captain Burr," as if to casually greet her annoying resident ghost. Just then, reflected in the opened cooler door, she clearly saw a man's legs and feet, as if he were standing right behind her. He was wearing brown leather work boots and heavy black pants that looked as though they were made of wool. Cindy spun around to confront the intruder, but nobody was there. Yet the legs and feet had been so clear! Nobody else was in the building, and the parking lot was empty. Besides, no customer would have come in wearing heavy wool pants on a hot summer day such as it was. She realized she must have summoned Captain Burr's ghost—or at least a partial ghost—just by saying his name.

Built at the bottom of a thirty-foot waterfall on the North Branch of Sandy Creek in 1801, the Burrville Cider Mill is one of Jefferson County's oldest establishments. For many years, the town of Burrville was known as Burr's Mills, for a sawmill and gristmill that have long since disappeared. In 1996, the Steiner family—Greg Sr., Cynthia, Greg Jr., and Tina—purchased the two-hundred-year-old mill, even after being forewarned that it harbored a resident ghost or two.

Sure enough, shortly after buying it, they were welcomed by two distinctly different gentleman ghosts whom they believe to be Homer Rebb and Captain John Burr. Cindy came right out and told the ghosts the night before opening day that they were not to scare her—she had enough on her mind without worrying about ghosts. Then, just to make sure she wasn't talking to herself, she asked them for proof that they even existed. A short time later, when she was putting sealer on the new tile floor in the kitchen, she dared the ghosts to leave a single footprint in the fresh sealer during the night. Greg Jr., her son, was working on his truck when Cindy left for the night, and he needed something from the mill, so he unlocked the door and let himself in. He had taken just one step into the kitchen when he saw that it had been freshly sealed and waxed, so he backed out. Cindy had no idea her son had been there after she left, so when she arrived the next morning and went into the kitchen, she saw the single footprint on the floor and thought the ghosts had fulfilled her request. Her son, meanwhile, saw her reaction and thought she was mad at him for stepping onto the floor. She cut him off in midapology and explained that she was shocked only because she had asked the ghost to do just what her son had done!

Homer Rebb was born around 1900 in Barnes Corners. His father, Charles, operated a sawmill and gristmill there and later purchased the Burrville Cider Mill, which Homer took over in the 1940s. An only child, Homer was mentioned numerous times between 1922 and 1934 in Lowville's *Journal and Republican* for confinement at home or in the hospital due to severe asthma, grippe, and bronchial ailments. But he also, according to news articles, enjoyed a life of luxury in his teens and twenties. In 1924, he took violin lessons. Later that same year, he purchased a new Studebaker. And still later that year, he left for an "extended trip to Florida," where he would remain for the winter, "if the climate and business prospects [proved] favorable." In 1936, he was treasurer of the Barnes Corners Cemetery Association. Several years later, he took over the Burrville Cider Mill and ran it in a conscientious, "very orderly way," even designing some of the mill equipment himself. Sometime in the 1940s, Homer Rebb converted the mill to cider production on a commercial scale, according to the mill's website, and he continued operating it into the 1980s, when he finally retired at a ripe old age.

You couldn't find an individual more in contrast to Rebb than Captain John Burr. He was as rough around the edges as Rebb was smooth and polished. Burr was a mysterious pirate who bought the old mill in 1802, and it's for him that Burrville and the cider mill were named. Rumor has it that in his day, he was quite the swindler, stealing goods from ships on Lake Ontario to pawn off on troops in Sackets Harbor. And if the following incident is any indication, Burr hasn't changed his ways in two hundred years!

One of the first inexplicable things that happened to the Steiners in their new enterprise was the disappearance of a twenty-five-pound bag of sugar. To this day, it has never been recovered. Tina Steiner had left the bag in the back room after the close of business one day, just before she locked up and left. She was the last person to leave, so she was certain the place was secure. But the next morning when she returned, the bag of sugar had vanished. None of the others had anything to do with the disappearance. The prim and proper Homer would never have pulled such a trick, so it must have been the ghost of Burr. Other objects have disappeared as well, such as a cordless drill, but they reappear moments later in the exact same spot, even though every employee denies having touched them. In 2005, Cindy Steiner told me that her husband, Greg Sr., had gone upstairs to clean the line on the cider tank. A screwdriver is supposed to remain next to it at all times, but for some reason it was missing. Very annoyed that it wasn't there, he went back downstairs for another screwdriver. He took a different one back up with him and was in the process of using it when he looked at the screwdriver in his hand, and it was the missing one. Not only was it back where it was supposed to be, but it was even in his hand! How's that for service?

Burr is also blamed for the sound of someone walking in the attic above the store when the Steiners are closing up for the day. They sometimes hear heavy objects dropping overhead as well, even though all that's up there is a number of empty plastic jugs. Nobody ever finds anything amiss when they mosey on up to investigate. The jugs are always still standing upright. But one day, as Greg Steiner was heading back down the stairs, a half-gallon plastic container hit him in the back of the head.

Cindy has also heard something lightweight bouncing across the first floor of the store. It sounds like a Ping-Pong ball, but she never finds anything to account for what she heard. The other unmistakable sound is that of the old double cider press in the basement operating when nobody is down there. It seems that this must be the work of Homer, because he ran the cider presses down there longer than anyone else.

From the basement to the attic, the Steiners have often heard sounds for which no apparent source can be found. And objects sometimes get knocked around by unseen hands. Cindy saw two candles fall down off the shelf right before her eyes. There was no breeze in the store, no freak earthquake or slamming door to blame . . . yet somehow the sturdy box holding the candles, which was six inches from the edge, suddenly just dropped off the shelf onto the floor right in front of Cindy.

According to Cindy, the spirit of the former pirate who once lived at the mill would insert into the sorting area three apples with perfectly discolored markings (scars) on the skins spelling out the letters "I-C-U," followed by a fourth apple with a rough skull image. That's exactly what a former employee discovered while sorting apples one day in 2006. "The employee just happened to be wearing a black shirt with a skull image on it that eerily resembled the skull on the apple," said Cindy. "He is now a believer in the supernatural!"

That same year, Cindy wrote to me about another bizarre spelling incident. Her ten-year-old granddaughter was helping her make fudge, when she sent the girl into the mill kitchen to warm some up in the microwave. The girl called out to Cindy to come into the kitchen, asking her why the microwave was saying "child." "I couldn't grasp what she was asking," Cindy wrote, "so I stopped what I was doing and went to check for myself. Sure enough, there on the digital readout of the microwave I had owned for years was the word 'child.' This word obviously isn't programmed into the microwave, so why would it have been on the display?" Was one of the resident ghosts concerned about having a child in the kitchen? It's another unsolved mystery from the mill.

Burr is also believed to be responsible for the smell of cigar smoke, as well as old cigars that are mysteriously found on freshly cleaned floors. One time, just after the floors had been swept clean and repainted, an old cigar covered in cobwebs appeared right in the middle of the floor. The staff couldn't recall anyone having been smoking a cigar in the store at the time. The Steiner women, especially, have noticed the fleeting pungent smell of cigar smoke in several places—the sorting room, the parking lot, and even under the kitchen sink. Cindy smelled it so strongly when she was driving home from work one night that it stung her nostrils. She was sure everyone would smell it on her clothes when she got home, but it had dissipated by then. It seems unlikely that Homer had a penchant for cigars, considering his serious respiratory ailments. So again this unexplained phenomenon sounds more like something Captain Burr would do. But that's not to say that Homer Rebb is not to blame for other strange incidents that go on at the cider mill.

Equipment sometimes fails for no apparent reason, and when it does, the women have learned to ask Homer for a little help. It seems that as soon as they say, "Homer, will you fix this?" the object begins working again. They also blame the doting gentleman for opening and closing cupboard doors behind their backs as they're doing dishes in the kitchen, because if they say, "Homer, go home," the activity abruptly stops.

Craig and Laurie, former members of the Greather Ithaca Paranormal Society and now of Empire State Paranormal, shared their possible Homer encounter: "In April 2008, the Greater Ithaca Paranormal Society conducted an investigation of the ghostly activity at the mill," they wrote. "During evidence review, it was discovered that the paper towels hanging on the kitchen wall seemed to unroll themselves. After examining the paper towel dispenser on a return visit to the mill, it was found to have a rubber stop that prevents the roll from turning on its own. Was this Homer lending a hand?"

In April 2001, I was interviewed regarding the Burrville Cider Mill by WWNY News from Watertown, and the reporter/cameraman paid the mill a visit after the interview to get some live footage. He got more than he bargained for. It was the reporter's birthday, so he jokingly asked out loud for a little birthday bonus from the ghost, if one was present. He was taking the video footage and interviewing Tina Steiner at the same time, and just he and Tina were inside. The camera was directed at Tina, who was standing in front of the swinging kitchen door. Unbeknownst to either of them, the door behind her opened very slowly and deliberately, then closed just as carefully. This is a door that takes some effort to open, so a breeze or draft couldn't have caused it to open and close like that. It wasn't until the reporter got back to his office and reviewed the footage that he noticed it. He called me up, so excited that he could barely contain it. The incident delighted viewers, who had never before seen such proof of a haunting as this appeared to be. This was before the advent of such shows as *Ghost Hunters* and *Paranormal State*, so it was groundbreaking in our little corner of the world. Another television film crew that later visited the mill was puzzled by outdoor lighting that began flickering overhead, right at the spot where they were filming.

One couple who had been married on the grounds of the Burrville Cider Mill, with the falls as a beautiful backdrop, approached me at a book signing one day to show me some of their wedding photographs. They had read about the cider mill being haunted in my first book and thought it would be a memorable place to hold their autumn wedding, especially if something paranormal occurred. They were thrilled to find orbs, ectoplasm, and other anomalies often attributed to spirit energy in many of their photographs. Thanks to Homer and Burr, the Burrville Cider Mill had yet another satisfied customer.

The year 2008 was a particularly active one for unexplained happenings, according to Cindy. She sent me the following email:

One night my grandson, Forrest, and I were at the mill after closing. We were waiting for two boys who were jugging cider for wholesale accounts to finish up. We turned out the lights in the retail store and were in the back room but had left the front door unlocked so the juggers could still get in. We then heard something fall somewhere between us and the store. I went to see if it was a customer and found nobody, nor any object that may have fallen. When I returned to the back room, Forrest asked me if I had heard someone walking in the attic! I had not. At that very moment, something fell again. Again I checked the store, and Forrest checked on the boys who were jugging cider. Again, I found nothing.

"One week later, I was in the store behind the cash register. I bent over to pick something up; standing back up, I saw the face of a cute little blond girl about three or four years old. There was no one else in the store at the time, so I assumed her mom was bagging apples outside. I walked around the counter to ask if her mom was outside, and nobody was there!"

Many of the ghost stories I write are works in progress, as the paranormal activity continues long after the book has gone to press. The Burrville Cider Mill appears to be a prime example. In August 2008, I visited the cider mill at the request of WPBS television to film a documentary called *Folklore and Frost.* The day started out beautifully for the two-hour drive from my house, but as I approached my destination, the sunshine yielded to overcast skies, and an ominous feeling permeated the air—perfect, of course, for the task at hand. I pulled into a minimart around the corner from the mill and heard a customer declare that a hailstorm was headed our way. The moment I stepped out of my car outside the cider mill, a light rain began. As I stood on the porch, Gerry Coleman, the PBS cameraman, and his assistant pulled up; it was decided that we would shoot the video footage outside for as long as we could, with the thunder in the background and the clouds rolling in, lending an authentic, spooky effect to the video. Gerry set up his equipment and pointed the camera at me, while I stood several feet away with my back to the main entrance of the mill's store. I began to recount the many types of paranormal activity that have been reported in practically every spot at the mill. Because the rain was becoming increasingly heavier and the thunder was drowning out my voice, I was practically yelling by the time I motioned behind me and described a male apparition that had been photographed near the sorting room. Just then, I realized Gerry wasn't looking at me any longer; he was looking over my head and behind me. He said, "The motion detector just went off behind you, and I got it on film." There was no explanation for it, as we were the only ones outside at the time. With that, a loud crack of lightning sent us scurrying inside. Captain Burr and Homer Rebb must have friends in high places to pull off the stunts they seem to manage: thunder, lightning, cryptic apple (and microwave oven) messages, motion detectors going off on cue . . . I have a feeling that every book I ever write regarding northern New York and New York State will include an update on the Steiners' Burrville Cider Mill.

So much has transpired since the night before opening day in 1996 when Cindy Steiner asked the ghosts for proof that the mill was haunted. In the years since, while the Steiners have owned the thriving cider mill, visitors and staff alike have experienced enough supernatural phenomena to fill a book of its own.

Fort Ontario

The ghost stories associated with Fort Ontario in Oswego origi-nated around 1900, when a sergeant named Fawdry began publi-cizing them in an effort to keep children off the property, according to an October 2002 article in the *Valley News*. That doesn't mean he made them up, as some sources have erroneously assumed. An article in the *Malone Farmer* dated January 23, 1907, said that even then the ghost stories were steeped in tradition and believed by all who were stationed there:

> Fort Ontario, Oswego, has become the interesting seat of a ghost. One of the new recruits saw the vision the other night when on guard, and on telling it, he was astonished to find that many others had seen the same thing. Shortly after taps is sounded, the sally port of the old fort opens, and the indistinct figure of a sergeant, with a ponderous musket on his shoulder and an unlighted lantern in the other hand, glides forth, "all's well," and retreats to the sally port with measured and dignified tread. It is one of the traditions of the fort, and, although the ghost does not make its appearance every night, it is seen upon occasions, and the men stationed there have full faith in the reliability of the vision.

Fawdry went so far as to guess, or fabricate, the names of the two ghosts he spoke of. One was a British lieutenant named Basil Dunbar, who has haunted the fort since losing a duel in 1759. Recent sightings of Dunbar's ghost have him wandering around the grounds dazed, as if he doesn't realize he's dead—which seems to be a common shortcoming among ghosts. And then there's

Corporal Fykes, who Fawdry—probably going for dramatic effect—said was a British soldier who died of hunger. In reality, Fykes was an American loyalist who died from disease in 1782. At any rate, his ghost has appeared to every new regiment for more than a hundred years, according to Lynda Lee Macken's *Empire Ghosts*, and a rapid drop in room temperature always seems to coincide with sightings of him. The assumed identities of Fykes and Dunbar as the two primary ghosts of Fort Ontario are based on the opinion of Sergeant Fawdry and the uniforms the ghosts were reportedly wearing.

Besides various spirits of men in uniform, a ghost baby has been heard both giggling and crying, and a female figure has repeatedly been sensed by psychics. Her essence may have been captured on film by paranormal investigators in 1998. The American Ghost Society's New York State representatives also experienced unexplained temperature drops in the men's barracks, where an argument once allegedly led to murder; erratic electromagnetic field (EMF) readings; and sounds for which no source could be found. When Fort Ontario became a training post in 1903, only one person was responsible for both guarding it and acting as its caretaker—one person and a ghost in the form of a little ball of energy that lingered around the night watchman's post, alternating between green and blue. Some say it's the spirit of a former guard manifesting as an orb. Guards ever since have reported not just the one peculiar orb, but also the sounds of doors slamming shut for no apparent reason and footsteps passing by when nobody can be seen.

Fort Ontario was built around 1755 on Lake Ontario and has been variously occupied by the British, French, and Americans. The United States has held it since 1796, and it is now owned and operated by the New York State Office of Parks, Recreation, and Historic Preservation as a museum that is painstakingly restored to depict life at the fort in 1868—a mild time period in its history. Harsher times prevailed in the distant past, such as in the winter of 1756. British troops occupying the fort at that time had become so desperate for food and warmth that they forcefully bound their commanding officer and left the site, seeking food and shelter at a nearby village. They were stopped dead in their tracks, so to speak, when a blizzard hampered their efforts, forcing them to return to the fort—and then kill and eat their comrades in order to survive. Had the Office of Parks chosen to depict a scene from life at the fort in the 1750s, it would have had to reproduce mounds of frozen and starved bodies. If it had depicted scenes from the fort during the Colonial wars and the War of 1812, hundreds of bloodied mannequins would have been appropriate. In light of such a morbid past—where countless lives were lost in bloody battles; disease, starvation, and hypothermia ran rampant; duels were fought and murders committed; and soldiers were forced into cannibalism—it's amazing the fort isn't haunted by scores of ghosts. It may have been decommissioned following World War II, but Fort Ontario has nevertheless remained a very "active" place—by paranormal standards, at least.

Haskell House

The historic house at 28 Tamarack Street in Massena was built by Captain Lemuel Haskell in 1826, making it the oldest structure in the town that is still used as a residence. It also is considered the town's first settlement and was called the Mile Square in 1792—a name that was changed to Haskell's Square Mile after the captain bought the site, complete with a sawmill on the Grasse River, from Amable Faucher. Lemuel and Polly Haskell had three young children, Martha, Laura, and Abel, when they moved into the stately stone house on prime river property near the mill. The mill became quite prosperous for the family—so prosperous, in fact, that legend has it that Captain Haskell hid half a million dollars somewhere within the three-foot-thick limestone walls before he died in 1870. Polly had passed away twenty years before him, so the house went to his only son when he died. Abel remained there until he died in 1909, leaving it to his descendants.

Alcoa acquired the house and property during World War I to provide living quarters to those who had been brought in to work at its plant. The Pilgrims Holiness Society then used the building as a house of worship, before selling it for use as a multiple-family residence. It was during this time that one of the teenage tenants was shot by her brother in the kitchen and killed. Joseph Verville purchased the home in the early 1970s, restoring it and bringing it to code for the several families living there. Then Barry and Allison Verville acquired it and moved in with their three children. They spoke to me about their paranormal experiences, which were numerous.

Haskell House is as solid and sturdy today as it was when it was built nearly two hundred years ago, having walls cut out of Grasse River limestone three feet deep. With a solid shell on the outside, hand-hewn pine timber was used to frame the interior. Clearly Haskell knew not only how to run a successful sawmill, but also how to build a home that would last. Many people, including the Vervilles, believe the handyman still inhabits the house—not in a malicious way, by any means, but mostly by aiding in construction and carpentry projects the men of the house undertake. One day, Barry was working on a cradle he was crafting in the basement, assisted by his friend Tommy. It had to be perfect, with the wood extremely smooth and polished, as an infant would be lying in it. Tommy had to go upstairs to take a phone call, and Barry ran his fingers carefully along the edge of the cradle to check for smoothness. Just as Tommy had rounded the corner at the top of the stairs, the electric sander on the opposite side of the basement from where Barry was working turned itself on. Nobody else was down there at the time, and the sander was in a dark area of the basement and hadn't been used yet for the project. As the realization hit Barry that he was not alone, he bolted up the stairs after his friend. Apparently the Captain thought an electric sander was in order for the task at hand.

The reason Captain Haskell is believed, above all others, to be haunting the house is because he put the most heart and soul into the property. He was the architect, builder, and first resident. It was the home in which his beloved wife, Polly, died and in which he also took his last breath. That's why when anything is missing or seems out of place, the Vervilles fondly point the finger at Captain Haskell. When the thermostat on the first floor was continually being manipulated, the family members accused each other, until they finally conceded that none of them had touched it. It was being turned up and down by unseen hands. The Captain also has his hands into the plumbing fixtures. Bear in mind that when he built the house, indoor toilets had not been invented yet, so it's no wonder he apparently finds them so fascinating. The Vervilles and friends who visited the home sometimes heard the toilet upstairs flush when nobody was up there. And when Barry, Allison, and their sister and brother-in-law were putting in a new kitchen faucet, an endless string of impossible events followed. First the water ran when the handles were in the off position, so they turned off the water main, but the water still ran. Then when they turned the water main back on, the water refused to run.

When working in the attic one day, Barry's brother-in-law nailed a sheet of plywood across the opening before going downstairs for a quick break, so that the young children wouldn't climb up there and get into the dangerous tools that were lying around on the floor. When he returned, the nails had all been yanked out, and the plywood had been removed and set off to the side. Nobody else had been upstairs in the short time he had been away from the work area.

Less-disturbing incidents were the norm for the Vervilles, such as a clock that they kept on top of the television set in the living room being constantly repositioned. Every morning for some time, Barry found the clock facing oddly to the left, so he straightened it out, only to find it again turned the next morning. This finally stopped when the television set was eventually moved to another spot in the living room, clock and all. Allison had a completely different experience in the living room. When she came home from shopping one day, she set a few bags of groceries on the coffee table in the living room before going into the kitchen to make some coffee for herself and her friend. Suddenly her German shepherd, Mata, started barking anxiously from the living room. When Allison went to check on her, she found a heavy bag of groceries strewn across the floor, and Mata seemed to be afraid of something. The strangest part of it was that the bag of groceries that had somehow ended up on the floor was the one in the middle of the table, surrounded by the other bags, yet none of the other bags had moved. After that incident, Mata stayed glued to Allison's side no matter where her owner went in the house. Maybe the poor, traumatized pup had never seen a captain's ghost before.

John Hoover Inn

"Romance in Which a Game of Cards Figured, With the Beautiful Madam as a Portion of the Stake—Finally Broken-hearted and Forsaken." That was a subtitle of an August 8, 1897, *Watertown Sunday Herald* article about Madam Ameriga Vespucci and an event that transformed her life, which occurred at the historic John Hoover Inn in Evans Mills.

More than 175 years ago, the John Hoover Inn was built by its namesake, Captain John Hoover, who had been stationed in Sackets Harbor during the War of 1812. Since then, the inn at 8497 South Main Street has seen a lot of action, a lot of history—and a lot of paranormal phenomena. Long after the last call for the night, a boisterous crowd has been heard, though not seen, hooting and hollering into the wee hours of the morning in the seemingly empty inn. Some believe it's a residual haunting from an incident that took place long ago—one that proved life-altering for the trio involved: Madam Vespucci, George Parish, and John Van Buren. The article detailed the true account of that fateful evening, as recalled by the bartender and several old patrons who were there at the time:

> On the main street corner of the little farming village of Evans Mills ... stands a time-stained and weather-beaten old brick tavern with great iron letters and figures upon its girth explaining the fact that it was erected by Capt. John Hoover in 1827, in the long, low wainscoted ball room of which was enacted one stormy winter night, some three score years ago, a most peculiarly romantic chapter in the checkered life of a lovely and accomplished woman, whose beauty and wit had dazzled the courts and capitals of two continents. ... At that old brick tavern the famous Madam Maria Helena Amerigo Vespucci first met George Parish, gentleman, then a

resident of Ogdensburg . . . and in the old ball room of that hostelry was played a game of cards which decided Madam's future and made her henceforth mistress of the historical Parish mansion at the corner of State and Washington Streets, Ogdensburg.

The article describes how the very wealthy Ogdensburg businessman George Parish was the young brother of Baron von Leftonberg of Saxony, whom Parish would succeed in 1856. Parish had come to this country representing "the great banking house of Hope and Company of Amsterdam" and had set up residence in Ogdensburg. Madam Vespucci had come to the country in 1838 seeking citizenship and a grant of land on which to settle. After all, she was a "direct descendant of Amerigo Vespucci, whose name the continent bears." As such, the black-haired, dark-eyed beauty with the false sense of entitlement was "courted, feted, admired, and honored." She was "young, radiant and beautiful, with all the charm of birth and breeding and the glamour of foreign courts about her." But soon her intimacy with President Van Buren's son, "Prince John," became the talk of the town, and it was rumored that she had come to America only after being "induced . . . to break off an intimacy with the Duke of Orleans, eldest son of Louis Phillipe, and leave the country." Such rumors caused her to fall from grace with "respectable society" of Washington, D.C., so she moved to Albany to be "taken care of" by the president's son. She accompanied John Van Buren on his fateful trip to the John Hoover Inn in Evans Mills in 1841 to meet with George Parish on business.

On a stormy winter day in January 1841, a big sleigh drawn by four fine horses came floundering through the snow drifts from Rossie, and drew up at Capt. John Hoover's tavern at Evans Mills. One of the fur-coated occupants of the sleigh was a man of most kingly bearing, young and noble looking, faultless in dress and with every mark of blue blood and breeding. He was George Parish of Ogdensburg. . . . Mr. Parish ordered a fire built in the fireplace of the old dancing hall, and three chambers to be prepared, as he expected to meet Lawyer John Van Buren of Albany there on business connected with his estates in that vicinity. About noon the famous lawyer arrived, driving through from Utica in a sleigh. He did not come alone, however, but was accompanied by a woman, tall, stately and handsome, who was magnificently dressed and who wore a profusion of jewelry. She spoke with a foreign accent and was introduced by "Prince John," who was a tall, stately and fine-looking man, as Madam Vespucci. After dinner, which was served to the guests in the old ball room . . . it was noticeable, even to the bartender who served them, that George Parish was much more deeply interested in Van Buren's fair companion than he was in his legal lore, and that the interest was mutual.

Van Buren had been drinking heavily all day, and as darkness fell, he stepped away for a time, leaving Madam Vespucci with her new acquaintance. When "Prince John" returned some time later, he proposed a game of cards with Parish, but he "lost steadily and finally wagered, sack by sack, $5,000 in gold, which he had received from a client to invest in Rossie acres." Dejectedly, he turned to Madam Vespucci and suggested that she might want to follow the gold; otherwise, he could neither pay nor play. She refused, nobly saying that she would stay with him through rich or poor, unless he made her leave him. Mr. Parish then proposed "to put up the $5,000 and as much more with it, the madam to go with the winner," and this was agreed to by all, so the game continued, as Madam Vespucci sat nervously at the table holding the sacks of gold.

Van Buren, probably because he was intoxicated, played sloppily, and Parish ended up with the winning hand. He offered the $10,000 to Van Buren, but the attorney declined. So Van Buren handed it to Madam Vespucci, who also tried to get Parish to take it, but again, he declined, telling her to hold on to it for the day when her "beauty faded or her friends failed." Van Buren then quickly ordered his horses up and left late that night for Boonville, "while George Parish and the madam drove away through the star-lit winter night toward faraway Ogdensburg and the brick-walled villa that was to be their home for the next sixteen years." Incidentally, local legend used to say that Madam Vespucci once haunted the Parish Mansion (now the Remington Art Museum) at 303 Washington Street, where she had spent sixteen years with George before being forced to leave in 1858, "while sobbing bitterly."

In 1856, when Parish's brother passed away, George had been summoned back to Germany to assume his proper title of Baron von Leftonberg and to marry "a daughter of the nobility." Madam Vespucci had been his longtime mistress, not his legal wife. Two years after his departure, she set sail for France, "a lonely, sad, and heart-broken woman, who but for her folly might have left a glittering instead of a clouded name upon the pages of history." Rather harsh words from that old newspaper account, but important information, from a parahistorian's point of view, if we are to understand who would have motive to haunt the John Hoover Inn.

Numerous tavernkeepers have come and gone since John Hoover's day, and in 2003, one of them, Stephanie Comini, shared her experiences with me. She had six rooms that she rented by the week, and she leased part of the upstairs to a beauty salon called A Step Above. The tenants upstairs were hearing people come and go below them in the bar area after the bar had closed for the night, when the place had been locked up. Stephanie was applying the final coat of a sealer to the new dance floor one night just before Halloween in 2003 and was working completely alone. She later recalled the time, because she had set the clocks back that night for daylight saving time. The next morning, one of her tenants asked her what time she had left the previous night, because it sounded as though someone had been having a good old time, laughing and clinking bottles, at about 5:30 A.M. in the dining room. Stephanie had been gone a full two hours by then, so it was perplexing, to say the least.

Early that morning, another tenant had heard the same thing, but when she went down to check it out, the noise abruptly stopped. So she turned around and headed back up the stairs. Just as she reached the top step, the sound of partying in the dining room below started back up. Thinking she would outsmart the partiers and catch them by surprise, she carefully crept down the steps. She tried this several times, but every time she approached the source, the noise stopped. The next morning, there were no signs of anyone having been in the dining room or bar, and nothing was out of place. Still damp and sticky with polyurethane coating, the new dance floor showed no evidence whatsoever of footprints. Someone would have to have been weightless to be partying in that room without leaving a mark on the freshly sealed floor.

Yet another tenant had a similar experience that night when he heard Victrola-type music coming from the beauty salon, but the music stopped as he approached the door. When he walked away from the door, it started playing again. Furthermore, Stephanie said that children of the beautician's customers often reported seeing a lady in the hall who would either tell them to "Shhh!" or wave nicely at them, depending on her mood. Who needs to give their hair a lift when they can have a hair-raising experience like that?

The regular customers and staff are also well aware of the paranormal activity, often saying that the old building is full of ghosts. It wouldn't be surprising. Local newspapers have reported several deaths at the tavern, such as that of old Patrick Cummings, who died in one of the upstairs rooms in 1910. The *Watertown Herald* of March 19 of that year said: "Patrick Cummings, one of the oldest residents of this vicinity, died at the brick hotel at Evans' Mills Tuesday morning, aged 96 years. For most of his life he had been a blacksmith in Evans Mills and had moved away just two years before he died. But, feeling that he was nearing the end of life's journey, he desired to be taken back to die where he had lived so long." Perhaps he refuses to leave the familiar grounds of the John Hoover Inn even now, more than a hundred years after his passing.

In the basement of the John Hoover Inn, people feel as if they are being watched from behind when they are completely alone. In the dining room, besides the aforementioned sounds of celebration, lights are turned on or off by unseen hands for no good reason. Though nobody knows who haunts the inn, it's fun to think that the, shall we say, *spirited* party that has been heard was that of Madam Vespucci and her two famous companions. Today, Gloria and Darcy Corey own the inn, which is open with a pub menu seven days a week from noon until closing.

Tug Hill Plateau

In my travels, I've heard many chilling stories about ghosts that have a propensity to follow or chase passing cars on desolate back-roads, including the following story about one that terrorized young residents in the Fort Drum–Watertown region in the early 1960s. It was reported in an unidentified newspaper clipping, dated June 22, 1960. The article is subtitled: "Apparition on Perch Lake Highway Follows Two Cars—Sheriff's Deputies Investigate." In this case, two visibly shaken teenage girls reported to authorities that a mysterious hooded figure chased the two cars they were riding in with six others down the Perch Lake Road northwest of Watertown, even as the cars neared fifty miles per hour. Because the girls seemed genuinely traumatized by the experience, sheriff's deputies took their report seriously, not necessarily expecting a crazed phantom on the loose, but possibly a prankster or somebody projecting an image on the roadway with a movie projector. The sergeant on duty told the young girls that they would question the other witnesses and send someone out there to investigate.

The investigation and interviews revealed that one of the girls and her boyfriend, a private first class from Camp (Fort) Drum, had seen the hooded figure several weeks earlier, so they brought six skeptical friends along with them this time for an impromptu ghost hunt. The cars, both driven by soldiers from Fort Drum, were headed southwest on Perch Lake Road at approximately 11:15 P.M., driving about twenty-five miles per hour, when a figure again appeared out of nowhere by the side of the road, half a mile from Bradley Street. Those in the second car were the first to see it, so they flashed their headlights at the first car to alert them to it, at which time both cars sped up to almost fifty-five miles per hour. All eight witnesses, who were interviewed separately, agreed that the figure looked like a woman wearing a long, white nightgown with a hood, though no facial features were discernible. Most alarming was the recollection that one hand appeared to consist of just three long fingernails, rather than an actual hand—a prelude to Freddy Krueger? Had horror writer Wes Craven, creator of the phenomenally popular *Nightmare on Elm Street* movie, gotten his idea for the razor-fingered Krueger after reading this very newspaper article? It's no secret that while Craven taught as a professor of humanities at Clarkson University, a student film project in 1968 that spoofed horror films using scenes from Potsdam's Elm Street became the inspiration for his 1984 box-office smash. Had he read about the apparition on the Perch Lake Road that had terrified teens several years before the film project? If so, perhaps it became his inspiration for the character of Freddy Krueger.

At any rate, one of the girls who witnessed the apparition said it moved like a character in an old black and white silent film—jerky, surreal, and just plain creepy. When it came between the two cars, the headlights from the second vehicle revealed that it was transparent. The witnesses said it was as if the figure were trying to force them off the road, going so far as to reach for the side of one car. So much for the sheriff's deputies' theory that the phantom may have been nothing more than a movie projector image. The apparition stayed with the cars for about half a mile before vanishing just as they reached Bradley Street.

Another disturbing story along this line is about a group of teenagers on their way to a prom in the Watertown area in the 1970s. They were driving down a dark road on the Tug Hill Plateau when they allegedly spotted an odd-looking figure wearing a long gown and walking along the side of the road in the same direction that they were traveling. As they passed her, they decided that perhaps it was another student on her way to the prom, so they did the neighborly thing—they turned around to ask her if she wanted a ride. But as they got closer, they noticed a strange, menacing look in her eyes. Something was definitely not right. Without hesitation, the driver did a one-eighty to escape the terrifying apparition, but as they sped down the road, they were horrified to see that the same figure had beaten them there, somehow teleporting itself ahead of them. The driver gunned the car, leaving the ghost lady in its dust. They say prom night is a night to remember, and I'm sure those kids will never forget that one.

Perry Residence

Several years after Bud and Bev Perry moved into the old brick house on Route 11 adjacent to the Union Cemetery in Adams Center, inexplicable things began to happen. Bud went downstairs to the kitchen one morning and found that the oven in his electric stove had been turned on. It was the beginning of a seemingly endless string of unexplained phenomena. For the next twenty years, lights turned on in the middle of the night, and television sets turned on between 2 and 3 A.M., full blast. The problem became so disruptive that the Perrys were forced to unplug them at night. They're lucky it worked—in some homes, even that hasn't stopped a determined ghost.

When the couple bought the house in 1978, they didn't mind that their home was just four feet away from a cemetery on one side. A fence in their backyard separated their property from the cemetery. But nobody told them that the man who built the house, Jay Harmon, had been found dead in his bed there, and that his chosen burial plot was right up against the backyard fence. Now the Perrys wonder whether it's the ghost of Harmon or one of the many others who were buried six feet under nearby who haunts their home.

In the early 1990s, Bud and Bev were going to bed one night when one of their twin sons came into their room and told them someone was making noise in the driveway. It sounded as if somebody were shoveling snow on the concrete driveway, he said, but it was the middle of the summer. Bud looked out his bedroom window at the backyard and saw about fifty small, white lights hovering above their lawn furniture and dancing up and down. They were nothing like fireflies; they were larger and remained continually lit. He shook his head and rubbed his eyes, but the little orbs were still there for another moment, then disappeared. During the experience, Bud found himself unable to look away or even speak to tell his wife and son to look out the window to see the bizarre light show.

Jay Harmon died in the month of February, which just so happens to be a particularly active time for paranormal phenomena at the Perry House. Coincidence? Several times, the Perrys have heard muffled, indecipherable voices but couldn't determine where they were coming from. Overnight guests have heard footsteps going up and down the stairs when nobody was there. Objects sometimes fall off the shelves and walls. And the family's pets have all stopped and stared at a particular chair near their front window, as if someone is sitting there interacting with them.

The Perrys believe they've also been visited by the spirit of Patches, their beloved dog, who lived to be nearly eighteen years old and died in 2001. A few years ago, Bev heard a dog crying on two separate occasions. Then one morning, Bud heard a dog, and it sounded as though it were right next to him. Patches had always loved the old carpet that had her scent all over it, so the Perrys think that perhaps she was upset about the carpet being replaced with a new one. When she died and was cremated, her ashes were spread around the cemetery, where she loved to walk with Bud. Now he worries that she is discontent on the other side, since she seems to be returning from time to time.

When the Perrys' son was young, he thought his parents should sell the house and move because of the unusual occurrences. Now, as an adult, he takes it all in stride. It's just your typical haunted home . . . nothing worth moving over. In fact, it keeps things interesting.

Spanky's Diner

Spanky's Diner at 3 North Main Street in Massena has become known as one of the North Country's most haunted places and has been publicized as such in newspapers, books, and on local news programs. It has been investigated by a number of psychics and paranormal investigators, often with astounding results. Situated on the corner of Center and Main Streets, it overlooks the Grasse River and a bridge leading to the heart of downtown. Massena's first hospital, founded by Dr. Louis J. Calli, opened in May 1940 and was located in the Horton residence, just north of the bridge on the land directly behind the diner where Route 37B now lies.

On a hill overlooking the backside of Spanky's is the very haunted Pine Grove Cemetery.

Given all this, it's no wonder if Spanky's seems to be basically a sitting duck for wandering spirits. Besides a haunted cemetery looking down on it, both the hospital and the river saw tragic deaths. After twenty-two-year-old Dominic Agresta was accidentally shot at a carnival shooting gallery in Massena in August 1940, he was taken to Dr. Calli's hospital, where his condition rapidly deteriorated. He died two days later. Donald Sutton was only ten years old in the winter of 1942 when he and his friend fell through the ice on the frozen river across the street. His friend was pulled from the water and taken to Calli's hospital, but Sutton drowned.

The oldest part of Spanky's is an old railroad car that the late Al Nicola converted to a small diner in 1956, when he had it moved to its current spot. The retro barstools that the diner's first patrons sat on are still in place, adding a wonderful sense of nostalgia. When it first opened, it was called the Massena Diner. Later the name was changed to the Diner. It ultimately became Spanky's Diner when Alex "Spanky" Krywanczyk purchased it in the mid-1980s. Krywanczyk's daughter, Valerie LeValley, manages the restaurant and spoke to me in 2001 about some of the more memorable paranormal incidents of recent times.

She had just hired one young man, whom I'll call Eddy, to be the dishwasher and closer. On his first day of employment, when he was the only person left in the building late at night, he heard something so disturbing that he wasn't even able to still his trembling fingers long enough to lock the door before bolting out of there. He tried, fumbling with the key and lock, but in his haste to get away from whatever had scared him, he gave up and ran home to call Valerie. He told her he quit—his first day on the job and he hadn't even worked a full shift. It wasn't the first time someone had quit because of the paranormal activity. Spanky's actually has a high turnover rate for its closers.

One employee told me that he watched in disbelief as a loaf of bread slid across the counter where he was preparing food, and Alex admitted to *Channel 7 News* that he has become accustomed to hearing sounds when he's alone in his diner that cannot be mistaken for natural, logical things. He knows they must be paranormal in nature, he said, because there's no other way to explain things like heavy footsteps overhead. He has seen items such as salt and pepper shakers get moved around, and he once watched a cooking tray rise up on its own and fly across the counter.

In the early 1990s, the *Pennysaver* ran a story about the diner in which two psychics were asked to investigate. Among the many spirits the two claimed they picked up on were a girl who had drowned in the river whose name began with an "L"; a man with a leg and hip injury, perhaps a patient from the original hospital; a tall, white-haired old man; another man, perhaps a former owner or employee, who was concerned primarily with the diner's business affairs and was believed to be the one heard walking around the diner; and a large man with a black mustache who had died of heart failure in his sixties. One of the women said that this last man spoke to her, saying he did not feel dead, even though they were telling him he was. The spirits the two encountered hung around mainly in the basement and were most active at night, when they felt the least disturbed and interrupted by the living.

A more recent investigation took place in 2001, when eight psychic investigators—including Ronnie Guindon of Toronto, Marjorie Thorpe of Cornwall, and Joanne Deruchia of Massena—armed with cameras, tape recorders, and their sixth sense, spent a memorable night after closing on March 2. Before the investigation had even officially begun, one member of the team experienced what he described as a spirit "walk-through," in which he felt an icy chill that he attributed to a spirit passing through his body. He believed it was a female spirit both he and another saw at about the same time that he felt the chill. She was dressed in red 1950s clothing and was seen both in the dining area and, later, in the basement. They said that another spirit kept asking when the owner would get there, apparently because it was very fond of him.

Once Alex had arrived and the investigation got under way, they all headed down to the basement. Though typically warm, they all felt a chill in the basement, possibly indicating that they weren't alone, which they were happy about. A female member of the crew walked toward a space between the wall and the storage room, where several of them sensed an unhappy spirit. It seems they were right, as the woman was shoved in the chest hard enough to knock the wind out of her. Later, all eight psychics agreed that this single entity was the only physically aggressive spirit on the grounds, and he stays in the basement area. They communicated with this spirit and learned that he was bitter because he had committed suicide and considered Spanky's his home; he considered all of them to be invading his space and wanted to be left alone. One female member, after listening to his story, told him that nobody there would hurt him, and he could take her hand and walk with her if he wanted to. Their report stated, "She was actually a little surprised when he took her right hand and went for a walk. Another member of the group was able to confirm that, compared to her left hand, her right hand was icy." After that, the aggressive spirit's energy changed, and it seemed as harmless as the rest of them. Shortly after, everyone returned upstairs to the dining room. Ronnie Guindon sketched the faces he had seen, and several matched the descriptions provided by the two psychics in 1991, of which he was not aware.

A week later, some of the members returned to Spanky's to drop off copies of the pictures they had taken. Their photos showed an abundance of spirit energy, such as blue orbs in the basement, unexplained streaks and lights believed to be ecto-plasmic in nature, and orbs in motion. They wanted to quickly check out the basement while they were there, to see if the same spirits were still down there. This time they were met by a defiant group of spirits, and one member heard the words "Get out!" tele-pathically. The basement was warm, but they could feel cold breezes whirling past them. Knowing it wasn't a good idea to remain any longer, they left.

The next night, four of the original investigators returned to spend the night again. The basement felt the same as the night before, with chilly air swirling around them in otherwise warm sur-roundings. As the group headed up the stairs, Guindon was the last one out of the basement. He was filming the others leaving and was right on their heels. But something didn't want him to leave. Every time he tried to take a step forward, the focus on the camera blurred, and he could tell that someone was blocking him. It took him three attempts before he was "allowed" to leave.

That wasn't the only spirit interference they experienced that night. The audiotape recorder they had carefully placed in the basement turned up no evidence of electronic voice phenomena (EVP) on their first attempt, so they repositioned it at a different spot and left. When they returned later, they found that the pause button had been pressed, even though they had been careful to ensure it was recording as they left. So they set it to record a third time. When one of the investigators returned to check on it later that night, he felt an invisible force blocking his way, and the air around him felt charged. His nerves were tingling, and the plastic covering the doorway was shaking. He sensed that he was being told, "No, not now." It was as if all the spirits were conspiring to destroy the investigation.

The next time they went to check on the tape recorder in the basement, it had been moved behind an obstacle that hadn't previously been there at all. But at least it was still running this time, so they left it there. (They later found that they hadn't captured any EVPs that night.) The focus on the video camera started blurring again, but only when they pointed it toward the stairs. At least they were able to walk back upstairs without being physically restrained by any unseen forces.

They concluded their action-packed investigation with a final message from one wise old spirit named Abe, who told them he had been a preacher in the area to the natives, but he died of "the fever." He told them that although he wasn't one of the resident spirits that stay there, he had been called upon to assist them in what apparently had become somewhat of a traumatic experience for them—having investigators there so often. The investigators' report said that the spirits "found our energies disruptive to their work. As Abe explained it, the diner is a sort of transfer point for spirits, and the group that stayed there continually was responsible for cleaning up the negative energies." Abe's parting comment provides food for thought: "We do not need any help. There are lots of things that you cannot see, and we are in one dimension, while you are in another; and we should not interfere with each other."

Clark Residence

Jeff and Kelly Clark have owned the house on the corner of Plumbrook and Mill Roads in Norfolk since 1989. Ever since his story was told in my 2003 book, *More Haunted Northern New York*, Jeff said his house has become known as the "haunted house"— for pizza delivery purposes, at least. He admitted that during the eleven years of remodeling he did on it, he heard a male voice call out his name at least a couple times a year in the middle of the night. Until he heard similar stories from other former occupants, he never thought much of it, assuming it was just his imagination. Now he knows better.

One former tenant told Jeff he always was hearing strange knocking sounds coming from the attic when he was in bed at night. One time, the tenant checked the front door just in case the sound was being thrown from that area, but nobody was there. He passed on checking the attic, where he was pretty sure the source of the sound was lying in wait for him. The same tenant once felt someone lie down on the bed beside him, and he assumed it was a roommate goofing off. When he opened his eyes, he didn't see anyone, yet he could vaguely make out an impression in his mattress that looked as if someone were sitting (or lying) there. By the time he fumbled in the dark to find the light switch, whatever had been there was gone . . . and so was the impression. But this was nothing compared with what happened to a tenant who apparently was singled out by a disgruntled spirit.

Gloria told Jeff she thought she was going crazy because of the nonstop unexplained incidents she was subjected to. One night as she lay in bed, she was awakened by the sound of her bedroom door slamming. The carpet is thick in that doorway, impeding any movement of the door, so it takes a little elbow grease to open or close it. Gloria asked whatever slammed the door, "Who's there?" The only response was a low growl, like a dog about to lunge. She jumped out of bed and raced downstairs to where her husband was asleep on the couch. Just then, she heard the same growl again— only this time it was in the stairwell landing, as if it were following her. A former owner of the house owned a German shepherd, so

it's possible it was the spirit of that pet; however, the man's shepherd was not aggressive or threatening in any way, so it didn't really
fit with what occurred. At any rate, it's no wonder Gloria refused to
go back upstairs the remainder of that week.

When she finally did go back up, she wished she hadn't. Her first
night back upstairs, she woke up flat on her face with the sheet still
neatly under her, only she was lying on the floor. It was as if someone had pulled her off the foot of her bed (which sat back in an
alcove) by her sheets. Regardless of how she had gotten there, she
had bruises and carpet burns to show for it. How do you explain
that one at the office? Another time, Gloria woke up to find her
necklace lying neatly on the pillow beside her head, in a perfect circle with the ends clasped, as if someone had removed it from her
neck and staged it beside her face on the pillow. Less disturbing,
but odd just the same, was the television going on repeatedly for a
period of time. All efforts to keep it off proved futile for Gloria, so
she finally conceded and let it stay on. Her brave little daughter,
who was eight years old when I interviewed her, told of a persistent
cold spot at the bottom of the stairs, where her mother had heard
the growl the second time. She told the ghost and his dog to leave
because they were scaring her mother, and that actually seemed
to work . . . for a while.

I recently spoke to another woman, Maggie, who is a friend of
the Clarks and visits the home often. She told me that since I first
wrote about this house in my earlier book, things have continued
happening there, leading the owner and occupants to believe it's
haunted. One day, Maggie was standing outside near the garage,
looking at the enclosed porch attached to the house, when she saw
a woman there very clearly and asked her friend who it was. Even
though her friend stood right beside her, she didn't see anyone on
the porch. Yet the woman looked so clear to Maggie that she
remembered every little detail about her description, even though
she had only watched the presumed phantom for about ten seconds before she disappeared. Maggie thought the woman was real
and that she would see her when she went inside a moment later.
She had just come back out onto the porch when a strong blast of
cold air knocked her against the wall. She said that it felt like a

"freezing force field" and described it as a wall of wind—except that there was no wind.

Several people, including a local historian, have told me that the home was once owned by the keeper of a gristmill who became involved in a love triangle with a minister's wife. The minister allegedly interfered, and someone ended up dying . . . my guess is that it was the miller. But efforts to find documentation of such a scandal have eluded me, mainly because the gristmill was there before the region had local newspapers, so I can't say for certain whether such a scandal ever occurred there. But then, sometimes things are better left unknown. If it did, it would offer a motive for at least one unsettled spirit to haunt the Clark residence.

Racket River Residence

In an early hamlet of Massena called Racket River, there sits a small, harmless-looking Cape Cod house with a big, bad attitude. Forget doors closing and opening or lights turning on and off, the typical phenomena reported in haunted houses. The former residents of this particular Cape Cod would have traded what they experienced in a heartbeat for such activity.

Built in the mid-1940s by a descendant of one of the area's earliest settlers, the house is located precisely where an Indian stockade was erected along the Racquette River some two thousand years ago, before highways replaced rivers for travel. It was sold so many times over the next six decades that you can't help but wonder if each owner experienced something similar to what the family who lived there in the 1960s endured: smothered screams, horrifying apparitions, and night terrors. The house typically goes up for sale about every two years, but sometimes as quickly as six months. Such a frequent change of ownership often suggests the possibility of a house being haunted or otherwise stigmatized.

Gracie, Julie, and Lisa were little sisters who lived there for approximately five years with their parents, which was probably the longest amount of time anyone managed to remain there—and they still have the nightmares to show for it. The girls shared the upstairs, which was a wide open single room with a small window at each end. Something about that upstairs haunted them nightly while they lived there, and continues to do so in their memories to this day. There was always a persistent chill in one spot of the stairway leading to their quarters, and heat had never been installed upstairs while they lived there, so in the winter, they shared beds in a living area downstairs, with two heads at one end and the third at the foot of the bed, lying between the two.

In the center of the upstairs room was a cubbyhole built into the attic wall, blocked off by a sheet of plywood. Whatever lay inside the cubbyhole, on the other side of the plywood, was terrifying to the girls, and to this day, Lisa, now in her late forties, still has a fear of open closets, because they remind her of that cubbyhole. Around the side of the cubbyhole was a plywood box about the dimensions of a bed that could be used for storage. Gracie decided she would put her mattress on top of that, since it would be a cool, different bed. The novelty wore off quickly when, one night as she lay there almost asleep with her cat, she heard a voice. Being half asleep, and only six or so at the time, her first thought was that her cat must be somehow talking to her. Then the voice said that someone was going to pull her hair, and a split second later, her hair was violently yanked. Several times after that, she saw a large, shadowy figure come at her in the darkness and put a hand over her mouth and nose, effectively preventing her from calling out to her parents. Each time the figure vanished as mysteriously as it came. Lisa, one year older than Gracie, felt hands on her often as she lay helplessly in bed trying to scream, but she too was unable to move or make any sound. All three of the girls, in fact, experienced the same paralysis and inability to scream or move many, many times. After the family moved, they never experienced it again, which should quiet those who would blame the phenomenon on the runaway imagination of small children.

Julie was only three or so when her night terrors started. For more than a year, her parents made their nightly sprint up the stairs to quiet the slight, sensitive youngster. Every single time, they found her terrified, screaming inconsolably, and the skin around her fingernails was always blistered; as if she had been warding off with her little hands a demon straight from hell that only she could see. Unable to awaken or console her, all they could do was hold her tightly until it was over, wipe the tears and sweat away, and put her back to bed. The next morning, Julie would come bounding down the stairs, none the worse for wear, with no recollection of the incident, and the blisters around her nails were always gone—until the same time that night, when it would happen all over again. That phenomenon also ceased the day the family moved out.

Lisa, the oldest, was subjected to a nightly visitation by an arm—that's right, just a single, graceful arm of a woman that looked as though it had been removed with surgical precision from her shoulder. The girls had a nightlight of a little boy wearing blue pajamas praying, and it was in the light of that nightlight that Lisa saw the arm. But as morbid as it seems, the arm didn't scare her. Not like the other things she had been subjected to, which had actually tried to harm her and her sisters. She was so used to the arm appearing out of nowhere, gently moving as it hovered nearby, that she was surprised one day to see a ring on the hand that she had never noticed before.

Had the girls' parents not had their own share of unexplained incidents, they might have attributed all this to overactive imagination, but they knew there was something wrong with the house, and they were determined to leave as soon as they possibly could. When they first moved in, there was a distinct change in the father's behavior whenever he had to work upstairs, according to his wife. He became uncharacteristically ill-tempered but was fine after coming back downstairs. The stairs themselves, the parents noticed, had that one freezing spot, no matter how hot and humid a summer day was.

More recently, a real estate agent had an incident regarding the stairs when she was showing the house—which was for sale again, of course—to a couple interested in buying it. The door to the stairway wouldn't open so that she could show the couple the upstairs. When her efforts to open it failed, the big strapping fellow gave it a shot, but it just wouldn't budge. So they went to look for a crowbar or something else to pry it open with, but when they returned to the door, it opened easily the moment the agent put her hand on the knob, and without any tools. The couple told me that the cold spot halfway up the stairs is still there.

While researching this story, I came across an old newspaper article that said a woman in her seventies once fell down those same stairs and became paralyzed. She died after never having fully recovered from those injuries. So her fall on those stairs played a role in her death. There have also been numerous deadly motor vehicle accidents at the intersection near the house. In fact, the girls remember their mother telling them to wait inside on three separate occasions, after hearing a loud crash, while she raced outside with blankets for the wounded. One accident took the lives of several teenagers right next to the house, and another claimed the life of a bicyclist who hit a bridge abutment head-on as he zipped down the hill toward the bridge nearby. A man is also known to have drowned in the river directly behind the house. On the hill behind the house, leading down to the riverbank, the girls and their neighborhood friends once heard an angry man's voice clearly telling them, "Get out!" It sounded as if it were coming from within the earth itself, so they thought that maybe it was coming from one of the little sinkholes dotting the ground. Then they heard in an even deeper, angrier tone, "Get out of here *now!*" Needless to say, they ran up the hill screaming.

Another woman told me she used to visit her teenage friend at the house before the primary subjects of this story moved in, and they played with a Ouija board often, just for fun. That may have invited in some undesirable spirits that were waiting in the wings until the next family moved in, which happened to be the poor couple with the three little girls. But that's not the only motive for the house to be haunted. As mentioned earlier, at least one woman died of injuries that occurred in the house, and a number of people died on the street beside the house. Furthermore, the property was once an Indian stockade. In fact, one day Gracie and Julie were running around the house kissing every doorknob, and when their mother asked them what they were doing, they replied matter-of-factly that they were kissing the doorknobs because the Indian boy told them to. Neither the mother nor the sisters were aware that the house was sitting on the grounds of an ancient Indian stockade until I told them.

After six years of little rest and too many disturbing incidents, the family finally grabbed an opportunity to leave when it presented itself. The mother told me that the day they moved out, she left some boxes of belongings in the basement and needed to return to get them. As she drove alone down the hill approaching the house, she was overcome with a sense of dread. Nevertheless, she unlocked the front door and stepped inside. The cellar door was immediately to her right, so she opened it and headed down the steps into the musty, dank, and dark basement. When she was about halfway down, she felt an icy grip on her shoulder and was shoved. She fell down a few steps to the bottom, banging her head on the stone wall. Somehow, even in her overwhelming fear, she pulled herself together enough to get up and run up the stairs and out the door. She never returned for the rest of her family's belongings.

The three sisters and their mother today still experience the same sense of dread whenever they hear about the house or drive past it. They feel as if whatever it was that caused all of the paranormal activity still remembers them and would hurt them, or worse, if they ever returned. People who have lived in haunted houses where the events were particularly disturbing and traumatic often describe this kind of fear. And all three of those girls, who are now grown up and have families of their own, continue to have nightmares that place them back in that house or outside of it being dared to go in.

Sheepfold Cemetery

Notice me! That's what the figure on the side of the road seemed to be trying to convey to Dianne as her car approached him one night in 1993 on a desolate section of Route 26 at Fort Drum. She couldn't see much in the dark, with the snow blowing hard in typical lake-effect fashion, but she could tell that it was a soldier, and he was trying to flag her down. "He just kept waving his arms until he realized I was slowing down," she told me. Just as she reached him, he turned and ran into the woods behind a single row of tomb-stones adjacent to the greater Sheepfold Cemetery.

Dianne couldn't see where he went, but she knew there were training spots back in that area. After all, she was in Fort Drum territory. She figured that someone had gotten hurt, and the soldier had gone back to get the person. She wasn't about to get out of her car, though, to follow a stranger into the woods. Especially when she had two small children with her. Instead, she waited a few moments, believing the soldier would return quickly for assistance. Her husband was in the military, and she would want someone to do the same for him if he were hurt. So she waited about twenty minutes, then beeped her horn and called out to the man, but there was no response. Feeling torn, she reluctantly continued on her way to her son's Cub Scout meeting, planning to come back as soon as she dropped him off.

A short time later, Dianne returned to the same spot where she had parked and waited earlier and got out of the car. She yelled into the woods that she was back, then waited in the car with her daughter for another thirty minutes, until it was time to go back and pick up her son. The stranger from the woods was nowhere to be found. After driving slowly past the spot one last time on their way home, Dianne finally gave up, but she was deeply troubled all night, wondering if she had left someone who needed assistance. The next day, she told the women she worked with what had happened, and one of them told her that the Sheepfold Cemetery, sometimes simply called the POW cemetery, was said to be haunted. POWs were buried in that single row of tombstones Dianne had seen the soldier run behind. The thought that she had encountered a phantom POW was almost as disturbing as the thought of having left someone in need in the woods. But what else could explain what she had experienced?

During World War II, Fort Drum was called the Pine Camp Military Reservation Area and housed three divisions: the 4th and 5th Armored and the 45th Infantry. It also served as a prisoner-of-war camp called Pine Camp. Up to four thousand German and twenty-five hundred Italian prisoners were kept here in comfortable stock-ade housing, where they were well fed and, toward the end of the war, even permitted to go to movies and restaurants. It has been said that conditions were so good for POWs sent to Pine Camp that some didn't want to leave. Sadly, seven never did.

The POWs buried at Sheepfold Cemetery died during incarceration in 1944 and 1945. Six were Germans who died of "natural causes," according to the Army, even though the men were only in their twenties through forties. Their names were Otto Edelmann, Karl Elert, Franz Heitmann, Heinrich Schmidtmeier, Joseph Mueller, and Christian Huppertz. The lone Italian was Rino Carlutti, who drowned in nearby Remington Pond. At the time of their deaths, their families could not be found right away, so their remains were placed respectfully in the small burial patch on Route 26, just over three miles past the intersection of Route 11 and Route 26 in Evans Mills heading toward Great Bend. The site is well maintained by Fort Drum crews. On November 17, 2002, Germany's National Day of Mourning, the German-American Club of Watertown held its first annual memorial for the POWs buried at Sheepfold. Now that they are receiving the recognition they deserve, maybe they can all finally rest in peace—including the soldier Dianne encountered who was begging to be acknowledged.

Plumbrook Milling Company

"The ghost that legend claims had for forty years haunted the old Plumbrook grist mill, near the southern border of St. Lawrence County, is without habitation, the frosts of the present winter having undermined the old mill's shattered, gaping walls and tumbled them down into the long empty mill pond . . ." was how a story in the *Ogdensburg Advance* from 1905 began. Ghosts don't seem to need walls to inhabit a place, however. They're apparently as happy to haunt ruins as they are to haunt populated buildings. So the legend lives on, fueled by the findings of a recent paranormal investigation.

In 2001, a Binghamton-based group called Paraphysical Scientific Investigations (PSI) visited the ruins of the Plumbrook Milling Company in Russell, a place I wrote about in *Haunted Northern*

New York. Along with soil samples that yielded some interesting findings, they also obtained audio recordings and photographic evidence to add credibility to long-held claims that the mill was haunted—and to help prove that the so-called legend is actually rooted in fact. One photograph taken in the lower level of the grist-mill, where a grisly double homicide is rumored to have occurred, showed three orbs and a localized mist. One of the three orbs is just outside the mist. The investigators set up three remote recorders, which yielded the voices of a woman and a man, as well as strange sounds coming from the top of the hill at the site. This was an all-male team, and the location of the ruins is too far from anything to have picked up passersby or neighborhood voices. There's no way to explain the voices, especially that of the woman, without considering the possibility that they are paranormal in nature.

The 1905 article, titled "Haunted Plum Brook Mill," told of an unsolved mystery that occurred in 1862 in the Plum Creek area, "about a mile above Russell Village," when a young woman and a teacher she had fallen in love with disappeared in the vicinity of the mill. The article is about "Tom Shanley, the club-footed miller, and the mysterious disappearance of Mary Millington, who had rejected his suit, and whose bones rumor whispered were ground in the mill to destroy all evidence of her suspected murder." According to the "History of Russell, NY," on a website called rays-place.com, there had been a small gristmill about half a mile from the mouth of Plum Creek near Russell in 1810; another was erected in 1863, a year after Tom Shanley left town, by Hiram Bartlett. By 1905, the old mill had, according to the website, become "little more than a pile of mossy stones and tangled mill irons," having been built in St. Lawrence County's pioneer days and abandoned on an old (now barely evident) backroad shortly after a new turn-pike was built. It was in the days of its declining prosperity that an Englishman named Tom Shanley purchased the mill.

Nobody knew much about Shanley, except that according to the 1905 article, he was "a cripple who wore nailed to the bottom of the dice-box shaped shoes that covered his club feet a couple of horse shoes, the caulks of which kept him from slipping as he hobbled around the mill. He was a widower, it was said, and in spite of his

deformity, was very vain and of an exceedingly jealous and vindic-
tive nature." He lived in a room over the mill, and it was rumored
he had a "hoard of money that he had brought from the old country [and] secreted somewhere in the mill." It was this supposed
wealth that caught the interest of one Mrs. Ann Millington, an elderly widow who lived nearby. Her plan was not to pursue the miller
herself, however, but to involve her beautiful nineteen-year-old
daughter, Mary. Mrs. Millington thought that if she developed a
strong friendship with Mr. Shanley, and fostered a relationship
between her daughter and the much older miller, she and her
daughter would be set, as it were. She encouraged a relationship
between her daughter and the man who was twice her daughter's
age for purely selfish purposes, baking him pies, doing his laundry,
and such. Mary seemed to be halfheartedly playing along, since
there apparently were slim pickings in that area at the time, until a
young schoolmaster from Ohio named George Ray strode into
town one day.

Ray was attending school at Ives Seminary in Antwerp, and he
accepted a job of teaching at the district school in Plumbrook in
the fall of 1861 to earn enough money to continue his studies. The
little red schoolhouse stood along the highway about a mile or two
from the hollow where the old mill stood. "Mary Millington," the
newspaper article reported, "attended the district school that winter, and it was soon noted by Shanley, the miller, that when she
returned by a path through a sugar orchard and across the pasture
from school at night, she was accompanied as far as the pasture
bars by the school master. Shanley also noted that Ray sat beside
Mary at the weekly singing school and escorted her to all the community events that winter." With this disturbing development,
Shanley "grew more morose than ever and ceased his visits to the
Millington cottage, flying into paroxysms of anger at the mention
of Ray's name." While all this was going on, the elder Mrs. Millington continued baking for the miller and doing his laundry, on the
outside chance that her daughter would come around and choose
the rich miller over the penniless schoolteacher.

At the close of the school year on March 16, 1862, word spread
like wildfire that the "young school master had decided to enlist in

one of the regiments being raised for the defense of the Union." By that time, Mary was wearing his ring, and she was thrown into a fit of despair over her lover's decision. Nevertheless, Ray bade adieu to the family who had boarded him while he taught at the district school, and headed out to the nearest train station. A neighbor later recalled that he had seen Ray through a window of the unlocked schoolhouse on his way out of town, but that was the last anyone had ever seen of him, and it was assumed that he had returned to Ohio and enlisted in the war from there.

Meanwhile, back at the ranch, as they say, the bridge below the dam that separated the Millington home from the mill had been washed out from the spring thaw, and all that was left were the stringer beams. Mary told her mother it would be safer for her to traverse the bridge than for her mother, so Mrs. Millington handed the usual basket intended for the miller over to her daughter and kissed her goodbye. Mary never returned that night, so her mother—keeping a positive attitude—assumed that the rest of the stringers had been washed away and that Mary was simply safe at the mill with Shanley. But the next morning, after locals had laid new planks across the bridge, Mrs. Millington rushed to the mill only to have Shanley tell her he had seen nothing of the girl. The miller refused to take part in the search for the missing young woman, claiming "she had joined her lover at the school house and fled with him out into the world."

People actually entertained this theory for a few days, until one night when "a country lad had gone to the mill for a bag of bran and had found a man, supposed to be the miller, frantically stuffing pitch pine wood into the roaring box stove and had been ordered out of the mill by the club-footed miller with such fierce threats that he had fled into the night in terror." The article reported that there was another witness to some strange goings-on as well: "All next day, which was Sunday, the mill was locked, and just as the chanticleers [roosters] in the farm barns on the ridge were proclaiming the midnight hour, a young farmer hurrying home from 'sparking,' along the gloomy crossroad heard the old mill gate hoisted, creaking in its grooves, and the mill stones begin to whirr, while through the cobwebbed windows, he saw Shanley, lantern in hand, dumping the contents of an ash sieve into the mill hopper." Hence the theory that Shanley was secretly grinding the bones of his victims, Mary Millington and George Ray, before their remains could be discovered on his property.

A few months after the disappearance of the young woman and her lover, Mrs. Millington moved to Upper Canada, and Shanley apparently tried to sell the mill, in vain. Then one morning in the spring, several months after Mary's disappearance, Shanley packed a "small bundle of clothing and hobbled away, no one knew where [to]." The cottage the Millingtons had lived in was moved away to an unknown location, and the old mill was abandoned to the elements, eventually becoming obliterated.

"Like nearly all such deserted and lonely old [places], the mill acquired the reputation of being haunted, the gossip of the neighborhood declaring that Mary Millington had been murdered on that March night in 1862 when she disappeared, that her body was burned in the great box stove, which would take in full length cord wood logs, and that the following Sunday at midnight hour, the ashes were sifted and the bones ground between the mill-stones into dust, that no incriminating clue might be found," said the *Ogdensburg Advance* article in closing. "More than one farm boy of the Plumbrook neighborhood will testify, just at the witching hour of twelve, as he has passed the old mill, he has heard the creaking wooden-cogged wheels start and the old mill-stones begin to grind, while the shattered panes of the old windows gleamed dimly as though lighted up by some ghostly hand."

Had the scorned miller, Shanley, murdered Mary Millington, then ground her bones to dust? Had the man Mary chose over Shanley met the same fate, as a 1973 *Ogdensburg Journal* article called "And All for the Love of a Maiden!" by George J. Moffat suggests? We can never know for certain. What we do know is that there appear to be two, if not three, spirits lingering at the site of the old mill . . . two within the mist and one just outside of it, based on photographs taken by PSI. Could it be the ghosts of the two victims and their tormentor? And EVPs captured by those same investigators revealed the voice of a young woman singing, perhaps that of Mary Millington on her way to the mill for what would be her last time, as well as a gruff male voice that could possibly be that of the miserable miller.

Regarding the photograph of the three orbs and the mist, which was published in *More Haunted Northern New York*, PSI member John Bang said, "It was a clear, relatively dry night with little or no breeze and no insects. It was far enough away from residences to prevent contamination by most outside influences." Furthermore, the atmosphere in that vicinity, based on soil samples they obtained, was "highly favorable for the detection of ambiguous energies." PSI had found the entire area to be rich in silica and quartz deposits, minerals conductive to electrical and magnetic energies, such as those that spirit energy is believed to manipulate. For a news article believed to be nothing more than a legend for more than a hundred years, there certainly seems to be enough evidence of paranormal phenomena to go along with it.

The Adirondacks

Paul Smith's College

In 1859, Adirondack guide, storyteller, hotelier, and land mogul Apollos "Paul" Smith founded the Saint Regis House in the town of Brighton, where Paul Smith's College now stands. After getting his feet wet, so to speak, in the hotel business with a small facility on Loon Lake, he purchased fifty acres on the Lower Saint Regis Lake (ten miles north of Saranac Lake) on which to build his "primitive hotel." As one of the first wilderness resorts in the Adirondacks, the Saint Regis House was intentionally bereft of such luxuries as bellboys and indoor bathrooms, but it did have seventeen well-appointed rooms and attracted an elite population eager to escape the chaotic pace of their urban lifestyles. With Paul's wife, Lydia, attending to every exquisite detail of the prospering hotel's amenities and decor, Paul Smith's Hotel—as they soon called it—became the most fashionable of all Adirondack resorts of the time period, judging by its list of clientele.

By 1900, the hotel had been greatly enlarged to a four-story frame structure with 225 guest rooms, as well as stables, a sawmill, store and casino, bowling alley, boathouse, and separate house for its sixty Adirondack guides. It was in his room in the guide house that an employee shot himself through the heart in 1905. Cecil Wright, a launch operator, was only thirty-three years old and had just finished playing a game of cards with several other guides when he went to his room and committed suicide. The *Malone Farmer* of November 15 of that year reported:

> He was evidently very unhappy because of his domestic relations . . . and he probably brooded over the matter until he had become insane . . . Wednesday he bought a new suit of clothes at Bloomingdales and drove to Paul Smith's for the night. There, he drew the money coming to him for his services, had supper in the guides'

building, and after supper, hitched up his horse and drove away. He came back after a couple of hours, put up his horse for the night, and joined in card games in the guide house. He asked for a room in the guide house and retired about 11:00 o'clock. That was the last seen of him alive. The next morning when the chambermaids went around to make up the beds, they found Wright dead in bed . . . Nobody heard the fatal shot because his act had probably been perpetrated in the morning after the guides had left the structure. The revolver was evidently held close to his body, for his shirt was burned over the wound.

Aside from that tragedy, the hotel was in its heyday in the early 1900s, and Paul and Lydia hosted such esteemed guests as Grover Cleveland, Calvin Coolidge, Theodore Roosevelt, P. T. Barnum, and E. H. Harriman. Paul Smith's vision of an Adirondack resort for the rich and famous had become a reality before his passing in 1912. His son Phelps then took over the business and continued running it until September 5, 1930, when a fire that began on the wind-swept roof quickly destroyed the hotel. Thankfully, the hundred guests escaped unscathed. But after more than seventy years of building his business, Paul Smith's Hotel had been obliterated in just twenty minutes.

When Phelps Smith passed away in 1937, his estate funded the construction of Paul Smith's College, ranked by *Newsweek* in 2005 as being the "most resort-like living college" in the country. Appropriately, the private college today continues to offer degrees in fields that the Smith family held dear to their hearts: hotel and resort management, the culinary arts, natural sciences, forestry, recreation, travel, and business, to name a few.

Images of the past seem to break through the thin veil separating the physical from the spirit dimension every once in a while at this site. A campus safety officer can attest to that. While working the graveyard shift one evening, according to Stephen Cobb from the class of 2001–02, in an article he wrote in 2004 for *The SEQUEL*, the Paul Smith's College newsletter, the officer was taking a catnap in his parked patrol car when he was suddenly startled awake by someone rapping on his window. A stranger stood outside his car door asking him if he needed assistance. After shaking his head, he realized that the man was dressed like an old-time stagecoach driver from the hotel's early days that he had seen in photographs. As he paused to absorb what he was seeing, the figure—along with the old hotel stagecoach he accompanied—vanished. Also according to Cobb's article, an electrician who had been hired during construction fell off the scaffolding in the Buxton Gym, where he was wiring ceiling lights, and died. Now he is believed to haunt the second floor by making rows of lights go on and off in a wave motion—a feat electrical inspectors say is impossible because of the way the lights were wired.

Equally impossible, it would seem, was a male student's run-in with a ghost believed to be Lydia Martin Smith in the hall of her name. Cobb's article said that the student came home one day, before the Lydia Martin Smith Hall had been wired into the college's network, and found his computer turned on, with his user name and password up. Since they weren't hooked up to the network yet, there was no reason for anyone to have attempted to access it, especially using his name—and how did they know his password? Stumped for an explanation, he deleted his password, shut the computer off, and left the room. When he returned moments later, the computer was back on, along with his personal information. In the same hall, a student came out of his room one day to find his term paper stuck on the wall, with nothing to adhere it there—as if an invisible hand were holding it against the wall. People theorize that the ever-proper Lydia haunts her hall because she isn't thrilled with the idea of co-ed buildings. One student claims to have actually seen her spirit sitting in a rocking chair in his room, looking at him, when he woke up one night. The moment he acknowledged her presence, she vanished.

Cecil Wright wasn't the only person to take his own life on the grounds—although he did it when it was a hotel and not the college. In 1963, a night watchman came upon the body of a twenty-four-year-old student who had shot himself in the head while sitting in his parked car on campus. So with at least two victims of suicide, a deadly fall, and a family with strong ties to the property they loved, is it any wonder spirits may linger still . . . or just pop in once in a while to make sure everything's okay?

Adirondack History
Center Museum

Like a character concocted by the darkly poetic mind of Edgar Allan
Poe, Henry Deletnack Debosnys was to nineteenth-century northern New York what the Zodiac Killer was to twentieth-century San
Francisco—a merciless murderer who left behind a deliberate trail
of visual clues and cryptograms, daring us to identify him if we can.
Until that time, he will likely continue to haunt—and taunt—individuals at the Adirondack History Center Museum, where the items
defining his final moments are on display . . . along with a shocking piece of the man himself.

When Debosnys, admittedly an alias, drifted into Essex shortly
after the suspicious starving death of his second wife, Celestine, in
Philadelphia, he swept the newly widowed and wealthy Elizabeth
"Betsey" Wells off her feet and married her within a month. Just
two months after they wed, he slashed the throat of the young
mother of three during a picnic by the side of the road. Then he
shot her for good measure, pocketed her jewelry, and headed back
alone to their house to ransack the property in search of hidden
cash from her first husband's estate and the deed to her house. It
was such a sensational crime in the late 1800s that the Adirondack
History Center Museum in Elizabethtown now devotes an entire
exhibit to Debosnys, where visitors can see, behind a glass enclo-
sure, a genuine ticket to his hanging, the noose that finished him
off, documents written by Debosnys and others regarding the case,
and the actual skull of the killer—which, incidentally, was passed
around to area schools as a teaching tool for years before finding its
way to the history center. But this may not be all there is to the
exhibit. Some believe it also contains the very spirit of Debosnys
. . . that is, inasmuch as one's spirit can be contained.

On July 31, 1882, witnesses placed the suave Debosnys at the
scene of the crime near Port Henry, where they had seen him and
Betsey Wells passing by on a horse and buggy. The next day, neighbors saw Debosnys alone in the same area, acting rather suspi-
ciously. So they searched the area and found the empty wagon with
the lifeless body of Betsey Wells nearby. Debosnys was picked up—

with blood on his hands and a pitiful excuse for it. He was quickly found guilty, convicted of first-degree murder, and imprisoned in Essex County Jail to await his hanging before the two thousand people fortunate enough to obtain a ticket for the event.

But if the good citizens of nineteenth-century Essex County thought they had Debosnys pegged as nothing more than a cunning, opportunistic, wife-murdering gold-digger, they were dead wrong. Debosnys spent his nine-month incarceration making sure he would never be forgotten, detailing forty-six seemingly extraordinary years of life in a number of lengthy memoirs and timelines. He used a fly's blood to color in a rose on one of the many intricate sketches he drew, drawings of the places he'd allegedly lived and the people he claimed to have loved that revealed a depraved mind at work. The poetry he penned was at once both demented and pretentiously sensitive, but always skillfully twisted. Take, for example, the following poems he wrote about his wife, Betsey, shortly after he killed her:

My Wife Last Home
She died so young and yet so cruelly, oh dear.
Her fleeting life was very speedily.
She died murdered and not a friend was near
To soothe there for her a dying bed.

To My Poor Wife
She died like a golden insect in the dew,
Calm and pure; and not a chord was wrung
In her deep heart, but love, she perished young
But perished wasted by some fatal flame
That fed upon her vital, and there came
Death sweeping lightly, like a stream
Along her brain, she perished like a dream!

Once he was sentenced to be hanged, he duplicated the latter poem to make it about his own impending death, changing the title to "The Solitary Grave" and all of the feminine references to male, and he ended the verse with "For Henry Debosnys." The twenty-five poems he wrote in jail had many references to death, which is understandable, but there were also stanzas that revealed a belief in an afterlife and spirits, as in the following passage from one such poem regarding his own death:

The City of Death
Strangers who pass near this grave
Let awhile your studious eyes engage in your head,
And when returning to your home, you may say,
We have seen the last home, where we have to go and stay.
From which is no return, no more, no, no more—
And never feel the splendor of the sun, no more.
They turned their head, and as he spoke,
A sudden splendor all around them broke
And they beheld an orb, ample and bright
Rise from the Holy well and cast its light
Round the rich city of the death, and the plain—
Shone out to bless the breaking of the chain

Among the twisted poems and many other vividly detailed musings Debosnys left behind must surely lie clues to his identity, if even an ounce of what he wrote had any truth to it. But he was determined to prevent his family from ever discovering his shameful alter ego or associating him with the crime that he was sentenced to die for, so he carefully kept his true name secret, taking it with him to his grave. Certain that nobody was as clever as he, Debosnys did however hint that clues to his real name might be found in the many cryptograms and "biographies" he produced in his jail cell. To this day, nobody has deciphered his elaborate pictographic alphabet, which appears, to the untrained eye, to combine some obvious Freemasonry symbolism, along with a hodgepodge of ancient hieroglyphics and a Semitic-type script. The things he wrote fluently in Italian, Greek, French, Portuguese, English, Latin, and Spanish would have us believe that Henry Debosnys was a highly educated, well-traveled man of a prominent Portuguese family who had served in seven wars before finally settling in northern New York, where he was wrongfully accused of murder. Or, more likely, that the talented linguist was also a compulsive liar—and a cold-blooded wife killer who spun tall tales effortlessly in many languages and whose smug attitude and deceptively suave appearance attracted plenty of female sympathizers to the jail to comfort the doomed prisoner. Amazingly, they didn't seem particularly scared of Debosnys, regardless of his heinous crimes, perhaps because he was rendered harmless behind bars. In fact, he's probably scaring more people today than he did a hundred years ago.

It seems that he certainly did his best to scare Jessie Olcott as she interned at the museum in 2001. Maybe it was because, unbeknownst to Jessie, one of her ancestors, Deputy Sheriff S. S. Olcott, had assisted in the Debosnys hanging. The first hint of what was to come was when the copier in the museum's Brewster Library apparently ran a copy by itself one day when nobody was in the room. It was a copy of a newspaper article about Debosnys that was published the day he was hanged. In 2003, museum director Margaret Gibbs told me, "The article was in the out tray of the copier when we arrived in the morning, but there was nothing in the copier—on the glass of the copier where the original article would have to be to make a copy. We did not know how it was copied. When we held it up and asked the other staff in the library if anyone had copied it, everyone said no, and at that same moment, the power went out in the building and surrounding area." At that point, Jessie didn't yet know who Debosnys was nor of the connection her family had to the famous case.

A short time later, Jessie and another intern were in the basement working on a bulk mailing when they saw a face in a glass table on the floor below. They said hello, but nobody answered, yet they were so sure they had seen somebody down there that they ran up to get Margaret to help them search for the person. The odd thing is that whoever it was would have had to walk past them to get to where they saw him, and the girls were certain nobody had. The face they saw looked remarkably like the image of Debosnys in the old newspaper article that showed up in the copier.

Jessie was becoming intrigued by the case. Her interest was further piqued when, during research on the crime, she finally discovered that her ancestor had aided in the hanging. By that point, her thoughts were often on the case, and she was putting together the Debosnys display for the museum, so it's not surprising that she had a bad dream about it. As she described it to me: "One night after researching the Debosnys newspaper articles, I had a dream that I was locked in the museum library, and people were coming out of the walls at me. I was screaming for someone to let me out when a girl with a blue skirt and shirt with stripes and a red thing around her neck touched my arm and told me it would be okay. It felt so real that it woke me up, and the next day at the museum, I discovered the box with Henry's poems and pictures in it." Among these, she found a picture he had sketched of three girls next to Betsey's grave. "The youngest girl was the one in my dream," she said, "but the thought of a ghost never came to me."

Jessie also told me of camera and film malfunctions while she and a couple of descendants of Betsey Wells tried to take photographs of Debosnys's skull and Betsey's gravesite. But the most frightening incident occurred at the museum one day at closing time. "I was turning off the upstairs lights for the receptionists. When I went to the last room on the right, I went to turn off the lights, which are special in this room, because they are like breakers that you have to turn off one by one. Well, I didn't get to turn out even one light before they all went out one by one, all by themselves!" The switch box was in a room across from the library, and when the incident occurred, the museum director was right out in the hall, so she witnessed it as well. She went to the switch box to see if it would happen again, but it didn't. "You have to switch one on at a time," the director explained. "It would be impossible to switch them all at the same time," with just two hands, or at least very awkward and difficult. This occurred a short time before the Debosnys exhibit opened.

After the lighting incident, Jessie said everything went back to normal, as in no more *para*normal experiences. Maybe the mysterious Henry Debosnys, whoever he is, has gone back into hiding . . . and maybe he's still waiting for a determined sleuth out there to finally crack the code he left in his cryptograms that supposedly tell his true identity. In today's virtual world, where information is readily available at our fingertips, anything's possible. It would be especially interesting to obtain some sort of paranormal evidence, such as an EVP or psychic impression, that might help identify the Adirondacks' most famous alias killer. The Adirondack History Center Museum is open Memorial Day weekend through Columbus Day, and it is located in the old school building at the corner of Route 9N and Church Street (7590 Church Street) in Elizabethtown.

Former Plattsburgh Air Force Base

The old Plattsburgh Air Force Base (PAFB) on the western shore of Lake Champlain is thought to be one of the North Country's most haunted places, and it's one that people frequently e-mail me about. One man who wrote to me had been stationed at the PAFB from 1993 until it officially closed in 1995. He heard many unexplainable sounds while working in the old headquarters building in front of the parade grounds. "There were many nights I worked late and heard footsteps and doors opening and closing, even though nobody else was there," he said. "Some of my friends who worked in the two buildings to the left of mine also heard weird things, like banging on the walls, screams, and footsteps. Many of them wound up switching to the day shift because they didn't want to be there after dark."

That didn't surprise Jerimy, a retired aircraft mechanic who worked on the base and admitted to seeing some "pretty weird stuff" himself. He worked sixty-five hours a week, including Saturdays. The one night it was his turn to take out the garbage, a ghost apparently was dawdling nearby. After going out the back door to the trash bin in the parking lot, he turned around to catch a fleeting glimpse of a man standing up against the building, about a hundred feet away, who appeared to be smoking a cigarette. He thought it was the new client he was expecting a bit later, so he hurried back to the office to prepare for their meeting. But the client never showed up, and Jerimy said, "My worst fear was that the client had entered the building without escort—security being a main issue in this program." But when he went back inside, he found nothing. He searched every corner to no avail, leaving him completely baffled as to where the man he had seen smoking a cigarette had disappeared to.

Just as mysterious were the sounds he and his assistant occasionally heard, such as footsteps approaching in the front hallway when nobody was there but the two of them. Sometimes they raced to open the door and look down the hallway, but even if they were standing right there, they never saw anybody that would account for the sound of footsteps. It got to the point that Jerimy's assistant would wait outside in her car until someone else arrived for work so that she wouldn't have to be inside alone. The sound of footsteps was that real. And apparently Jerimy and his assistant weren't the only ones who experienced something strange while working on the flight line. When he left that position, he met others who had worked on the base who confirmed that they too had heard unexplainable sounds. Considering the extensive dynamic history of the base, it's not surprising. Residual hauntings seem to come with the territory of military forts and bases.

A cemetery on the old side of the base is said to be haunted by the specters of soldiers lying in unmarked graves from the 1814 Battle of Plattsburgh, as well as ghosts of babies and children that were buried in the early 1900s. It's habitually rumored that base police have seen apparitions in this cemetery, as well as in the adjacent crematorium allegedly called "Building 666." There's also a rumor that a surgical ward for prisoners during the Revolutionary War was once located in the basement of the military finance building. The story goes that the walls were painted red to hide the bloodstains. I'm not able to confirm that legend; but I do know that following the Revolutionary War, the base, then called the Plattsburgh Barracks, remained devoid of military activity for more than thirty years, until the War of 1812. From 1812 until 1944, the Army was stationed at the base. From the mid-1940s until 1953, it was used for college student housing. Then in 1954, the Plattsburgh Barracks became the Plattsburgh Air Force Base when the government converted it into a Strategic Air Command bomber base. And from the 1950s to 1995, Plattsburgh AFB was heavily utilized for countless military purposes. On September 30, 1995, it was officially closed for good, as a result of the 1993 Defense Closure and

Realignment actions. That year, the Plattsburgh Airbase Redevelopment Corporation was formed to manage the five-thousand-acre industrial complex formerly known as the Plattsburgh Air Force Base and attract business to its expansive grounds.

In a compound where many highly visible occupants of the industrial, business, and residential kind coexist, many who have lived and worked there have reported intangible occupants as well. The base has long been thought to be haunted, especially the old gym, the main entrance, and one particular office. Rumor has it that the gym was once a morgue, and gym staff have admitted to hearing pounding coming from the doors, as well as screams in the night echoing through the empty gymnasium. Local historians have not confirmed or denied that a morgue once existed there, but that doesn't dissuade staff from believing the gym is haunted. A Revolutionary War soldier allegedly still stands guard at the entrance to the old base, between the original two pillars, and a woman in white is said to haunt the woods nearby.

I've received an amazing number of photographs depicting spirit orbs and unusual mists that were taken on the base, as well as notes recounting people's own unexplainable experiences there. Still, they speak fondly of their time in the Plattsburgh area and, specifically, of the old Plattsburgh Air Force Base. And of all the stories I've heard regarding the base, none has ever been about something terrible or malevolent . . . just what apparently is harmless residual energy left behind by someone at some point in the old base's lengthy, diverse history.

Meron's Restaurant

"It's just Maynard." That's what they say at Meron's Restaurant in Plattsburgh when things go bump in the night. Grace Bergman is the owner and proprietor of Meron's Bar and Restaurant on the corner of Beekman and Bailey, a business that has been in her family since 1931 when Henry Meron opened it during Prohibition. When I spoke to Grace in 2003, she and her mother, Elizabeth Meron "Betty" Bergman, were living on the second floor of the restaurant, and both shared their paranormal experiences with me. Sadly, Betty passed away in 2007 at the age of seventy-six. But while she was living over the restaurant with her daughter, she and Grace felt the presence of Betty's brother, Maynard Meron, often and found it comforting.

"Uncle Maynard," as they called him, had run the restaurant for fifty-three years, since he was fourteen. He died in 1984 at the age of sixty-seven, but Betty and Grace believed he continued watching over them from the spirit world. They were sure he was the only one haunting the place, because it had always been his ritual to go down to the bar each morning for coffee, bacon, and cinnamon rolls. Even though the bar no longer has bacon and cinnamon rolls available, the same two smells have continually turned up over and over in the twenty-three years since he died. Furthermore, after he died, his family got rid of the coffeepot because he was the only one who used it. Even so, the very distinct aroma of Uncle Maynard's coffee continues to permeate the air now and again, especially near the bar after closing. Grace said the smells are strong and occur very frequently, but they are not at all scary.

It might have been difficult to identify who the spectral visitor was had it not been for the familiar scents that can only incriminate Maynard. The only other ghostly antics that occur are benign as well. Bottles and glasses sometimes fall from shelves at the bar. The television set comes on by itself when nobody is in the room. One bartender said she felt as if someone were standing right behind her when she was in the basement; yet she has never been particularly afraid. (Everybody knows about Maynard.) And it isn't just the feeling of not being alone that makes the employees believe the restaurant is haunted. Employees who are in the basement fetching more bottles of liquor sometimes hear footsteps walking around upstairs, even though nobody else is in the building with them. Grace and Betty often heard footsteps going down into the basement when Meron's was closed, but they were never startled. They knew it was Maynard "doing his thing," which was puttering around making sure everything was in order. After all, he was barely a teenager when he took over Meron's Restaurant, so it was all he ever knew. Old habits die hard, and it seems that sometimes they don't die at all.

SUNY's Hawkins and Macdonough Halls

In my first book, *Haunted Northern New York*, I included a story called "Haunted Halls" regarding the State University of New York at Plattsburgh. Based on information I was provided at the time, as well as countless other misguided sources, I said that "around 1905 a grief-stricken janitor hanged himself in the basement" of the Normal School (where Hawkins Hall stands today) and his body was discovered by a group of pupils sent to the basement to find out why the heat wasn't working." Wow . . . was I ever off the mark. Thanks to the volumes of archived newspapers now available online, I found out what really happened; and I realized just how easily the truth can be distorted as time marches on and information is passed from individual to individual. That's why I'm so grateful for such newspaper archives as the Northern New York Library Network's "Northern New York Historical Newspapers" to help sort fact from fiction. Don't get me wrong—the janitor's death was actually even more gruesome than I first reported, but he didn't hang himself, and a group of students didn't find his body. Here's what really happened—and why Hawkins Hall is now presumably haunted by a janitor who took his own life. According to the *Plattsburgh Sentinel* of March 16, 1917:

> John Blanchard, for many years janitor at the Plattsburgh State Normal School, committed suicide by inhaling illuminating gas in the room of the night watchman some time Tuesday night, his body being found by Willard Parnaby, assistant janitor of the building when he went on duty about 7:20 o'clock Wednesday morning.
>
> James Atwood, the night watchman of the building, desiring to attend a meeting of Plattsburgh Lodge, F. & A. M., on Tuesday evening, arranged with Mr. Blanchard to perform his duties for the night. Blanchard went to the building early in the evening and was at that time in his usual spirits. That was the last seen of him until his body was found by Parnaby Wednesday morning.
>
> Soon after entering the building Wednesday morning and while at work in the basement, Parnaby noticed a strong odor of gas and started an investigation. He went to the private room of the night

watchman and there found not only the cause of the odor but the body of Blanchard, which was in a sitting position in a chair, the head wrapped in a blanket resting on a desk.

The principal of the school was notified, and the death was decisively deemed suicidal in nature because of the following considerations.

> The coverings of the bed in the room were disturbed, showing that it had been occupied, and the supposition is that after having decided to take his own life, Blanchard turned on the gas and lay on the bed, but that possibly fearing that the desired result could not be accomplished by this means, he arose, went to the toilet, where there were several heavy blankets, and taking one of these, he wrapped it around his head, sat in the chair and placed a gas tube either in or near his mouth and thus speedily accomplished his purpose.
>
> During the investigation by the coroner Wednesday afternoon, it developed that Mr. Blanchard had been acting strangely for the past few weeks, and there is no doubt but that the rash act was committed during an attack of temporary insanity.
>
> Because of the suicide and the strong odor of gas, which had penetrated all parts of the building, there were no sessions of the Normal Wednesday.

Blanchard was about sixty years of age at the time of his death, and he was survived by one son and three daughters. Just four months earlier, he had experienced the sad, unexpected passing of his sister, Mrs. Theodore Callanan. It may have been for her that Blanchard was grieving, rather than his wife, as some sources say, because the timing of his sister's death was so close to that of his own.

The three-story-high Plattsburgh State Normal School was built in 1890–91. The large basement housed the gymnasiums, study rooms, boiler rooms, closets, storage rooms, night watchman's private room, and janitors' apartments. It was here in the night watchman's room that Blanchard presumably took his own life.

Twelve years later, a devastating fire of unknown origin began in a boiler room in the basement, resulting in a total loss of the impressive Normal School building—and the near loss of the lives of six students. The January 29, 1929, issue of the *Plattsburgh Sentinel* describes a scene of chaos, as the police tried to piece together the sequence of events leading to the fire.

> Parnaby—the same janitor who had discovered the body of Blanchard—was questioned by police, since he was the janitor on duty when the fire broke out; but he hadn't seen anything suspicious that could help shed any light on the disaster. It was generally believed that the fire was a result of spontaneous combustion in the boiler room. Six students of the Normal School band were trapped in the burning building with their instructor. When the smoke became too thick to find their way through, the instructor dropped each child out the window of their room. One suffered a fractured skull in the ten-foot drop, another injured his ankle and yet another his leg, but nobody died.

After the ruins of the Normal School were removed, there was a sense of urgency to replace it with "a more modern and even more beautiful one, where the work of education may continue," according to a resolution adopted by the City Town Hall and the mayor on January 26, 1929. So the new Normal Hall was built in the 1930s, today making it the second-oldest building on campus. In 1955, it became Hawkins Hall, named in honor of George Hawkins, the principal of the Normal School for thirty-five years. Today the entire building has been renovated and restored, and it really is a more modern and beautiful building than the first Normal School on the property. But a little piece of the past apparently remains within its walls, according to some who believe Hawkins Hall is haunted.

Not long after Blanchard's untimely demise, reports started surfacing of people seeing his ghost walking through the upper halls and on the edge of the roof where the flagpole stood, as if he continued to go about his duty, even though he made a conscious decision to end that routine. Those particular sightings ceased in 1929, when the great fire leveled the building, but the legends of the unfortunate janitor live on.

Macdonough Hall is the third-oldest building on campus, being built in 1948, soon after New York State established the State University of New York higher education system. It would be the first actual college building and the first state-owned dorm. Shortly after

groundbreaking, during excavation of the property on which Macdonough now sits, two antiquated tombstones were unearthed.
The workers set them by the side of the road to take care of at a later
time. The stones belonged to the city's earliest white settlers, a
woman and child, who had been buried in a family plot on the
marshy farmland. The following morning, the stones were missing.
Since then, students have had numerous paranormal experiences
in Macdonough Hall, such as lights that mysteriously flicker, unexplainable sounds, and "funny feelings." There have also been reports
of piano music emanating from an empty room, frightening images
in reflective surfaces like mirrors, and the sounds of a woman
screaming and children laughing or crying, when everyone knows
there are no young children on campus.

Besides the Macdonough and Hawkins Hall ghosts, there is also
apparently a helpful ghost in another dorm room at SUNY Plattsburgh. Just before Thanksgiving 2003, a young lady named Amanda
Armstrong became lightheaded while showering, and after stepping out of the tub, she cracked her skull when she fell. Because of
a severe subdural hematoma, she was rushed to Fletcher Allen
Medical Center in Burlington, Vermont. Her neurosurgeon, after
seeing her remarkable recovery after just one month, told her
"someone from up there" must have been watching over her.

Sometime later, while Amanda and her friends were taking
group photos of themselves in their dorm room, a series of photographs may have revealed who that "someone from up there" was.
Jared Greene took a photograph of Amanda leaning against the
wall, combing her fingers through her hair, oblivious to what was
coming her way. With one friend to her left and two to her right,
Amanda was smack in the middle of the group, with a white,
teardrop-shaped anomaly appearing several inches away from her
head. The next two photographs show the image moving closer,
and then it finally settled, resting on top of the college student's
head. The fact that there is such a brilliance to it—and that it
appears to have deliberately targeted Amanda before finally landing smack on top of her head—indicates that it must have been
some sort of supernatural phenomenon. The last image looks very
much like an angel on her head, because it's easy to make out a

central area that looks like the head and chest, as well as two very obvious wings. Furthermore, in the first two photographs, it looks like something—a bird or an angel—from a side profile, as it moves over to Amanda. These images were not seen at the time the photographs were taken, and none of the students having their pictures taken were aware of their spectral visitor.

There are several possibilities as to what this angel-like apparition may have been. For one thing, Amanda's beloved dog Charlie Thor had passed away, and he was called Thor for the Thunder God character in literature and art, who wears a silver Viking cap with gold wings on the sides, thus resulting in an angelic silhouette. Perhaps her dog had come back to watch over her as he did in life. Likewise, it could have been the spirit of one of her two grandfathers, who had passed away within the five years prior to when the photograph was taken. Or maybe the "someone from up there" is really an angel watching over the students, especially those recovering from severe injuries and illnesses.

Koen Residence

When Mitchel C. Koen purchased the house at 1732 Main Street in Parishville, he knew he got a bargain, as most people in that giddy honeymoon stage of new homeownership believe, but little did he realize that he had gotten even more than he bargained for. The house was one of the earliest buildings erected in the town of Parishville, which was established in 1814, making it nearly two hundred years old. Originally it was used as a dry-goods store, and it had three floors, rather than the two that are there today. But it was also a doctor's office, and it seems that its walls may have absorbed the residual energy of untold suffering from that time period, so maybe that's why discontented spirits apparently are still haunting the house today.

Shortly after Barb Beamish moved in with Mitchel, her then-fiancé, she had her first paranormal encounter, with many more to follow. As Barb reported, "I was out on the porch hooking the dog to his tie-out when I felt someone behind me. I turned around to walk back to the door, and something or some*one* was standing in my way, so I ducked through whatever or *who*ever it was. I instinctively ducked as if I was going to hit it." In hindsight, she is sure that it was a spirit.

Another time, Barb's mother, Nancy, was sitting at the kitchen table after dinner while Barb did the dishes. They were the only ones there. Even so, Barb's mother said, "What are those girls doing up there?" Barb asked, "Up where?" And her mother told her to listen; she could hear them running around upstairs. Just as Barb explained to her mother that they were alone, and the attic was overhead, she too heard the sound of scampering footsteps. Barb's children, Jenna and Morgan Sauve, were also affected by the ghosts of the Koen residence. They heard their names spoken by unseen presences, and they felt as if someone were always watching them, to the point where they were afraid to sleep in their rooms alone.

One night, when Mitch was away in the Southern Tier on a hunting trip and Barb was in bed, she heard what sounded like wood being thrown violently around in the basement. She could hear it hitting the furnace, walls, and pipes and was understandably hesitant about going down to investigate all by herself. By this point, she realized the house was haunted, so what good would calling the police do? They would find nothing, and she would feel foolish. Besides, she said, "It didn't really scare me. It just intrigued me." The clanging and banging continued all night and culminated with the bedroom door handle shaking practically off the door, as if someone wanted to come in. She checked but found nobody there. Everyone else was sleeping upstairs, so it was a little unnerving. On the other hand, did she really *want* to find someone there, in spirit form or physical? When she checked the next day, she said that for all that ruckus, "not a stick had been disturbed." That night, Mitch returned from hunting and was treated to the same show, finally making a believer out of him.

According to Barb, the doorbell would ring a song that wasn't even programmed into it when the spirit was feeling mischievous, and the spirit (or spirits) seemed to enjoy tormenting her daughters when no adults were home. While living at the house in 2005 and 2006, she often saw movement out of the corner of her eye, heard unexplained footsteps, and saw lights turn off by themselves and doors shutting unaided. Most recently, she was awakened one night by a very bright light shining in her eyes, but the second she opened her eyes, the light was gone. Still, she actually found all of it rather amusing, although her children would probably beg to differ.

Life has a way of changing, but one thing never can: the memories Mitch, Barb, Jenna, and Morgan share of the paranormal activity that occurred in the house they once shared in a historic old house in Parishville.

The House on Elm Street

Most of the time, there's nothing unusual about one particular house on Elm Street in Plattsburgh. It's a lovely home in a pleasant neighborhood. But every once in a while, a dark, menacing being appears, and apparently it's looking for a fight.

One tenant had lived there for more than a year before a supernatural encounter left him too afraid to sleep without a knife under his pillow. He had often thought he'd seen shadows out of the corner of his eye while living there, but it wasn't particularly alarming—most of us experience that sensation once in a while. Then a tall, dark figure appeared in his room one night, wielding a knife and obviously ready to do battle. It was a real-life "nightmare on Elm Street." For an instant, the tenant hoped the form he could make out in the moonlight in front of his bedroom window was Connie Repas, his landlord at the time. She was the only person who had access to his apartment. But for God's sake, why the knife? He knew almost immediately that it wasn't Connie, and the thought left him too terrified to move. He was face-to-face in the dark with an unknown intruder intent on doing him harm. Realizing his life was in imminent danger and the armed and dangerous figure had the upper hand, all he could do was lie there and watch . . . and wait.

The tenant remained frozen for probably six to ten minutes. He knew that the thing—whatever it was—was watching him, and he was sure it could smell his fear, so he consciously struggled to show no reaction, even though his heart was pounding. When the dark form suddenly slithered across the room, the tenant's heart was in his throat, but thankfully the figure disappeared through a sealed-off door into the bedroom of another apartment.

Connie had inherited the house, which was built in 1895, when her mother passed away, and it had been in her family since 1957. Nobody had died there while Connie and her family owned it, but Connie admits that before that, it's anyone's guess. Aside from the occasional paranormal incident, it was a very comfortable, peaceful home. There were two apartments upstairs and two down, and Connie mostly lived downstairs. When she lived in one of the upstairs apartments, she too had a couple of unforgettable encounters with the unknown, as did a roommate of hers.

In 1978, Connie was out of town and her roommate was in the spare bedroom—the room into which the dark figure had slithered. One night, he woke to find the room filled with smoke, so thinking that the house was on fire, he searched frantically for the source before realizing that it didn't even smell like smoke. It didn't smell like anything, but rather was some sort of smokelike haze. So he raced downstairs and woke up Connie's mother to help him. When they could find no explanation for the atmospheric anomaly, he refused to sleep in the apartment that night. In fact, he never slept there again unless Connie was home.

In that same spare room, Connie woke one night in 1980 or 1981 to find what she describes as a tall, dark, shrouded figure looking down at her from the foot of her bed. At least she assumed it was looking down at her, even though it appeared to have no eyes. She could tell by its outline in the dark that the faceless figure was hooded and cloaked . . . and she sensed that it was pure evil. Believing that it would only gain strength if she showed fear, she began praying, reciting the Apostles Creed out loud. She sensed that she was winning the mental battle this entity was waging, so she continued reciting her prayer; and the figure soon vanished back into the shadows.

Connie has also experienced other phenomena while living there. She saw shadow people—that is, entities perceived in the peripheral vision that are now thought to be a paranormal phenomenon in and of itself. Connie had never paid much attention to them, however, since they never felt threatening to her. Another manifestation involved a framed photograph of Weezer, Connie's Jack Russell terrier, that sat on an old wooden radio next to the window in her dining room. She had the picture facing into the room so that people would see it as they walked through the house. In a two-week period, Connie found the picture turned completely around, facing out the window—three times. The dust beneath it was undisturbed, meaning that somebody had to have lifted the picture up off the radio, turned it around, and carefully set it back down. But she had been the only person in her apartment for three straight months.

John and Laura, Connie's friends and former tenants, moved into the second-floor apartment with the notorious spare room in 2000. Though the room was painted antique pink and nicely decorated when they moved in, they used it only for storage. When I talked to Laura, she confessed that there was something uncomfortable about the room, even though it's attractive. She was unaware of Connie's experiences in that room at the time, but she and her husband had some unexplained incidents in the other rooms of their apartment, such as John's baseball caps repeatedly going missing. If they did turn up later, it was always in an obvious place that wouldn't have been overlooked while he was searching for them. And once John felt someone sitting on the foot of their bed, but he knew Laura was asleep on the couch. So he figured it was Bear, their large black Lab. Sometimes Bear put his paws up on the bed, and it felt like that. But the dog was nowhere in sight. Thinking that Laura must have awakened and come in and sat for a second before leaving, he got up and checked, but she was still fast asleep on the couch. On another occasion, he had turned off all the lights and the television set before going to bed, as he always did, but in the middle of the night, he woke up when the TV turned itself on.

One time, Laura found Bear blocking the bathroom doorway so nobody could go in (or out). For no reason, the dog then turned his attention to the dining room, planting himself firmly there while looking at something nobody else could see. Bear also figured prominently in an incident that involved a friend of Laura's who was staying with them at Christmastime one year. Laura's friend had the master bedroom, while Laura and John slept on the couch. The next morning, the friend came out of the bedroom and said she'd had a really strange experience during the night. She had been looking out the window, and the curtains kept moving back and forth, so she thought Bear's tail must have been wagging against them. But the curtains continued to move like that, even after she realized it wasn't Bear, so she checked to see if there was a draft. There was no explanation for the movement. It was just another on a long list of unexplained incidents in the house on Elm Street.

Pulpit Rock

"You probably don't even know who I am, or what I look like . . ." A former student wrote those poignant words in a note to Mabel Smith Douglass in 1933. Thirty years later, Mabel's remains seemed to whisper the same words . . .

An apparition of a woman was seen several times near Pulpit Rock in Lake Placid prior to 1963. Then, in September of that year, two divers exploring the bottom of the lake at that very location discovered what they first believed was a discarded store mannequin. They soon learned it was a human body. The water temperature where the body was found, more than a hundred feet below the surface, was a frigid 34 degrees. Combined with the high calcium salt chemical composition of the water, it was a recipe for "adipocere," a physiological reaction in which chemical minerals and salts replace body tissue, forming a somewhat effective barrier against total decomposition of a submerged cadaver. The result is a waxy, petrified shell of the individual who once inhabited the body.

According to reporter Barney Fowler in his 1974 *Adirondack Album—Volume Two*, the scuba diver said the body was found lying on its right side "in a deposit of silt," with a rope knotted around the neck. On closer examination, the divers found that the other end of the rope was attached to an old-fashioned anchor. The rope disintegrated unexpectedly when the divers touched it, and the body, naked but for an unusual pair of shoes and a thin strip of elastic around one thigh, detached from its rope and anchor and began to float up, while the anchor settled deeper into the silt. The divers then gently guided their gruesome discovery to the surface, where they temporarily affixed it to a buoy while preparing to bring it on their boat. In that short amount of time, several speedboats went by, tragically causing large waves to jostle the buoy. The jarring of the fragile remains caused the corpse to fall apart. The head, neck (with attached rope), and left arm and right hand all broke off the cadaver, returning to their murky grave.

Another diver was immediately sent to retrieve what he could, but the remains had plunged into the silt, making them difficult to find. All he was able to recover after an extensive, exhaustive search was the head. But it was in far worse condition than when the body had originally been discovered. For thirty years, the corpse had lain on the placid lake bottom undisturbed, allowing it to remain remarkably well preserved. The facial features had been recognizable when it was first found, but the trauma suffered by the remains in its short journey to the surface had caused the features to erode and vanish, as if someone had wiped them right off the head. Worse, the jawbone—so crucial in identifying the victim through dental records—had become dislodged in the hasty recovery of the head from the silt, sending it back into the murky sediment.

Early in the course of their investigation, state troopers and the local coroner were tipped off by a Lake Placid tour boat operator that their dead woman might be the famous Mabel Smith Douglass, who had disappeared in that general vicinity in 1933. While they were pursuing that lead, an autopsy was being performed on the remains, revealing that the body was that of a Caucasian woman who had been approximately five feet, five inches tall and weighed about 140 pounds. She had given birth at least once, and there were no signs of external injuries to what remained of the now-atrophying tissue. In other words, no foul play was suspected. All that remained of her clothing was the thin strip of elastic around her right thigh, like that found on panties, and a pair of once-expensive shoes that a local shoe expert dated to the thirties.

As the investigation continued, with more and more evidence mounting daily, officials became convinced that they had finally found the long-lost woman. They learned that Mrs. Douglass was the founder and first dean of the New Jersey College for Women, now known as Douglass College, the women's college of Rutgers University. The college had opened in 1918 as a result of her dogged pursuit of funding for the institution and her determination that women of all economic classes deserved a higher education. She had given so much of herself—her time, her money, and her energy—and yet hers was a life fraught with tragedy.

Born in Jersey City in 1877, Anna Mabel Smith was a highly intelligent and giving child, traits she carried with her throughout her lifetime. She received her bachelor's degree in arts from Barnard College in 1899 and was one of the first graduates of that school, a sister school of Columbia University. Always a supporter of education, she taught elementary school in Manhattan until 1903, when she married William Douglass. The couple had two children, a son and a daughter. All was right with their world.

Then, in 1911, Mabel decided that the all-male Rutgers College should open a sister college for women. She became so dedicated to this cause that she used her own money, along with the money she raised over the next five years, to see the project through. By the time her dream was realized, and the New Jersey College for Women had finally opened, her husband and mother had both passed away. Five years later, her son committed suicide. All she had left was her daughter. By the early 1930s, her health had begun to deteriorate, and in 1932, she requested a leave of absence, which concerned friends and colleagues of the indefatigable Mabel Smith Douglass. About the same time, she suffered a tremendous setback in the stock market. In May 1933, she resigned as dean and moved to her camp in Lake Placid in the Adirondacks. Four months after resigning, she vanished. Witnesses spotted her in a St. Lawrence skiff rowboat near Pulpit Rock in Lake Placid some time before her capsized boat was found. Her disappearance made headlines, and a massive search for her body was undertaken, but no body was ever found . . . until the two divers came upon it unwittingly almost thirty years later.

Ultimately, after a lengthy investigation, Mabel's death was ruled accidental, even though much evidence pointed to the possibility of suicide, and many people to this day believe that it was. The official police statement issued by the Bureau of Criminal Investigation in Saranac Lake reads as follows:

> State Police investigation into the recovery and identification of an unknown body from Lake Placid by members of the Lake Champlain Wreck Raiders Diving Club, has identified the body as Mabel Smith Douglass, who vanished September 21, 1933. The investigation reveals no evidence of a criminal homicide.
>
> The investigation does reflect ill health and an extreme nervous condition of Mrs. Douglass, but since positive factual evidence is lacking, and the rope the skin divers saw around the neck disintegrated when touched, examination of a knot or accidental entanglement in an anchor rope cannot be determined.
>
> Therefore, the official coroner's verdict is accidental death.

Many believe that spirits refuse to rest in peace when their true cause of death is incorrect. Mabel's body was claimed by Douglass College and buried in Brooklyn's Green-Wood Cemetery at 500 25th Street, beside her husband and children—and six hundred thousand other "residents." Not only is she thought to have haunted Pulpit Rock in Lake Placid, but some students say that the spirits of either Mabel or her children still haunt the Little Theater on the campus she founded, where unexplained phenomena are known to occur. And historian Jeff Richman tells of Mabel Smith Douglass's petrified remains as he recounts tales of "murder, mayhem, spirits, and ghosts" in his annual Halloween at Green-Wood Cemetery Tour. Mabel's legacy will live on, but her soul certainly deserves the eternal rest it presumably sought at the bottom of a lake called Placid.

McCargar Residence

Dr. Gideon Sprague, one of Hopkinton's earliest settlers and its beloved physician, owned the two-and-a-half-story home at 2831 State Highway 11B in Hopkinton in the 1800s. Today the historic home is adjacent to the village's museum and park and is owned by Jared and Maureen McCargar. The McCargars purchased their home in 1999 and began renovating it as soon as they moved in. According to Maureen, several years ago, a lot of strange things began happening once they began to remodel. But first, a bit of history. The following account regarding the McCargar residence is from Franklin Benjamin Hough's 1853 *History of St. Lawrence and Franklin Counties*:

On the last of February, 1814, after the British party had returned from their incursion to Malone, and had arrived at French Mills, they learned from a citizen-spy . . . that a large amount of flour belonging to the United States Army was stored in a barn in the village of Hopkinton, and that there was no guard at that place to protect it . . . Thirty soldiers, who proceeded in sleighs . . . arrived at that place early in the morning before the inhabitants were up. They first posted sentinels at the door of every house, and proceeded to search for arms in every place where they might be suspected to be found, and succeeded in obtaining about twenty stand, which had been distributed among the inhabitants. It is said that several muskets were saved by being hastily laid in a bed, which had been occupied but a few moments previous, and thus eluded the search that was made for them. Their case has been described by the poet:

> "'Tis odd, not one of all of these seekers thought,
>   And seems to me almost a sort of blunder,
>   Of looking *in* the bed as well as *under*."

They found some three hundred barrels of flour stored in a barn owned by Judge Hopkins, and occupied by Dr. Sprague, but having no teams for conveying away more than half of that quantity, they began to destroy the remainder, but being dissuaded by the inhabitants, they desisted, and distributed the remainder among the citizens.

At one time, the barn raided by the British in 1814 stood in the McCargars' backyard. Their backyard was also the local cemetery for years, perhaps even since the first settlers inhabited that land. The founder of the town, Judge Isaac Hopkins, owned the property containing the cemetery until Dr. Sprague acquired the house, barn, and burial ground in 1814. Dr. Sprague practiced medicine and lived in that house until his passing in 1859. The burial ground between the house and barn was no doubt especially convenient when Sprague was county coroner in 1834. But by 1840, there was no more space for additional burials, so the cemetery was dug up and moved around the corner to the Hopkinton–Fort Jackson Cemetery on County Road 49. The McCargar residence may conceivably harbor a ghostly straggler from the burial ground that was once on their land, since it seems some spirits like to hang around the spot where they were buried.

Several years ago, during a period of heavy renovation, Maureen and Jared were relaxing on the couch in their living room when they both felt something whoosh right past them. Jared compares it to being a spectator at a track meet where you can feel the breeze of someone racing past you, although there was no sound. It made a believer out of the usually skeptical Jared. No doors or windows were open, so there was no chance that it was a draft or breeze. It's easy to picture Dr. Sprague on an urgent house call, grabbing his medical bag as he sprinted for the front door. In fact, the McCargars believe that their living room may have been Sprague's office, as it is located at the front of the house overlooking the street. Regardless of its past uses, it does seem to be the most active part of the house with regard to paranormal phenomena.

Unexplained phenomena occur throughout the house, however. When the McCargars are sitting in the living room, they sometimes hear the sound of footsteps, as if someone is walking around the bed on the floor directly above them. It makes a very distinct, unmistakable sound. Jared's mother felt someone get into bed with her in the guest bedroom several times when she was staying over. The spare room was always the coldest part of the house. Even if they opened the bedroom door so that the heat from the rest of the house could help warm it, the McCargars could see their breath in that room in the winter. But after they made it their toddler son Sammie's room, it seems to have flip-flopped and become a tad too warm, regardless of the season. The McCargars also noticed that the curtains on the window in that room were always shifting from the way they'd been left, as if someone kept opening and closing them.

Maureen's friend Amy happened to be sleeping over one night when Maureen had a very vivid encounter with one of the spirits of the house. She was lying in the bedroom above the living room—where footsteps have been heard on the wooden floor—when something prompted her to look up. She did, and saw a feminine form standing in the doorway. It was a woman with her hair in a bun, wearing a long dress that Maureen said was gathered like a prairie dress. The apparition was not transparent or fuzzy or ghost-like in any way. It looked so solid that Maureen assumed it must be her friend, so she asked, "Do you need something?" Without responding, the silent figure just turned around and walked away. As she lay there thinking about it, Maureen realized that her friend would never dress like that, and she certainly never wore her hair in a bun. The next morning, her friend confirmed that it definitely had not been her.

Many people have come and gone—and lived and died—in the home, including Dr. Sprague's first wife, Maria Pier, who died there in 1826 at just thirty-four years of age. She had given birth to five children in that home. The youngest was only two and the oldest twelve when Maria died. Then Dr. Sprague married Maria's sister Laura, who dutifully helped raise her nieces and nephews. But she too died young, in 1834, when she was just forty-three. The most likely person to be watching over the McCargar family, especially the children, in spirit would be either Maria or Laura Pier Sprague, or both. The female apparition that Maureen encountered may have been the ghost of one of the sisters. It seems that maternal instincts must transcend even the boundaries between life and death, if the many cases reportedly involving female apparitions watching over living infants and toddlers are any indication.

There also seems to be a playful, childlike ghost in the house. Maureen once felt someone tap her on the shoulder while she was in the upstairs bathroom. Simultaneously, she heard the voice of a small child and turned expecting to see Sammie, but nobody was there. Sammie was still down for his nap. Their other son, Carson, was just an infant at the time, so it surely wasn't him. The McCargars have both heard the voice of a young child that wasn't one of their sons on several occasions in different rooms. Sometimes it only says, "Mommy." But it says it very clearly. They believe the ghost that has been turning on toys that shouldn't be able to turn on is also a child ghost. Some of those toys haven't even had batteries in them when they suddenly turned on! Maureen said that Sammie used to tell her someone was playing with his toys in his room.

Children and animals seem to sense spirits with far greater ease than adults, so we should never discount what we call their "imaginary friends." There may be a lot more to imaginary friends than what psychiatrists would have us believe. Maybe they're not so imaginary after all, but instead are spirits or other ethereal beings that enjoy the children's company and unconditional acceptance. Imaginary friends can't turn off nightlights after the child falls asleep. And they can't adjust the thermostat high up on the wall to keep the room temperature just right. Yet that's what apparently has happened in the McCargars' home.

The house seems to have at least two or three spirits, including at least one maternal type and a young child. Maybe they stayed behind when the cemetery was relocated. Or maybe one or both of the Pier Sprague sisters have returned to offer maternal support in the place where they once mothered young children. Maybe they're spirit guardians passing for imaginary friends. But as long as they can coexist with today's residents, the McCargars, does it really matter what their story is?

McKim Boardinghouse

"Kosterville, Nov. 25—The southern part of Lewis County is greatly interested in some strange developments which have occurred at a house in this village which is claimed to be haunted . . ." So wrote the *Watertown Herald* in 1887.

Kosterville is a hamlet west of the village of Lyonsdale in the southeast part of Lewis County. The John McKim family had a love-hate relationship with the boardinghouse for the employees of their pulp mill, thanks in large part to their resident ghost. In 1887, the *Watertown Herald* reported that the large building housing the McKims' employees, as well as their own family, was haunted by Mrs. McKim's sister. Since her sister had died in 1883, family members had heard strange noises in the building during the night. They kept the somewhat disturbing news to themselves, until the supernatural sounds became so loud that neighbors were asking about them. Mrs. McKim then admitted, according to the newspaper article, that "one day she heard a sound resembling the noise made by her sister when she died—that of groaning and sighing—but that she thought but little of it at the time."

As time went by, however, the same death sounds were heard more and more often, and not just by Mrs. McKim, but also by her father and mother, who were living with them at the time. Interestingly, her father, Mr. Hamblin, passed away before the family ever determined with certainty what was causing the sounds. After he died in 1887, the groaning and sighing actually intensified, but that was nothing. "Tuesday night three or four persons who occupied the same room claim that at about 11 o'clock they saw a chair move and tip about halfway over," the article continued. "The chair was pushed back, but it persisted in moving about for an hour or more and then raising itself from the floor three times, it whirled around and around."

Mrs. McKim told a visitor that her mother and a girl who was there with them that Tuesday night had just gotten into bed around 10:30 P.M., while Mrs. McKim remained sitting up, visiting with several others in the same room her mother was trying to sleep in. Suddenly they all heard a distinct rapping noise two times in a row. Mrs. McKim said, "Mother, talk to it," thinking it might be her deceased sister, Amanda. So Mrs. Hamblin said, "Amanda, is it you?" One rap was the reply. "If it be you, father, rap three times," Mrs. Hamblin said, since he too was now deceased. As requested, there were three successive raps. So it was determined that one rap meant no and three raps meant yes. Mrs. Hamblin, thinking she was on a roll, continued: "Can you talk with us?" There was one rap. Just then, a pitcher of water that had been sitting on a stand in the corner of the room lifted up off the surface and crashed to the floor "by some mysterious agency." The crash woke the entire family.

There seems to be no doubt that the boardinghouse was haunted. What we don't know is by whom. Was it really Mr. Hamblin, or was it a mischievous spirit pretending to be a deceased family member?

The next information I've been able to find about the McKims and their haunted boardinghouse was from eleven years later, so I don't know when the family first moved from the boardinghouse and whether it was on account of the poltergeist activity. But in 1898, two Lowville newspapers reported the McKims' return. From the October 20 issue of the *Journal and Republican*: "J. McKim has removed his family and household goods to the Koster boarding house at Kosterville." And the November 19 *Democrat*: "Mr. and Mrs. John McKim, who removed some time since from Kosterville to Port Leyden, are about to return to Kosterville, where they will resume control of the boarding house for the employees."

Perhaps the boardinghouse still harbored the same mischievous ghost, because the McKims didn't last long there this time. Less than three years later, the *Democrat* reported, "Mrs. and Mrs. J. McKim, who have for some time kept the mill boarding house at Kosterville, are about to remove to their small farm near Port Leyden." And that was the last time the haunted boardinghouse was ever mentioned in the papers.

Spicer House

In the spring of 2003, just six months after Marc and Sarah Spicer married and moved into their 180-year-old home at 19 Wellington Street in Malone, Marc was awakened by a hearty sneeze coming from downstairs one morning. This would not ordinarily be a big deal, except that Marc was certain he was the only one home at the time. Sarah was visiting her parents, and his son, now seven, was with Marc's ex-wife. So it was just Marc and the two cats. Yet he was sure the sound that woke him from his slumber was a man's loud sneeze, and it definitely had come from inside the house below his second-floor bedroom. Marc sat up and grabbed the cordless phone. He asked the police officer he called to stay on the line while he searched the house, because he was certain someone had broken in. Both embarrassed and relieved to find nobody there, he apologized to the officer and told him that it must have been a vivid dream. He hadn't even considered at the time that his house might be haunted. It would take a lot more than a sneeze to convince Marc of something he'd never believed in. But as it turned out, there *was* a lot more where that came from.

In 2005, when the Spicers were in the midst of heavy remodeling, they noticed a dramatic increase in unexplained phenomena. They saw shadowy movements in the corner of the reading room on the second floor, and the two cats seemed especially drawn to that spot, climbing over boxes to get to it, making it seem likely that it was the spirit of an animal lover or a small child that the pets would instinctively be drawn to. In fact, Marc and Sarah both heard the pitter-patter of little feet running across the upstairs when the entire Spicer family, including the two cats, was downstairs in the living room. Furthermore, their daughter, now three, started pointing and speaking to what she calls "nice baby" and "pretty baby" after she began to talk. This always happens at the top of the stairs, just outside her bedroom door. Sometimes she reaches out her hand, seemingly as if to caress the baby's face, according to Marc, while at the same time enthusiastically saying, "Hello, baby!"

One night, Marc woke to the voice of a woman calling out, "Jane!" Assuming he was hearing things, he fell back asleep, but he was quickly awakened again by the same woman's voice calling out the name again. The windows were all closed, it was the middle of the night, and the voice was unquestionably coming from inside his house. He said it sounded like a concerned mother calling for her child. So up he got, just as he had with the sneezer, and searched his house from top to bottom, again finding nobody. The next morning, still shaken by the entire incident, he was changing his daughter when she called out in her wee, two-year-old voice,

"Jane! Jane!" Marc was astonished. She had repeated the same words with the same inflection that Marc had heard the night before, even though he hadn't mentioned it to anybody, including his little girl. Was Jane the "pretty baby" his daughter often encountered outside her room? If so, then the woman who was calling to her might be Jane's mother, grandmother, or nanny.

The bathroom seems to be a hotspot of paranormal phenomena. Both Marc and Sarah have watched as the two upstairs bathroom doors opened and closed right before their eyes. The doors are secured evenly and require an intentional push or pull to move them. Sarah has often experienced dizziness in the bathroom, and I also felt it when I visited them. Quite strongly, in fact. The feeling, according to Sarah, is most intense at the rear of the shower. Marc also recalls that a strange, sewerlike smell emanated from under one of the two upstairs bathroom sinks for a period of time in 2006. The couple asked several plumbers and contractors to try to find the source, but nobody could get to the bottom of the mystery. Whatever was causing it, the odor vanished following a visit to the home by Reverend Belle Salisbury, a well-known psychic and spirit investigator.

Belle's visit to the Spicer home answered a lot of questions and confirmed much of what the couple had already come to suspect about their house. She was not provided with any details about the Spicers' experiences prior to her walk-through of their home, preferring instead to start with a clean, unbiased slate. A bathroom may seem like a strange place to start, but Belle was immediately drawn to it, and that made perfect sense to the Spicers, because the bathroom was hands-down the most active room in the house, paranormally speaking. So up the stairs they went. Flanked by two of her eager students, Belle pointed into the bathroom and asked the Spicers if either of them had ever experienced dizziness there. When Sarah admitted that she often did, Belle pointed to the rear of the shower and said that a vortex—a doorway from this world to the spirit realm—was located there. It is thought that heightened spirit activity around such portals creates a huge drain on the energy of the living in the immediate vicinity, causing them to feel dizzy, just as battery-operated and electrical equipment often seems to suffer myriad disruptions and malfunctions in locations believed to be spirit-infested.

The next stop was the bedroom belonging to the Spicers' daughter. At exactly the spot where their daughter stops and appears to pat an unseen baby outside her bedroom door, Belle felt the presence of what she believes is an eighteen-month-old girl, as well as an older lady who had served as the child's nanny. Belle also sensed that long ago, a rocking chair had been in the corner, right where one of the students who accompanied her was unintentionally swaying back and forth. All involved in the case think that it was the nanny's voice Marc heard calling to Jane, and Jane is likely the eighteen-month-old "pretty baby" that their daughter is so fond of. Belle believes that Jane succumbed to illness, since she did not feel like a "healthy" presence. Of the other presences Belle sensed during her investigation, one was a handyman type, very tall and frail. He may be responsible for the sneeze, as well as the unexplained hammering and whistling sounds that have been heard. Another was a teenage boy, unrelated to the house or its people, but with ties to the land. Belle believes he was killed long ago in a farming accident.

Shortly after Belle's departure that day, the putrid smell emanating from the upstairs bathroom finally disappeared. Although Belle told the Spicers that these spirits would probably all leave if they were asked to, the couple sees no reason to ask them to go. Like most people who live with harmless ghosts, the Spicers have accepted theirs as part of the house and find them, in some ways, comforting to have around. Marc summed up their attitude with a question: "How can we ask them to leave? This house has been their home a lot longer than it has been ours."

Hand House

In the late 1990s, two newly ordained Franciscan friars were sharing a bedroom at the Hand House on River Street in Elizabethtown following the ordination ceremony in Westport. At the time, Hannelore "Hanna" Kissam, the stepmother of one of the friars, was the executive director of the Bruce L. Crary Foundation, which owns the historic house. With its five bedrooms, and Hanna at the helm, it was an ideal venue to help accommodate the influx of attendees in town for the ceremony. The bedroom to which the two friars had been assigned was furnished with twin beds and was quite comfortable . . . at least until one of the young men was awakened by the sound of footsteps coming down the hall toward his bedroom sometime during his first—and only—night there. A passing car cast just enough light into the room for him to see the doorknob turning and the door slowly opening. And even though he didn't see anyone enter, he heard the footsteps continue to come toward him.

To his horror, he felt something sit—then lie—right down on top of him. After what seemed like an eternity, but was actually only about ten minutes, he felt the weight lift off his body. He yanked the blankets up over his head—something he had been too paralyzed by fear to do when it all began—and listened as the door opened and closed and the footsteps receded back down the hallway in the direction they had come from. Needless to say, the poor cleric didn't sleep a wink that night, and at the first sign of daybreak, he hastily grabbed his belongings and left. Meanwhile, Hanna's stepson slept through all the excitement.

The Crary Foundation—a nonprofit organization that has offered college scholarships to over six thousand North Country students for more than thirty-five years—has owned and maintained the elegant Hand House since 1979, when it was acquired from the Hand family. The foundation has done major restoration over the years, authentically refurbishing the house to its original appearance and furnishing it with original possessions of the Hand family. Hanna started working for the foundation in 1984 and had the pleasure of spending more time in the house than anyone else in recent times while she was executive director. She was in the house on a daily—and sometimes nightly—basis, including a six-week stint spent convalescing in a bedroom on the second floor following surgery. She said she had encountered the apparition a number of times, so she was not surprised by the friar's eerie experience. She too had heard doorknobs turn and footsteps outside her bedroom door, and she had seen shadows out of the corners of her eyes. One night, she saw what she described as "a vaporous, misty, smoky figure," which went through the door to the servants' quarters just down the hall from the room she was staying in. But at least she never had a ghost recline on top of her!

In the 1980s, when the house was home to the Adirondack Council and Nature Conservancy, several summer interns staying in the servants quarters, like the friar, left in the middle of the night and never returned. They were in the same room Hanna had seen the smoky figure drift into, so who can blame them for leaving? Three's a crowd, especially when one happens to be a ghost! But who is this ghost, and what is its affiliation with the Hand House?

Judge Augustus C. "A. C." Hand and his wife, Marcia, moved from Vermont to Elizabethtown in 1831 and built the brick Greek Revival home in 1849 to better accommodate their family of seven. Beginning with A. C., a lawyer for forty-seven years who served in Congress, as a state senator, and as a judge of the New York State Court of Appeals, the Hand House has seen six generations of Hands follow in the patriarch's footsteps. Marcia and A. C. had five children between 1831 and 1839. Daughters Ellen and Marcia Augusta both married well, but they died young. Ellen married Matthew Hale and died at thirty-two years of age, and Marcia Augusta married Jonas Heartt and died when she was just twenty-five. Sons Clifford, Samuel, and Richard all studied law with their eminent father before moving on to their own successful legal careers. Clifford set up practice in New York City and Samuel in Albany, while Richard remained in Elizabethtown, taking over his father's practice and raising his own family of four in the Hand House.

A. C. died at his home on March 8, 1878, but generations of Hands continued to occupy the house, first as a year-round residence and later as a summer home, until the 1950s. The house, needless to say, witnessed a number of births, marriages, and sad passings in its hundred-year Hand reign. And besides the Hand family members, servants and caretakers also occupied the home in its early years. If a spirit lingers from the past, it could be that of any number of people, but I tend to agree with Hanna, who believes it to be the ghost of one of the Hand women. Life was cut tragically short for A. C.'s two daughters, so it would make sense for one or both to return to the safe haven of their parents' home, where they had lived a pampered life of luxury.

The younger daughter, Marcia Augusta, was married on October 9, 1861, at her father's home and moved to Troy with her husband, Jonas S. Heartt, Esq. Just nine months later, she was dead at the tender age of twenty-five. Residents of Elizabethtown were shocked and saddened. According to the *Elizabethtown Post* of July 17, 1862:

> The grave has rarely closed over so much of virtue and loveliness as centered in the person and character of Mrs. Heartt. To a highly cultivated mind and prepossessing person, she added all womanly and Christian graces and virtues in rich profusion.
>
> But a few months since married, under auspices that promised all of happiness and usefulness that life can give, she passed from the paternal roof and from her native village to a new sphere of love and duty. Who then could have anticipated the sad, sad blighting of so many hopes and so much promise?
>
> The sorrow of husband, parents, brothers, and sister is sacred from our intrusion; but outside this circle, there is another wider circle of loving and mourning friends and neighbors, of her seniors who have known and cherished her from infancy, of her own youthful companions, to whom she was in life so dear and is now so precious a memory, of children whose earliest recollection is of her sweet and affectionate address, and with these at least we may mingle our tears.

Hanna believed the spirit she encountered was a young woman, because she sometimes walked through what seemed to be an invisible cloud of cool air tinged with a subtle scent of perfume. The fragrance was intermingled with the distinct smell of a woman who apparently hadn't bathed in a while, as was common in the late 1800s. She noted that one of the Hand women—she didn't say which—had died at a young age during childbirth, though the death hadn't occurred at the Hand House. If the woman she spoke of was Marcia Augusta, as I believe, does this daughter's ghost return on occasion to her beloved father's house? The female presence may not be the only spirit who visits the old Hand residence. After all, other family members, including A. C., passed away at home. And a tragedy also occurred right behind the Hand House that may have left a spirit or two behind. According to the *Ticonderoga Sentinel*, three youngsters drowned in the Boquet River near the Augustus Hand "cottage" on September 8, 1921:

> The children, in charge of a French nurse, were playing on the bank of the Boquet River a short distance from Judge Augustus Hand's summer cottage. As they were floating a toy boat in the stream, one of the children slipped from a shelf of rock into the water, which was over its head. When the other two children tried to give assistance, the struggling child grabbed them and drew them both into the current. All three sunk to the bottom. The nurse, screaming for help, jumped into the water after them and in a moment or two, had one of them out on the shore. Mr. Olney, the father of two of the children, Judge Hand, and A. Wadhanis, hearing the nurse's cries, rushed to the river and quickly got the children out on the bank. First aid measures were resorted to, and two physicians were soon on the scene, but all efforts to rekindle the spark in the little bodies were fruitless.

Wherever people have lived and died, spirits may reside. And the Hand House on River Street has certainly seen many people come and go . . . some more prematurely and tragically than others.

Tallman House

Spirit rapping: a form of communication between living persons and the spirits of deceased persons by tapping out messages on a table, board, or the like. [Origin: 1850–55]

—*Random House Unabridged Dictionary*, 2006

Malone is a small rural community of about fifty-nine hundred in upstate New York, but in 1897, it made big-city news. Granted, the article in the *New York Times* began rather condescendingly. The *Times*, in its October 9, 1897, article about "spirit rapping" in upstate New York, automatically assumed that it was dealing with a naive, unworldly population far removed from the city that couldn't possibly know what they were dealing with, adding that they should, at the very least, try to make money off their alleged claims, like others had been doing for nearly fifty years:

> Malone, this State, is a town so far away from New York—and almost everywhere and everything else—that one can pardon or excuse its residents for any ordinary exhibition of naiveté, but Mr. Thomas Tallman, a prominent and hitherto respected Maloner, has rather exceeded the limit of permissible simplicity. Spirits of the most satisfactory kind have chosen his house for a home, and are rapping on the walls potential yeses and noes enough to answer all the questions in the world . . . Mr. Tallman at first yielded a skepticism which is, we hope, more characteristic of the age than of Franklin County, and attempted to "investigate" the mysterious noises. . . . In this case, the ghosts were kind. They neither materialized nor vanished, but continued to rap . . . [Mr. Tallman] has become stricken with unmanly and unprofitable fear . . . He doesn't know a good thing even when it comes to live with him. His heirs-in-law ought to have him put under restraint and then proceed to turn the manifestations into hard cash in the usual way.

Apparently "the usual way" was a reference to the financial gains gleaned by the Fox sisters of Hydesville, at the height of their fame in the mid-nineteenth century. Unfortunately, the three sisters died alcoholic and penniless, after first admitting their alleged communication with the dead had all been a hoax—the sounds of "rapping" created by cracking their own toes under the table—and then retracting their admissions and saying it had actually been real, leaving many to wonder whether there had ever been any truth to their claims. Regardless, the women were undeniably instrumental in founding the Modern Spiritualist movement, and because of them, interest in connecting with the other side became intense, widespread, and enduring.

The movement was alive and well in October 1897, when the Tallman family sought the help of their neighbors in finding the source of the loud knocks that had begun emanating from their seriously ill teenage son's room, where he was confined to his bed with heart trouble. But according to another *New York Times* article dated October 8, 1897, their friends and neighbors were able to offer no explanation. "Those who came to scoff went away puzzled. Hundreds of persons visited the house. They tried every conceivable panacea for quieting the noise, but the 'rapping' continued." Word spread rapidly, and every local newspaper jumped on the media bandwagon to give their version of the incredible story.

The unwanted attention the rappings drew to the family, the character-marring accusations—and indeed, the persistent, unexplained rappings themselves—were extremely upsetting to Mr. Tallman. Hysterical and driven to desperation to make the disturbing noise stop, he renounced his own Protestant religion for his wife's Catholicism before a crowd of people, hoping it would appease the angry spirits. His reasoning had to do with a promise he'd made to his mother-in-law on her deathbed, which was clarified by a friend of the family in a letter to the editor printed in the *Potsdam–St. Lawrence Herald* on October 15, 1897:

> Thomas Aubrey, a neighbor, had conversed with the spirit and found that it was the spirit of Mrs. LaSabe . . . a Catholic [who had] brought up Mrs. Tallman, and after the marriage she lived with the Tallmans for years. Mr. Tallman was a heathen and Mother LaSabe tried often to get him to join the church, but he said he was not ready to do so, as he could not believe in Catholicism. Just before death [fourteen years earlier], she called him to her bedside and he, with her hand in his, promised that he would become a Catholic if she would return from the other world and tell him which was the better religion. Now she has come and fulfilled her promise, and Tallman seems to believe it intensely, as do hundreds of others.

When his efforts failed to silence the rappings, Mr. Tallman packed up one day and left the family. The *Plattsburgh Sentinel* of November 12, 1897, said he had "reached almost the stage of nervous prostration on account of the rappings, and has left the family and gone 'down east.' The father took the matter seriously and could see no possibility of a trick, which some surmised was the case, in the hope of inducing him to change his religion."

Many people began to believe that the Tallman boy, sixteen-year-old Arthur, was responsible for the rapping sounds, and the *Sentinel* was harsh in its opinion on the matter. It stated that the boy had become well enough to leave home and had been a guest at various houses in Malone. Interestingly, the rapping sounds followed him. They stopped at his own house on Edward Street as soon as he left but were subsequently heard in the other homes that he visited, causing speculation that the young Tallman was, in fact, a gifted medium, tapping effortlessly into the spirit world. This theory was further substantiated when the boy played a trick on a young lady friend shortly before he was apparently told to move out. According to the *Sentinel*: "While she was sitting seven or eight feet from the bed occupied by him, he suddenly asked, 'Where is your ring?' Raising her hand to show him, she is said to have been surprised to find that she had lost it, whereupon the boy laughingly held it out to her, having in some mysterious way secured possession of it." The article berated Arthur Tallman, accusing him of "amusing himself at the public's expense," saying, "If he gets amusement out of getting possession of a ring by some magical process, he may have some contrivance by which he makes the rappings everywhere he goes." If that were the case, according to the article, then it would seem the rappings and the magic tricks were "a little bit more *natural* than supernatural."

I disagree. Whether young Arthur conjured spirits that were responsible for the rappings and sleights of hand or had the mental ability to pull off those seemingly impossible stunts himself, there was nothing natural or ordinary about it. The dictionary defines the supernatural as something that can be "attributed to a power that seems to violate or go beyond natural forces." Since no source was ever found for the rappings in Malone, I would say that the word *supernatural* pretty accurately portrays the whole unexplained ordeal.

Wellscroft Lodge

"You have a lady in a red dress who sits in the window watching for someone," said a psychic who was called in to do a house reading on Wellscroft Lodge in Upper Jay shortly after Linda and Randolph Stanley purchased the property. That made sense to Linda.

A mysterious Lady in Red had actually been seen by a visitor some time before the psychic had been called. That individual had seen the apparition in the window of the Green Room (now sometimes called the Spirit Room), and that's the same room the psychic pointed to when she saw the lady in the red dress. And the young son of the people who owned Wellscroft Lodge in the 1960s was adamant that he had once seen a woman floating down the grand staircase. He said the woman liked men and wore her hair in a Victorian style. Linda has never seen the apparition, but she has seen imprints on chair cushions in the Green Room that look as if someone had been sitting there, even after the cushions had been fluffed and the room had been vacant. Who could this Lady in Red be?

Jean and Wallis Craig Smith of Saginaw, Michigan, had Wellscroft Lodge built as their summer home in 1903. Jean's parents were Upper Jay natives who came into wealth in Minnesota with the discovery of a large iron ore mine. Her father invested his fortune from the mine in the timber industry, allowing his family to enjoy all the perks that go with prosperity. Wellscroft was constructed as a summer home for the Smiths, a very elaborate summer home with a distinct English Tudor Revival flavor, built as a duplicate of an estate they had fallen in love with in Scotland. The residence was complemented with a caretaker's house, firehouse, powerhouse, icehouse, carriage house, children's playhouse, maple syrup house, golf courses, stables, gardens, and walkways. It was a self-contained seasonal retreat on the grandest scale of the time in the Adirondacks. The mansion is an impressive seventeen thousand square feet—not bad for a "summer home." Its worth in today's market would be in the area of $10.5 million, but in 1903, the price for that slice of heaven was just half a million.

For several decades, the Smiths vacationed and entertained at Wellscroft. Then the stock market crashed, taking much of the Smith family fortune with it, and they had to give up their Adirondack mountainside retreat. The property was sold in 1942, after which it saw periods as a public resort and periods of neglect and abandonment. Linda and Randolph Stanley purchased Wellscroft during a period of abandonment in April 1999. They had been searching for a place with bed-and-breakfast potential and found it at 158 Route 9N, thirteen miles from Lake Placid.

It has been a monumental task to restore the neglected, vandalized estate, but what a great place to toil away one's day! Linda used a stack of photographs she collected of Wellscroft's former days to help the couple accurately restore the lodge to its original appearance. One such photo of Wellscroft as it appeared when they first bought it shows an orb drifting across the ceiling of the dining hall. That was their first clue that Wellscroft harbored a spirit or two. Next came the otherworldly music. During renovations, before the Stanleys even had a radio anywhere on the premises, a visitor asked if they could turn off the radio. Keep in mind that Wellscroft Lodge sits up on the side of a mountain, too far from the road to pick up radio music from a passing car or other nearby residence. No source could ever be found for the sound. Likewise, no source has ever been found for the beautiful music several guests have claimed they heard, sometimes during the night. They described it as instrumental, soft, and even enchanting.

Another occasional unexplainable sound is that of a group of people entering through the main door, all talking at once. The front door at the carriage entrance is the original and is loud and heavy, so it makes a distinctive sound on opening and closing that differentiates it from all the other doors in the mansion. Once when Linda heard it open then slam shut, she went to see who had arrived but found the door locked, like all the other doors of the mansion. Her son heard the same thing one time, only what followed that sound, in her son's case, was the sound of a group of people arriving. Nobody had. And one employee quit when he had a similar experience. The painter heard doors opening and closing but knew that every door on the first floor was locked, and none of the doors on the second floor had even been hung yet! Poor guy left that day and never returned. Linda said she has also heard the old original light switches clicking on when nobody is anywhere near the switch, and she demonstrated to me how they make a very distinctive sound that can't be duplicated by any other means.

The psychic who informed Linda about the Lady in Red in the Green Room spoke of another spirit she saw who dwells in the yard between the powerhouse and the old firehouse. She said he wears an unusual hat, much like the one Frank, the original care-taker, was known to wear. It was a big-brimmed straw hat that made him instantly recognizable to the townspeople. Frank was also known for keeping Wellscroft in immaculate condition. Maybe he returns now to ensure that the Stanleys have been as conscien-tious as he was with maintenance of the property. He needn't worry. They have been.

There have been numerous caretakers over the years. According to locals, one hanged himself in one of the barns. The caretaker's cottage is farther up the mountainside, where the original struc-ture burned to the ground years ago. The town of Jay's deputy his-torian, Amy Shalton, said she remembered being in the original caretaker's cottage before it burned and feeling a chill pass by as she stood there. She recalled one incident a previous caretaker's teenage son experienced at the main lodge. He had been trying to open a door in the kitchen area, but it took some time before it would even budge. When it finally did, he saw stairs leading down into the basement, where he didn't particularly care to go, espe-cially alone. So he closed the door. Then the same door that moments before wouldn't budge for him kept opening, but now, when it opened, the stairs were leading upward. Startled and shaken, he ran up to the second floor to find his mother, who was cleaning. She came back down with him, wondering what he was talking about. *What door in the kitchen?* When they got to where he had found the door, it was gone. There was no sign of a door ever having been in that place. It was nothing but a bare wall. It's possible that he simply had become disoriented in a mansion with so many nooks and crannies and doors and windows, but he insists to this day that he knew precisely where the door had been, and exactly what he had seen behind it.

The last spirit the psychic picked up was a man standing in the doorway to the old "men's dorm" on the third floor. His arms were crossed in front of his chest in a no-nonsense way. The third-floor attic space is massive and as wonderful as the rest of the premises. Originally, it was used as the servants' quarters, so the first owners must have thought well of their hired help, because their quarters were fit for a king. The walls, floors, and ceilings are still lined with the original hundred-year-old hardwood, which is in mint condition, and every servant (Linda believes there were about thirty) working and living at the lodge had a view to die for from the window in their room. That may explain why they might linger.

Aside from such benign paranormal incidents as those described above, Wellscroft, now fully restored, is truly a marvel and a testament to the Stanleys' labor of love. They've spared no expense to ensure a comfortable stay, and it's no wonder they have so many returning customers. Though most people stay at Wellscroft Lodge for the sheer luxury of it, those interested in perhaps seeing or hearing something of a paranormal nature should request the Green Room suite, where the spirit dubbed the Lady in Red occasionally pays a visit. There are no guarantees that you'll experience anything supernatural, but there is a 100 percent guarantee that you'll feel pampered and spoiled while you try.

BrightSide on Raquette

More than a hundred years ago, a couple checked into a hotel on Indian Point in Raquette Lake in the middle of a blizzard. Shortly after their arrival, the man set out across the frozen lake for the village, presumably for supplies. He never returned to the resort. And it seems that his heartbroken wife has never left it. It is said that after his disappearance so long ago, she kept continuous watch by the window of their guest room—an effort in futility, though this apparently hasn't stopped her even after all this time. For whatever reason, the only thing that could pull her away from her silent vigil was the sound of the old Vose and Sons piano playing in the Great Room, and there are claims that she makes her presence known in that same room today whenever someone plays the original piano. Many believe the woman's spirit also continues to haunt the room above the kitchen, which she briefly shared with her beloved, as she awaits his return, and there may be evidence to support that thought.

When the Light Connection purchased the BrightSide in 2001, renovators found an old-time woman's coat hanging on a coat rack in the storied room. Regardless of its obvious age, it was in perfect shape, yet nobody could fathom why it was there, and the workers weren't aware of the couple's tragedy. What's more, a few months after they found the lady's coat, a man's coat from the same era appeared on the rack beside it. According to the BrightSide's website, nobody "knows where, when, or how it got there," so obviously, they can't help but wonder whether it has something to do with the above ghost story. And that's just one of the many ghostly tales that the BrightSide, a vacation complex on Raquette Lake that is accessible only by boat, shares on its website.

The 122-year-old Adirondack resort is a treasure trove of history and hauntings. The resort was an intense labor of love for Joe and Mary Bryere, the enterprising couple who built it in the late 1800s. But no two people were better suited for such a major undertaking, according to the website: "In terms of stamina, Joe and Mary were a good match. Mary could swing an axe and pull a crosscut saw on par with any man, and legend has it that Joe killed a 1,200-pound bull moose with his bare hands in his younger days in Canada."

By the time it opened as a hundred-acre vacation complex, the BrightSide consisted of the hotel plus a number of cabins, a boathouse, and a water tower. Besides all the modern conveniences it boasted in 1891, the resort also offered golf, tennis, and water sports. Not only was Joe the builder, owner, and operator of the BrightSide, along with Mary, but he was also a sought-out carpenter whose Adirondack-style furniture still graces the resort compound. And the tireless couple who bore and raised four children at the BrightSide somehow managed to remain active in their community. Joe even served a stint as county coroner, back in the days when it was a common practice to bury bodies in the loose soil of basements when the ground outside was frozen.

The BrightSide enjoyed prosperity and recognition in its heyday and was a favorite resort of many wealthy guests and colorful characters, which was no doubt delightful for the Bryere children. But as time marched on, the children grew up and moved away. Joe had been running the BrightSide for fifty years when he passed away in 1941. His daughter Clara, a nurse in France during World War I, returned home after receiving word of her father's death to run the BrightSide. Every bit as capable as her parents, Clara not only continued to run the resort for sixteen years, but she also made some much-needed improvements, earning her the moniker "Miss BrightSide." In 1957, when she sold the inn to BrightSide on Raquette Lake Incorporated, she donated many of her father's handcrafted wooden creations to the Adirondack Museum in Blue Mountain Lake.

In 2001, the Light Connection, one of three telecommunications firms owned by Frank Grotto, purchased the property. Under Grotto's direction, modern plumbing and additional bathroom facilities were established on each floor, coal-burning furnaces were replaced by propane ones, and window, foundations, and roofing were either replaced or repaired. New furnishings were brought in to accompany the original antique pieces, and a fresh coat of paint on the outside of the resort was the icing on the cake. The resort has since been used as a corporate training facility and for special events for Grotto's companies. But it also is offered to other companies and private groups for company retreats, annual meetings, training seminars, and special events. The BrightSide, with its contagious atmosphere and culinary delights, is guaranteed to leave its guests with something to talk about, even if they don't have a paranormal experience while there. But if they do have such an experience, there's a good chance it will happen in the Ghost Room. That's right, one room—the room above the kitchen—has been designated officially as the Ghost Room, and a running list of ghostly happenings at the BrightSide called "The Ghost Update" is posted outside of that room.

There was the young girl who decided to retire early to bed one night, only to change her mind when her bed started shaking so hard that she could barely hold the book she was reading. She was unaware of the ghost stories, but the rest of her group and staff were quick to tell her that she wasn't the first person who'd had such an experience in that room. Another woman swore that she heard her camera, on the other side of her room, snapping pictures one morning while she made the bed. A couple weeks later, when she got her film developed, she was stunned to find three photographs that were somehow taken from the exact position at which her camera was sitting at that morning, each showing blue orbs. Think about that for a moment . . . it means that a ghost was taking pictures of a ghost!

Another guest was also witness to the famous BrightSide blue orbs. At breakfast one morning, he mentioned to his companions and staff the bluish spheres that had mesmerized him in his room the night before, saying they must have been reflections off the lake from boat lights. The only problem with that theory, he was soon reminded, was that his room didn't face the lake, or any source of water, for that matter. Furthermore, he was informed that paranormal investigators called the Mohawk Valley GhostHunters had captured similarly colored orbs in photographs they took during their investigation of the grounds in August 2002. This guest didn't take the news so well and made an early departure. But a copy of the GhostHunters' report, stating that they found the original building to be very active, is available for all guests of the BrightSide to enjoy.

Western
New York
and the
Finger Lakes

Holiday Inn

New York State's most famous hotel ghost is Tanya, a little girl who allegedly haunts the Holiday Inn Grand Island Resort and Conference Center at 100 Whitehaven Road, Grand Island. The six-story, 263-room hotel overlooking the Niagara River was built in 1972 and renovated in 1999. According to legend, on the very foundation the hotel was built on, a young girl once died in a horrific house fire, and her resilient spirit now frolics about the hotel looking for playmates.

In the 1830s, the property on which the hotel was eventually built was called the Whitehaven Sawmill Settlement, a sixteen-thousand-acre community that included a beautiful mansion known as the Riverhaven Lodge, as well as a store, school for workers' children, church, warehouse, and lumberjack sleeping quarters. The sawmill, managed by Stephen White, for whom the settlement was named, cut the property's white oaks into desirable timber using the largest steam saw in the world, then shipped it to East Coast shipyards via the Erie Canal. In 1848, Grand Island's first town supervisor, John Nice, purchased the property, and he and his wife raised ten daughters at the mansion. The family is buried in the Whitehaven Cemetery. The mansion was then rented to various tenants before being purchased by Fred Mesmer, a restaurateur who converted it into Mesmer's Supper Club in 1946. In 1962, the restaurant—the old Riverhaven Lodge and Nice residence—burned, but thankfully nobody died in the fire. Ten years later, the remains of the mansion were razed, and construction of the Holiday Inn began on the site. A single stone building from the old sawmill settlement still stands on the property, identified by a sign designating it as a historic site.

Though I could find no records to support the legend of a girl dying in a fire—and no records of a girl named Tanya dying by any means on Grand Island—scores of people have reported encounters or experiences with a suspected child ghost that roams the halls of the popular resort. Google hits number into the tens of thousands for the girl ghost dubbed Tanya. With numbers that high, the legend shouldn't be dismissed merely on the basis of a lack of historical evidence. After all, many girls have lived in the vicinity since its days as a sawmill settlement. And there's no law that says a ghost can only haunt the place at which the person died. It also seems that ghosts often return to places they were once fond of.

As far as the Holiday Inn ghost being called Tanya, well, when a ghost is seen often enough, it seems only fitting to give it a name, even if it's not the name the spirit went by when alive. The popularity of the name Tanya peaked in 1974, when it was ranked forty-six out of a thousand, and that time period correlates with the first sightings of the girl ghost. Conversely, the name was ranked two hundred in the popularity index of 1962, the year of the only recorded fire on the property. In the Nice family's time at the mansion, Tanya was not even listed in the top thousand girl names. This leads me to believe that the name was given to the resident ghost simply because it was a semipopular name at the time, although it may have been divined by a psychic or by means of a Ouija board.

Employees and guests of the Holiday Inn have long reported apparitions of a spirited little girl, between five and ten years old, skipping down the hallways, bouncing a ball, and sometimes waking guests. Housekeepers, especially, have had countless run-ins with the little ball of energy, such as hearing their name called out in a child's voice while making up a room or walking down the hall. Tanya has been seen running across the grounds and disappearing around the corner of the building into thin air. Like my own seven-year-old daughter, she's a constant flurry of motion. On the fourth floor, purportedly Tanya's favorite "haunt," so to speak, another spirit has been seen, though much less frequently: a tall, sullen man who stands beside beds looking down at a select few guests. Nobody knows what connection he has to Tanya, if any, primarily because we don't know who Tanya really is. What we do know is that her hair is consistently long and wild. She sometimes dons an old-fashioned white nightgown, but other times she is seen in a red velvet dress and high, black button-up shoes. And even when she is not actually seen, she is quite often heard—by some accounts every night. It seems that at any given hour of the night, someone, somewhere in the resort hears the patter of little feet traversing the length of the corridor outside his or her door, but the guest simply shrugs it off as just the unruly child of an inattentive parent.

One woman I spoke to stayed at the Holiday Inn during a scientific convention she was attending. She recalled being repeatedly awakened by a child running up and down the hall past her door one night. Growing increasingly annoyed, she finally got up, opened the door, and prepared to chastise the child she was sure she would see. But alas, no child was anywhere in sight. Strangely, however, it still *sounded* as if a child were there. As she stood there looking up and down the empty hallway, she could have sworn she felt a slight breeze brush past her as the sound of little footsteps continued merrily on their way down the corridor.

Durand-Eastman Park

For years, Rochester-area residents have told stories about the White Lady of Durand-Eastman Park, who frightens young men as they park on Lake Shore Boulevard and other roads in the vicinity. In all fairness to the opposite sex, women are equally scared when they see her. There are several variations of the story. In one version, a semitransparent ivory apparition is seen, accompanied by two dogs, barely skimming the surface of the water as they float in from Lake Ontario toward the shoreline to confront young lovers and put an end to romantic interludes. The reason? The apparition is believed to be a woman whose teenage daughter vanished as she walked to the beach along Lake Ontario long ago, before the shoreline property was bought out by philanthropists Henry Strong Durand and George Eastman and converted into a public park, which they donated to the city of Rochester. The girl's body was never found, nor were any clues to her disappearance. It is said that the mother spent the rest of her days searching in vain for her lost daughter, who she believed had been raped and killed by a local farmer. When it became apparent she would never see her daughter again, the woman threw herself off a ridge into either Lake Ontario or Durand Lake and drowned. If true, this all took place before documented records were kept for the area, such as newspaper clippings, so that version can't be confirmed . . . or rejected. There were a number of farms on the massive park grounds that Eastman and Durand purchased prior to 1907, so it's possible that such a tragedy did occur. An incident did occur in 1936 that had a somewhat similar theme, so maybe someone along the way tied it to the White Lady sightings.

Irondequoit is a major suburb of the city of Rochester, bounded to the north partially by Lake Ontario and the city of Rochester and to the east by Irondequoit Bay. Durand-Eastman Park is surrounded by the town of Irondequoit on three sides and Lake Ontario on the other. It belongs to the city of Rochester and is connected by an easement along Culver Road. Oklahoma Beach is across the Irondequoit Bay from Durand-Eastman Park, and it too has Lake Ontario as its northern border. In 1936, eighteen-year-old ballet dancer Winifred Schenk was gunned down by her own father after she attempted to retrieve a purse he had stolen from her mother, his estranged wife. It had $17 in it. Winifred had been at a lakeshore party with her brother when she decided to leave and fetch the purse. She went to her father's home on the lakefront in Oklahoma Beach to get it, but her father became so incensed that her brother told two male friends who had accompanied her to take her away in one of their cars before her father hurt her. The young woman and her two companions from Irondequoit left quickly, but her father chased them in his own car and eventually forced them off the road near Forest Lawn. He shot all three, killing his daughter and mortally wounding the two young men.

Imagine Winifred's mother's horror upon learning that her only daughter was killed by her father while attempting to get her mother's purse back. The night had started off nicely with a beach party on Lake Ontario and ended with three dead over $17. Perhaps Winifred returned to the last place she had been, the beach near Durand-Eastman Park, before sealing her fate by returning to her malicious father's house. Maybe she's checking parked vehicles even today, still searching for her two companions who lost their lives trying to save hers. After all, she was the first one shot and may not realize they soon followed her to the afterlife.

In *Spooky New York*, S. E. Schlosser said the White Lady is a very vengeful spirit that dislikes men because of what she believed happened to her daughter. So she returns from the grave to avenge her daughter's death by confronting parked cars in both Durand-Eastman Park and along the Lake Ontario shoreline. She has never hurt a female, but witnesses have reported the apparition chasing males straight into the lake or shaking their vehicles until they leave the park, in an effort to prevent any other mother's daughter from the same fate she and her own daughter met.

Unfortunately, she wasn't able to scare the Alphabet Murderer away in the early 1970s, when three little girls from the surrounding communities of Churchville, Webster, and Macedon were abducted and later found raped, beaten, and strangled. Wanda Walkowicz was only eleven years old when she vanished on April 2, 1973, after walking to a grocery store for her mother. Her battered body was found near a bridge that crosses Irondequoit Bay the next day. Carmen Colon, age ten, and Michelle Maenza, age eleven, met the same fate—all within two years of each other. Apparently one of the killer's criteria for his victims was that their names have the same first and last initial, along with the same initial of the town their bodies were found in. Wanda Walkowicz was found in Webster, Michelle Maenza was found in Macedon, and Carmel Colon in Churchville. The Alphabet Killer, about whom a movie is being made and filmed in Rochester, has never been found, at least not in Rochester or in connection with the Rochester-Irondequoit-area slayings.

It's hard to say who haunts Durand-Eastman Park. The apparition sometimes is seen as just a drifting white mist. There's something strangely romantic about calling such a mist over open water a White Lady, but the ghost that allegedly shakes parked vehicles and chases people into the water could as easily be a man or young boy. It just doesn't sound as good to call a ghost the White Boy or White Man. In fact, I don't think I've ever heard a ghost dubbed that, out of the thousands of stories I've read or written about! But there have been other tragedies in or near Durand-Eastman Park that didn't involve a white woman at all. In 1944, according to the Albert Lea, Minnesota, *Evening Tribune*, a fifteen-year-old Boy Scout named Robert was showing his friends "what not to do" on a raft in Durand-Eastman Park, when he fell off and drowned while attempting to swim to shore. All I'm saying is, usually there is more than one possibility for the spirit responsible for haunting a place, especially a place as large—and frequented—as Rochester's Durand-Eastman Park.

Fort Niagara

Fort Niagara in Youngstown is believed to be one of Western New York's most haunted sites, home of Henri the Headless and a hideous hobgoblin. With construction of its first structure, the French Castle, in 1726, Fort Niagara is one of our country's oldest forts. And long before it was even built, around 106 A.D., a succession of Native American forts stood there. Fort Niagara, overlooking the Niagara River, was always a highly desirable strategic location. Whoever had control over it controlled access to the Great Lakes, so four nations continually vied for it. It was at various times occupied by France, Canada, Great Britain, or the United States. Before it became Fort Niagara, and after it had been the site of Native American forts, it was a trading post that French explorer Sieur de La Salle established for trade with the Iroquois Nation. With a history like that, it seems that Fort Niagara was destined to one day become ghost-infested, and the moment Henri LeClerc's head hit the floor, that day came.

Samuel DeVeaux was first to describe the legend of LeClerc in a small publication written in 1839. As the story goes, LeClerc agreed to a sword fight with another Frenchman over the affections of an Indian maiden during the Battle of Fort Niagara in 1759. The maiden favored LeClerc, but he lost his balance during the sword fight, giving his opponent a small window of opportunity to decapitate him. LeClerc's head was then allegedly tossed into either a well or the river, but wherever it was thrown, its body was left somewhere else. It is said that his headless body came back as a ghost and was seen wandering around the French Castle, as if dazed and confused. Hardly surprising, given that it could not see or think.

Paranormal activity had been reported at the fort for nearly a quarter century before DeVeaux described the ghost of Henri LeClerc. In 1815, a hobgoblin, an ugly little goblin or elf that harasses the living, was first reportedly seen in the fort's cemetery. It was also observed in the dungeon of the mess house, a rather appropriate place for a miserable little monster. According to *Historic Landmarks of America* (1907):

> The dungeon of the mess-house, called the black hole, was a strong, dark, and dismal place; and in one corner of the room was fixed the apparatus for strangling such unhappy wretches as fell under the displeasure of the despotic rulers of those days. The walls of this dungeon, from top to bottom, had engraved upon them French names, and mementos in that language. That the prisoners were no common persons was clear, as the letters and emblems were chiseled out in good style. In June, 1812, when an attack was momentarily expected upon the fort by a superior British force, a merchant, residing at Fort Niagara deposited some valuable articles in this dungeon. He took occasion, one night, to visit it with a light; he examined the walls, and there, among hundreds of French names, he saw his own family name engraved, in large letters!

Today there are still many varied reports of paranormal activity throughout the compound. Staff, visitors, and paranormal investigators have all reported creaking doors and floorboards, disembodied voices, unexplained footsteps, vague apparitions, dark moving shadows, muffled battle sounds, moving objects, and so on. Video footage shows the mysterious moving shadows, as well as dancing orbs. But all of the personal experiences and physical evidence are par for the course in a place such as this, where mayhem and misery once ruled.

Mount Hope Cemetery

Like many college students interested in the paranormal, Christie, James, and others they know occasionally visit places nearby that are believed to be haunted. Across the road from the University of Rochester, there happens to be such a place: the sprawling Mount Hope Cemetery in Rochester, founded in 1838. Among the 350,000 dead that have been buried, entombed, or cremated are Col. Nathaniel Rochester, the founder of the city; Susan B. Anthony; Jonathan Child, first mayor of Rochester; Indian torture victims; Civil War veterans and generals; Buffalo Bill Cody's three children; a Titanic victim; and George Eastman. With a third of a million bodies beneath the ground, it's not surprising that Mount Hope is considered to be one of the most haunted cemeteries in the region.

Many people have taken photographs within the cemetery that depict not only spirit orbs, but also some pretty amazing apparitions. One such photograph, taken by the college student Christie, appears on my website, www.theghostauthor.com. She wrote to me in January 2008, saying that she and two of her friends had visited the cemetery the previous summer, and she wanted my opinion of the only photograph they took that appeared to have some anomalies. "I took three pictures," she wrote, "but by the third one, my friend James told me that he had a bad feeling and said to stop taking them, so I did. Later we went back to his house, and I looked at the pictures. The first one had nothing. The second didn't either, but the third one had something—what looks to be a man in old-fashioned clothing crawling or sitting on the ground. Everyone I show it to can see the man."

I've received countless photographs depicting alleged spirit energy, but I have to say that this photograph taken at the Mount Hope Cemetery is one of my all-time favorites. Two of the students were walking down the cobblestone road in the darkness after closing time, with their backs to Christie, who took the photograph. There are four obvious orbs very close to the camera lens; one is much brighter than the others and clearly in motion. The faint outline of tombstones can be seen in the distance, but on the ground not far from the two who were walking ahead of Christie is the upper torso of a man, from the chest to the top of the head. He appears to be wearing a tux and has a hat on or a mass of very dark hair. He is looking straight at the unsuspecting camerawoman. And it looks as if he is leaning against something, perhaps a tombstone. Christie saw the man's face easily, because it stands out so well, even in the darkness; so she assumed it was someone sitting or crawling. But when I increased the brightness of the photograph, it revealed a lot more clarity in the darkness, and we were able to tell that the image of the man on the ground was actually a partial apparition, of the upper torso only. It's as if he is projecting up out of the ground.

Christie didn't see the orbs or apparitions while she was walking along taking photographs, but one man who drives by Mount Hope on a regular basis did. He stopped at a traffic light one day on Mount Hope Avenue when he saw an old man begin to walk across the road . . . and then vanish right in front of his car.

There's also a legend of "the hounds of Mount Hope." It is said that these hounds—much like the "black dog of death" phenomenon—bark and growl at night if people are in the cemetery when it's closed. Some say they've seen red, glowing eyes and heard something circling around them, like a pack of wolves closing in on its prey. One second it's in front of them, and the next instant it's beside them. How's that for incentive to keep out?

In 1837, Silas Andrus had just paid $323 for a fifty-four-acre piece of property a mile and a half from the city center, when he was approached by the city of Rochester and offered a whopping $5,386 for the same acreage—a hundred bucks per acre. After a deadly cholera epidemic five years earlier, the city's small cemeteries had become overcrowded and filled beyond capacity, and the city was in dire need of a new burial ground outside of the city. The city's conundrum made Andrus a very happy man.

The first interment was in August 1838, and that same year, a four-year-old child died during the cemetery's official dedication ceremony in October, making him the first "official" burial. In 1865, an additional 78.57 acres were added to the original property, bringing the overall total today to 196 acres. There are currently five hundred to six hundred burials each year at the Mount Hope

Cemetery, and the property cannot be expanded any further, because it is bounded by residential neighborhoods and Strong Memorial Hospital. But for now, the Friends of Mount Hope Cemetery, a volunteer organization founded in 1980 to preserve and restore the historic cemetery, does a fine job of repairing and protecting various structures, including gravestones, Victorian monuments, the cobblestone road, gazebo and Gothic gatehouse and towers, miniature Greek temples, and so on. The public is always encouraged to visit and stroll about the wooded grounds, searching for famous names from the past or the recently departed. A pocket guide with a map of the grounds is available at the gatehouse for this purpose, as are the guided Tours in Mount Hope Cemetery, led by knowledgeable local historians and tour guides. The community is also invited to adopt a plot, agreeing to reclaim, beautify, and maintain old, long-forgotten family plots so that future generations can continue to appreciate the historical and sentimental value of the cemetery. One man who called himself the Wizard took the invitation to a whole new, sordid, level in the mid-1990s. He was found by police in a mausoleum, "sleeping with skulls," according to my source, who said the incident made the local news.

The bottom line about Mount Hope Cemetery is that it is a fascinating place filled with history and trivia, and if you bring along your camera for the tour, you just might capture a real live piece of the past like Christie did.

Van Horn Mansion

Sleep Malinda, sleep; sleep calmly here
Where flowers bloom and zephyrs sigh
Where I may come to shed the tear
That streams unbid from sorrowing eye.

Malinda Van Horn was barely an adult when she gave birth to James Van Horn III on January 13, 1837. And before the end of that same fateful day, the young woman who had just turned twenty-one ten days earlier would succumb to the dreaded childbed, or puerperal, fever, which was tragically common in the nineteenth century. She would never experience the joy of holding her baby or watching him grow at the mansion where she died when he was born.

Or would she? Some say her spirit looks out over the grounds from one of the windows, like a mother watching her young child at play. Had she, in spirit, been right there watching him grow, after all? Her son moved to California as a young man and is long since gone. But perhaps Malinda's spirit is bound to the property where she took her last agonized breath, and all she has left is the hope that her child will return, not realizing—in her unchanging spirit form, where time as we perceive it doesn't exist—that he has died and moved on. Countless people have experienced paranormal phenomena at the historic Van Horn Mansion in the hamlet of Burt, and most attribute it to Malinda's restless spirit.

The Van Horn Mansion on State Route 78 (Lockport Olcott Road) in the town of Newfane was built by James Van Horn Sr. in 1823, and a year later, the very first Newfane town meeting was held in its living room. Around 1852, James Sr.'s son Burt assumed control of the two-story brick house and farm, while Malinda's husband, James Jr., took over the family's mill operations. In 1881, Burt Jr. moved into the Van Horn Mansion, and in 1900, he remodeled it extensively, installing the breathtaking stained-glass domed skylight over the foyer, an open staircase, and various other additions. The house remained in the family until 1910, when it began a stretch of various ownerships and periods of vacancy. In 1949, it became Green Acres Restaurant, and then it was purchased by the Fitzgerald family, who lived there for five years. In 1959, the Fitzgeralds sold it, and the Van Horn House became an apartment complex until 1967. Several years of vacancy followed, during which time the property was vandalized. In 1972, it was purchased and used as a residence again, until 1977, when Noury Chemical Company bought the house. Noury kindly donated the run-down house to the Newfane Historical Society in 1987, along with a generous monetary gift to use toward its restoration. With volunteer help from the community, the Van Horn Mansion has been restored to its original splendor and today houses the Newfane Historical

Society, ensuring that the history of the home and town will be appreciated by the public for years to come.

Before her tragic death, Malinda had lived in the mansion with her husband, as well as his parents, James Sr. and Abigail, and a number of other siblings (the elder Van Horns had twelve children between the two of them). The Van Horns were well respected by the community, with James Sr. serving as judge, and James Jr. (Malinda's husband) serving as both the town clerk and the town supervisor for twenty years. There are several rumors regarding Malinda's death, with one saying she died after being struck by a tree branch, another saying she hanged herself, and still others saying she died under mysterious circumstances. But there's nothing mysterious about her official cause of death. Volunteers at the historical society learned that she died of childbed fever, an aggressive, often fatal infection of the reproductive system following childbirth also known as puerperal fever or puerperal sepsis. Though the condition is rarely seen today, thanks to the common practice of using antiseptics and antibiotics for medical procedures, in the 1800s it could turn maternity wards into morgues. Malinda's death was cruel and swift. According to Herbert Edward Buffum's *The Household Physician* (1905), germs, "if introduced into the little lacerations and wounds which are liable to ensue during labor, set up a violent form of blood poisoning, which, for its severity, rapidity of development, and direful consequences, surpasses all other infectious diseases." Malinda likely suffered from, in rapid succession, fever, chills, sweating, an intense headache, foul-smelling discharge, and stomach pain. Once the infection spread to the abdominal cavity, according to Buffum, death came quickly "to end the frightful scene."

Malinda's gravestone was found in the carriage building when the historical society began restoration in the late 1980s, so it was brought inside to prevent further wear from the elements, since it already had one crack in it. When the graves of the rest of the Van Horns were moved from the property to Glenwood Cemetery in Lockport in the 1950s, Malinda's grave had been left behind, perhaps because it had become separated from the tombstone that had marked its location. And that's precisely when the paranormal phenomena and Malinda sightings began. The Fitzgerald family, who lived there from 1954 to 1959, said that their tenure at what was then known as Green Acres was the most joyful time of their lives, even though the children refused to sleep in one of the bedrooms, according to Rick of the Paranormal & Ghost Society. In the early 1970s, some carpenters working on reconstruction of the mansion allegedly refused to go back into the house to retrieve their tools after they saw an apparition materialize before their eyes. One nearly fell off the roof in the commotion, according to legend, and another swerved to avoid hitting an apparition in the road. Since then, Newfane Historical Society volunteers and visitors have had many run-ins with what they believed was the ghost of Malinda Van Horn, along with several other apparitions.

Bruce and Dorothy Ludemann have devoted a website to the paranormal experiences they had at the Van Horn Mansion in the late 1980s, as well as another concerning their cadaver dogs. On their website, they mention how their dogs—very perceptive by nature—on one occasion growled while looking toward both the library and the stairway to the second floor and refused to go near them. That same evening, several people standing outside the house, including a local police detective, a college student, and Dorothy, heard the distinct sound of someone tapping crisply on one of the upstairs bedroom windows, at exactly the same moment that one of the dogs inside growled while looking up the stairway. Nobody was upstairs at the time, but many people over the years have seen a feminine form in the window and assume it is the ghost of Malinda. Her apparition has also been reported near the front door, next to the road, and in rooms that were undergoing remodeling. The Ludemanns tell of a couple people who were wallpapering during restoration in the late 1980s and never returned after seeing her ghost appear in the room they were working in. Another volunteer, Pam Wilkins, corroborated that incident, saying that a new volunteer was scraping wallpaper while her three-year-old daughter ran around the house; the woman later called the head of restoration, Grace Kirk, telling her that she wouldn't be back. When asked why, she said her daughter had told her on the way home in the car that she was a good girl and did not take candy from the lady. Her mother assumed she meant Grace, but the little girl said, "Not Grace, Mommy, the other lady." When her mother asked what other lady, the child replied, "She said her name was Linda." Which sounded a little too much like Malinda for comfort.

Pam Wilkins also took what is perhaps the most remarkable—and famous—photograph of a Van Horn ghost captured to date. She volunteered at the house from 1988 to 2005 and recently shared her experiences with me. Pam owned a photography studio in 1987, which made her perfect for the task of taking before-and-after photographs of the Van Horn restoration . . . and also an expert at discerning photographic anomalies, which would come in handy after she took her legendary photo of what looks like a genuine apparition. When she arrived before anyone else at the mansion the first morning of restoration, she had to wait outside until someone arrived to unlock the doors, so she used that time to obtain video footage of the exterior of the house. Playing back her video a few hours later, she noticed what looked like a woman's figure in the dining room's bay window, although she couldn't make out her face. She stopped the video and took a still from it to enlarge in her darkroom, but she couldn't make the image any clearer. So she returned to the dining room to see if anything were propped against the window to create the illusion of a woman in white standing there, but nothing was there. For the next four days, she attempted to re-create the place, time, and angle of the original image she had captured but was unable to. More experiences would soon follow.

One day, when Pam was talking to Grace, the two women heard a creaking noise directly overhead but didn't think anything of it. Later that day, Pam had to take a box to the maid's room, and when she stepped into the room, she heard the exact same creaking noise she had heard earlier, which would have required someone actually stepping across the floor. Then some young college girls told Pam they had seen a lady dressed in white by the mulberry tree in the side yard one night, but they didn't stick around long enough to find out who—or what—it was, because they fled as soon as the figure began to walk toward them. Two days after that sighting, the late Bill Tollhurst, then chief of Special Forces at the Niagara County Sheriff's Department, came upon the site of a grave that is presumably Malinda's, and it was at the exact location where the girls had seen the woman in white.

Nobody knows why Malinda's tombstone and remains were not beside the rest of the family's graves, but she was clearly loved by her family, as the poetic script on her tombstone, given at the beginning of this story, indicates.

In 1987, at the behest of the Historical Society, Bruce Ludemann and Bill Tollhurst brought in their cadaver dogs to scour the property in search of Malinda's grave. First Dorothy Ludemann and Bill used dowsing rods, narrowing the area to have the dogs sniff down to the southeast corner of the property. As they began to dig, the dogs showed an interest in one particular area, and further digging at that location "revealed bones, wood, and nails, indicating that a body had been buried there," according to Wilkins. They promptly covered the grave back up to prevent disturbance of the remains and set Malinda's stone over the top of it. As word of the discovery spread, people donated flowers to plant a garden and erect a rose arbor at the site. Though forensic analyses of the discovery were not done to confirm that these were the remains of Malinda, it is generally believed that they are hers.

A plaque that was placed at Van Horn Mansion when her remains were found states that since that time, there have been no more sightings of Malinda, but many people, including Pam Wilkins, would disagree, since all of her personal experiences occurred between 1988 and 2005.

St. Bonaventure University

St. Bonaventure University (SBU) in Allegany was the brainchild of Nicholas Devereux, an Irish financier who founded the town on land grants in the 1850s. The pious Devereux, for whom the campus's most haunted hall was named, was generous with the fortune he acquired as a merchant. Most of his donations went toward the construction of churches and colleges, and he was adamant that his newly founded town have excellent religious instruction. So with the assistance of the first Roman Catholic bishop of Buffalo, the Most Rev. John Timon, he solicited several Franciscan friars to Western New York in 1855 to build a monastery in Allegany with his $10,000 donation. That monastery became the college and seminary of today. With those first Franciscan brothers prepared to teach religion, and the land and financing for a college donated by Devereux, St. Bonaventure College was born. The cornerstone was laid on August 20, 1856, less than a year after Devereux passed away. The *New York Times* reported his death of December 29, 1855, as follows:

> Another of the oldest and most influential of our fellow-citizens was this morning removed from our midst. . . . Of cheerful disposition and given to hospitality, the example and the influence of [Mr. Devereux have] exercised a decided and wholesome influence upon the community in which [he] lived, promoting unity and liberality of feeling among those of different race and religion. . . . The deceased was possessed of a vigorous and enterprising mind, and of late years has been largely interested in lands in Allegany and Cattaraugus Counties. . . . The immediate attack of disease from which Mr. Devereux died commenced on Friday last, which terminated fatally at about 6 o'clock this morning.

The school was dedicated on October 4, 1858, and named for the patron of Franciscan studies and learning, St. Bonaventure of Bagnoregio. The first class of fifteen, taught by just three friars, graduated in 1860; today's staff numbers three hundred and graduating classes typically number twenty-seven hundred students. The college became a university in 1957 and is now one of the most prominent Catholic universities in the country. In fact, it is the largest Franciscan-order educational institution in the English-speaking world. But as with any institution so large and old, SBU has experienced its share of tragedies, and tragedies are often where and when rumors of hauntings begin. For example, on March 4, 1908, the *Marshfield [Wisconsin] Times* reported that a well-loved former SBU priest, Father Leo Heinrichs, had been murdered in Denver, Colorado, by Giuseppe Alia, an avowed anarchist. Because of failing health, the priest had been transferred from SBU to Denver, "where, at the chancel rail of St. Elizabeth's Church . . . he was shot and killed." His body was returned to SBU and laid out in the monastery, where ten thousand people attended the viewing and funeral. "The body rested in a white, satin-lined casket with silver trimmings. The martyred priest wore the plain brown garb of his order, the feet being enclosed in sandals, while about the neck was a purple and gold stole. . . . All creeds and nationalities were represented in the throng which sought admission to the church."

Father Heinrichs had been the pastor at the SBU monastery for years. Perhaps he occasionally watches over the students of the university today, for many people claim to have seen a robed figure looking down at them, wearing the traditional garb of the Order of Franciscan Monks.

In June 1908, the main building of the college was destroyed by a mysterious fire. The *Syracuse Herald* reported on June 30 that the fire started in "a small, unused corner room," and that the Jesuit Father who was in charge of the college at the time could not account for it. Losses, between the building and its contents, were estimated at around $110,000. But at least no lives were lost, since the school year was over and the building was "untenanted." The article said:

> The fire was discovered at 4:30 this morning. As far as could be ascertained this morning, nobody connected with the college had been in the room where the fire started for some days. This, coupled with a Black Hand letter received recently by Father Butler, threatening that the college would be burned, has caused a strong impression to gain ground that the college was burned because Father Butler would not submit to a demand for $10,000 blackmail.

Black Hand was the symbol and name of a secret terror society associated with the Mafia and the Camorra in the late 1800s and early 1900s. At the turn of the twentieth century, nine out of ten Italians living in New York City, where the Black Hand was especially active, had been blackmailed by letters bearing the mark of the society. Even the pious and moral, such as Father Butler, were targeted by the forces of darkness. Because he stood up to them and refused to pay the blackmail, the main college building was destroyed, but at least his life was spared, unlike many victims of the Black Hand who refused to pay the terrorists.

After the fire, the building was rebuilt as the Father Lynch Hall. But on April 18, 1933, Lynch Hall—then the oldest building on the campus—was once again destroyed by a devastating fire. This time, the cause was believed to have been a lightning strike to the clock tower, where flames were first seen. Again, no lives were lost, but six firemen were injured battling the blaze, and one was left in critical condition after the bell tower collapsed on top of him. Damage was estimated to be at $60,000, and the two hundred students who had been housed on the third and fourth floors of Lynch Hall had to temporarily occupy the still-standing Devereux Hall until new quarters could be built for them. When Lynch Hall was rebuilt and reopened yet again, its name was changed to the De La Roche Hall. The fire of 1933 marked the third fire at SBU in three years. A large barn had burned to the ground in the early 1930s, and on May 5, 1930, the monastery, seminary, and church were destroyed by fire. Remarkably, none of the fires in the university's history resulted in fatalities that were reported in the papers. But the priests at SBU did express their sympathy to the twenty-year-old firefighter, Raymond Hirsch, who was critically injured by the bell tower collapse, as well as Captain John T. O'Hara, who suffered severe blood loss from his injuries, so they may not have survived their firefighting injuries, even though they didn't actually die on the property or immediately.

Many of the ghostly legends associated with SBU involve a student who allegedly died in one of the fires at De La Roche Hall, where an apparition has been seen still trying to frantically complete a paper he was typing when a fire broke out, killing him. No students perished in the fires at De La Roche, however, but it's possible that the spirit so often reported is an alumnus or former employee who, for whatever reason, has left an imprint at that spot where he once sat, causing a residual haunting. Today science, math, and computer classes are held at De La Roche Hall, which is reportedly one of the two most haunted buildings on campus. The other is Devereux Hall, completed in 1928.

Devereux Hall—or Dev, as they call it—is one of the most popular dorms for students to live in, mainly because of its unique appearance and character. But part of what gives the building its intriguing ambience is its haunted history. Many current and former residents have experienced paranormal phenomena of one type or another at Dev, especially on the fifth floor, where a Black Mass, a service worshipping Satan, was attempted by a misguided trio of students in the 1960s. After the fire of 1930 destroyed the monastery and chapel at SBU, a west wing was immediately added to Dev, which became the temporary quarters for the friars until 1961, when the new friary in Doyle was created. The football team was housed on the fifth floor—military-barracks style—from the late 1930s to the 1950s. In 1939, three SBU students on the football team died within days of each other, and a memorial for them—a statue of St. Bonaventure, the college's patron saint—was placed in the center of the lawn in front of Devereux Hall facing the highway. Two of the deceased were returning home from a game against Canisius in Buffalo when they were involved in a fatal car accident. The other student was fatally injured during a game against Niagara University. Have those three departed souls returned to their quarters on the fifth floor of Dev, unaware that they died prematurely long ago? The students certainly believe someone haunts the fifth floor of Dev, but many people believe it has more to do with the Black Mass in the early sixties that was foiled when a friar walked in on the three culprits. Still . . . had the mass progressed far enough to invite an evil presence to SBU?

After the football team had moved out of Dev's fifth floor in the late fifties, fraternities began using the space for meetings. Then, sometime in the early 1960s, a few students stole some unconsecrated hosts from the friary and took them, along with three instructional books on the occult, to the fifth floor to perform the rituals necessary to attempt to conjure evil spirits. But a friar walked in on them, cutting short their ceremony, and the students were expelled from the university. One required psychological counseling, either because of the great guilt and shame he was burdened with or as a direct effect of the ceremony they performed, such as near possession or some other supernatural influence.

Dev's fifth floor was closed down for several years, leading students to wonder whether it had something to do with the possible evil unleashed from the Black Mass ceremony. Administrators insisted it was closed because of high insurance costs and the fire hazard it presented—and the university had certainly seen enough fires in the past to make them on edge about such things.

Even with its ominous history, efforts were continuously made to reopen and utilize the fifth floor. So in the 1970s, a recreation room was opened on that floor, along with a typing and study lounge. That stint lasted only a few years, before the floor was closed abruptly once again. This time, it was due to lack of interest. But it also may have had something to do with what sounded like an explosion emanating from Fifth Dev that prompted residents to flee the building for a short time. After careful investigation, no source for the sound or evidence of an actual explosion was ever found.

Some of the paranormal phenomena reported by students over the years have included sightings of a friar jogging up and down the hallways of the third floor of Dev in the middle of the night or early in the morning. A shadowy, hooded figure has been seen in the closed-off fifth floor by a number of students, as well as at the foot of one student's bed on the second floor. In the latter case, the student saw a hooded figure wearing a black robe just standing there, and in an instant, it disappeared into thin air. The figure has also been seen by more than one individual in the courtyard outside of Dev. The apparition always wears a black or dark-colored robe, like that of a friar, and it often has a hood pulled up over its head. If it weren't for the fact that the figure vanishes into thin air, it might be difficult to distinguish it from the living. But there are other reasons to believe Devereux Hall is haunted. Footsteps are often heard in the middle of the night, when there shouldn't be any. Water faucets have turned themselves on, and doors sometimes rattle and shake.

There has been so much paranormal activity at SBU, in fact, that in the early 1970s, the late Father Alphonsus Trabold taught a paranormal activities class designed to study the supernatural abilities of humans, a lifelong interest of his, besides theology. Between the foiled Black Mass on the campus and the tragedies that have befallen alumni, former priests, students, and firefighters, it's no wonder St. Bonaventure University is surrounded by tales of hauntings. Thankfully the paranormal activity has never been threatening or too disturbing. After all, if ever there were a harmless ghost, it would have to be a Franciscan friar.

USS *The Sullivans*

There is a long-standing superstition that a Friday occurring on the thirteenth day of any month will be an unlucky day. It certainly rang true for the Knights Templar when they were arrested on Friday, October 13, 1307. It rang true for the Uruguayan rugby team—on whom the movie *Alive!* was based—after the Andes plane crash on Friday, October 13, 1972, killed twenty-nine of their own. And it rang true for the Sullivan brothers and their shipmates when the vessel they were serving on during World War II was torpedoed on Friday, November 13, 1942.

On Thursday, November 12, the *Juneau,* classified as a light cruiser, arrived in Guadalcanal after escorting reinforcements to the region. That afternoon, it shot down six Japanese torpedo planes but held its own. Then, barely two hours into Friday the thirteenth, the Battle of Guadalcanal began in earnest in utter darkness, with the Japanese practically on top of the American ships. The melee later was blamed on bad weather and miscommunication—in other words, pure bad luck. Especially for the Sullivan family, who lost five sons in the tragedy. The *Juneau* was struck once on the port side by a torpedo, but she limped along at eighteen knots, retreating from the area for repairs. Then a second strike from a Japanese submarine torpedo hit her just after 11 P.M., instantly splitting the vessel in two, sending it to the depths within just twenty seconds. Many died immediately, but the hundred survivors of the blast who had been abandoned by other retreating ships and left to fend for themselves in open seas met a worse fate. Because of their injuries, shark attacks, and the elements, only ten remained by the time rescue crews arrived eight days later. Four of the Sullivan brothers died the moment the ship was struck the second time, and the fifth died within several days.

The Sullivan brothers of Waterloo, Iowa, ranging in age from nineteen to twenty-seven, had all been willing to enlist or reenlist in the U.S. Navy in 1942 under one condition: that they be allowed to serve on the same ship. Navy policy regarding multiple family members serving together was disregarded, since it wasn't being strictly enforced at that time. So the brothers all served aboard the USS *Juneau* together—along with thirty other pairs of brothers and four brothers from Connecticut—and they all died together. Al, Frank, Joe, and Matt Sullivan died at the moment of the torpedo impact. George, the eldest, died after four or five days adrift in a raft at sea. One survivor who was rescued said George had become delirious from heat and thirst and decided to swim naked around the raft one night, or perhaps try to make it to shore, but the movement attracted sharks, and the survivor never saw him again. The Sullivan family's tremendous multiple sacrifice, and the undesirable public attention it attracted, encouraged all branches of the military to design "sole survivor policies" to spare other families—to the best of the military's ability—from a similar fate of losing all their children in battle.

The Navy has named two destroyers in honor of the Sullivan brothers: The USS *The Sullivans* (DDG-68) was launched in 1995 and still is in active service, and the USS *The Sullivans* (DD-537) was launched in 1943, four months after the Sullivan family tragedy; it was decommissioned in 1965 and donated to the city of Buffalo and the Erie County Naval and Military Park in 1974 as a public memorial. Though the USS *The Sullivans* (DD-537) saw intense combat in both World War II and the Korean War, through all of its many battles, not a single soul was lost. For what it's worth, a shamrock was painted on her forward smokestack, supposedly in honor of the Sullivans' Irish heritage, but it may have been for good luck, in an attempt to offset the Sullivan tragedy, which had occurred on a very unlucky Friday the thirteenth. And it seems to have worked. Or maybe the Sullivan brothers were watching over their ship and protecting its crew from a similar fate.

Apparitions bearing the likenesses of the brothers, especially George, have been reported. Sometimes five hazy apparitions are seen together drifting down the corridors. Whispers are heard when nobody else is around, along with the faint sounds of men playing cards and chains being dragged across the floor. Locks come undone, and objects are found that appear to have been thrown. Photographs taken of the Sullivan brothers' portraits in the gallery at the memorial occasionally have white spots blocking out George's image, as if setting him apart from the others, since he was not with them at the moment of passing. Even if the spots are just a reflection on the glass from the flash, it's still interesting that George's image always seems to be the one affected. A security guard who claimed to see the bloodied and ghoulish apparition of George floating across the deck of the USS *The Sullivans* was so shaken by the incident that he quit. Hatches have come unlocked aboard the ship, and objects have begun shaking and rocking for no apparent reason. Far too many people have seen or sensed the presence of the Sullivan brothers on the ship to discount the stories.

Valentown Historical Museum

In my line of business, I see a lot of photographs and video footage purporting to be evidence of paranormal activity. Some can be quickly dismissed with a scientific explanation; some are iffy—maybe they do show something supernatural, but it's pretty indiscernible. It may have a logical, scientific explanation—or not. But then other times (and it's happening more and more often these days), something absurdly supernatural jumps right out at you, leaving you with no choice but to concede that it has to be paranormal in nature. When Western New York Paranormal investigated the Valentown Historical Museum in Victor in 2006, they captured one of the best apparitions I've ever seen on video. It can easily be viewed online with a quick Google search of "Walking Ghost Caught on Tape?" The woman holding the camera was unaware of what was transpiring—the spirit walking stiffly toward the foreground—

until after the investigation when the video footage was reviewed. You can easily make out a semitransparent male form approaching from behind, walking briskly to the foreground, and then disappearing out of the camera's range. The paranormal investigators viewed the amazing video footage in various modes to see if they all showed the same apparition, and they sure did. It didn't matter if the footage was viewed in black and white, negative, or infrared—the same downright creepy apparition was visible no matter how they looked at it!

So what exactly is Valentown? For many years, it was just an abandoned old shopping center in the town of Victor, but the historic landmark has been steadily revitalized since it was saved from demolition in 1940. Today it's a large, three-story wooden museum containing historical artifacts from the region, but it was built in 1879 by Levi Valentine as a shopping and community center when it was rumored that the railroad would be running right by his farmland. Valentine planned to develop an actual town on his property to attract rail travelers, but when he found out that the railroad had run out of financial resources to reach Victor, further development of his town ceased, as it was too far out in the middle of nowhere to thrive without the easy access of rail. For a time, the building was a hub of activity, with Valentine running the grocery store in the building, followed by two other grocers. There was also a cobbler's shop that Seth Cole ran until 1905, a leather goods store operated by Aaron Longyear until 1910, a school of music, and a community room into which all of these shops opened. On the third floor was a ballroom, where the fifty-four-piece Valentown Band played. But one by one the shops closed, and nobody rushed to fill their vacancies. And eventually Valentown went the way of other failed enterprises, becoming abandoned and forgotten. Valentine's dream community became a little ghost town . . . and, boy, does it have ghosts all right!

In 1940, eminent local historian J. Sheldon Fisher purchased the neglected building and turned it into the Valentown Hall. He had never been a handyman, but he quickly became one as he tackled the restoration and preservation of the old building, even reopening the old ballroom on the third floor with a band for community dances. Following World War II, Fisher moved his family of five to the second floor of Valentown Hall, and they lived there for nineteen years. Fisher ran, at various times on the first floor and in the basement, an antique shop and antique refinishing workshop, and a seasonal restaurant. Finally, in 1953, the town of Victor was making plans for its 140th anniversary celebration, which would include a stop at the Valentown Hall, so Fisher set out on display his vast personal collection of local artifacts and heirlooms that he had been fervently collecting since he was a child. The fruits of his lifelong passion were greatly appreciated by all who visited Valentown. Thus the Valentown Historical Museum was born, and it became wildly popular, especially among school groups.

In 1997, five years before Fisher passed away at the age of ninety-five, his beloved Valentown Historical Museum, complete with contents, was acquired by the Victor Historical Society, which continues to operate it today. The society is carefully restoring and preserving the structure, primarily through volunteer efforts, to ensure that it continues to be an asset to the community, as Valentine and Fisher would have wanted. It wouldn't be surprising if one or both of the men who poured so much of their hearts and souls into Valentown still pay a visit once in a while from the other side. Evidence certainly seems to indicate that *some*one lingers there in spirit form. Valentown Museum now offers public "ghost hunts," in which anyone can visit and investigate the building and grounds following a basic set of commonsense ground rules; visit the Valentown.org website for more details.

Some of the paranormal activity that the general public, investigators, and employees have reported includes: voices and subtle music coming from locked, empty rooms; inexplicable footsteps and knockings or rappings; sounds of something scraping or dragging along the floor; moving shadows, both dark and white, passing through doors; the antique doorbell tinkling in the general store when nobody has come in; apparitions in reflective surfaces such as windows; lanterns swaying; objects moving inside enclosed display cases where it's impossible to disturb them; and lights turning on and off. Besides the investigators' amazing video footage of the walking apparition, investigators and laypeople have yielded EVPs, an abundance of photographic anomalies, and many aberrant EMF and temperature readings.

Villa Serendip

Frances Ambroselli never set out to buy a fixer-upper. She wasn't even in the market for a home in 1996. And she certainly had never entertained the idea of opening a bed-and-breakfast in the Finger Lakes region; she'd never even stayed in one herself. Yet something—or someone—kept drawing her back to the same dilapidated, old Victorian that she'd stumbled upon accidentally one day after taking a wrong exit off the thruway on the way to her daughter's house in Canandaigua. She ended up, as fate would have it, on Route 371 (River Road) between Cohocton and North Cohocton, where she found herself parked on the side of the road, staring up in awe at a house that she said reminded her of the Bates Motel from the movie *Psycho.*

After nearly three years of purposely taking the "wrong" exit on the way to her daughter's house just to see the vacant mansion again, she finally conceded that she was hooked. When that Italianate villa at 10849 River Road went up for sale in 1998, Fran seized the opportunity to buy the house she had unwittingly become obsessed with. She soon found herself restoring a run-down house in the country into a stately Victorian bed-and-breakfast—her dream home. Thanks to ten years of hard work, luck, and happenstance—and perhaps a little help from some unseen force—what friends and family had thought might become "Fran's Folly" actually turned out to be the inviting, enchanting, and elegant Villa Serendip Bed and Breakfast at the Woodworth House.

In 1860, Samuel Fitch Woodworth, a well-to-do farmer whose direct descendants from Massachusetts were among the first settlers in America, moved his family into the large house he had built for them on River Road. Their lives were apparently somewhat uneventful, but for the untimely deaths of at least two family members in the house. One was their three-month-old baby girl, and the other was Henry Paterson Woodworth, who fought at the Battle of Bull Run and died at home from his injuries shortly after the Civil War ended. Fran and her guests have good reason to believe that those two family members, and perhaps a few deceased Woodworth-family granddaughters, now haunt their former abode.

Fran told me about the first time she was visited by the ghost of Henry, whom she now affectionately calls her Blueberry Ghost. She had just picked some fresh berries at Blueberry Hill in Arkport and was baking a nice, homemade pie. As the aroma wafted through the house, she heard someone whistling in her parlor. It was about 10 P.M., and she thought she was the only person there. Assuming that a late customer must have arrived, she walked into the parlor to greet the person, but when she got there, the parlor was empty and the whistling had moved to the kitchen. Puzzled, she returned to the kitchen, only to find that the whistling had again moved into the parlor. So she called a friend to tell her she thought she had a ghost . . . there seemed to be no other explanation. Instead of being afraid, she said to her friend, "I wish it would either show up or shut up!" With that, the whistling abruptly stopped.

A week later, Fran again returned home from picking blueberries to find that her whistling ghost was back, leading her to believe two things: One, her ghost had a penchant for fresh blueberries. "Frozen blueberries don't seem to affect it one way or another," she said. And two, the whistling specter had to be the ghost of Henry Paterson Woodworth, because it repeatedly whistled a Civil War melody, and Henry was known to have died in the house as a result of his war injuries.

Fran also believes the ghost of an infant, perhaps the baby daughter the Woodworths lost, haunts the home, because guests often tell her that they heard an infant crying during the night, but there are no infants in the home, or even cats for that matter, that could make such a sound. Although she has never heard the sound herself, carpenters, staff, and guests have. One woman staying at the inn told Fran she had a dream of a woman named Anna Elizabeth, not knowing that this was the name of the mother of the baby who died.

Besides these two spirits, there also seems to be a helpful presence that Fran can't quite put her finger on. She said that her friends used to call her kitchen table the Serendipity Café, so she named her bed-and-breakfast Villa Serendip, which sounded more appropriate for the Italianate structure, plus there was already another Serendipity Inn, and she wanted her own unique name. So she used the word it was derived from instead; she then learned that one of the original granddaughters had actually been a missionary in Ceylon, which is Sri Lanka, the home of the original Serendib or Serendip. That's why she feels the Woodworth granddaughters have something to do with the endless coincidences she has experienced during her time here. "It seems that all I have to do is wish for something for the inn," she said, "and it just shows up from out of the blue." Ah, if only life were so simple for the rest of us!

Before they began working on the inside of the house, Fran and her family had to clear the tremendous amount of brush surrounding it, and she mentioned to her grandson that she would have to remember to bring over a rake. No need, her grandson told her, because there was—lo and behold—one ready and waiting in the property's smokehouse. This may seem minor, but taken in context with the sheer volume of similar incidents, it does make one wonder. Once Fran had raked up a huge brush pile ready to burn, only to realize she had no matches or a lighter. The cigarette lighter in her vehicle wasn't cooperating, so she was about to call it a day, dragging the hose and rake back into the garage, when what to her wondering eyes should appear but a box of matches, sitting on top of a dusty old box. They were damp and dirty, but they still lit, so she burned her pile of brush that day after all.

What really made her think someone was watching over her was that when she needed a wood chisel, which she kept forgetting to buy, an entire set miraculously appeared. "It literally fell out of the walls," she said. "We had removed the verge boards around the perimeter of the house to clean out all of the debris that had fallen through when they cleaned out the house before I bought it, and *voilà*—a brand new set of six wood chisels of various sizes!" Next, she said, thirty-seven bottles of aspirin also dropped out of the walls during remodeling, leading Fran to jokingly tell guests, referring to the deceased Woodworth granddaughters, "The girls wanted me to know this was a major headache, but they have me covered. I cannot tell you how many of those thirty-five-year-old aspirin tablets I actually took, and they still work." Also during renovation, out of the blue one day, they came across an old greeting card that said, of all things, "Welcome to Your New Home!"

After opening her B&B for business, Fran purchased a Victorian settee without looking at it first for her dining room, and when she went to pick it up, she was pleasantly surprised to see that it came upholstered in the very same fabric she already had used to cover her dining-room chairs. Seriously, what are the odds? Speaking of the dining room, Fran had her heart set on finding a large crystal chandelier for that room, ever since a guest had pointed out that such a fixture would be perfect in there. Several months later, Fran showed up two hours early at a nearby estate sale, because she had gotten the time wrong. So she was the first customer to see a big, beautiful signed crystal chandelier, which she subsequently purchased for the dining room. And when she decided that her B&B needed a small desk where guests could sign in and check out, she found one that fit in the spot perfectly at a local garage sale—for just $1. More recently, she mentioned to a guest that she needed two wingback chairs for her reception room, and he told her his parents just happened to be moving and had two wingback chairs they were planning to sell. It seems that Fran's every wish is the granddaughters' command. It's truly amazing, she shared, that "I don't have to venture off to showrooms or stores to find the little things the house needs. They just have a way of showing up when I need them."

With any life-changing venture, we're bound to have occasional doubts, and it was no different for Fran when she first opened for business. She had concerns that all the time, effort, and money she had invested into her bed-and-breakfast might not pay off, and it might end up being "Fran's Folly" after all, as some had predicted her endeavor would be. But for Christmas that year, her innkeeper gave her a postcard with a picture of the Woodworth House that Fran had seen some time before at an antique shop but had thought was too expensive to purchase. At the time, Fran hadn't read the back of the postcard, but when the innkeeper gave it to her, she discovered that the postcard was actually a reservation of sorts. Dated March 17, 1874, the writing on the back said, "Son Samuel, Wife and I and Mr. A. Billings and wife purpose visiting you this week Thursday. Will be at your house to dinner, stay overnight, visit Wetmore's Friday & return home Saturday. Your father, CVK Woodworth." Fran was thrilled, taking this as a sign that she was on the right path after all. And sure enough, business these days is booming. Fran's dream has become a reality. The dilapidated old Woodworth Mansion, which had been infested with various vermin the day she bought it, is now the elegantly restored Villa Serendip, retaining "the charm, romance, and gracious hospitality of the Victorian era."

Though you won't find any ghosts of the scary variety here, if there's a blueberry pie in the oven, you might just be lucky enough to hear happy whistling coming from the parlor.

Rush Rhees Library

"And it didn't hurt a bit." Those were the infamous words uttered by Pete Nicosia, a twenty-five-year-old Italian mason's helper, *after* he plunged to his death in 1929 during the final phase of construction of the Rush Rhees Library tower at the University of Rochester. It is said that he returned to collect his final paycheck several years after he died, and he has been seen sporadically since then. Unlike the majority of hauntings of the residual or noninteracting type, Nicosia's ghost has actually mingled blatantly with the living.

The story began when the River Campus of the University of Rochester was being built; more specifically, when the $1.5 million Rush Rhees Library on Oak Hill overlooking the Genesee River was being built. At the time, the striking nineteen-story tower behind the main library building was the highest such structure in the world, according to the university librarian back then, Donald B. Gilchrist. But it came at a high price, both in dollars and in the invaluable life it claimed. Gilchrist features prominently in this ghost story because he was the one people asked about the man they had seen, and he was the one who tracked down Nicosia's foreman, James Conroy, to ask if he knew of a former employee fitting Nicosia's description. But since Gilchrist didn't tell Conroy that his former employee had been seen wandering around asking about Conroy, the foreman couldn't understand how they could possibly have described the dead man to a tee. It would all make sense soon.

Conroy's reply to Gilchrist's letter came handwritten on the back of two time cards. In it, he said that the man Gilchrist described could be none other than Pete Nicosia, and then he proceeded to describe Nicosia's tragic death in detail. He said it happened while Conroy was running a lift up the I-beam in the center of the tower one day in 1929. Nicosia had been taking concrete up in a wheelbarrow one day when they were nearing completion of the tower job. He rolled the wheelbarrow into the lift, and Conroy ran it up to the top with a mechanical lift. Once it was at the top, Pete rolled the full wheelbarrow onto the platform, as he'd done so many times. But this time it started tipping, like heavily burdened wheelbarrows are wont to do. Pete did his best to keep it from going over the edge, but it was just too heavy, and he couldn't hold it. He had been pulling so hard to keep it from falling—like a deadly game of tug-of-war—that when he lost his grip, the momentum caused him to fall backward. He flipped over the side of the guardrail and fell 150 feet down onto the solid concrete below. "He never knew what hit him and was all crushed to hell," said Conroy. So he signed Pete's death certificate and used his young employee's remaining wages to pay for a funeral mass at Nicosia's church, St. Monica's, and a proper burial, since he had just come from Sicily six months earlier and had no known family.

Four years later, Pete Nicosia apparently returned from the dead, as jolly and sociable as he'd been while alive. Between 1933 and 1948, professors, students, and staff all had similar encounters up close and personal with Pete, usually in the library tower from which he fell, in the stacks, on the quadrangle, or in the basement. He was always dressed in an old sweater, workmen's overalls, a cap, and sometimes a coat that was rubber on the outside, and he almost always said he had to find Conroy, who had moved on to another construction job in Minnesota when his work at the University of Rochester was done. Perhaps 1948, when the last sighting occurred, coincided with the time Conroy died, and maybe the reason the sightings stopped was because the persistent Pete finally tracked his foreman down on the other side. At any rate, while they lasted, the Nicosia sightings were unforgettable and far more interactive than spirit encounters generally are.

Word of the hauntings first surfaced in the news media in March 1934, when the literary magazine of the men's campus, *The Soapbox*, ran a sensational story called "Concerning Pete Nicosia." A short time later, on March 16, 1934, a story called "Mystery of Pete Nicosia Probed by Faculty, Students, Campus," made front-page news of the university's newsletter, *The Campus*. That article included a photograph of the deceased Italian, and those who had seen and spoken to the man recognized him immediately, saying that if it were not him, it was an identical twin brother—if he had one, which was really a stretch.

The first person to report an encounter with the ghost, George Maloney, had been walking across the quadrangle one cold fall morning in 1933 when he met a short, stocky man in front of Morey Hall. When Maloney greeted him, the stranger looked surprised and then asked Maloney, in a thick Italian accent, if he had seen his boss. Maloney asked who his boss was, and the stranger said it was Conroy—whom Maloney had never heard of. Then the Italian proceeded to tell Maloney he had never checked out at the end of the day and hadn't turned in his time card, and his boss still owed him some money. Then he continued on his merry way. A man washing windows at Morey 305 also saw the stranger talking to Maloney but had never seen the Italian before either. A few weeks later, Maloney and Joe Stull were walking through the tunnel under Morey, and just as they came out under the library, the Italian stranger appeared and greeted the men with a nod and a smile. He actually walked alongside them and accepted a cigarette from Stull. After a bit more small talk, he said goodbye and left. A couple weeks later, he was again seen by Stull and again bummed a cigarette off him, before saying he was still looking for Conroy.

The following October, Maloney and Bob Metzdorf decided to go up to the platform of the library tower to take in the view. They borrowed the key from Gilchrist, the librarian, and headed up. To their surprise, the window they were to climb out was already unlocked, and standing there was Pete Nicosia. After talking for a while, the two *living* men headed down to the bottom to see how the book conveyor worked, and the man believed to be Pete said he was going to stay behind for a bit. A moment later, he appeared out on the steel platform far above them and asked them how high up he was. They responded that he must be about 150 feet up, and he seemed impressed by that. When Metzdorf and Maloney returned the key to Gilchrist, they mentioned the man still on the tower. The librarian asked for a description and then became annoyed, saying he was going to go out and talk to him, because the same stranger had been hanging around the library for a couple years, and nobody knew him or why he was there. Gilchrist didn't know if he was some kind of nutcase or what, but enough was enough. When he went out to confront the man, however, there was nobody on the tower at all.

Since the stranger kept insisting that Conroy was his boss, Gilchrist decided to track down the construction foreman, whom he had known, and get to the bottom of it. He located Conroy in Minnesota, who responded as stated above, confirming the description of Pete Nicosia and giving vivid details about the man's death. So apparently it *was* him. But the man everyone had seen looked so solid, so alive, that nobody could believe he was a ghost. On the other hand, there were no other explanations that made any more sense than the ghost theory. Many people wanted to believe that it was just a remarkable lookalike, or maybe a twin brother, or someone playing a practical joke on everyone, but this had been going on for a few years . . . How and why would anyone keep up such a scam for so long?

Two weeks after Gilchrist received the letter from Conroy, Maloney encountered Pete's spirit again. This time, keeping in mind what Conroy had revealed, he thought he'd humor the ghost—if it was, in fact, a ghost—and ask him if he knew anyone named Pete Nicosia, just to elicit a reaction. The man didn't miss a beat. He simply said, "Sure, that's me, Pete Nicosia." When the stunned eyewitness was about to tell him that he had been killed, Pete cut him off and said, matter-of-factly, that it was true: He had fallen 150 feet and "it didn't hurt a bit." Then, with a jovial tilt of his cap, he was off again. In the same time period, the professor of sociology, the superintendent of buildings and grounds, and the musical clubs director also met Pete Nicosia near the library. It was quite the topic of discussion for some time in the early to mid-1930s.

Following a relatively quiet streak of several years, Pete's ghost resurfaced in 1948, apparently to make sure he would not be forgotten. In the May 21, 1948, edition of *The Campus*, reporter Bob Weiss described his encounter with the ghost in an article called "Hark! Pete Nicosia's Back—and Rush Rhees Has Him." Weiss said he had been sitting alone in the newspaper room in the basement of the library doing research, when suddenly something made him look up. A man presumed to be Pete was staring at him from across the table. The man was dressed in an old sweater and workmen's overalls, and he politely introduced himself to Weiss as Pete Nicosia. He then retold the story of his death, which was already well known around campus, and asked the young reporter if he would be sure to write his story, which Weiss did. Perhaps that's all the closure he was looking for—to have the story of his life and premature death recorded somewhere so that he would never be forgotten. Pete, this one's for you.

Seneca Falls Historical Society Museum

In 1961, the Seneca Falls Historical Society moved into its three-story, twenty-three-room Victorian mansion at 55 Cayuga Street in Seneca Falls. Restoration of the home into an upper-class family residence circa 1880 so authentically depicts the late-Victorian-era culture and lifestyle that some of those who once lived there physically may have no desire to leave the familiar, comfortable surroundings. Though the museum staff insists that their ghost is a benevolent presence, it is a ghost, nonetheless.

According to the museum's website, the site originally had a simple, one-room wooden house in 1823. Edward Mynderse then built a two-story brick house on the ten-acre estate in 1855, and he and his family lived there for twenty years. The next owner, Mrs. Leroy Partridge, purchased the home in 1875 and transformed it from a two-story Italianate-style house to the three-story, twenty-three-room Victorian it is today. In her fifteen years there, Mrs. Partridge added beautiful touches such as stained-glass windows. But when the original owners of the house moved out, they may have left a couple of friendly spirits behind. The Norman Becker family, who bought the home in 1890, reported strange incidents that began as soon as they started renovations. Pictures hanging on the walls were found to be turned around, facing the walls, which is quite a feat, even for a ghost. Disturbing noises were heard, doors opened and closed and locked and unlocked seemingly unassisted—sometimes leaving the Beckers out in the cold—and furniture somehow got moved around by itself while they were outside trying to get in! The Beckers raised six children in the home, with the help of their nanny and cook, Mary Merrigan. Their family remained there until 1961, when the Seneca Falls Historical Society purchased the house.

Since the historical society acquired the home, even more paranormal activity has been added to the list, but it still involves the doors locking themselves. Some staff members have found themselves locked out, with doors that have been locked from the inside—and with hooks and latches, no less. And a closet door sometimes feels locked and won't budge, but no lock is even on it. Employees and volunteers have heard the sound of a young girl sobbing on the back steps of the building, but they never found a source for the sound and don't have any idea who the young girl might be.

The basement harbors a spirit that someone recognized. A silent and solemn woman wearing a gray uniform appeared in the basement as workers were installing a heater. She stood there staring intently at them as they went about their business, which was unnerving enough that the men got the job done quickly and left. One worker later noticed her likeness in a portrait in the house. It was Mary, the Becker family's cook and nanny. When Mary appeared, which was more than once, she always appeared solid, though silent. In fact, her apparition once tricked the Beckers, of all people—before they knew she had died.

Mary had been loyal to the family for many years, until she became afflicted with severe dementia and had to be admitted to the Willard State Hospital, where she spent her last days. Moments after she died, she showed up in the Beckers' living room wearing her standard gray work uniform—the same one the men in the basement saw the female apparition wearing. Unaware that she had just passed away, the Beckers assumed Mary had left the hospital without permission, but as it was late in the evening, and they still had a tender spot for their former cook, they told her to go up to her room on the third floor and get some sleep. They would take her back to the hospital in the morning. But the next morning, just moments after they realized Mary was missing, the hospital called to tell them that Mary had passed away the night before. As it turned out, her time of death was exactly the same moment she had appeared in their living room. They say that home is where the heart is, and apparently Mary so loved the Beckers and the house that she returned there at the moment of her death, rather than returning "home" to heaven.

And she may still be there today. According to Susan Smitten's *Ghost Stories of New York State*, a tape recording made in Mary's third-floor room by a visitor yielded an unidentified feminine voice saying, "Excuse me. You hit me." There was nobody else in the room at the time but the visitor and a historical society employee, and neither of them had said any such thing. Plus the mysterious voice sounded "cultured," as if it were from another era. Had one of them unknowingly walked right into her ghost, or right through it? If so, she may have thought it was quite rude of them, if she doesn't realize nobody can see her and that she is no longer among the living. Of all the authentic historical relics a museum can possibly acquire for people to get a real sense of the past, a recording of that nature is a priceless treasure.

Old Sutcliffe House

In 1915, an eight-foot-tall, shrouded figure terrorized residents of the Clark Street area in Auburn as it floated around the old, abandoned Sutcliffe House. At the time, the neighborhood at the west end of the city of Auburn was occupied predominantly by Italians. The *Syracuse Herald* ran a story about the haunting that year, saying, "Superstitious Italians are keeping their lights burning nights while, around the chimney corners, they talk in low tones of the nightly ramblings of spirits and the ghostly groans that are said to emanate from within the walls and boarded windows of the old Sutcliffe house on Clark Street."

The Sutcliffe House looked the part of a stereotypical haunted house, with its black exterior, boarded-up windows, and a yard that hadn't been tended for years, all surrounded by giant trees—any one of which a spook could easily hide behind. Because so many people had allegedly heard the groans or seen the floating figure, most chose not to go out in the evenings—which meant a loss of business for the local theater, all on account of some pesky ghost. Ever since the house had been vacated, there were rumors that it was haunted, making it difficult for the local real estate agents to sell it, for "whenever a customer seemed right, the stories of the 'haunt' that hangs like a shroud over it . . . caused the prospective buyer to change his mind." And just when they thought things were quieting down enough to begin pushing the property again, after a few months of no new reports of ghost sightings, the haunting started back up in earnest.

Residents of the neighborhood told police they saw a white, shrouded figure, roughly eight feet tall, floating around on the unkempt front lawn of the Sutcliffe House at midnight. Furthermore, they heard "the faint strains of soft waltz music and hollow laughter" emanating out into the darkness from inside the house. Then someone posted phony bulletins around town saying the police were offering an $800 reward for anyone who would spend the night in the haunted house and determine what was going on. Next thing they knew, half a dozen Italians showed up at the police station to apply for the job! The whole affair had become a headache for the Auburn Police Department. First it was the nightly reports of ghosts at the Sutcliffe House from frightened neighbors that had to be investigated, and then it was the poster about the haunted house that created a short-lived stir in the community from wannabe ghost busters. The police couldn't catch a break—and they never did catch their white, shrouded ghost either.

Belhurst Castle

The Billiard Room at Belhurst Castle in Geneva is one of the most memorable rooms I've ever stayed in, and it isn't just because of my own possible encounter with the fabled White Lady that cold October night in 2004. The ambience of the room is rich, the furnishings and woodwork are elaborate, and the unique floor plan is the icing on the cake. The room boasts its own private balcony accessed by climbing five carpeted stairs to the right of the bed that lead to a landing and a door to the balcony. The headboard reaches up to three conjoined windows that look out onto the balcony (if one were to stand up on the bed, which I did not). There's an oft-told legend that an apparition of a woman dressed in white has been seen on that very balcony, overlooking the estate, as well as floating across the front lawn of the castle and the Seneca Lake shoreline. She is believed to be the spirit of an opera singer who fled from Spain with her lover to avoid scandal. It is said that the amorous couple perished when a hidden vault or tunnel beneath the castle in which they were hiding collapsed.

It was just about midnight, and I was having trouble falling asleep, even though the room was very comfortable and quiet. All of a sudden, on the windows directly above me, I heard a series of eight very distinct, evenly spaced taps on the windowpane. Being so close to the source, I was certain of where the sound came from. So I fumbled with the light switch and got out of bed—on shaky legs—to see what it was, thinking perhaps the wind was to blame. There was nothing astray, nothing touching the windows, and no breeze to speak of. I can't help but wonder if that unexplainable sound was the White Lady, giving me my own experience to write about. Her musical background would explain the nice, steady beat with which she got my attention. But she isn't the only ghost thought to haunt Belhurst.

Though the Seneca Indians were the first to inhabit the property where the castle was built, they are not believed to haunt it. In the early 1800s, there was a glass-manufacturing company on the grounds, and in 1820, Joseph Fellows built the first residence there, which he called the Hermitage. William Henry Bucke, aka Bucke Hall, was first to live at the Hermitage. Similarly to the opera singer, Hall had fled from London to Geneva to avoid prosecution for embezzlement. It wasn't until he died of blood poisoning in 1836 that his criminal past was uncovered. As treasurer of the famous Covent Garden Theater, he made off with substantial theater funds.

After several other owners, the Hermitage and grounds were sold in 1885 to the ambitious, well-heeled Carrie M. Young Harron, from New York City. Three years after her arrival, she had divorced her husband and married a Captain Collins. There is a photograph that shows her dressed in a long, white gown, so the White Lady could be the ghost of either the first owner of Belhurst Castle or the opera singer. The first thing Carrie did was to hire fifty men to raze the Hermitage and build, in its place, the elaborate four-story Belhurst Castle. During its four-year period of construction, one employee went insane while roofing, and another fell off the tower and perished on the grounds. Then in the 1930s, a friend of the owner died of a heart attack at Belhurst. What could three healthy men have seen to make one go crazy, another lose his footing and fall to his death, and a third have a heart attack?

After a forty-year stint as a successful restaurant and casino, Belhurst Castle was converted in 1975 into the lodging establishment that it is today. Under the capable ownership of the Duane Reeder family, the opulent castle boasts a four-diamond rating and has been voted "one of the most romantic places in New York State." If it is haunted, this apparently hasn't hurt business. A brochure about Belhurst says, "Tales persist of the romantic past, of secret tunnels, hidden treasures buried in the walls and on the grounds, of ghosts and haunting. Fact or fancy? No one knows." And the facility's website today mentions that the Hermitage, where "many believed there was an escape tunnel built by Bucke Hall as a means of escaping if the authorities found him," was haunted, so the rumors have persisted for some time. Customers have posted photographs of orbs in their rooms at Belhurst Castle online and shared their unexplainable experiences. Many people claim to have heard the subtle sound of an infant crying, along with a woman singing soothing lullabies in the Billiard Room and throughout the castle. A male apparition has reportedly been seen in the men's room several times. Is it the opera singer's lover? The roofer who died of his injuries after falling off the tower? The English embezzler? The man stricken by a heart attack? Like the brochure said, nobody knows. But employees and visitors alike would be willing to bet that somebody haunts the castle, and I'll heartily second that bet.

Syracuse, Central New York and the Capital District

Syracuse City Hall

Syracuse's City Hall certainly looks the part of a haunted landmark. Built between 1889 and 1892 on the site of the first City Hall, the five-story fortress made of Onondaga limestone looks today like the archetypal European castle of old: stepped dormers, stone-barred windows, and towers and turrets of all sizes, with one rising high above the rest—a 165-foot bell tower. It reminds me of a line in Gordon Lightfoot's 1969 pop hit "If You Could Read My Mind": *"In a castle dark or a fortress strong, with chains upon my feet, you know that ghost is me . . ."* It's not hard to imagine a ghost or two in a place such as this, but mere imagination can't push the buttons on an unmanned elevator to operate it. Mere imagination can't open and close doors in a vacant room or create the unmistakable sound of footsteps echoing through the corridors of an empty building. The imagination theory can only go so far when trying to explain the unexplainable.

Long ago, the land on which City Hall now sits was submerged in the South Basin canal. The city had the area filled in, because the swampy land was deemed a health hazard, and built a public market there in 1846 called Market Hall. This became the original City Hall, with stalls for the market on the first floor and a public meeting hall on the second floor. The name changed from Market Hall to City Hall in 1848. In 1857, an expansion became necessary, and the first floor was converted into office space that housed the city's first public library, the city clerk's office, and the city council rooms. The second-floor public meeting hall became the assembly chamber. Also during the 1857 expansion, a bell tower was added, and the brass bell was used as both a fire bell to summon firemen when needed in an emergency and an instrument to commemorate events significant to the community. If people heard the bell, they knew something important was happening.

In the late 1880s, when the first City Hall was razed, the brass bell was temporarily installed in a tower in Columbus Circle to await completion of the new building. But architect Charles Colton didn't want such a passé object "defiling" his new bell tower—and half the public felt the same—so he butted heads with Syracuse Mayor William B. Kirk over it. Kirk, who was determined to have the bell reinstalled in the new City Hall one way or another, had Colton removed from the project. The bell was installed, as the mayor wished, and stayed in use until 1939, when it was removed and ultimately melted down for use by the Allied troops in World War II. Many believe that Mayor Kirk lost the next election because he had upset half of the voters by firing Colton. But at least he won the battle of his beloved bell. In 1987, the Rotary Club donated an electronic bell to City Hall for its bell tower, but a brass-plated aluminum bell was installed as well—to fill the void left when the storied old brass bell was removed . . . or perhaps to appease the former mayor's spirit.

Employees of City Hall believe the old building is haunted, according to their September–October 2003 community newsletter. And if it comes from the mayor's office, it must be true, right? One employee named Elke, who had been working in the maintenance department for twenty-six years at the time she was interviewed in the newsletter, had experienced enough to convince even the staunchest skeptic that there are ghosts at City Hall. What else could have operated the rear elevator in the middle of the night when she was the only person working? City Hall has always had an elevator at the front of the building and another at the rear for the public's convenience. But the old manually operated pulley elevators weren't changed until the major modernization and restoration work of 1977 and 1978, at which time they were replaced by new electronically operated elevators. Elke stated in the newsletter that she occasionally heard the rear elevator start on its own, and the maintenance crew chief admitted that it did seem to have a mind of its own, such as taking people to the wrong floor or operating with nobody on it. Other employees had similar experiences with the elevator, to the point where they had mechanics examine it a number of times trying to determine what was going on, but no one could figure out why it acted up. Modern-day conveniences do seem to intrigue ghosts and are among the most commonly manipulated objects in hauntings.

Some people believe the ghost is a former prisoner from City Hall's jailhouse days, because prisoners were then housed in the basement, which is arguably the most haunted area of the entire colossal structure. There, cold drafts pass through people, who are simultaneously overcome by a palpable feeling of being watched. It sounds harmless enough, but if you ever experience the sensation of being watched in a place that's said to be haunted, you'll understand why it's so disconcerting to those who have been subjected to it. Elke said there were times when she was sitting alone in the basement at night and not only felt a cold chill go through her, but also heard the door to the basement open and someone coming down the stairs. The maintenance people at City Hall, for whatever reason, nicknamed the ghost Charlie and speculated that he perhaps was a former inmate that had been housed in the cells in the basement long ago. I could not find an explanation for the name they chose or when it was first attributed to the ghost. Was it a psychic revelation? Intuition? Whatever the case, I think they may be onto something.

On July 31, 1893, a detective named James Harvey was in pursuit of two men he believed were burglars. According to the *New York Times* of May 15, 1894, "They walked along quietly with him until within 200 feet of the police station [at City Hall]. Then suddenly, one of the men hit the detective on the head with the butt of his revolver, and the other shot him in the head. The detective was killed instantly." The two men, who were brothers, then ran off. One, Lucius "Dink" Wilson, was captured in less than ten minutes. He was electrocuted for his crime on May 14, 1894. The other brother was caught on August 24, 1893. And guess what his name was? That's right, *Charlie*. According to the same newspaper article, Lucius made the following antemortem statement two hours before he was executed: "I desire to make as my dying statement, as follows: That Charlie F. Wilson, otherwise known as George Calhoun, his real name being Charlie F. Wilson, and is my brother . . . is entirely innocent of any connection with said Mr. James Harvey's death."

So Charlie was his name, and regardless of his brother's dying words, he was sentenced by Justice Wright to be electrocuted the week of June 17, 1895, at Auburn, just as Lucius had been. But on June 11, Governor Morton "commuted to life imprisonment the sentence of death imposed upon Charles F. Wilson in Onondaga County." Charlie was remanded back to his cell at the Syracuse City Jail for life. Could it be his ghost that haunts City Hall? It's certainly possible, considering the amount of time he spent there. Or is James Harvey, the officer Charlie and his brother killed near the jail, the one haunting the building? After all, it was his final destination, and he had almost made it there before being gunned down. Maybe he picked up his ethereal body, dusted himself off, and continued marching right on into City Hall and down the stairs to the holding area in the basement, as if the shooting never occurred. If so, it may be a residual haunting, replaying over and over for an indefinite period of time, causing people such as Elke to swear they hear the door opening and footsteps coming down the stairs toward the cells. Or perhaps the ghost is the *other* Charlie that plays a prominent role in the whole City Hall drama—the original designer and architect, Charles Colton, who was dismissed prematurely over a tiff with the mayor regarding the bell.

Suffice it to say, there are a number of people who may haunt City Hall. And according to the summer 2004 community newsletter from City Hall, you can still see the old jail cells where the likes of Charlie F. Wilson were imprisoned for life, death—and maybe even eternity—in the basement.

1834 Herkimer County Jail

Mrs. Druse, who murdered her husband and cut up and burned the remains, was yesterday sentenced by Judge Williams to be executed on Wednesday, November 24.

—*Lowville Journal and Republican*, October 8, 1885

A Herkimer correspondent claims that the ghost of Mrs. Druse now haunts the cell in Herkimer jail in which she was last confined, and tells of moans and murmurs and cries of "Oh! Oh!," such as Mrs. Druse uttered when the black cap was drawn over her head.

—*Fort Covington Sun*, July 7, 1887

On the hundredth anniversary of the infamous Chester Gillette murder trial, a historical marker was dedicated in front of the 1834 Herkimer County Jail in Herkimer. Gillette had been imprisoned at the jail in 1906, and his murder trial was held at the courthouse across the street. The jail is best known for holding Gillette, who was convicted of murdering Grace Brown in 1906, and most people automatically assume that if someone is haunting the old jail, it must be Gillette. Two other prisoners housed at the jail, however, committed crimes as sensational as Gillette's: Jean Gianini in 1914 and Roxie Druse in 1885. Druse was the only one of the three to be executed on the grounds, so it would make sense that her ghost is the one haunting the jail, contrary to the popular belief that it is Gillette's. If Gillette haunts anywhere, it would more likely be the Auburn Prison, where he was electrocuted in 1908.

Chester Gillette met Grace Brown while they were both working at a skirt factory in Cortland in 1905. By the spring of 1906, their relationship had been consummated, and the twenty-year-old Grace revealed to Gillette that she was pregnant. She returned to her parents' home but couldn't bring herself to burden them with the news of her pregnancy. When she heard rumors that Gillette was running around on her, she returned to Cortland, which no doubt put a damper on his amorous activities. Gillette devised a plan to take Grace on a trip to the Adirondacks, under the impression that he was either going to propose to her, as she had been begging him to do, or, as some historians theorize, that he was going to deliver her to a home for unwed mothers in upstate New York. This point has never been determined. A bittersweet letter Grace penned to Gillette just six days before she was murdered indicated that she was troubled by the predicament she found herself in and not looking forward to leaving her family behind for good. She wrote, "I know I shall never see any of them again. And Mamma! Great heavens, how I do love Mamma! I don't know what I shall do without her . . . Sometimes I think if I could tell Mamma, but I can't. She has trouble enough as it is, and I couldn't break her heart like that. If I come back dead, perhaps if she does not know, she won't be angry with me." Surely she couldn't have imagined what fate had in store for her. Or had she?

The final stop on the couple's Adirondack trip was Big Moose Lake. On July 11, 1906, they were seen out in a boat on the lake. What hadn't been witnessed, but the trial would reveal, was Gillette raising a tennis racket over his pregnant lover's head and bringing it down with a powerful blow. Whether the stunned young woman was then pushed over the side of the boat or the blow itself had knocked her overboard no longer matters, because her lifeless body was found the next day, and Gillette—who further incriminated himself with differing explanations of Brown's disappearance—was arrested at Inlet and taken to the Herkimer County Jail. He remained incarcerated there until the culmination of his trial six months later, at which time the twenty-four-year-old murderer was transported to the Auburn Prison to await execution. The sensational crime became the basis for *An American Tragedy* and *A Place in the Sun.*

In 1914, a sixteen-year-old boy named Jean Gianina was placed in the same cell Gillette had occupied eight years earlier. Gianina had murdered his former teacher, Miss Lydia Beecher, by clubbing her ferociously with a wrench and stabbing her repeatedly, because she was trying to get him reenrolled in a school. The young teacher was on a mission to help her wayward student, whose father was at his wit's end in trying to keep the boy in line, since his mother had died when he was very young. The father had been the clerk of the village of Poland and was held in high esteem in the community. He, Jean, and a daughter had lived in one of the finer residences, but he admitted that his son was "not up to the average mentally," according to newspaper accounts at the time. So after the boy was expelled from the school at which Lydia had taught him, she sent a letter to the George Junior Republic reform school, saying, in part, according to the *New York Times* of April 1, 1914:

> Have you room for another citizen, a boy of 15 years? He is a good-hearted boy, one of my pupils last year and one of my most interesting boys . . . If he could get into some place like the George Junior Republic, where he received a little kind treatment as well as hard work, it would be fine for him. He responds to kindness very readily. *He is not a bad boy by any means.* He is simply unhappy at home, but is ambitious, and has other fine qualities that would develop if

he only had a little guidance to show him that he really could amount to something if he chooses to.

The trial was groundbreaking in that it was the first in the United States to employ the Binet-Simon intelligence test as a defense. The verdict "not guilty due to criminal imbecility" came about after the boy's defense team, including a lawyer named McIntyre, convinced the jury that being committed to an asylum for the rest of his life would be punishment enough. But the boy had confessed to the crime, and there was no doubt he had committed it after careful planning. The verdict shocked the community. An article from the *Ilion Citizen* that was reprinted in the June 11, 1914, Lowville *Journal and Republican*, called "Jurymen Failed to Do Duty," was scathing:

> We doubt if there was ever rendered a verdict in Herkimer County which gives such general dissatisfaction as that handed up by the jury in the case of Jean Gianini, the self-confessed murderer of his teacher . . .
>
> The common feeling is one of astonishment and disgust and is best expressed in Gianini's own words. "Now how the hell did they bring in *that* verdict?" It is very significant that more than nine-tenths of the people feel that way . . .
>
> Gianini was guilty as a dog. He intelligently and deliberately planned the murder. He intelligently and knowingly committed it. That the jury allowed a smart lawyer to befuddle them does not change the facts at all . . . it gives our county a bad name; it holds us up to the contempt of men of sound judgment. It puts a shadow on the lives of the 12 men who brought in that imbecile verdict. But it guarantees that there will not be another such miscarriage of justice in many years . . .
>
> Meanwhile, young Gianini has not yet recovered from his surprise . . . He knew he ought to go to the chair and expected it . . . the Judge knew it and expected it and was so surprised he did not thank the jury for their services . . .
>
> As another proof of his "imbecility," Jean Gianini, when he went from Chester Gillette's cell in the Herkimer Jail left behind him some verse . . . many of them were of obscene nature and not fit to print, but the following forms just one more little sidelight on the verdict of "not guilty on the ground of criminal imbecility":

My name is Gianini, I would have you know,
And I always have trouble wherever I go:
To be thought a tough, it is my delight,
And I am thinking and planning both day and night.
I killed Lida Beecher with an old monkey wrench,
And they took me before the judge on the bench;
The sentence they gave me, it caused me to smile.
It was, "He is not guilty; he's an imbecile."
Now here is thanks to the jurors who let me go free,
The foolishest men I ever did see;
When they came marching in, it raised up my hair,
I thought sure they'd say, "He must sit in the chair."
Now soon I must leave you and bid you adieu,
And the dollars I've cost you, they won't be a few;
I never will fear if I can find McIntyre,
I really believe he could save me from hell-fire.

So these are two ruthless criminals who were once held at the 1834 Herkimer County Jail. But I saved the worst for last, and it's her ghost that is most likely haunting the jail now: Roxalana "Roxie" Druse brutally murdered her unsuspecting husband, William, in the kitchen of their house in the town of Warren on December 18, 1884, with the help of her children and nephew, whom she threatened with the same fate if they didn't help and if they ever spoke of the crime. With her daughter Mary sneaking up behind her father as he sat eating his breakfast, Roxie pulled out a revolver and shot him, then called to her nephew to continue shooting. When he fell to the floor, she grabbed an ax, and just as he uttered his last words while looking up at her—"Oh, don't, Roxie!"—she brought the ax down on his head once, cracking open his skull, and again, decapitating him. She then quickly and competently—obviously with much forethought—disposed of the body, using a razor, knife, and ax to chop it into small pieces, boiling it, and feeding it into the stove. After that part of her plan was accomplished, she threw the ashes and remaining bone pieces into a clump of bushes and covered them with snow. Then she repapered the blood-spattered walls, washed down the floors with a hose, and threw a bucket of paint across the floor to conceal any stains. She warned the children involved to say that William had gone on a trip, if anyone asked where he was.

But the neighbors had smelled the foul odor of burning flesh coming from the chimney the day of the murder, and when they went to inquire about it, they were turned away at the door. The nephew was first to break down and confess his knowledge of and participation in the crime. Roxalana and the children were taken to the Herkimer County Jail. Her daughter Mary pleaded guilty to murder and was sent to the Onondaga Penitentiary for life, but she was pardoned in 1895. Her young son and nephew were released because of their age. Roxie was convicted of first-degree murder in October 1885 and sentenced to be hanged. After two reprieves, the hanging finally took place on February 28, 1887, on the gallows behind the jail, with heavy security to prevent onlookers. Twenty-five people witnessed the first woman being hanged in Herkimer County and the last in New York State.

The day before the execution, the *New York Times* described the state of affairs at the Herkimer County Jail, saying, "Mrs. Druse, the woman who will die upon the scaffold tomorrow, took part in a choral service this evening. The service was held in a large room which adjoins her cell." It went on to say, "The preparations for the execution are complete. The woman will be dressed in black, relieved at the neck and wrists by narrow bands of white linen. The execution will be witnessed by less than 30 persons, as none of her relatives will be present."

From the known facts of the crime, we can glimpse what kind of person Roxie Druse was psychologically, but what did the woman who had committed such callous, monstrous atrocities look like? A *New York Times* article published the day of the hanging gave the following physical description:

> [Her eyes] were unusually large and black in color. They possessed, though their gleam is somewhat dulled now, a snakey glitter that was repulsive, while it also had a measure of attraction . . . She was of medium height, rather spare, but of good figure; had an abundance of long black hair and a pair of eyes that exercised over "Bill" Druse, as he was called, the fascination of a serpent.

In 2006, the Ghost Seekers of Central New York investigated the jail and determined that they believed it to be haunted by an entity that was "negative in nature." Of the three criminals described above, Roxie was the only one actually hanged at the jail, and her crime was the most twisted and demented of all (not to diminish the callousness of Gillette's and Gianini's crimes). At one point during the Ghost Seekers' investigation, the gaussmeter reading spiked just before a team member was shoved to the floor in a cell. It would be interesting to find out if this were in the same cell in which Roxie had been incarcerated. The investigators stressed how unusual it is for someone to be touched, let alone shoved to the ground, during an investigation, which led them to believe something negative had manifested. Both digital and 35-millimeter photographs they took in front of the Gillette and Gianini cell appeared to depict spirit energy. And a photograph taken outside the jail showed a very large orb. Keep in mind that Roxie Druse was hanged on the grounds outside.

The stately limestone Federal-style building, located at the historic Four Corners intersection of Herkimer at 400 North Main Street, served as a jail from 1834 to 1977. But today it is the headquarters for the Herkimer County Historical Society and is listed on both the State and National Registers of Historic Places. In 2005, the nonprofit Preservation League of New York State, headquartered in Albany, placed the old jail on the "Seven to Save" list of the state's most threatened historic places. That designation will help the Friends of Historic Herkimer County obtain publicity and funding for restoration of the jail. Ultimately, they plan to keep the old cells intact but turn the former sheriffs' quarters in the front area into office space. There is currently a gift shop, which is open July through August. Even without the general consensus that the jail is haunted, it's still an extremely intriguing place to visit for its storied past.

Forest Park Cemetery

Forest Park Cemetery on Pinewood Avenue in the town of Bruns-wick was established in 1897, after a group of wealthy Troy busi-nessmen solicited a design from architect Garnet Baltimore and had the cemetery incorporated. What was originally intended to be two hundred acres of rolling hills, wooded trails, and beautiful landscaping—a garden-variety cemetery of the type popular in the Victorian era—ended up consisting of just under twenty-two acres, which today lie vandalized and forsaken. In 1914, the Forest Park Cemetery Corporation went bankrupt, after spending too much money on drainage systems, architect fees, and the granite above-ground receiving tomb, which was large enough to hold 128 corpses through the winter to await burial but is now in ruins. So the cemetery, as originally envisioned, was never completed. The undeveloped property was sold to the Country Club of Troy, whose property was adjacent to the cemetery. In 1918, investors from New York City and Chicago acquired the remaining acreage of the cemetery and reincorporated it as Forest Hills. But by the 1930s, the Forest Hills Cemetery Corporation became insolvent, like its predecessor, and the name reverted to Forest Park Cemetery.

Since nobody was officially designated as caretaker of the property at that time, it was considered an abandoned cemetery. Through the admirable volunteer efforts of the elderly William Christen, at least the thousand or so burial records were main-tained, and he did his best to tend the grounds until his death. But for the most part, upkeep and maintenance of the grounds and cemetery plots were lacking for the better half of a century. Munic-ipal laws of the state required the town of Brunswick to assume responsibility for the cemetery in 1990, so the Forest Park Cemetery Advisory Council was created by the town in 1991, but it was dis-banded three years later. Then in 1997, the town made another attempt, appointing a new advisory council to lay out a plan to restore the cemetery. What is it about this cemetery that makes every effort to preserve it fail? It is hoped that this time the new advisory council's efforts will be enduring and successful.

Besides its string of misfortune, the cemetery has another problem to contend with: its reputation, whether deserved or not, of being the most haunted cemetery in the state, if not the nation. Although "Gateway to Hell" is its popular nickname, especially since all the paranormal publicity, and some refer to the cemetery as Pinewood Cemetery because it borders Pinewood Avenue, its proper name is Forest Park Cemetery. Were it not for the tales of bleeding statues and phantom babies, along with the token urban legend or two perpetuated by news media and the rumor mill, it likely would have remained an unfamiliar site to most. Instead, the urban legends have garnered enough publicity to ensure that Forest Park Cemetery will always be revered . . . and feared.

The cemetery was established at the site of a previously existing obscure little graveyard that some allege had once been an Indian burial ground. Sadly, vandals have toppled tombstones and decapitated some of the monuments of angels and other figures, leading to tales of statues bleeding from the neck. Such claims are certainly sensationalistic, but a botanist and biologist who investigated the phenomenon said the so-called "blood" is actually a type of moss that turns red in humid weather when rubbed. People also have claimed to have heard a baby or child crying, but skeptics shoot that one down by blaming the eerie sound on feral cats or wild turkeys. Another disturbing story is that of a large, looming apparition reportedly seen by people as they approach the receiving tomb, and they say it bounds away into the woods with superhuman agility. The town historian, Sharon Zankel, said this is most likely a deer being spooked and fleeing, which makes sense. I can tell you from firsthand experience that deer most certainly do have "superhuman agility," but that's another story.

A group of paranormal investigators from Central New York called IMOVES has visited the cemetery twice, once in 2001 and again in 2002. The team's investigations yielded photographs with a number of unexplained anomalies, such as orbs, possible apparitions of an Indian in the trees, and an apparition standing next to the Roth headstone. They captured video footage of white floating images near the receiving tomb that drifted from the rear of the ruins toward the cameraman. Numerous danger readings appeared on their Extremely Low Frequency (ELF) meter, which measures electromagnetic fields, and some of their batteries drained prematurely. Voice phenomena included the sound of a woman screaming, "Help!" as they stood near one of the headless angel statues. They speculated that perhaps it was a nearby domestic dispute, as the cemetery is in a residential area and they heard sirens some time later, but they are not the first to report hearing an unidentified woman screaming for help in the cemetery. One person posted a message on an online forum on Ghostplace.com asking if anyone else had ever heard loud screams of a woman saying no and crying. The individual had just returned from a visit to the cemetery and heard the screams just as he or she approached the same headless statue at which the investigators heard their distress call. The story behind the headless angels is that one was beheaded by a demented man who believed the angel's eyes were following him, and the other was a copycat crime by someone apparently trying to outdo the first desecration.

To top it all off, Brunswick, like many other localities, has its own version of the "hitchhiking ghost" story associated with the Forest Park Cemetery. According to an article in the October 27, 1996, *Troy Record*, a cab driver once told the local historian that he had picked up a young girl dressed in party clothes at the Emma Willard School one night. She said she needed a ride home to Pinewood Avenue. Just as they neared the cemetery, the girl vanished from the front seat, without paying the driver or even opening the door. Some cabbies complain about deadbeat fares, but this one seems to have been simply dead.

College of Saint Rose

Several years ago, a nun at the College of Saint Rose in Albany had a very disturbing encounter with what her priest told her was a phenomenon known as St. Elmo's fire, so named for the patron saint of sailors, who often witnessed such balls of fire from their ships' masts during storms at sea. Since the nun was obviously not a sailor nor at sea, he explained that seeing St. Elmo's fire was a sign that she would do something important in her life.

Her encounter, as described by Ashley Melsert in the college's *Saint Rose Chronicle* of October 18, 2006, occurred when she was alone in Carey Hall and going down the stairs from the second floor to the first. Suddenly a ball of fire came up the stairs at her and seemed to follow her as she froze in her steps and started backing up. She fled in terror back to her room. The next day, she went to her priest to ask what it could have been. According to the *Columbia Encyclopedia*, St. Elmo's fire "sometimes plays about the head of a person, causing a tingling sensation. The phenomenon occurs when the atmosphere becomes charged and an electrical potential strong enough to cause a discharge is created between an object and the air around it." In the sister's case, had the atmosphere become charged because of a meteorological condition—or by the presence of spirit energy? Could the ball of fire actually have been a spirit orb? Carey Hall, a residence hall at 944 Madison Avenue, is rumored to be haunted, along with a number of other residence halls on campus.

The College of Saint Rose is a private co-ed college founded by the Sisters of Saint Joseph of Carondelet in 1920. Its primary function originally was to prepare women for teaching, business, and other professions, but in 1969, the college became co-educational. Today about forty-five hundred men and women from diverse cultural and religious backgrounds are enrolled each year, and enough students experience something considered paranormal that freshmen are routinely informed of the hauntings during orientation to prepare them in the event that they should experience something unexplainable. It is stressed that the spirits mean no harm; they're simply lonely and looking for attention.

That opinion didn't comfort one young man, who refused to go back into Carey Hall when it was being used to house men one year. He was packing to go home and had left his room for only a moment to take one suitcase downstairs. When he returned to his room, he found his other neatly packed suitcase empty, his clothes strewn around the room. According to Melsert's article, the same thing happened more than once to that individual. Nevertheless, most of the students and resident assistants (RAs) who have reported sensing a presence in that hall feel that it is the gentle spirit of someone watching over them.

The Communications Department's online "Journalism Page" posted an article by Meg Senecal called "Albany Hauntings: Fact or Fiction?" in which she interviewed a student who had been an RA at Carey Hall for two years. The RA said that although she had never encountered a ghost in that house, there had been a strange incident involving a window shade. She was telling a student who lived there a ghost story she had heard when the shade suddenly flew up. She still refused to believe that it was something paranormal, but to have it occur at the exact time that a nonbeliever is telling a story about the resident ghost to a curious student makes one wonder. The RA told the reporter that she had heard various stories about who is haunting Carey Hall. Some say it's the ghost of a mother whose baby died in the house and remains to keep watch over it; while others say it's a man who had grown up in the house who didn't die there, but was called off to war and returned postmortem to a more agreeable environment. Still others have told her that they heard it's a young girl. Whoever it is, the RA didn't consider the house to be scary in any way, just "protected" by a benevolent soul.

Quillian Hall at 953 Madison Avenue is allegedly haunted by a seven-year-old girl who died in a fire, if the Ouija board the students used to contact her is to be believed. After the contact with the deceased child, evidence of charred wood when renovations were being made to the stairs lent credence to the story of a fire. The spirit of the young girl is blamed for locking students out of their rooms in Quillian and for saying, "Play with me," in the middle of the night. If they reject her requests, it apparently sounds as if she is playing jacks alone while they try to get back to sleep, according to what one man told *Capital News 9* on Halloween Day 2004. The students say they can actually hear a ball bouncing and the sound of someone scooping jacks off the floor. Sometimes students have been unable to get into their rooms when the doors become jammed, yet when they called security to help them, the doors easily opened. This has been going on since the 1970s, according to that news report.

Morris Hall is said to currently be the most haunted hall on campus, according to the college's newspaper. The Melsert article stated that students have heard flute music there and believe the hall is haunted by a priest. Students claim to have seen a priestly apparition with its back to them, as if giving a sermon, where the altar of the former chapel used to be when the building was a convent for the Sisters of Mercy. Some reported seeing a priest in the reflective surface of mirrors and windows in Morris Hall, and one student had a ghostly priest approach him in the hall. Students have also reported a poster-loathing spirit on the first floor of Morris Hall that removes their posters from the wall and piles them neatly in the middle of the floor in their absence. What's more, items have flown off the windowsill and landed in the middle of the floor. Apparently the spirit has strong feelings about how a student's room should be decorated . . . maybe it *is* a priest. Whoever it is seems hell-bent on getting attention. A student was once awakened at 3 A.M.—often called "dead time" and said to be when evil spirits become more active, because 3 A.M., being opposite the time of Christ's crucifixion at 3 P.M., mocks that religious event. She heard the mirror on the back of her door rattling, but no source for the vibration could be found anywhere. Her friend had an even more disturbing experience when he felt and saw the impressions of an invisible being walking around him on his bed one night, according to Melsert's sources.

Other halls said to be haunted at the College of Saint Rose are the Charter Residence Hall at 923 Madison Avenue; Cabrini Hall at 399 Western Avenue, where the college's human resources, community relations, and events scheduling and administration offices are located; and the Fontbonne Residence Hall at 935 Madison Avenue. Whether the college is truly haunted or not, the ghost stories continue to amass, and the students continue to pass the stories on to incoming freshmen each year.

Beardslee Castle

Restless Native American spirits, a suicidal previous owner, a transparent figure carrying a lantern along the side of the road, a skeletal ghost, two ladies wearing old-fashioned gowns, and four disappearing diners—these are the ghosts said to haunt Beardslee Castle, a famed restaurant on Route 5 between Little Falls and St. Johnsville. Beardslee Castle was built on the foundation of a homestead from the 1700s that had tunnels underneath it, suitable for storing gunpowder and munitions during the French and Indian War. One long-standing legend is that a band of Indians infiltrated the tunnels one night, planning to raid the weapons stockpile. But the flames of their torches allegedly ignited the gunpowder, resulting in a horrific explosion that killed them all; hence the belief that Indian spirits remain eternally trapped in the tunnels. Later the same tunnels were used as part of the Underground Railroad.

Augustus Beardslee, a wealthy New York attorney, purchased the property in 1860 and built the Irish-style castle that houses the restaurant today. Like his father before him and his son Guy after him, Augustus was a hardworking mover and shaker. We can thank the Beardslees for many things, including creating the first rural electric power in the country. In fact, after Guy Beardslee commercialized power in the surrounding towns, he sold the business in 1911 to Adirondack Power and Light, which eventually became Niagara Mohawk. Guy was certainly an enterprising and intelligent entrepreneur, but he had a lapse in common sense as a young man, shortly after graduating from the United States Military Academy at West Point. Guy was commissioned and assigned to Fort Niobrara in Nebraska, where the Army was preparing to seize land from the Sioux. While he was there, he took several souvenirs and returned home with them to East Creek, the Beardslee settlement. They were sacred Sioux artifacts—three war bonnets, tomahawks, knives, and ceremonial artifacts—and their presence any place other than in Sioux hands was considered to be sacrilegious. The artifacts were destroyed in a fire in 1919, giving the spirits of the Indians who had lost their lives in the explosion in the tunnels many years before good reason to be angry.

The tunnel explosion isn't the only tragedy the castle walls have endured. In the 1950s, a previous owner hanged himself at a side entrance to the structure. He was despondent over a terminal illness, and after several repeated attempts to end his life, he finally succeeded. Is he having second thoughts about that decision, even to this day? Some people claim that they've seen an apparition in the very spot where he was found. Another male apparition is sometimes seen on the roadside, appearing semitransparent and carrying a bright lantern. He wears a top hat and black suit, leading some to believe it might be the venerable Captain Beardslee himself. At least he was wearing something, unlike the skeleton ghost whose bones were clearly visible that yet another individual saw. There is also at least one female apparition, according to various reports. A blond lady wearing an old-fashioned long gown was seen in the ladies room. Another was dressed similarly, but she was carrying a bed tray as if up a stairway that no longer exists.

Though the number of apparitional sightings is remarkable for one place, Beardslee Castle has also had its share of more mundane ghostly phenomena: unexplained footsteps, passing shadows, unfamiliar whispers, and orbs of various colors flitting by. A relatively high number of motor vehicle accidents have occurred on the road in front of the castle over the years, allegedly because of mysterious lights that emerged from the woods, blinding the drivers. And the staff tells of occasional flying silverware, bottles and glasses breaking, and tables and chairs being rearranged in the middle of the night when nobody is there. Employees have stated that unknown ghostly voices seem to have encircled them. It probably didn't help matters when several employees used a Ouija board to summon the spirits of the castle, and just when the lights went out, one young man was thrown across the room by an invisible force. Another group of employees once heard a hideous howling noise that sent them running from the castle, and the owners admit that some of their employees, after experiencing something paranormal, have quit on the spot and never returned. It would make a good venue for *Fear Factor*.

Ghost Seekers of Central New York investigated Beardslee Castle in 2007, garnering physical evidence of ghostly phenomena to complement eyewitness accounts. In a now-vacant mausoleum on the grounds where the original Beardslee family was interred, physical sensations were reported and gaussmeter readings spiked. One member of the team who was holding a tape recorder felt her hands get hot, just as a psychic sensed a female presence indicating that they were not welcome there. Ghost Seekers captured two EVPs in the dungeon of the castle, as well as 35-millimeter photographs depicting ectoplasm. But regardless of the incidents that would make some people cringe, Beardslee Castle, according to the current owners, is still "a beautiful and compelling building that has a powerful, true sense of place," and say, "We are honored to share this castle with our guests, from this dimension and any other."

Cohoes Music Hall

From the day the restored Cohoes Music Hall reopened in 1974—on its one-hundredth birthday—apparitions have been reported, seemingly awakened by the extensive renovations. If it had been haunted during the first half of the century, nobody would have known, because the building was vacant during that time period. The most active ghost by far is a woman seen in the balcony, but she has been described many different ways, suggesting the possibility that it's not always the same ghost. Some who have seen the apparition say she was wearing 1930s-era clothing, and others saw a woman with angry eyes wearing a black dress. Still others say the apparition was a dead ringer for Eva Tanguay, the highest paid, best-known vaudeville star of her day, who got her start in Cohoes.

Eva was born to French-Canadian parents who moved to the United States from Marbleton, Quebec, when she was very young. Her father's early passing left Eva and her mother in dire financial straits, but by the age of eight, the girl was already earning money performing. As a teen, she and her mother lived in Cohoes, and Eva's road to stardom actually began on the stage of the Music Hall, where she was allegedly booed during her first performance. Fortunately for history, the young "queen of vaudeville" and musical comedy was plucky enough to keep going. When, at twenty-six years of age, she sang the song "I Don't Care" on Broadway, her celebrity reached a new level. She was making up to a whopping $3,500 a week by the time she became one of the Ziegfeld Follies girls in 1909, setting her high above any other vaudeville performer of the time. People were intrigued by the woman's jolly disposition and daring outfits and songs, such as "I Want Someone to Go Wild with Me," and when she took her show on the road, it was a phenomenal success.

Too phenomenal to last, however. Eva lost her fortune, an estimated $2 million, in the 1929 stock market crash. A few years later, as if things weren't bad enough, she became plagued by serious medical complaints, including arthritis and blindness. A friend paid for her to have eye surgery to restore her vision, and she had hoped to make a comeback so that she could pay her friend back, but fate had turned against her. She was plagued for the last twenty years of her life with crippling arthritis, confining her to her home in Hollywood. She died following a stroke on January 12, 1947, and had left no will, for her estate was only worth a total of $500 by then. She had been seen by her doctor the night before her death, and he was quoted in the *New York Times* as saying that she was in good spirits, speaking "as she always did, of the past in which she lived." In fact, she died surrounded by bedroom walls "papered with yellowing photographs of herself" in her prime. As she closed her famous eyes for the last time, had she been looking at a photograph of herself on stage at the Cohoes Music Hall, where she had captivated an adoring audience? Some believe that Eva has been drawn back from the dead by her fondness of the Music Hall, as well as the love interest she allegedly once had while there.

Besides the balcony ghost, many people believe there's a paranormal explanation for the malfunctioning elevator in the Music Hall. It got so bad one time that management had to disable it, because it kept opening and closing repeatedly without any riders. As often reportedly happens in haunted theaters, objects set beside the stage prior to performances often turn up missing, while other objects that have nothing to do with the show appear out of nowhere next to the stage, especially old props that were used by Buffalo Bill Cody, Tom Thumb, and—you guessed it—Eva Tanguay. It is said that a former stage manager died when a sandbag fell on him many years ago and is still trying to run his stage. A male apparition has been seen in the aisles and on the stage by several individuals. Others haven't seen the apparition, but they have heard a disembodied male voice for which no source could be found.

The Cohoes Music Hall building at 58 Remsen Street was constructed in 1874, at the behest of newspaper publisher James Maston and textile manufacturer William Acheson. The first floor originally held three large stores and a post office, to give you an idea of how large the building was; the second floor consisted of the ticket office, as well as a storage room and eight other offices. The entire third floor of the expansive hall was devoted to an elaborate theater area. The vaudeville era proved lucrative for the Music Hall, with some of the biggest names of the time gracing its stage, but the prosperity was short-lived. Just four years after construction, James Maston sold his $30,000 interest in the Music Hall to Mary Acheson for a mere 25 cents; he was that sure that the future was bleak for the music hall, with so many others being built nearby. By 1905, business had trickled to the point that the National Bank of Cohoes, who owned the building at that time, was forced to close the theater, saying that it needed extensive repairs that were not economically justified.

For more than six decades, the building was sealed up and neglected. Then in 1969, the city of Cohoes purchased it for only $1. Five years later, it reopened as the Music Hall, fully renovated, and it took its rightful place on the National Register of Historic Places. Today, besides its resident ghosts, it houses the RiverSpark Visitor Center and C-R Productions, a nonprofit organization headed by Jim Charles and Tony Rivera whose mission is to revitalize the hall, attracting high-quality performances to ensure that the cultural and educational landmark will be enjoyed by many future generations.

Split Rock Quarry

In the nearer zone, women were in hysterics, fleeing along the roads and streets of the city. Last night it was thought that only half a dozen persons had been killed, but daylight disclosed scores of bodies in the blackened ruins.

—*New York Times,* July 4, 1918

Today all that remains of the Semet-Solvay Munitions Plant at Split Rock Quarry in Onondaga is its fabled rock crusher, along with several man-made tunnels that are now dead-end hidden shafts, foundations, and caves concealed by overgrown brush. The area is said to be one of the eeriest places to visit in the Syracuse area, whether one is aware of its gruesome history or not. After all, the air very probably is rife with gut-wrenching residual energy of a tragedy that occurred there long ago—residual energy that many have sensed in the form of apparitions, unexplained sounds, and atmospheric anomalies.

Gilbert Coons was the first to operate a quarry at the Split Rock location in Onondaga County in 1834, recognizing the value of its large deposits of limestone for use in the construction of buildings, locks, and the Erie Canal. In 1881, the Solvay Process Company acquired Coons's quarry grounds, because large amounts of limestone (as well as coal and salt) were needed for its lucrative soda ash production process. Overhead cables were fabricated to carry large buckets of limestone from Split Rock quarry to the company's factory on Onondaga Lake. In 1912, Solvay Process vacated Split Rock for a larger quarry at Jamesville, but in 1915, the Split Rock location, dubbed the Rock, was modified, expanded, and reopened as the Semet-Solvay Munitions Plant for mass production of TNT explosives during World War I. There was such a huge demand for munitions by some of our allies—France, Great Britain, Italy, and especially Russia—that a larger site became necessary. When the United States entered the war in April 1917, demand for munitions increased so greatly that the twenty-five hundred employees of the Rock were working three shifts around the clock. Had the war ended just five months earlier, the tragedy at Split Rock would not have occurred. After the war ended on November 11, 1918, the munitions plant was no longer needed, so it was permanently closed. But its history can never be rewritten.

The *Syracuse Post Standard* put out a special-edition newspaper just one hour after the main explosion, titled "Explosion and Fire in Split Rock Plant Kills 5, Injures 45," but the true extent of the tragedy was not realized until the following morning, once the darkness of the night, as well as the smoke, lifted. The fact was that at least fifty men had perished and another one hundred had been injured in the massive explosion at Split Rock Quarry that shook the city of Syracuse and its surrounds on the night of July 2, 1918. It started around 8:30 P.M., when a worker in one of the towers noticed that the water pressure had become dangerously low. Before he could tell anyone, an overheated gear in a grinding machine apparently set the chemicals on fire, and Plant #1 went up in flames, leading to the first small explosion. A fire whistle was blown to alert the rest of the plant, and the forty fire patrolmen assigned to that building quickly set about getting the fire under control. Every shift had one hundred fire patrolmen on hand, since fires were common and could be expected in such an industry. Their sole job was to contain a fire before it could reach any of the explosive agents on the site, especially the mother lode—four hundred tons of TNT stored in warehouse magazines not far from the main factory. Four hundred tons of TNT is enough to take out the entire city of Syracuse and then some. As it was, they would soon find out just how devastating a mere ton or two of the explosive could be.

When the wind shifted, drawing flames up and out of the roof of the tower they were in, the fire patrol realized the fire was getting away from them, and worse, they realized the water pressure had failed completely. Their efforts were futile, and the heat of the fire drove them back. In the midst of the chaos, the power failed, throwing everyone into darkness, leaving each person to fend for himself and try to find a way out. Some gallant heroes refused to give up hope that the water pressure would return, so they held on to their hoses, determined to keep the fire from reaching the TNT warehouse across the way. They were found dead in the ash the next day, still holding the melted nozzles on their hoses. A series of small explosions sounded over the pandemonium for the next hour, and then at 9:30 P.M., a twenty-two-hundred-pound vat of volatile toluel exploded with a deafening blast. A huge black mushroom cloud shot up over the site, spewing debris and ash as far as three miles from the blast and shattering store windows. Residents throughout the vicinity believed that the Germans were bombing them or that there had been an earthquake, until police using bullhorns canvassed the neighborhoods, alerting people to report to the morgue if they knew anyone working at the munitions factory. It was Syracuse's longest night.

About 11 P.M., an hour and a half after the last explosion, and with Plant #1 still in a state of chaos as the living searched for survivors, the munitions plant received orders to resume production (until the end of the war) of its picric and nitric acids, which were crucial for the war effort, at Plants #2 and #3. But many workers just coming on shift turned away for good when they saw the death and destruction the explosion had wrought. The official death toll reached at least fifty, though some reports said fifty-two. Dozens of critically injured workers were taken to seven area hospitals throughout the night and into the morning hours.

The dead and wounded suffered horrifying injuries. The strength of the final blast lifted one man high up off the ground and held him pressed against a concrete wall engulfed in flames, "like a human torch." Many others were burned beyond recognition, and some were crushed beneath the rubble of the explosion. Some were blown to pieces, their body parts later found around the perimeter of the site, and others succumbed to the toxic fumes of picric and nitric acids that the company produced in large volumes. These chemicals are extremely volatile and highly corrosive to the skin and airways. In fact, many of the workers at Split Rock had pitted skin on their faces from their exposure to picric acid prior to the fire. Both picric and nitric acids cause burning and yellowing of the skin, hair, and eyes, and that fact would be repeated often in the years following the disaster, when people puzzled over apparitions at Split Rock Quarry that seemed to have a yellowish or greenish glow about them. Sixteen- and seventeen-year-old workers were told at daybreak to pick up bodies and body parts that had been blown onto the grass, so that a mass funeral and burial in

Oakwood Cemetery could eventually be held for them. When all was said and done, besides the tremendous loss of lives, property loss was estimated at $1 million. The fire had destroyed three TNT plants, one nitric acid plant, the main office, a laboratory, and a boiler house, according to E. L. Pierce, vice president of the Semet Solvay Company. He reported that "the men had the fire under control when the water supply gave out, and this permitted the spread of the flames."

As news of the explosion spread, people demanded answers. The *New York Times* reported that District Attorney John H. Walrath ordered a double investigation because of "several peculiar circumstances, including the breakdown of the water and lighting systems." Walrath said, "There is a rumor that the tragedy, the worst in the history of Syracuse, was the work of spies," adding that the truth must be known. That rumor was never substantiated. The article, called "60 Killed by Blast in Syracuse Plant" and dated July 4, 1918, described the horror:

> The night was one of terror after the big explosion. A general exodus followed the blast. Besides the fleeing workmen, many families moved away from the scene. Some pushed wheelbarrows containing their children and a few household goods.
>
> Besides the buildings of the plant, the small homes of workmen about the hillside and in the valley were wrecked. Many women in these houses had narrow escapes. They rushed out in panic, some with children in their arms.

It's not surprising, considering the nature of the tragedy and the number of lives that were affected by it, that many consider the abandoned Split Rock Quarry to be haunted. The most common reports are of glowing apparitions seen on top of the rock crusher; the ethereal sounds of moaning, unexplained footsteps, and rocks falling; and feelings of being watched. Numerous reports online are from individuals describing an immediate drop in temperature and a sensation of static electricity when standing inside the rock crusher, the only remaining structure, which sits within a limestone cliff flanked by tunnels. Lord Rick of the Paranormal & Ghost Society said that during his solo visit to the site, he had "multiple supernatural occurrences, such as [hearing] footsteps, voices, cold spots, and feelings of being watched as [he] looked up into holes in the ceiling," and stressed that Split Rock Quarry is one of the scariest places of the hundreds he's investigated.

Pierce Homestead

WANTED: Pierce—The Camden Murderer. Height, 5 feet 8 inches; weight from 150 to 160 pounds; light auburn hair, slightly inclined to curl; light brown whiskers; eyes, blue. He was last seen with a gun on the track of the Central Railroad, going in a westerly direction.

—*New York Times*, April 10, 1873

Robert Pierce was a thirty-year-old man who murdered his wife, Fidelia "Delia" Beeman Pierce, in front of their children at their home on the Oak Opening–Camden Road in Vienna, just south of Camden. He then fled the scene, leaving the three young children behind to fend for themselves in their mother's blood, and he was never seen again. As with any sensational story that various newspapers of the past hastily tried to scoop first, sources vary somewhat on the details of the crime, but for the most part, the details were eventually pieced together quite well, considering the resources available in 1873, when the grisly murder occurred. The *Journal and Republican* was one of the first papers to run the story on April 16, 1873:

Terrible Murder Near Camden—A terrible murder came to light near Camden on Sunday last. The wife of one Robert Pierce was found dead on the floor, having been horribly mangled by an axe which lay nearby covered with blood. The horrible crime was probably committed on Friday last. There were three children in the room, the youngest of which is less than twelve months old. The two older ones were in bed, and all were nearly dead from cold and hunger and may die. The eldest child says she saw her father strike her mother with an axe and then take his gun and go away. He is still at liberty. The crime was discovered by a little boy, a brother of the supposed murderer, who was sent to the house on an errand. He returned and reported that his brother's wife was asleep on the floor. The scene of the crime is about five miles southwest of the Village of Camden.

Mary Clark Norton, who wrote about the history of nearby Elpis in 1960, offered additional insight on the murder, beyond what has been reported in newspapers, as a local who knew descendants of both the Pierce and Beeman families. Alexis Beeman, the murdered woman's father, was hired to run the sawmill at Elpis. Besides Delia, he and his wife had five other children. The Pierces were a family of eleven, with Robert being the youngest son. After Robert married Delia Beeman, said to be a very pretty woman, the young couple moved into a house on the Oak Opening–Camden Road between his parents' home and that of a man named Peter Audus Jr.

On Good Friday 1873, Delia and Robert had just returned home from visiting Robert's brother when an argument broke out. Many people believe that because of his wife's beauty, Robert became violently jealous about something—possibly his next-door neighbor Peter Audas, with whom he had been working in the woods that day. Robert had just sharpened his ax that day, and in his moment of rage, he brought it down on the head of Delia, then hit her several more times over the breast and heart area. The poor young woman was said to be pregnant at the time, so hers was not the only life snubbed out prematurely. Robert massacred his wife in front of the children, locked the door, left the ax on the back steps, and walked away . . . from the wife he murdered, from the children he left toddling through her blood, and from his life. On Easter Sunday, two days later, two of the children were in the front yard when Delia's young brother stopped by to pay an Easter visit. After the gruesome discovery, he raced home to tell his parents. The children were cold and starving, the baby was covered in its mother's blood after crawling through it to be near her, and the oldest told everyone who asked that his father had killed his mother with the ax, then left with his gun.

Pierce, according to Norton, was traced to the mill at Elpis—possibly in an effort to track down Delia's father, whom he was said to hate, but thankfully, Mr. Beeman wasn't at the mill when the murderous man arrived. Then Pierce's gun was located on the other side of the Wendell Farm's stone wall near North Bay Road, where it had presumably been thrown. The trail of the killer stopped across the lake at South Bay where his sister lived. A week after the grim discovery of Delia's body, Robert Pierce's parents were arrested and taken to Camden as accessories to the murder, after the fact. It was rumored that Pierce had been hiding in the woods near the murder scene, and that his parents, who lived next door, had been seen bringing food into the woods for him. His brother reportedly said that he wasn't worried about Pierce being caught, because his appearance had changed so much in a week's time that nobody would recognize him. The brother callously added, as if to taunt those involved in the manhunt, that Pierce had on him more money than people realized, implying that he had enough to live on for a while, if necessary (which immediately brings to mind the fact that the murder was premeditated). Pierce's parents were released the following day, after questioning.

The baby girl was taken by a family near Bernards Bay; the boy, who had witnessed the crime and told authorities who did it, was taken in by a Westdale family; and four-year-old Cora was taken in by Reverend Johnson of Whiskey Island. Cora died at the tender age of eleven and was buried beside Delia in the Maple Flats Cemetery.

A year after the crime, the *New York Times* ran a blurb that simply said, "Robert Pierce, who murdered his wife with an axe at his home in the town of Vienna, Oneida County, N.Y., on the 11th of April, 1873, is reported to have been captured at Chicago." But apparently it wasn't their man. The same thing happened twelve years later, when another *Times* article appeared called "Caught after Twelve Years: Arrest of a Man Who Hacked His Wife to Pieces in 1873." That article said:

> The crime had almost been forgotten until yesterday, when some boys who were hunting in a swamp in Madison County, not far from the scene of the murder, came upon a rude hut made of boughs. Almost at the same moment, a rough voice from within warned them to leave the place on pain of death. The boys ran off and alarmed the neighborhood, and soon a body of farmers had surrounded the place with two constables from Oneida. The man was told to come forth, and he reluctantly did so. He was a villainous-looking fellow, stoutly built, with a long beard . . . several persons in the party declared that it was the missing Pierce . . . He said his name was John McGinnes.

After further investigation, however, they determined that "Mc-Ginnes" wasn't their man either, and no further mention was ever made of finding the real Pierce. The story of the murder eventually faded from the spotlight, but the farm where the murder occurred earned a deleterious reputation of being haunted, because of the murder—and perhaps another tragic death that occurred next door. An article in the *Watertown Herald* of January 29, 1910, called "So-Called Haunted Farm Was Sold for an Insignificant Sum on Account of Its Uncanny Reputation," said, "The so-called haunted farm of 500 acres in the town of Vienna, Oneida County, New York, which a few years ago was sold for $4,500, was Saturday knocked down at auction in Utica for $535, and for good measure, a complete sawmill outfit was thrown in. The farm was the scene of a famous murder a number of years ago. Its uncanny reputation depreciated the value of the property, inasmuch as it was impossible to secure tenants."

It would not be surprising if Delia Pierce remained firmly planted in spirit form in the house in which she was murdered, waiting for Robert Pierce to be captured and made to pay for his crime against her and their children. But there was another poor soul with a good reason to hold a grudge as well, this one related to the Audus House next door. Pierce's sister, now Mrs. Audus, as well as his younger sister, Fanny, were there on October 27, 1863—a full ten years before Fidelia Pierce's murder—when a cold, exhausted German named William Schlenburg appeared on the doorstep. Schlenburg had spent the day trading in Camden with a Mr. Deveresse and his son. After dark, it began to snow, and the rough road became coated with whiteness. The two men and the boy stopped at the Craig House on their way home, and they left the boy and their oxen to find shelter and rest. The two gentlemen, Deveresse and Schlenburg, decided they should continue on their way so as not to worry their wives. But by the time they reached the Peter Audus Jr. home, next door to the Robert Pierce residence, Schlenburg was too exhausted and cold to go on. Deveresse asked the young Mrs. Audus and her sister to open the door, because he had a man with him who needed shelter immediately, but Mrs. Audus refused, saying her husband wouldn't allow her to let a man in the house while he was away. Regardless, Deveresse left the ailing Schlenburg on the Audus doorstep, hoping Mrs. Audus would reconsider, unbeknownst to the two Pierce women inside. The next morning, Mrs. Audus opened the door and found poor Mr. Schlenburg lying there, frozen to death. He had merely been trying to get home on a frigid autumn night to his wife and three young children when he met his end.

In a bizarre twist, the following summer, the very same Mrs. Audus that had refused to shelter a freezing man became ill with the "ague," a fever of unspecified origin. She fought the chills of a high fever but was unable to get warm. When she died of the ague—just a year after she had left a man to die on her doorstep—she too left behind three young children. So you can see why the Pierce home and its surrounds, including the mill and the Audus property, could be haunted. There were no less than three distinct, untimely deaths of entirely different natures between two adjacent properties within ten years' time.

In 1960, when Norton wrote her history of Elpis, she said that the Pierce House where the heinous crime had been committed was gone, and the house next door—that of the elder Pierce—was gone as well. All that remained to indicate the houses had ever been there was lilac trees and rose bushes on the north side of the road between the Fields Brook and the radio towers.

New York State Capitol

BODY RECOVERED—Samuel Abbott, Victim of Capitol Fire in Albany—The body of Samuel Abbott, the human victim of the state capitol fire was found in the southwest corner of the building where the flames raged fiercest. The body was charred beyond recognition but identified by means of a watch. Workmen clearing away the ruins of the southwest cupola, the only part of the exterior wall to give way, found the remains of the aged night watchman in a little corridor on the fourth floor. That portion of the building was honeycombed with temporary partitions and floors and since the flames did not reach it until nearly an hour after the fire started, it is believed that Abbott was overcome by smoke before the fire touched him or that he lost his life in a vain attempt to rescue some of the state's valuable relics.

—*Lowell Sun*, March 31, 1911

Albany's version of the proverbial "haunted house on the hill" sits majestically atop State Street Hill in Capitol Park. The imposing New York State Capitol is not a house, per se, but try telling that to a ghost who is believed to have taken up eternal residence there. Some have dubbed the harmless specter George the Janitor, while others believe it is Samuel Abbott, the ill-fated night watchman who died in the disastrous fire that consumed the entire western portion of the building in 1911. I tend to believe it's the latter. But either one— a janitor or a night watchman—would explain the keys that are often heard jangling when nobody is around, the doorknobs that are sometimes heard rattling, and the doors that occasionally are found to be open after being closed and locked for the night.

The elaborate capitol was considered a modern marvel of nineteenth-century architecture when it was completed in 1899. Built of white Maine granite in Renaissance-Romanesque style and inspired by the City Hall in Paris, it was among the greatest buildings in the world and considered the most expensive government building of its time, twice as costly as the United States Capitol. It cost about $27 million to build—more than $1 million per year of its construction, which spanned nearly three decades. That's equivalent to half a billion dollars today. But the real value was in the priceless records and original documents, such as the old English and Dutch Colonial records it contained. Then calamity struck in the wee hours of March 27, 1911, twelve years after the state capitol opened. A devastating fire that began in the assembly library rapidly consumed the entire west wing, causing an estimated $10 million in damage to the structure itself (not including the value of the contents). Some three-quarters of a million historic books and original manuscripts were destroyed.

There was no insurance on the building or its contents, because the capitol had been considered "absolutely fireproof," according to a March 30, 1911, *Post Standard* article. In fact, "so firmly was this idea imbedded in the brains of most Albanians," the article said, "that when they were roused from sleep early this morning and told that the city's architectural pride was afire, they laughed and expressed the belief that you might as well look for a spectacular fire at the North Pole." True, the granite exterior hadn't burned, but much of the interior had been consumed, since the fire started in the State Library, where there was plenty of combustible material to fuel the flames: "wooden shelving, books and pamphlets and loose papers."

The fire was believed to have been started "by the fuse of an electric push button becoming electrified" at around 2:45 A.M., according to some sources. But another theory mentioned in the *Post Standard* was that it was caused by a careless smoker. "They blamed it on a carelessly thrown cigarette, and it was asserted that the desk of a clerk and the book case near it was observed to be on fire when the flames were first discovered." Nobody ever determined with absolute certainty what caused the deadly fire, but two men who happened to be in the capitol when the fire started said that around 2:15 A.M., when they were working on the third floor, a clerk and a night watchman (Abbott, perhaps) went frantically running through the corridor yelling, "There is a fire in the Assembly library!" The two men ran to the door of the library and saw the desk in the corner on fire. They said that had they had just one bucket of water, they could have put the fire out then and there, but they could find nothing to put water in, and the fire wouldn't wait, so they closed the door, hoping to contain the fire in that room until firefighters arrived. Unfortunately, the night watchman had to run all the way downstairs to sound the alarm, as there were no other fire alarms in the building.

Twenty minutes later, the State Library had caught on fire—providing a smorgasbord of paper products for the hungry flames. Among the documents consumed were "the most valuable genealogical works in the United States, together with relics and priceless documents," among them thousands of volumes of law and code books, including the original "twenty-three manuscript folio volumes of the famous official records of the governors of the city of New Amsterdam, covering a period from 1630 to

1674." The departments destroyed included the Court of Claims, the Bill Draughting Department, the Bureau of Weights and Measures, the State Regents' Rooms, the State Prison Commission Office, the State Department of Education, the Attorney General's Office, the State Excise Department, the Office of the State Treasurer and Tax Commissioner, the State Board of Charities, and the Commission of Lunacy.

All of those losses of material things were bad enough, but the greatest tragedy of it all was the loss of Sam Abbott, whose troubled spirit a psychic once sensed still lingering in the corridors ... which would certainly be understandable, considering the horrific circumstances of his death. In the years since that devastating fire, employees claim to have heard voices after hours and swear they've seen unexplainable shadows moving through the corridors. One described a shadow she saw as a "grayish blur" that approached her and passed right through her with an icy chill, before hurrying past another employee so fast that her skirt blew up in the breeze the disturbance caused, according to an account in Arthur Meyers' *Ghostly Register*. Perhaps Sam Abbott continues to repeat his last desperate race to escape the flames, save some priceless state documents, or tell everybody to get out on the night of the fire that took his life.

Rensselaer Polytechnic Institute

West Hall at Rensselaer Polytechnic Institute (RPI) in Troy was originally the Troy Hospital from 1871 to 1914. In that capacity, the building saw the gamut of human emotions within its walls, from the joy of successful childbirth to the sorrow of debilitating accidents and incurable fatal diseases. Is it any wonder that ghosts are believed to now roam its halls, when so many people are known to have died there?

The infamous West Hall Ghost has been widely publicized since at least 1985, when an article called "Is Betsy Roaming West Hall?" ran in RPI's newspaper. Grand marshal Eric Lambiaso relayed an often told story about a Civil War–era nurse named Betsy who allegedly went crazy from being around her feeble-minded patients for too long in the basement ward, where the insane were supposedly sequestered. According to Lambiaso, it was said that Betsy would do away with patients who got on her nerves in the middle of the night, and that her spirit now haunts the halls and has been heard whining, slamming doors, flushing toilets, and such. In 1880, five nurses, Sisters of Charity, were living and working at the Troy Hospital, though none was named Betsy or Betty or anything even remotely similar. The 1900 census lists one "Bessie McMahon," however, a twenty-four-year-old woman who lived at the hospital performing "house work." Most of the nurses listed in the census were named Mary and Anna, and Bessie was the only name I could find that is similar to the legendary Betsy. So could Bessie McMahon be our spectral darling of West Hall?

Today West Hall, as it's been called since 1953, houses Rensselaer's Arts Department and Music Association, as well as the Office of Research Administration and Finance, credit union, and real estate management department. But it has served many functions in its 140 years. In 1866, the Roman Catholic managers of the original old Troy Hospital on the corner of Fifth and Washington realized the need for a larger, quieter facility to serve the growing community of mostly Irish immigrants. So they purchased a plot of land on the east side of Eighth Street at the head of Fulton and began construction of the four-story brick structure that ultimately became West Hall, laying the cornerstone on June 28, 1868. A year later, patients and employees of the old hospital moved into the new facility, operated by the benevolent Sisters of Charity. The Civil War had ended three years before the hospital even went up, so if there ever were a nurse named Betsy, she wasn't caring for insane patients during the Civil War at West Hall, as is commonly rumored, because the building didn't exist until after the war was over.

I also was unable to corroborate the story about the basement being used exclusively to house the insane. Census records do list two or three insane patients residing at the hospital at any given time. But with the Marshall Infirmary for the insane nearby, why admit the feeble-minded to a regular hospital? The people who were actually patients at the Troy Hospital in the late 1800s and early

1900s, according to historical documents, suffered from—and succumbed to—maladies common to that era: "consumption" (tuberculosis), paralysis, debility, rheumatism, "sore eyes," "old age," whooping cough, smallpox, scalding, "water on the brain," measles, factory accidents, and horse-and-buggy or railcar accidents. There were also war veterans, abandoned children, and vagabonds in need of food and shelter. The Sisters turned away nobody in need, regardless of background. As a hospital, obviously, many people died there during its forty-three years: Mary Dwyer, age forty-two, and Jeremiah Connors, twenty-eight, both of consumption, and Mrs. Connors, twenty-five, of smallpox, to name just a few actual examples. And where there has been death, it seems that spirits often linger, so it's not surprising if West Hall is rife with paranormal phenomena.

After its reign as the Troy Hospital, the building served as a War Department training facility for a brief time in 1918, but when World War I ended that same year, the training facility was immediately vacated. The diocese of Albany then purchased it to house Catholic high school students in 1925. But when the school's enrollment increased beyond capacity in 1952, the diocese sold the building, now on the National Register of Historic Places, to Rensselaer Polytechnic Institute, which was also in need of additional space for its own growing populace.

In 1991, a much-needed restoration project was undertaken on West Hall to begin updating the facilities to code. The sum of $11 million was allotted for the work, which was to include repair of the roof, windows, dormers, and masonry—all substantial jobs, considering the impressive Second Empire–style features of the building. But after less than $1 million had been spent, the project was abandoned and put on the back burner until 2004, when a grand-scale renovation effort got under way on West Hall's exterior facade. That restoration is expected to be completed in 2009. Since West Hall's initial renovation in 1991, reports of unexplained phenomena and antics attributed to Betsy have increased dramatically. Remodeling often seems to increase paranormal activity, with tools being moved, equipment malfunctioning, and doors slamming for no good reason. The West Hall ghost also unabashedly whines to anyone who will listen.

People using the building at night, especially janitorial staff, often tell of unusual thumping noises, the sounds of ethereal whining and screaming, and doors opening and closing unexplainably. A couple students once spent the night in the basement with a tape recorder to see if anything would present itself. Thinking it had been an altogether uneventful evening, they left disappointed, only to discover later on playback of their tape that they had captured an EVP of the now-famous "three-second whine." In 1997, two custodians working together in the building heard the sound of glass breaking in the middle of the night, when they were the only ones there. Though they searched everywhere for something that could explain the sound they clearly heard, nothing was ever found. The same employees have smelled cookies and unfamiliar chemicals on their rounds, and one night they left the building in a hurry when they heard a moan on the other side of a door they were trying to open. Printers in the credit union at West Hall have operated on their own, and on one occasion, all of the toilets in the restroom flushed at the very same time . . . 3 A.M., also known as "dead time," when the spirit world is most active. In some European folklore, 3 A.M. is considered "the witching hour," when supernatural beings such as ghosts, demons, and witches are believed to be at their most powerful. And in the 2005 movie *The Exorcism of Emily Rose*, 3 A.M. is said to be the "anti-hour," because Christ is traditionally believed to have died at 3 P.M., so 3 A.M. would be the exact opposite time. Therefore, the film explained that 3 A.M. is the hour each night when demons mock Jesus and the Holy Trinity. Since that movie's release, Internet message boards are saturated by forum members detailing their own supernatural experiences that have occurred at 3 A.M.—many of them downright chilling. When the toilets flushed in unison at 3 A.M. in West Hall, there were skeptics who said that because RPI's plumbing is connected to the Troy sewer system, heavy rain downpours could have caused water to erupt from the toilets "at unusual hours." But with twenty-three other hours in the day, why did this occur at precisely 3 A.M.?

In 1997, paranormal investigators Ed and Lorraine Warren performed an investigation of West Hall. Lorraine, a psychic intuitive, immediately sensed the pain and suffering from its days as a hospital, at one point feeling weak in the knees, and at another point feeling a light tap from something unseen. The Warrens adamantly believe the building is haunted, based mostly on Lorraine's sixth sense. In 2006, their nephew John Zaffis, an acclaimed paranormal investigator himself, and Christopher Moon, president of *Haunted Times Magazine*, presented a joint lecture following their investigation of West Hall. A number of very convincing EVPs were recorded, including one that said that about eighty different spirits dwell in West Hall. Abnormal electromagnetic field readings were taken in several locations, and many students captured spirit energy in the form of orbs in their photographs that evening. It was enough to convince even the most hardened skeptic that there's definitely "something strange in the neighborhood."

The fact is that many people died in the building long ago when it was the Troy Hospital, and many others passed through in various states of extreme emotional duress. Thus it's likely that West Hall is haunted, based on its history and the continually mounting evidence that has been witnessed, recorded, and filmed by staff, students, and paranormal investigators alike.

Professor Java's Coffee Sanctuary

Though many paranormal investigators have requested permission to investigate Professor Java's Coffee Sanctuary in Albany, and many customers have asked if they could spend the night on a "ghost watch" there, to date none of them have been granted permission, according to the manager, Charles Pemburn. But he was kind enough to take the time to share his understanding of the ghost lore surrounding the coffeehouse with me.

The building at 217 Wolf Road that houses the Coffee Sanctuary was originally someone's home, and then a hair salon, before finally becoming the popular coffeehouse that it is today, when, as Charles told me, "One man had a vision to create a café that would serve the community by providing great service, freshly roasted coffee, and a perfect relaxed atmosphere where those who enter can forget about the bustle of life outside and just enjoy themselves."

Regardless of the comfortable café that it truly is today, the building hasn't always been so pleasant in the past. Back in the days when it was a home, there was, at one time, a working meth lab in the basement. Equipment found supports that claim. The story goes that when the lab was raided by authorities, a dog (either a police dog or the owner's dog) was accidentally killed. Years later, when the house had become the Sanctuary, employees and customers could hear a dog barking late at night. Charles mused, "To be honest, it has been fun to see them run outside in search of a barking dog, only to realize that the sound grows quieter as you leave the building. The barking came from within the Sanctuary walls." And the basement, where the tragedy occurred, still sends shivers down some employees' spines, though not for any tangible reason. The manager admitted that it's still a very eerie basement, and some employees are leery about going down there, but he said it was even more so in the past before it was renovated.

"Little has been heard from the dog in some time. We believe this is due to the love the owner has shown to all dog kind. At one point, the owner opened his doors to allow dog lovers the opportunity to bring in their four-legged friends. He went so far as to create a line of healthy dog treats that were baked on-site and offered as part of the menu for his canine clients. This got him the title of the K-9 Chef of Professor Java's Barkery . . . that even led him to having a Sunday evening segment on *News Channel Nine* in Albany, where he expanded his recipes to include healthy dog meals.

"Sadly, the 'barkery' has closed and the K-9 chef has left the airwaves. Still, there have been few new reports of the ghostly barking emanating from the Sanctuary. Although quiet, our ghostly canine is not forgotten, and on some rare occasions, he may still be heard barking into the night."

Charles admitted that people have long reported ghost stories associated with Professor Java's Coffee Sanctuary, and having been at the Sanctuary longer than any other employee, he too has experienced things that could not be explained. In July 2008, he said: "We were doing some large catering orders for a flight arriving from Germany, and I was in nearly every day early in the morning. Most days got me to the shop before 4 A.M. The owner arrived within an hour of me, so I was alone for at least 45 minutes. One day I was in the basement working in the office around 4:10 A.M. when I heard footsteps above me. I took it that the owner had gotten in early that morning. That was seemingly confirmed when I heard the sinks running; he must have been washing up or getting water ready to boil. I went upstairs expecting to see all the lights on, only to find it was still dark. I walked around, and the owner was nowhere in sight. Nobody was. I stood in the dark of the shop and wondered. Logic would say it was just the building creaking, making the sound of footsteps. Reason can tell me that the pipes were just running water through them, fooling me into thinking the sinks were on. But while down in that basement, I would have bet there was someone overhead. Not seeing them upstairs made me wonder, if only for a second, if maybe I did have a visitor with me that morning." Still, he insisted, "For the record, I am not one who strongly believes in ghosts. I am writing this as someone reporting on lore that has been witnessed (unexplained or not) and stories relayed through the art of oral reproduction." A man after my own journalistic heart. "In the past, employees of the Coffee Sanctuary were deathly afraid of the 'Java Ghosts.' Some even refused to go into the basement because they were so afraid. One employee who was hired called in and quit before her first shift even started because she was scared of ghosts." To her, "every creak was the ghost, every noise was the ghost, and every blinking light was the ghost."

That's not to diminish the truly unexplainable, such as the dog barking, for example, or pictures falling off the wall, dishes rattling, and appliances that purportedly turn on and off, according to a *Capital News 9* report. That same article tells of a Sanctuary employee's knowledge of a female apparition with long hair that has been seen walking into the back room, but is nowhere to be found when employees go in after her. And she's not the only apparition. There seems to be an entire family. Charles told me that a "wandering gentleman," fiftyish, wearing an "old world suit and tie with an overcoat" has even been seen by the owner. This apparition enters the café and heads directly to the library where, like the woman in the back room, he simply disappears before anyone gets there. The owner had a closer encounter with this one than most.

He was washing his hands in the men's room, when he looked up to see the male apparition in the mirror. By the time he spun around to face him, the figure was gone. According to Charles, it would just "move about the Sanctuary from room to room always vanishing at direct sight." And to make the family complete, there's the ghost of a young child, who appears to be between eight and twelve years old. Some say it's a girl with short hair, others say it's a boy. It "likes to play about and run around the Sanctuary. Employees have noted furniture having been moved and laughter coming from various places within the Sanctuary," said the manager.

I don't know whether it's that ghosts tend to come out in quieter times, such as the dark of night, simply because they're inherently shy, or they're actually around us all the time—even in crowded rooms, when it's much harder to sense the subtleties of spirit presence—but I like Charles's final thoughts on the matter: "From feeling a presence behind you to a chill run by you, unexplained reports at the Sanctuary haven't been silenced. It just takes a quieter time to realize what has just occurred. As for the Wandering Gentleman, he still catches the wait staff wondering where their customer ran off to, and the Young Child still gives a giggle when its latest game has befuddled the employees."

Landmark Theatre

The historic Landmark Theatre, first called Loew's State Theatre, at 362–374 South Salina Street in Syracuse, has a mysterious silent patron in its balcony. They call her the Lady in White. Like most theater apparitions, the Landmark's Lady in White infuses both awe and a hint of unease into an already-charged atmosphere. The stately theater was designed for Loew's by Thomas W. Lamb, whose vision was to build a grand venue that would provide city residents with a lavish place to escape from the grim news of the day, if only for a few hours. To that end, he spared no expense to detail. The theater, which opened on February 18, 1928, was truly a movie palace, with a three-thousand-person capacity. It saw people through the Great Depression and World War II. But in the 1950s, the theater's popularity waned, when smaller movie houses and cinemas sprouted up all over, and by the 1970s, attendance had dwindled so low, and the building was in a state of such disrepair, that there was even talk of razing the old landmark to make way for a new parking lot and shopping center.

Luckily, a group of concerned citizens called Syracuse Area Landmark Theatre (SALT) quickly managed to get the property placed on the National Register of Historic Places in 1977 as a Classical Revival, but one of the group's members said it was the first "great Oriental-style" movie theater. Their determined efforts to acquire the designation of a historic landmark opened the door for government funding to restore their beloved theater. SALT purchased the theater, changed its name to the Landmark Theatre—to stress the reason they resolved to save it—and began renovations. That was when the Lady in White, whom they subsequently called Claire, made her first appearance.

Claire has been seen in the balcony, weaving in and out between aisles or simply sitting silently. She doesn't appear to be all there, meaning she doesn't look quite solid, but rather fuzzy around the edges. She appears in a long, white gown and has vanished before onlookers' eyes. Ushers have even been known to approach the peculiar woman, thinking she was an actual living person, to ask her to leave a prohibited area, but before they reach her, she disappears into thin air. There may be days when she doesn't feel like fully manifesting into an apparition and instead chooses to flit about in the simplest manner for a spirit—as an orb. Apparently a blue orb, in her case, unless there's another spirit haunting the theater. The blue orb has been seen floating throughout the theater: along the catwalk, on the stairs to the dressing room, and, most often, along the back of the auditorium.

Besides the orbs and apparitions, there are said to be unexplainable cold spots, as well as strange voices and whispers when nobody but a lone employee is in the building. People often smell a pleasant lilac scent when there's no apparent source for it. In fact, according to a 2005 article in the *Post Standard*, a telephone repairman who walked into the tunnels beneath the building was suddenly surrounded by the smell of lilacs near the door. Thinking it was odd enough to warrant a second look, he returned to the door a few moments later, only to find it locked. One legend is that Claire, or Clarissa, fell off the balcony to her death years ago—though I could find nothing to confirm this story. Nevertheless, the apparition allegedly has a penchant for lilacs—and a dislike of cigarettes. So there you go.

Apparently, people have learned these bits of trivia through trial and error. A psychic brought in to discern information regarding the Landmark ghost was the first to sense that the spirit's name was Claire. She divined that Claire had been married to a Loew's employee and had hoped to become an actress but—as fate would have it—died before she ever had the chance to perform on the Landmark stage. Again, that's a tough one to confirm with historical records, so I wasn't able to corroborate that legend either, simply because I would have to somehow find every former male employee's name over Loew's roughly fifty-year term, and then find out if his spouse ever had a dream of becoming an actress before she died. Good luck with that, right?

Management doesn't necessarily believe the Landmark Theatre is haunted—at least, not at the current time—even though people still tell of fleeting white shadows believed to be the Lady in White. But that didn't stop the board of directors from suggesting it might be haunted at a Halloween fund-raiser that offered a "ghost hunt" of the grounds. And whether it's because the air is supernaturally charged or simply the anticipation of seeing a great performance, you can feel the electricity in the air when you enter the theater.

The Landmark Theatre is still open today, offering concerts and performances, and also hosts other community events and happenings for special occasions. Way back on opening week in 1928, Loew's ran an ad in the *Syracuse Herald* thanking the public for its tremendous support of the theater during its first week in operation. I'd like to take this opportunity to reiterate their closing sentiments: "To the citizens of Syracuse, Loew's State Theater is *yours*. May it bring you endless days of pleasure and happiness."

Ancestors Inn
at the Bassett House

After an exhaustive search for a property in the Syracuse area that they could convert into a bed-and-breakfast, Mary and Dan Weidman settled on the Italianate-style, red brick home at 215 Sycamore Street in Liverpool known as the Bassett House. In honor of their own ancestors, they decided their inn would be called Ancestors Inn at the Bassett House, using their forebears' preferences in choosing the design theme and name for each guest room. Little did they know that someone else's ancestors wanted to be acknowledged in the house as well.

When the house was built in 1860, its first owners, George and Hannah Bassett, some of Liverpool's earliest settlers, moved in. When George died, the house was passed on to the couple's only son, Henry, who planned to move his mother into a more suitable home he had built for her nearby, but Hannah wouldn't budge. She insisted on staying in the house her husband had built until the day she died. Some believe the stubborn woman, along with her beloved George, still remains even to this day.

When the Weidmans started converting the house, which at one point in its history of six owners was a dentist's office, tools were mysteriously misplaced and lights turned on and off inexplicably. Knowing what the lights had a propensity to do, Mary got in a habit of going through the house and double-checking to make absolutely certain every light was off before leaving. Yet sometimes before she even got out to her car in the driveway, the light in what was believed to have been the original owner's master bedroom had been turned back on. A ghost who's afraid of the dark?

By the time the inn opened for business in 1998, paranormal activity was in full swing. Guests reported seeing a frail little man sitting in the parlor, and one couple said he even joined them at their table for a few moments before getting up to leave. Not so unusual, except that no man fitting that description was staying there when witnesses insisted they saw him. A visiting psychic told the Weidmans that they have a friendly spirit named Tim, who was a servant to the Bassetts in the nineteenth century. He still watches over the property and its current family, just as he did more than a hundred years ago. He may be the spirit responsible for jangling guest room doorknobs in the middle of the night, as if to make sure they're locked and secure.

Mary told me that the Valentine's Room, named for her great-uncle Valentine Diehl, is the most haunted room at Ancestors Inn, and she knew there was something peculiar about it even while they were remodeling it. She knew right away that she wanted to call it Valentine's Room, because she planned to decorate it in opulent wallpaper that was red and black with gold highlights. Dan was a bit uncertain about the color scheme, but Mary was determined, so he helped her start stripping away layers upon layers of old wallpaper to prepare for the transformation. When they got down to the very first wallpaper ever hung on the walls, they got the surprise of their life (well, one of them). It was the exact wallpaper Mary had envisioned her Valentine Room would have. If that weren't strange enough, the same thing happened in Charlotte's Room, named after Mary's grandmother. Mary had pictured the walls covered in bunches of violets, and days later, when she stripped the walls in that room, she discovered that the original wallpaper was just what she had envisioned. Does Mary have some sort of psychic connection to the first lady of the house, or was Hannah Bassett's spirit reaching out from beyond, whispering ideas into Mary's subconscious mind?

One of the spirits haunting the inn appears to have a camera fetish. Guests often complain that their cameras have disappeared, and they either never turn up at all or appear in the wrong rooms. If the guests are lucky enough to leave with the cameras they came with, there's a whole other issue with the film. The ghost seems to want Mary or Dan to be in every photograph taken on the grounds; otherwise, the pictures may not come out. Sounds as though Tim, the eternal servant, is kicking his loyalty to his masters up a notch.

Hudson Valley
and the
Catskills

Shanley Hotel

In 1845, carpenter Thomas Ritch built a hotel at 56 Main Street in Napanoch that he boasted was the best in the Hudson Valley area. When it was sold in 1851, and the name was changed to Hunderford's Hotel, it was again called "one of the most beautiful and commodious public houses to be found in any section of the country," according to www.shanleyhotel.com. The hotel was a lot of things to a lot of people at the time. With its close proximity to New York City, it was a favorite summertime destination for city folk. With its close proximity to the railroad, it was a regular stop for train passengers passing through. And with its central location in the heart of the town, it was a favored watering hole for Napanoch residents and transient construction workers alike. In 1895, after the hotel had passed through the hands of several more owners, including Adolph Wagner and George Grosselin, a fire at a house adjacent to the property spread to the hotel, burning it to the ground. Thankfully, no lives were lost. And like the legendary phoenix that rose from the ashes, a brand new three-story hotel was built on the very same spot and opened in November that same year.

In 1906, fate (disguised as a health condition) drew Irishman James Louis Shanley to the Hudson Valley, where he purchased what was by then called the Napanoch Hotel. James, who was born on Halloween 1874, and his brothers were already successful restaurateurs and hoteliers, with elegant holdings around the country, so it didn't take him long to get the Napanoch Hotel up to his standards. Shanley and his wife, Beatrice, were well known and well admired throughout the community, and their hotel was the envy of the region. Just two years after acquiring the hotel, they had added a bowling alley, barbershop, and billiard room to it, and Shanley's hotel and restaurant became a resort of choice among the rich and famous, including Eleanor Roosevelt. Also during the

1930s, but not related to Mrs. Roosevelt's visits, the hotel was apparently sidelining as a speakeasy and bordello. Though the Shanleys' lives certainly seemed blessed, they (and their employees) suffered their share of tragedy. Beatrice had much to envy—expensive clothing and accessories, the best perfumes and silk bedding, a magnificent hotel—but as they say, money can't-solve all one's problems. She lost her three beloved infants before they ever turned one. An obituary in the *Middletown Daily Times-Press* on January 9, 1912, said: "Kathleen, infant daughter of Mr. and Mrs. James Shanley, of Napanoch, died on Saturday, after two weeks severe illness of spinal meningitis. An only child, six months old, the affliction is a very severe one for the parents."

In a poignant twist of fate, Beatrice soon found herself raising her sister-in-law's little girls, Kathleen, age five, and Marie, six. Their mother, Esther Faughnan, who lived in an apartment at the Shanley Hotel with her husband and daughters, died giving birth to her third child. Nobody is immune to life's trials and tribulations. Not the Shanley family, and not its employees. The hotel's barber, Peter Gregory, suffered a great loss when his four-year-old daughter fell into a well on the nearby Hoornbeck Farm and drowned. "The child had lifted up the lid and fell head first into the spring [and the] body was found two hours afterward," reported the *Middletown Daily Times* of May 31, 1911. Then in 1937, James Shanley—for whom the hotel is still named today—died of a massive heart attack on August 26 at the age of sixty-two, leaving the stunned community reeling from the sad news. Calling hours and funeral services were held at the hotel. Eleanor Roosevelt sent her condolences to her friend, the widowed Beatrice. On Easter Sunday 1941, a fire once again threatened to destroy the Shanley Hotel, but firefighters from Ellenville and Napanoch finally managed to contain it after about an hour. The structure had suffered damage, but it was saved. Though she had given it her best shot, Beatrice Shanley's heart was no longer in the hotel business, and it was proving too much for her to handle or worry about.

Al Hazen—another Halloween baby, like James Shanley—acquired it in 1944 and ran it for many years. Today the lucky owners carrying the torch for the historic hotel are Cynthia and Salvatore

Nicosia. And the enterprising couple has every reason to believe that their Shanley Hotel is haunted by a number of former occupants, workers, and patrons. The evidence certainly seems to validate their claims. This spirit-infested hotel celebrated its grand opening in June 2008, and in a marketing plan sure to thrill anyone reading this book, the Nicosias invite the public (in a big way) to visit the Shanley Hotel, where, they say, "The Spirits are Inn." Their website shares EVPs, spirit photographs, and the personal experiences of many people, along with the most common legends and names of various spirits said to still remain at the hotel. There are paranormal workshops, in-house psychics, a gift shop, and ghost tours of which the *Times Herald Record* dared, "If you're brave enough, reserve a spot."

Photographs have depicted apparitions, including "screamers" (elongated ghostly faces that appear to be screaming) and orbs in motion. EVPs on their website include what sound like some of the following words and phrases: "murdered," "No!" "take care," "Betty," and "I said answer me." Mysterious footsteps are often heard going up and down stairways and hallways, doors open and close unassisted, and strange sounds are often heard: bar music, talking, crying, and so on. People have reported being pinched on the derriere, poked, and even hit on the side of the face, and earrings have been pulled off by unseen hands. Apparitions have been seen of a beautiful woman with long, golden hair, dressed in Victorian clothing, that floats down the hallways or past the bar. The same apparition has been seen and photographed in a third-floor window. Rocking chairs are sometimes seen rocking when nobody is anywhere nearby, the sound of clocks (that don't exist) chiming are sometimes heard, and fleeting cold (and hot) spots seem to accompany a strong sense of being watched or that one is not alone. The seductive room believed to have been the bordello is by far the most haunted room in the hotel, and it causes its own unique sensations. There, according to the website, people experience sensations associated with amour, sexual conquest, and defeat: feelings of lightheadedness, or a sense of heaviness, shortness of breath, and an overwhelming sense of either joy or sadness (guess it all depends). There are thirty-five other rooms to investigate, but the bordello is the scene of the most activity.

Of the many possible culprits who haunt the Shanley, some have scared people enough never to return—like the barmaid who went to the back room to fetch something, and the next thing her customers knew, she was racing out the front door. Or the patron who came running, terrified, out of the bathroom with his pants still down! He never returned, either too afraid or too embarrassed. But mostly, the Shanley Hotel attracts a never-ending stream of visitors and investigators who would relish the opportunity to come face-to-face with a bona fide ghost . . . or many.

Bull's Head Inn

If ever a ghost needed a motive to haunt a place, it would have plenty to choose from at the Bull's Head Inn at 2 Park Place, near Main Street and the historic district in Cobleskill. Today the inn serves up food and drink as a popular tavern, but it has served the village of Cobleskill well in many other capacities during its two hundred plus years.

In 1752, George Ferster built a log cabin where the three-story Bull's Head Inn now stands. According to John M. Brown's *Brief Sketch of the First Settlement of the County of Schoharie by the Germans* (1823), a quarter of the population in the region in 1752 consisted of outlaw Indians, "naturally inclined to revenge and murder against the white people and among themselves." Brown recalled one Indian who "killed an Indian in Cobleskill, in the house of George Ferster, on the place where Lambert Lawyer now lives," and said such bloodlust continued until the start of the American Revolution. That ferocious stabbing was the first recorded death that took place on the Bull's Head property. Shortly after, the log cabin burned to the ground, not once, but twice, during the French and Indian War, and each time, a new cabin was built. After the second cabin burned, Ferster built a tavern in its place and sold it to Lambert Lawyer, one of Cobleskill's first settlers. Lawyer's tavern met the same fate as its predecessors, and when it too burned to the ground, it was rebuilt and sold to Seth Wakeman in 1802.

Wakeman was the first to call the Federal Georgian–style structure you see today Bull's Head Inn. It was during his tenure that the inn served as the community's town hall and courthouse, because of its location near the center of the growing village. In 1837, Charles Courter, an enterprising Schoharie businessman, moved to Cobleskill and married into the prominent Lawyer family. In 1839, he and his wife, Helen, purchased the Wakeman property and converted the inn back into a residence and its barn and sheds into storage houses for his mercantile business. Not only was Courter the president of the newly organized First National Bank of Cobleskill, but he was also responsible for having the Lutheran church built, as well as many notable residences in town. Because of his efforts to transform the quiet village into a booming business area, he was elected to represent Cobleskill on the Board of Supervisors in 1841 and 1842. After his success in Schoharie County, Courter continued to wave his magic wand in other parts of the country, until he was stricken with pneumonia on a business trip in 1878. He returned to the Bull's Head Inn, which was still his residence, where he died on New Year's Day 1879.

In 1920, the booze-loving John Stacy and his booze-loathing wife purchased the house and remained there for the next forty years. Most people attribute the ghostly happenings at Bull's Head to Mrs. Stacy, because she had a fierce opposition to liquor that has apparently transcended time and dimensions. The kicker is that what once was her bedroom in the basement of the house is now the inn's Timothy Murphy Pub! It's enough to make a staunch member of the Women's Christian Temperance Union, which Mrs. Stacy admittedly was, roll over in her grave. According to society's website, www.wctu.org, in those early days of the movement, "Normally quiet housewives dropped to their knees in pray-ins in local saloons and demanded that the sale of liquor be stopped." No wonder reports of paranormal phenomena began in earnest when Monty Allen purchased the house in 1966 and reopened it as a tavern under its former historic name, which it retains to this day. Tami and John Van Leuven, the current owners, purchased the inn from Bob Youngs, who was responsible for placing a microbrewery at the inn, and they continue to operate it as an eatery and pub. Is it any wonder that Mrs. Stacy is spitting mad today?

Former managers, bartenders, owners, patrons, and staff have had countless encounters with the ghosts of Bull's Head Inn. In a typical phantom tantrum, ashtrays, wine glasses, dishes, silverware, and napkins are inexplicably moved or thrown around—though thankfully, nobody has been hit by flying objects. Lights and other objects, such as a decorative phone that isn't plugged in, the cappuccino machine, and the water faucets have been known to turn on and off on their own. Chairs that are straightened out at the end of the night are found to be moved around the next morning. But most exciting of all are the actual encounters with an apparition believed to be Mrs. Stacy. One former manager said she had seen images in mirrors that looked like a woman, but the images—true to ghostly protocol—are fleeting and disappear by the time the person who sees them does a double-take. A bartender was mesmerized one evening when he saw a transparent, white humanoid shape hovering over the bar before moving straight through it. The spirit had no clear facial features. Several lucky witnesses have seen a woman in an old-time long, white gown sitting in a rocking chair in the ladies' room, looking so solid that they believed she was the restroom attendant; but most see the apparition as a feminine form in white that walks right through solid objects such as walls and tables. Nothing can stop a woman on a mission to rid the world of alcohol, especially when it's being served in her own bedroom!

Bardavon 1869 Opera House

The Bardavon on Market Street in Poughkeepsie is everything an opera house should be—majestic, well appointed, and regal. In a word, *magnifique*. But as the oldest continuously operating theater in the state, the Bardavon may also be something executive director Chris Silva admitted in a news article that old theaters are infamous for—being haunted.

James Collingwood, one of nineteenth-century Poughkeepsie's wealthiest men, built the Bardavon on land that originally served as the uptown branch of his thriving coal and lumber business. It opened as the Collingwood Opera House in February 1869, attracting the likes of Edwin Booth, Franklin and Theodore Roosevelt, Helen Hayes, and General Tom Thumb to its stage or audience. In 1923, it was transformed into the Bardavon Theater, a popular movie palace of the time that hosted silent films, vaudeville, and finally, the modern talking film. Houdini, Frank Sinatra, Milton Berle, and countless other elite personalities of show biz came to perform at the Bardavon. In 1976, the theater was saved from the brink of demolition by the Concerned Citizens to Save the Bardavon. It became a nonprofit corporation called the Bardavon 1869 Opera House and was placed on the National Register of Historic Places, hosting everyone who's anyone in the entertainment industry. Think Gregg Allman, Joan Baez, Harry Belafonte, Ernest Borgnine, Carol Channing, Cher, Natalie Cole, and David Crosby, to name a few . . . and I'm only up to the Cs.

Considering its extensive roll call of distinguished entertainers, one can't help but wonder whether a performer from yesteryear has returned to haunt the Bardavon's stage. But the two *primary* ghosts the staff believe haunt the building are a man they call Roger, who they believe was a former stage manager allegedly caught in the crossfire of a gunfight between two patrons in the late 1800s, and an unnamed little girl thought to have been killed by a coal trolley when the opera house property was the Collingwood coal yard. (The marquee that the audience walks under today when entering and exiting the theater was a driveway for coal wagons back in the day.)

I searched long and hard to find anything that might lend credence to the legends of Roger and the little girl. Although I had no luck corroborating the story of Roger—or anyone who actually died on-site, for that matter—I did come across a number of news articles that could explain the little girl who is said to haunt the massive building. Jason Adams, technical/lighting director, told me that the girl ghost is believed to be six to eight years old and wears a pink, frilly southern dress. He may have caught a glimpse of her walking along the balcony landing himself one time (he works alone at night), but said he can't be sure, and he conceded that nobody knows whether the story about her alleged demise is true.

While searching for a little girl who matched her description, I found some *New York Times* articles about a former orphan child in a traveling show that could be related.

A March 19, 1895, article in the *Times* called "The Sad Plight of a Youthful Actress" described the circumstances in which nine-year-old Lillian Graham found herself when she fell ill and was removed from the luxurious surroundings of the Collingwood Opera House to the miserable confines of a nineteenth-century pesthouse:

> The little girl was a member of an "Uncle Tom's Cabin" troupe which appeared at the local theatre [Bardavon Opera House] Saturday. She played the part of Little Eva. Saturday morning she was discovered to be ill, and the manager of the company took her to Vassar Hospital and tried to secure her admission there, but was refused, as it is only an emergency hospital and not equipped for treatment of infectious diseases. He then endeavored to have her cared for in some private house, but failed.

The health officer then ordered her sent to the city pesthouse, a shelter for those infected with contagious diseases.

> A colored girl in the company volunteered to remain behind and nurse the child, and the two were sent to the pesthouse in a carriage. On their arrival . . . the nurse and her little charge got out of the carriage and found the building locked. They waited in the cold for someone to come and, after an interval, were noticed by the Superintendent of the Poor who sent one of his keepers to inquire what the trouble was. When he learned the situation, he directed his men to break the door in and build a fire and care for the ill and half-frozen little girl . . . The two were given such shelter as a half-rotten building, which had been unused for six months and was damp and cheerless . . . The little girl was put to bed in bedclothes that have been in the pesthouse a long while and have been used by people afflicted with all sorts of diseases. The last case there was one of scarlet fever, which resulted fatally, and the bedclothes used by that patient were given to Lillian Graham.
>
> Dr. Porteous of this city, learning the facts of the case, offered to take the little girl to his house and permit his daughter to nurse her. The Board of Health would not consent to this unless the house was quarantined. So she is still in the pesthouse, and, if she recovers, it will be in spite of her surroundings and the treatment she has

received from the officials of the Board of Health . . . A member of the Board of Health said this morning that the pesthouse, as at present conducted, is a disgrace.

What makes Lillian Graham's case all the more pitiful is that her mother is dying from consumption in a hospital in Chicago, and her father is traveling with a show in the West and does not know of her plight. All the money she made she sent to her mother.

On March 26, the *Times* reported:

The nine-year-old actress who was taken to the pesthouse a week ago suffering from diphtheria is very weak, and her chances for recovery are very poor. Her father, Barry Adams of White Plains, attempted to see her today, but was prevented by the Health Officer. Mr. Adams obtained a divorce from the mother of the little actress several years ago and had lost trace of her until he read of her being quarantined in the Poughkeepsie pesthouse.

That was the last article I was able to locate regarding the fate of Lillian Graham. A sketch of the child in the March 31, 1895, edition of the *Times* depicts her much as Jason described the child ghost: around eight years old, wearing a frilly southern dress. When death became her only means of escaping the appalling conditions of the pesthouse, did her spirit return to the Bardavon—a far better place? We can't blame her if it did. The pesthouse was half a mile from the nearest street, in the middle of an open field, fully exposed to all elements, with no access except through the fields. It was a tiny, one-story, dilapidated structure with only a sitting room, two little bedrooms, and a kitchen on a damp, uncarpeted ground, heated by just one stove. And there was no water or sewer. In stark contrast, the early Bardavon, where Lillian Graham was performing at the time she fell ill, was a comfortable, cavernous music hall with a stage easily twice as large as the pesthouse and a glorious dome similar to those seen in cathedrals and buildings of great prominence. It cost $50,000 to build at the time, compared with the $200 spent constructing the pesthouse.

Although Lillian Graham is the only actual person I was able to tie to the Bardavon as a real potential ghost candidate—since she was, after all, taken from there on her deathbed—Roger is the ghost that gets all the hype and credit for haunting the place. In 2005, the

Poughkeepsie Journal ran a story called "Hudson Valley Hauntings," in which reporter Alice Hunt interviewed Silva. Roger is described as a stage manager who was fatally shot in the theater in the nineteenth century and is now blamed for myriad baffling things, such as turning the water and lights on and off.

Jason said that as with the little girl ghost, he doesn't know whether the story about Roger is true, but when unexplained events occur—and they admittedly do—Roger is the "catch-all." Yet for all his ghostly antics, he has never seemed to be associated with a feeling of malice. In fact, he is so highly esteemed that his name is memorialized in the Esplanade Walk of Fame beneath the Marquees, a pavement roster of sorts to support the Bardavon's "Campaign for the New Century." It includes granite paving stones engraved with names of past performers who have graced the Bardavon's stage, as well as those who otherwise played an important role in the theater's history and those who have contributed financially to its continuing restoration and preservation. Apparently someone thought highly enough of the opera house's beloved ghost that one stone bears a single name, Roger. I think it's only fair that a Good Samaritan similarly purchase a stone for Lillian, or "Little Eva," as she was known on the Bardavon stage.

Smalley's Inn

Smalley's Inn on Gleneida Avenue (State Route 52) in Carmel was first established in 1852 as Smalley House, a hostelry owned and operated by forty-year-old Sheriff James J. Smalley and his wife, Emily Philips. It catered to early businessmen, many of whom were associated with the Hudson River Steamboat Line. James Smalley himself was quite the businessman, serving variously as sheriff, treasurer, and coroner of Carmel. In fact, his stint as coroner plays prominently in the steady stream of speculation about who is haunting Smalley's Inn and why. There is a rumor that the basement of Smalley's was used as a morgue back in his day, which adds a little extra oomph to the ghost stories associated with the inn. The Smalleys' children, according to a *New York Times* obituary for one of them, dated July 6, 1942, included James J. Jr., Joseph B., and Ada. Any other children they may have had were not listed in that obituary, possibly because they had died many years earlier. James Smalley died in 1867 at the age of fifty-five. The following year, Barnabus and Horton GaNun opened a small store in the Smalley Hotel, but Horton died in 1869, perhaps while working at the hotel. The following year, the Putnam County National Bank moved in to share the Smalley building with the store, until both grew too large to remain there.

Smalley's Inn is located in the business district at the center of town, across the road from the historic circa 1814 county court-house, where a young man named George Denny was executed in 1844 for shooting an elderly Philipstown man. Because the decision to convict the youth was made hastily in a second trial that followed one in which he was deemed innocent, and because his attorney was inexperienced—and finally, because he was forced to sit on his own coffin with the noose around his neck in front of four thousand merciless onlookers prior to the execution—some believe Denny may haunt the street and Smalley's now, because of the injustices done to him then. Perhaps he's the ghostly male figure that has been seen or the one responsible for slamming the door to the restaurant shut so hard one day, with current owner Tony Porto Jr. as a witness, that the key popped out. Denny certainly has reason to be an angry ghost.

Just as Smalley House had been a family-run business, with the children pitching in to help out, today's Smalley's Inn has remained in the Porto family for three generations. Tony Porto Jr.'s father pur-chased it in 1968, just six years before a fire demolished it. And this was not the first devastating fire at Smalley's Inn. On November 18, 1924, the *New York Times* reported on a fire the previous day that had destroyed the three-story Smalley's Inn, where six guests were forced to climb out onto the roof to escape, as well as much of the town, including the historic old Putnam County Courthouse, a bank, the jail, and a newspaper office. The article, called "Historic Court House at Carmel Is Burned," said the fire "threatened to wipe out the entire business centre." Smalley's Inn at that time was owned by the com-missioner of charities, Bird S. Coler, who leased the property out.

The devastating fire had begun in the inn's kitchen and quickly spread to the surrounding wooden structures, as a result of high winds. No lives were lost, but six fire departments battled the blaze, and losses were estimated at $150,000. All of the affected historic buildings had to be rebuilt, including Smalley's Inn. Almost exactly fifty years later, on October 22, 1974, an article appeared in the *New York Times* called "Center of Carmel Destroyed in Fire." Once again a wind-fueled fire devastated the town, destroying six stores in the heart of the business district, and six fire departments battled the blaze. And once again Smalley's Inn burned down. The 1974 article contradicted the 1924 article, which said that Smalley's had been destroyed in the first fire. The more recent article said Smalley's had "escaped with minor damage in the blaze a half century ago" but was "left in total ruin by last night's fire," which had only spared the sign stating that the inn was established in 1852. Thankfully, no lives were lost in the second fire either.

Many investigations have yielded evidence of paranormal activity, but nobody knows who haunts Smalley's or why. There had been speculation that one spirit was the young daughter of James J. Smalley, but he had only one daughter, Ada, and she lived to a ripe old age. However, Tony Porto Jr. admits that a Ouija board was used in the 1980s to divine any spirits that might be there—and they may have gotten more than they bargained for. Ouija boards are believed to often attract more unwanted paranormal activity than the desired results. And there has certainly been a lot of activity since the eighties. Porto's wife once heard a little girl giggling beside her when she was by herself in the building. And Porto has seen a little girl, probably the same one his wife heard giggling, wearing an old-time dress, playing hide-and-seek in the basement. While vacuuming and looking down, he once saw a pair of feet standing right beside him for a fleeting second.

He and his wife are not alone in experiencing the unknown. Staff, guests, and investigators alike have heard things they can't explain, such as banging and footsteps. They've seen apparitions of men, women, and the mysterious little girl. And according to Porto, in an October 19, 2007, article in the *Times Herald-Record*, once all of the phones in the building, including everyone's cell phones, started ringing at the same time, with each call coming from a single phone in the building. The article, called "Ghost Encounters with the Hudson Valley Paranormal Investigations," described the findings of that group's investigation of Smalley's Inn. The team captured orbs on film and witnessed a vacuum cleaner "taking off" down the steps to the basement! They also heard pots and pans flying off the shelves in the kitchen, and their medium was said to have made contact with the spirit of the little girl Tony Porto had witnessed on several occasions, who appeared drenched and said she was afraid to leave. The article said photographs taken at the moment of contact revealed a small child's face.

After all this time operating as a restaurant and tavern—and surviving two devastating fires—Smalley's Inn just keeps on going. Today Italian American fare is masterfully served, with spirits à la carte.

Bannerman's Island

A thousand feet from the Hudson River shoreline, between Breakneck Ridge and Storm King Mountain, is an island formally called Pollepel, but more often referred to as Bannerman's, for one of its more notable past owners. It's a little island with a big attitude.

Pollepel Island has historically been a force to be reckoned with. Excavations have revealed evidence of early Native American encampments on the island, but very few artifacts were left behind, which seems to indicate a hasty departure. Many historical accounts say that something on the island made the Indians believe it was haunted, and thereafter, they refused to go near it. Perhaps it was the violent environmental conditions surrounding the island—the mysterious and deadly undercurrents, choppy waters, and fierce winds—that led the natives to believe that the spirits of the dead had created a natural force field to keep intruders away. The early Dutch explorers also thought the island was inhabited by supernatural beings, such as goblins and fiends, that they believed were responsible for the deadly squalls that appeared from out of the blue, sinking their ships.

But Francis Bannerman, the country's biggest surplus arms dealer, wasn't interested in, or hindered by, such folklore. He had a booming wartime business to operate and needed adequate, isolated storage space in which to store his volatile war stock. After all, it wouldn't do to have stockpiles of black powder overflowing at a storage facility in the middle of a city like New York. But Pollepel Island, with its unique, natural, built-in security system would do nicely. So Bannerman purchased the island in 1900 when the volume of surplus equipment and ammunition he had acquired from the Spanish-American War became too large to contain in his Brooklyn and Broadway warehouses. Pollepel Island offered six and a half secure acres on which to construct storage buildings. The only drawback was safely getting building supplies and war stock onto the island.

Long before Bannerman purchased the island, it had been used during the American Revolution in a futile attempt to hinder British troops from entering the Hudson Highlands by placing sixty-foot sharpened logs, pointed up, just below the surface of the surrounding water to gouge the hulls of incoming British ships. Surprisingly, for a time in the mid to late 1800s, locals allegedly used the island for recreational purposes, such as swimming and camping. Talk about scary campfire stories! Then Thomas Taft purchased it for his black market liquor-trading operations. What better place than a remote, intimidating little island for such clandestine activities?

Finally, the twentieth century heralded in a new keeper of the island, the Bannerman dynasty, and it was renamed Bannerman's Island. Though many buildings were erected, including the famed Bannerman Castle, which contained a massive collection of historic weapons and ammunition, there was also the family's residential castle, a lodge, three additional storage buildings, employee apartments, a powder house, workshops, and an icehouse. Docks were constructed by sinking old ships next to the island's shoreline and then covering them in cement. This process is rumored to have created one angry ghost. A tugboat captain who sold his old boat to Bannerman requested that the workers wait until he was well out of sight before sinking his beloved vessel, since he couldn't bear to see it go down, but he had not even turned around to walk away before his boat started sinking. He cursed Bannerman and his workers and told them they hadn't heard the last of him. Years later, workers heard a ship's bell double-ringing (indicating it was going in reverse) when they were standing in a lodge that was built above the sunken tugboat, and they recalled the last words of the angry captain.

Though Francis Bannerman died in 1918, his family continued spending summers on their island until the 1930s, when they vacated it. In 1967, it was sold to the state of New York and is now owned by the Office of Parks, Recreation and Historic Preservation. In 1969, a tremendous—and mysterious—fire destroyed or damaged most of the buildings, and the island's ruins were deemed unsafe for the public. Had the scorned captain gotten his last revenge on the Bannermans, destroying all they had worked so hard to create? Hundreds of photographs of the abandoned Bannerman buildings reveal orbs and spirit faces, adding corroboration to the ghost stories and Indian legends associated with the island. Today the Bannerman Castle Trust is exhaustively restoring, stabilizing, and preserving Bannerman Castle and other buildings on the island for future generations to enjoy. Their mission: "To preserve and protect Bannerman Island for the public to experience as an educational, cultural, historical, and recreational facility for promoting heritage tourism." While their ultimate vision is to "be a premiere destination for people to experience and enjoy the ambiance that was Bannerman's once again," for now the public will have to remain patient. Conditions are still considered unstable while work is under way, so access by the general public is forbidden. But it still inspires awe to see the huge concrete words "Bannerman's Island Arsenal" on the side of the castle while passing by the island.

United States Military Academy

Over the years, ghosts have been spotted from time to time at the United States Military Academy at West Point. One man was awakened by a beautiful woman in a long, white dress standing over his bed—not a bad thing for a lonely man to wake up to, if the woman had been *alive*. This one was definitely a ghost, however, judging by the way she walked straight through the solid door. Some told the cadet that the apparition he'd seen was an Irish cook named Molly, who had worked for Colonel Sylvanus Thayer, the "father of the Military Academy." Others said it was a professor's wife, whose spirit was unsettled because her husband had married her mother after the young woman died. That same disturbed—and disturbing—apparition is believed to be responsible for chasing several young girls from the academy's Morrison House in the 1920s.

Built in 1778, West Point is the nation's oldest continuously operating military post. It served as Washington's headquarters during the American Revolution and has seen such historic military figures as Ulysses S. Grant and Robert E. Lee pass through. Some of its other renowned cadets have included Dwight D. Eisenhower, Douglas MacArthur, George S. Patton, and Edgar Allan Poe, the master of horror himself, who would have reveled in the ghost stories associated with his former school, even if he didn't have a hand in writing them.

Besides the two female apparitions described above, the most well-known apparitional encounter took place in 1972. Several cadets of Company G-4 were in Room 4714 in the 47th Division Barracks of the 4th Regiment, when an apparition of a soldier dressed in a cavalry uniform of the 1830s manifested right before their eyes. He had a handlebar mustache and was holding an old musket. The cadets described him as a shimmering ghost that came out of a wall near the closet, then turned and walked right back through the wall. Just prior to the sighting, there had been a sudden, distinct drop in room temperature that everyone present had felt. In the same room, a ghost was allegedly once seen rising up out of the floor. Knowing his cadets were prohibited from lying under the Cadet Honor Code, the commanding officer had the room turned into a storage room. Today it remains unoccupied, at least by the living. Thayer House, the superintendent's residence, is allegedly haunted by the ghost of a former superintendent, according to a tourist service.

New York City
and
Long Island

Kings Park State Hospital

"Disappointment in love," "abuse of husbands," "disappointed ambition," "seduction," "remorse," "anticipation of wealth," "perplexity of business," and "anti-rent excitement" were just a few of the alleged causes of mental illness that landed thousands of people in lunatic asylums in the mid-1800s. No wonder asylums in the nineteenth century were so overcrowded. The reasons touted as causes of insanity back then would pretty much cover all of us today. In 1885, the Kings County Farm, or Kings Park Psychiatric Center, was established on a 924-acre tract on the north side of Long Island to provide care for the mentally ill, indigent, and homeless, according to an 1884 *New York Times* article. Initially the property off Route 25A included three wooden buildings valued at $20,000, which would, the paper said, "be used for housing the pauper laborers who will be put to work on the farm as soon as the purchase of the site is complete." There was only enough room for fifty-five patients. The need for beds remained consistently greater than the number of beds available, and as each new building was added to the compound, it was quickly filled.

In 1895, the state took over the asylum and changed the name of the self-sufficient farming community first to the Long Island State Hospital at Kings Park, and then in 1916 to Kings Park State Hospital. Up to 90 percent of the patients were put to work on the farm, as the combination of light manual labor, fresh air, and sunshine was the accepted remedy of the day for the feeble-minded; it was a gentle, moral method that ensured a restful sleep. By 1900, the number of patients had risen to 2,697, and that number more than tripled to its peak population in 1954, when the hospital was filled beyond capacity. By then, the number of buildings had increased to more than 150, including a rec hall, laundry, bakery, library, nursing school, and repair shops. There was also a cemetery—now said to be haunted—a morgue, and even a designated railroad for delivering supplies to the hospital . . . and eventually for the transport of patients to other hospitals.

In the 1920s, as the patient population soared out of control, resources, including staff, were stretched to their limit. Drastic therapies intended for immediate results replaced the earlier one-on-one concept consisting of relaxation and open air. Controversial remedies such as lobotomies and electric shock therapy became the nightmarish reality for many patients, including a seventeen-year-old girl named Marie who, according to legend, died while undergoing electric shock therapy and whose shrill death screams have been heard ever since.

In 1929, Governor Franklin Roosevelt ordered an investigation of conditions at the state hospital after charges of disease, malnourishment, and abuse of "inmates" (patients) became public. At the time, Roosevelt admitted that he wouldn't be surprised if those accusations were found to be true, because it was a known fact that Kings Park State Hospital was nearly 50 percent overcrowded, and the lack of proper accommodations and treatment was obvious and inevitable. Mercifully, the 1950s saw the advent of psychiatric drugs such as thorazine, which proved far more effective and cost-efficient than any previous treatment. With the proper medications, patients who had required constant supervision were able to be released from the state hospitals and blend back into mainstream society. At the same time, the Mental Health Study Act called for the closing of state hospitals, which could no longer be financed at the rate they were going. The elderly were sent to nursing homes, the serious mental cases were sent to Pilgrim State, and those who could be medicated and released were deinstitutionalized. With only a few patients remaining, the top three floors of colossal Building 93 were closed in the 1970s, and by 1996, when no patients remained at all, Kings Park State Hospital was finally closed and abandoned.

The ghost stories started almost immediately, as seems to be the case with most abandoned hospitals and asylums. After all, here is a place where thousands of disturbed and distraught people—many of whom didn't even belong there and were wrongfully admitted against their will—died in various manners and were buried on the grounds. I pulled the names of the following individuals who died at Kings Park State Hospital out of the obits of the *New York Times* for just the month of June 1898: Lizzie Murray, age nineteen; Mary Walters, age forty-one; Teresa McCabe, age fifty; Helen Crain, age one; and Catherine Apmann, age eighty-eight. Causes of death were not listed, nor were the reasons they were admitted. Was it "disappointment in love," or "remorse," or some other absurd reason used to lock up people—many who were simply down on their luck—for the rest of their lives? One *New York Times* article from 1922 was called "Love Wrecks Girl's Mind: Musician Insane after Suppressing Affection for a Married Man." Twenty-seven-year-old Vera Anderson had been committed to the state hospital after doctors there deemed her a "mental wreck," saying she was incurable. Many others were placed in the asylum and later released after being found sane, as the following headlines state: "Sisters Describe 10 Years in Asylum—State Hospital Commission to Investigate Confinement of Sane Women" (*New York Times*, March 20, 1920); "Woman Sues Brothers—Charges She Was Placed in Insane Asylum without Cause" (*New York Times*, August 8, 1923); "Jury Awards $15,000 for Term in Asylum—Former Gardener for H. L. Pratt Wins Damages on Charge Employer Caused Detention" (*New York Times*, January 29, 1938). And that's just a smidgeon of the articles regarding unjustified incarcerations in the state hospital that actually made the news.

One of the persistent rumors about Kings Park is that there are remnants of torture chambers in the tunnels beneath the hospital, where paranormal activity appears to be higher than usual. But there's no evidence that torture chambers ever existed there, and who knows what props have been planted over the years by mischievous trespassers hoping to deceive others into believing such chambers did exist. Still, bona fide investigators have felt cold spots and reported unseen hands pushing them in the tunnels, and photographs taken there have shown unexplained mists that can't be attributed to any of the usual sources, such as dust, smoke, or water vapor. The tunnels were used for steam when they were active, according to the online "Long Island Oddities," so when the hospital was still open, it would typically be over 100 degrees down there. In that sense alone, the tunnels could be considered to be "torture chambers," if patients ever were, in fact, confined there for any period of time. But again, there's no documented evidence of such a scenario ever having occurred.

That said, there were numerous cases of abuse and even homicide of mental patients at the hands of hospital aides and staff. In 1899, the general superintendent of the asylum at Kings Park discharged "keepers" Connors and Griffin "pending investigation into the death on Nov. 12 of Frank Mitchell, a [patient] whom, it is alleged, was roughly handled." And in 1928, an attendant named Jeremiah Houllihan was held on charges of first-degree manslaughter for allegedly causing the death of Michael Caprise, a seventy-two-year-old patient at the hospital, by kicking the elderly man in the ear and head. There were other tragic deaths, as well, that might account for the hauntings. In 1933, a twenty-five-year-old patient was instantly killed when he threw himself under the rear wheel of a truck operated by a hospital employee as it passed him. Means of death at the hospital were clearly diverse, and some were more unexpected, shocking, and tragic than others.

Paranormal investigators have also reported hearing banging and clanging echoing throughout the corridors of the abandoned hospital, but that's not so surprising, considering the labyrinth of old pipes and the typical creaking and settling of old buildings. Some people have seen misty apparitions and orbs in motion, especially in Building 136, the old medical center. And the cemetery on the grounds is said to have a ghost that chases people away if they get too close . . . another enduring legend about Kings Park.

In 2000, a large part of the northern Kings Park grounds became the Nissequogue River State Park, and several other land-use proposals have been submitted for consideration by the state since the hospital closed. Wisteria House, or Building 15—the building that allegedly harbors a screaming, sobbing ghost—is being converted into government offices.

Though many people have admitted to feelings of dizziness and terror when visiting the abandoned hospital, that's a common reaction to visiting a place one has heard such awful things about. Still, in this case, many of those awful things are actually based in fact. Many people were confined at Kings Park, some wrongfully; many suffered when the hospital became overcrowded; and many died alone and afraid and are buried on the grounds. So could it be haunted? Absolutely. Not only *could* it be, but it *should* be.

White Horse Tavern

"Seventeen whiskies. A record, I think." Those are allegedly the famous last words of Dylan Thomas, who was such a regular at the White Horse Tavern in the 1940s and early 1950s that his presence attracted tourists hoping to catch a glimpse of the eccentric Welsh poet. He was such a regular that some people called the tavern his "stateside headquarters." He was such a regular that in 1986, the St. David's Society ceremoniously placed two plaques, dedicated by fellow Welshman Keith Baxter, in Thomas's honor at the White Horse Tavern: one in the main room, which was renamed the Dylan Thomas Room, and the other at a table near the window where the poet always sat—and where he was sitting the day he literally drank himself to death. Is it any wonder, then, that his portrait hangs on several walls of the establishment, or that paranormal activity there today is blamed primarily on Dylan Thomas? Who else would be responsible for mysteriously rotating the table at which he once sat, just as he commonly did while alive?

The White Horse Tavern was built in 1880 at 567 Hudson Street at West 11th in Manhattan and hasn't changed much in appearance or ambience. Its customers have certainly changed over the years, however. Originally it was considered a longshoremen's bar, and the regulars were the sailors and laborers you would expect to see near the docks. In the mid-1900s, it became a literary center, like Chumley's, which was frequented by authors, poets, screenwriters, and songwriters. Some of its most famous patrons included Bob Dylan, Jim Morrison of the Doors, Norman Mailer, Edna St. Vincent Millay, and the Clancy Brothers. It also became a popular meeting place for labor organizations and liberals. Today it's a neighborhood hangout of some celebrities, like James Gandolfini's television wife, Edie Falco, from *The Sopranos*. But mostly it receives locals, tourists, and New York University students.

On November 5, 1953, Dylan Thomas, admittedly an alcoholic, staggered out of the White Horse Tavern and returned to the Hotel Chelsea, where he collapsed. Though the bar denied that he drank a lethal amount there, the seventeen shots of whiskey, combined with several prescription medications such as morphine and cortisone, had rendered him comatose. His mistress called for an ambulance, and he was taken to St. Vincent's Hospital, but his condition deteriorated rapidly when pneumonia and emphysema added to the complications. The *New York Times* on November 6 said that he was at the hospital "with a serious brain ailment." He died at 12:40 P.M. four days later, in the company of fellow poet John Berryman, while being bathed by a nurse.

Only six days before, Thomas was celebrating his thirty-ninth birthday. Just two years earlier, he had written one of his most famous poems, about his dying father, called "Do Not Go Gentle into That Good Night." It was about not dying without a fight. Thomas was such a part of the history of the White Horse that his portrait adorns a number of walls, and on the anniversary of his death, the staff offers the exact same meal he had eaten that fateful night in 1953.

Just because the manager and bartender deny that the tavern is haunted doesn't mean it's not. Many people have seen a cloaked, shadowy figure believed to be Thomas's spirit. And if anyone haunts the White Horse, it would have to be someone who loved the place—and the booze and the beer—as much as he did.

Lefferts–Laidlaw House

The house, which is destined to hold a conspicuous place in the annals of local ghost stories, is a neat two-story frame house, with an extension. The main house has a castle-like roof, and in front are three large pillars extending to the roof, topped with Corinthian capitals. Like the other houses in the block, there is a space of a couple of yards between it and the adjoining ones. It stands back about forty feet from the street, and a high iron fence encloses it . . . The neighborhood is a most respectable one, and a ghost could not select a more quiet locality for its operations.

—*Brooklyn Eagle*, December 20, 1878

In the Wallabout neighborhood of Brooklyn, south of the Navy Yard, there is only one structure currently designated as a New York City landmark, even though the area is known for having the most pre–Civil War frame houses in the entire city. It's the authentic Greek Revival house at 136 Clinton Avenue, which was built from 1836 to 1840, during a period of rapid population growth and residential development in Brooklyn. The house was restored to its original condition with clapboard siding and a temple front in the 1970s and early 1980s, and in 1985, it was listed on the National Register of Historic Places. It was built by Rem Lefferts and his brother-in-law, John Laidlaw. In 1855, the two enlarged the stone, brick, and wood building by moving a preexisting small house and adding it to the rear of their original structure. Lefferts's sister-in-law, Amelia, along with her three children, then occupied the fine home. One of her children was Marshall Lefferts, the Civil War commander and inventor.

In 1876, the house was put up for sale "in consequence of the death of the proprietor, on very easy terms and at a reasonable price," according to its advertisement in the *Brooklyn Eagle*. It was quickly snatched up by Edward F. Smith, who occupied it with his wife and two daughters, as well as another boarder and his wife. Everything was "quiet and uneventful," said a December 20, 1878, *Brooklyn Eagle* article, until early that month—two years after they had all moved in—when suddenly the house seemed to become haunted. The first night the paranormal activity began, Smith responded to the ringing doorbell three or four times, only to find nobody there. Then, as soon as the doorbell stopped ringing, the two back doors rattled so hard that it seemed they would be shaken off their hinges. For three weeks straight, every single night, beginning around 5 P.M., the same scenario played out—and every night, it would continue until around midnight. Because of the close proximity of neighbors, the people on either side of the Smith residence had their sleep disturbed by the ringing of the loud bell as well. "Though the knob of the bell is held, the jingling goes on all the same," reported the *Eagle*. "One peculiarity of the mystery is that though the front door is never moved, the two doors that lead into the yard and into the alley are shaken one after the other. The knocking is very violent."

Smith tried to explain it away as just the wind or "some bad boys [that] might be playing tricks on the family," but the rest of the family was unconvinced and began staying up until the wee hours of the morning, too afraid to go to sleep. To put an end to it, Smith sought the assistance of a Detective Price and a few other men. They surrounded the house and waited for the usual noise to begin. One man was positioned at the front door and held on to the doorknob. The detective stood in front of one rear door, and a third gentleman stood at the other. All bases were covered. Detective Price was first to hear the rapping at his door, and he immediately opened it, but "nothing could be found or seen which was not there before." After the other two men experienced a similar phenomenon, they all left the house around 10 P.M., certain that there was truly a mysterious force at work in the Smith House. They determined then and there that "the bell will be tied, and if it rings then, it will be pulled down, and if it rings then, it will be destroyed." Nothing could be done to the doors, but Smith said he didn't care, because as long as he didn't actually *see* the spirits responsible for the impositions his family was experiencing, he would keep right on sleeping through the night, as he had been.

Besides tying the doorbell to see if that would stop the incessant ringing, ashes and flour were sprinkled at the entrances to detect if any "earthly feet approached the door." No imprints were made in the ashes or flour, even in the midst of the nightly noise, lending more credence to the supernatural theory. It was time to call in the big guns. Captain McLaughlin of the Fourth Precinct was a no-nonsense man and a nonbeliever in anything supernatural. With his usual smug attitude, he said, "I will go to the house this evening with my detective, and take my word for it: we will capture the ghost if it has flesh and blood and is visible to mortal eyes." So he and his man set up watch at the Smith House, and, sure enough, right around 5:30 P.M., the sounds began:

> Again and again the mysterious knocking occurred, and neither the Captain nor the detective, with all their ingenuity and agility, could discover the agent by whom it was produced. Price finally went outside and took up a position a few yards from the door, at which he fastened his eyes; but there, right in his very presence, three distinct

and heavy blows, one after the other, were rained on the door by unseen hands. The few hairs which the detective has on his head fairly stood on end, and he hurried into the house and exclaimed, "Cap, this is no case for me. I cannot pretend to explain it."

The noise stopped at 10, "and the Captain and his detective returned to the station house with more belief than they had ever entertained before." The lawmen were determined to keep their investigation and their findings quiet until they had reached a satisfactory conclusion. The next night, Captain McLaughlin returned to the Smith residence with three other officers, as well as his faithful detective. The three officers were posted outside of each of the three doors and were instructed to keep alert for any movement or sound, while the captain and the detective guarded two of the doors on the interior side. The arrangement seemed to make the spirits "even more active and demonstrative," because this time, besides the usual ringing and knocking, a brick was hurled through the dining-room window—as if for added emphasis. But the brick could have been thrown through that window only from the alleyway, and the alleyway was carefully guarded at that moment by officers. Again, no person was found to lay the blame on.

The next evening, the captain returned again—this time with an entire squad—and the house was lined from one end to the other with officers, including one on the roof. Detective Price had searched the house thoroughly beforehand to ensure that there were no hidden wires and such. By this point, crowds of self-proclaimed psychics and curiosity seekers were becoming disruptive to the neighboring homes—and indeed, hindering the investigation by law enforcement personnel. The *New York Times* reported that the crowds were "periodically dispersed by the police, and periodically returned again, dividing the time between chaffing the officers and telling the most awful ghost stories that ever lifted one's hat." It continued:

> The throng finally became so noisy and clamorous for the ghost to appear that Capt. McLaughlin undertook to disperse them. One powerful German refused to "move on," and when the captain arrested him, he fought desperately. During the struggle, the angry man caught one of the Captain's fingers between his teeth and bit till

the blood came. He was finally overpowered and locked up, and Capt. McLaughlin now has a sore finger to keep him in remembrance of "the Clinton Avenue ghost," which Mr. Smith thinks is the devil.

"The Brooklyn Ghost—The Proprietor of the Ghostelry Determines That It Is Old Nick Himself and Drives Him Off with a Prayer" was the headline of a story the *Times* ran on December 21, 1878. Smith claimed at that point to have finally solved the little problem he had with his house being haunted. According to the article, "He is now convinced that the invisible cause of all the phenomena is no less a personage than his Satanic Majesty himself." Through prayer, the devout Mr. Smith believed he had exorcised the "evil one" and was confident there would be no further noise problems at 136 Clinton Avenue. They had managed their first night in three weeks with no phenomena of any sort. Still, the captain, the detective, and all of the officers involved weren't willing to agree that Satan had been responsible—there was no concrete evidence of that. But they were willing to "swear that they [had] heard and seen the startling demonstrations" and were certain it was "beyond all human probability that any earthly hands pulled the bell, pounded the doors, or threw the brick through the dining room window." In other words, they knew it was supernatural in nature; they just couldn't accept Smith's theory that it was the Devil, rather than some other disgruntled spirit, without proof.

As it turned out, there were two other theories the locals were throwing around to explain why 136 Clinton might have been haunted. For one thing, rumor had it that a lawyer who had occupied that address long before the Smiths had committed suicide, "and there are plenty of superstitious Brooklynites," the *Times* article said, "who need nothing further to enable them to explain the whole mystery." The other possibility was that, according to the *Brooklyn Eagle*, "in the adjoining house, No. 140, spiritual séances" had been given a few years earlier, "so that the spirits may have lingered in the neighborhood." No further articles reported on the events that had transpired for three harrowing weeks, so it seems safe to assume that Smith's prayers worked to persuade the unsettled spirits to move on. The historic house continues to be privately owned and should be respected as such.

Blissville

Don't let the name of this little neighborhood at the eastern edge of Long Island City fool you. All has not always been blissful in the two-hundred-resident community. Today the area is zoned for manufacturing, so new homes can no longer be built there; however, current residents may continue to live there as long as they wish.

According to the Queens Historical Society, Blissville was named after Neziah Bliss, a Brooklyn businessman who founded the area. It was accessible only by boat until the Borden Avenue bridge was built in 1869, and even today, residents must go to Sunnyside, across the Long Island Expressway, for most services. Two cemeteries—Calvary and New Calvary—border the neighborhood to the east and west, reminding residents of the flip side of the state of bliss. In the late 1800s, Blissville was downright bleak:

July 1, 1875: A Blissvillian named John Van Hasset was killed instantly while working in Calvary Cemetery when the soil caved in on top of him, breaking his neck, as he stood in the very grave he was digging.

February 25, 1878: Blissvillian William Owens fell overboard while rowing a boat in the cold waters of Newtown Creek and drowned.

December 21, 1879: Blissvillian George Reinhardt died from a fractured skull after allegedly falling off a wagon on his way home. There was strong suspicion that he was murdered in a drunken brawl but insufficient evidence to prove it.

June 21, 1882: Blissvillian Ferdinan Teupner was killed by a train near the Greenpoint crossing in Blissville, after telling a youth who was trying to warn the drunk man of the oncoming train to "go to hell" and that he could take care of himself.

February 13, 1883: Blissvillian Henry Walker, the deputy collector, was shot in the back by a double-barreled shotgun and killed after confronting another resident named Dave Fraley, who was operating an illicit distillery. Walker lived just long enough to name his killer and tell the reason for his murder.

Is it any surprise, after a decade of such crime and freak accidents—and in an area so small and with so few residents—that the ghost stories would begin? The *New York Times* ran an article on March 9, 1884, called "Ghost-Hunting in Blissville," which began by saying, "Blissville is in a shudder of ghastly excitement. Blissville, be it known, is a suburb of Long Island City, and its chief landmark is Calvary Cemetery. Heretofore, the respectable persons interred in the cemetery have rested quietly in their graves. Now the inhabitants of Blissville are convinced that a ghost has broken loose, and they are determined to hunt the rascal down." No mention or suggestion was made of Van Hasset, the laborer who was killed at the gravesite he was digging, and the first experiences with the Blissville phantom were purely audible, making the identity of the ghost harder to determine. It was variously heard saying, "Oh, ho!" "Ah, ha!" and "Hmph, hmph!" The funniest part of the article said, "No one has ever heard [the ghost] swear or ask for a drink, which is regarded as very strange in Blissville." Maybe the ghost wasn't a true Blissvillian.

Though most of the audible encounters occurred at or near the Calvary Cemetery, the first visitation reportedly came from a house where someone had committed suicide. The elderly James Flaherty was "on his way home from Laurel Hill. When passing Blissville and a Bohemian settlement in Thompson Avenue, he was accosted by a loud voice . . . which cried out, 'Oh, ho!'" The voice was described as "shrill," and Flaherty believed it was a woman in distress, so he rushed into the house the sound seemed to come from and searched for the source. He found nothing, so he went home and told his son, a strapping young man named John Flaherty, who gathered up a posse of ten other brave young men to search for it. The young men heard the same thing—a shrill "Oh, ho!"—but they also saw an apparition to go along with it, and it seemed to be sitting right on top of a fence at Calvary Cemetery. The young men decided to wait until they had the much older, wiser men with them the next day to pursue any further ghost-hunting.

> At Bradley's Hotel, Blissville, on Friday evening at 9 o'clock, one hundred of the boldest hearts in Blissville assembled. . . . Every man was armed with a six-shooter, a musket, a slingshot, a sand club, or a dagger. Determination was in every eye, and a small bottle of encouragement in every pocket . . . They had not gone far when the spiritual soprano turned on her works. "Oh, ho!"

The ghost sounds were once again coming from the "suicide house" (rather than the cemetery), so ten men were sent in to search the house, but as soon as they entered, the sound shifted again, and it was coming from the nearby cemetery, this time saying, "Oh, ha!" And every man agreed that it was definitely "the voice of a dead woman." In fact, of all the upstanding citizens that had heard the voice—the aldermen, the cemetery superintendent, and other prominent men—they exclaimed that "only a disembodied spirit could produce such a sound." Still, there were those who speculated that it was a "colored barber of Laurel Hill" who had as powerful a voice as the specter. A police officer believed it was kids goofing off, and Justice Kavanagh said it must have been an owl. The article concluded by saying, "And no man knoweth to this day what the ghost is. And he don't try very hard to find out either." But the next day . . .

The next day, the *Times* ran another article, this one called, "A Red-Haired, Blue-Eyed Ghost: The Stoutest-Hearted Citizens of Blissville Filled with Terror." John Powers, the proprietor of a hotel opposite of St. Raphael's Church, reported that on his way home from the liquor saloon in the basement of the City Hall at 11 P.M. the night before, he met a "little woman" in the road behind the DeBevoise homestead. He could tell, in what little light the moon cast through the clouds, that she was dressed all in black, and "there seemed something so weird and unearthly about the mysterious traveler" that it made his knees shake and his heart jump into his throat. Still, he managed a polite "Good night" to the black figure as he passed it, but when he turned to take one more look at the mysterious little woman, she was gone. "He had looked away but one brief moment, but in that moment, the black figure had vanished utterly. There were no houses, trees, nor fences near; nothing that even a cat could have concealed itself behind, and yet the weird apparition had disappeared and left not the slightest indication of its presence."

Thomas Culvert Jr. met what was presumably the same black figure the following night. He reported that she was extremely short—not more than three feet tall—but her hair and features bore stark contrast to the black she was cloaked in. He saw a tiny woman, about twenty-five or thirty years old, with "red hair . . . and long curls [that] hung down her back." Her countenance, he said, was one of deep melancholy, as reflected in her eyes, which were "of a stony blue that chilled his very blood, and she fixed them upon him for a single instant." Unlike the hotel proprietor, Culvert couldn't bring himself to look back at the unusual figure, and instead raced to the safety of his home and bolted the door shut behind him. That same night, a number of people near the "suicide house" heard frightening sounds coming from within the abandoned building.

For the second day in a row, there were some who were still convinced the mysterious sounds were being made by Rollins Johnson, the village barber from Laurel Hill, for he had the loud, booming voice that would seem otherworldly with the slightest hint of shrillness to it. But when questioned, he insisted that he was too afraid to leave his house at night, just like the other Blissvillians. Two days later, however, Johnson was caught red-handed by John Flaherty (whose father was the first to hear the ghost) while Flaherty was on his way home from Laurel Hill. The *Times* reported on March 12, 1884, "When half-way down the road, he heard the 'Oh, ho!' coming from behind a large tree a short distance in front of him. He at once drew his six-shooter and ordered the banshee to surrender or he would 'kill it dead.' The banshee at once threw up his hands and exclaimed: 'Don't shoot, boss; I is the ghost.' Flaherty at once recognized Rollins Johnson, the negro barber of Laurel Hill," just as some had suspected. (And they trusted this man with a razor at their scalps?) Flaherty gave the man a good tongue-thrashing in exchange for a promise that his nightly antics would cease.

The plot thickened. Five days later, on March 17, 1884, the *Times* reported, "Blissville is not yet rid of the ghost." Apparently, Johnson, the alleged ghost, had the hotel proprietor, John Powers, arrested for assaulting him in the road. Remember Powers's story of walking past a black figure and only managing a "Good night" to it? Well, according to the barber, that "little lady in black" was him, and he got a lot more than a "Good night" from Powers. Powers conceded to the judge: "I did strike a colored man who assaulted me on my way home on Friday night. I did not know who it was, as

I never saw Johnson. I fired two shots to frighten him. I did not intend to hurt him, and I intended that he should not hurt me." Talk about trying to weed out the truth from fiction! No further mentions were made in the papers about that particular "Oh, ho-ing!" ghost, so perhaps it was the barber. But still, how did two witnesses get a three-foot-tall female apparition out of a strapping large man with a powerful voice?

For a while, all was quiet in Blissville, as far as ghosts go. And then, in 1885, an employee at a yeast-manufacturing company in Blissville saw the angry spirit of his former boss, Owen Geoghegan. It had only been a year since the previous ghost hunt, and residents were still a little leery of new reports of ghosts. After all, there had never really been convincing proof that all (or even, any) of the prior paranormal phenomena could be blamed on one individual. So the employee's claims were ignored. "The scoffing world," the article said, "rather than believe that the tomb in which it saw Geoghegan riotously inurned has opened to let him out again, will suspect the trusted employee of having invented Geoghegan's ghost."

Flushing Old Quaker Meeting House

"Ah, brother, why dost thou believe in such nonsense? Thee should'st know better." That was the answer a *New York Times* reporter received from a member of the Society of Friends in response to a question regarding the alleged ghost sightings at the Old Quaker Meeting House in 1884. The meeting house at 137–16 Northern Boulevard (formerly Broadway) in Flushing has been used as a Religious Society of Friends house of worship for more than three hundred years . . . and reports of it being haunted span nearly two hundred. From the original floorboards to the hand-hewn timber beams on the ceiling, the structure still looks much the same as it did the day it opened its doors to Quakers—charming, simplistic, and peaceful. John Bowne, whose own house is said to be haunted and is included in this compilation, donated land for a burial ground on Northern Boulevard in 1676, and then in

1692, he and John Rodman purchased three more acres of property adjacent to the graveyard on which to build the meeting house. It is believed to be the state's oldest house of worship and the country's second-oldest Quaker meeting house.

The first Friends meeting was held there in 1694, after Bowne and other Quakers completed its construction. Not only did the meeting house shelter Quakers who had been fighting for religious freedom for nearly forty years, but according to its website, it also "saw the beginnings of the abolitionist movement and the first school in Flushing." The school was established in the meeting hall in 1703 in direct response to the rapid increase in attendance at Friends meetings in town. Then, in 1716, the abolition of slavery was called for by John Farmer at the meeting house and was followed up two years later by the publication of one of the nation's first antislavery addresses. By 1767, the Quaker Meeting House in Flushing had condemned slavery, and several years later, Quakers were asked to no longer purchase slaves. In fact, members were banned from owning slaves in 1774.

Like other homes and public buildings, the meeting house was seized during the Revolutionary War and used for storage and as a hospital and a stable. The Flushing Quakers were punished for refusing to aid the British or engage in military service to either side, choosing instead to hold true to their idea of peace, even if it meant prosecution and confiscation of their property. During the Civil War, they were clearly sympathetic to the Union cause and operated one of the first Underground Railroads in the country to assist slaves in escaping through Long Island and upstate New York. Many of the Flushing Quakers became early movers and shakers of the nation, and some of them are buried in the graveyard behind the meeting house. Quakers of the seventeenth and early eighteenth centuries did not believe in using tombstones or burial markers when they were interred, so it's hard to say how many of the earliest Quakers were buried on the grounds or where. Then, in the late 1800s, burials within local churchyards, such as the one behind the Flushing Meeting House were forbidden because of city regulations. So nobody really knows how many Quakers were buried there, or how many Hessian soldiers, for that matter. One person who lived nearby in 1884 told the *New York Times*, "When I was a boy, about fifty years ago, I remember very well that there was a ghost in the meeting house. You see, where the meeting house now stands, was a burial ground during the Revolutionary War, and there are over 500 Hessians buried there."

In the year 2000, just before Halloween, the cemetery caretaker noticed that a tombstone was missing. It was the first time the sacred grounds had been vandalized since the first burial in 1676. Unfortunately, nobody was able to give the police a description of it or say whom the stolen gravestone belonged to, because they were unable to find any records of the burials or photographs showing that particular plot, and Quaker tombstones were very simple, unremarkable slabs of white stone—making the task of locating it even more difficult. It had to be a stone from the eighteenth or nineteenth century, but that's all that was known at the time.

By the late 1800s, there were only about twenty venerable old Quakers still attending meetings at the meeting house and still continuing—to the best of their ability—to perform charitable acts. It was during this time of relative tranquility in both the meeting house and the town of Flushing itself that a few ghost sightings put the entire town and surrounding communities in a tizzy. In April 1884, a reporter spotted what he described as a male apparition dressed in white with a sword hanging on its side coming out of the meeting house. He said the phantom moved along quietly, as if oblivious to anyone around it. The reporter ran to the police station and told Chief Hause that "the devil just came out of the Quaker meeting house," according to the *New York Times* and the *Brooklyn Eagle* of April 20, 1884. "It was about 1 o'clock in the morning, and the Chief, who knows, or *pretends* to know, something about ghosts, was surprised that any kind of respectable ghost should be out at that unusual hour." (It's even funnier when you read that line a second time.) Nevertheless, he grabbed a few men and hurried back to the meeting house with the reporter.

> As they approached, the Chief was astounded at the sight that met his gaze. It was a moonlit night, and he could plainly see the strange form disappear in the meeting house. They approached the house cautiously but found the doors and windows fastened. At this time,

the party had increased to ten, and one of them looked through the keyhole of the front door. He only looked for a second and then ran at breakneck speed through the vacant lot adjoining the house. The others, of course, ran after him.

Of course. When the sufficiently spooked party caught up to the fleeing man on Northern Boulevard, he was breathless, as were they, I'm sure, and "turning a deathly pale." They revived their failing friend with a drink of water from a flask, and he came to with a start, saying, "My God! Let us go home. After what I saw through the keyhole, I never want to go out again after dark." Poor Chief Hause couldn't contain himself any longer and blurted out, "Well, come, tell us what you saw!" The man said, "What I saw! Well, I saw three big men dressed in white and with swords hanging to their sides. When I looked in first they were closer together, and one of them seemed to be explaining something to the other two. Then they commenced to dance, and I ran away." After that disturbing development, the chief and another officer had to escort the other men home.

For the next few days, the chief placed a couple of his officers in the meeting house around the clock, but nothing more happened. Then on Friday night, another young man who insisted he knew nothing about the meeting house ghost or ghosts was passing by the building when he saw an apparition that fit the description of the earlier witnesses' sightings. The chief had tried to keep the entire episode quiet, but with the young man's ghostly encounter, the haunted meeting house became the talk of the town. That was when some of the much older residents admitted that forty or fifty years earlier, it was understood that the meeting house was haunted.

A tongue-in-cheek article (at least, I *think* it was meant to be tongue-in-cheek) a couple days later said, "Public opinion in Flushing is convinced that the three ghosts are Quakers. We must then believe that, in the other world, Quakers become addicted to gorgeous white clothing, that they wear swords and presumably use them, and that they become so worldly and reckless that they actually dance in Quaker meeting houses." Then, with the reporter's humble understanding of karma, he added, "There is evidently in the life of the *just* Quaker a lack of swords and dancing, which is made up to him in the future world in order that his character may be well and evenly balanced." On the other hand, he went on, it was not even certain that the three ghosts were Quakers. After all, the property had been used for other purposes early on, including a hospital, stable, and storage house. And then there was the burial ground with all its possible restless spirits of Quakers, Hessians, and others. So the reporter to the *Times* in that 1884 article threw out another idea to ponder: "The Flushing ghosts may be the ghosts of three deceased pirates who buried money in Flushing and thereby contracted chills and fever, and the dancing in which they are said to have indulged may have been simply the involuntary motions which ghosts suffering from chills are wholly unable to control." Everybody's an expert.

After the whole ghost flap thing of the 1880s, the twentieth century arrived like a lamb. The remaining Flushing Quakers have continued to partake in the national Quaker effort to provide peaceful assistance, such as holding vigils outside of the meeting house in support of Martin Luther King Jr.'s desegregation efforts and holding peace vigils protesting the Vietnam War. The meeting house was listed on the National Register of Historic Places in 1967 and declared a national and city historic landmark. If ever a historic place deserved those recognitions, the Quaker Meeting House in Flushing does.

In 1970, with its three-hundredth birthday looming, extensive restoration efforts were undertaken, and the burial grounds were restored to their lovely, tranquil setting. Let's hope there are no more bad apples out there who would desecrate the burial ground like in 2000. Fund-raising efforts will remain an ongoing necessity, in order to maintain and repair what its website calls "one of the oldest and most fragile places of worship in America." So please, if this story interests you, consider making a donation toward the meeting house's $300,000 goal. The Old Quaker Meeting House is open every Sunday for tours from noon until 12:30 P.M. Other visits can be scheduled by appointment.

Gusterin's Flat

My wife and daughter got up and shivered and trembled. Was I afraid? No, Sir; but it was terrible. *Terrible,* I say! I am glad we escaped with our lives. Will I visit the beach next summer? Never, Sir—that is, I always go to the Catskills in the summer. Good day, Sir; good day.

Those were J. Weller's actual parting comments said to a *New York Times* reporter on January 9, 1896, regarding a haunted four-story double flat he had rented from Augustus Gusterin on Fair View Avenue (now Beach 84th Street) in Rockaway Beach. The reporter had followed the shaken man to the train station, where Weller and his family were awaiting the first train out of town. The reporter said that Weller "lost no time in putting miles of track between him and the haunted house" and wouldn't relax until he was back "in dear, old, *quiet* Brooklyn." Apparently the haunting surprised the people of Rockaway Beach, because the haunted property was a modern flat, rather than the "old manses and ancestral halls [that] have always been the dwelling places of authentic wraiths."

Weller had planned to rent the large frame building for his family in the middle of the winter of 1896, even though it had been built primarily for summer occupancy. Though the flat was only two years old, it already had a tragic history that set it up for future haunting. An old man named Quinby who had rented it the summer before fell down its stairs and died from his injuries. Several months later, another tenant, a young girl, disappeared from the beach and was never found. The noises began after Quinby was buried and were so disturbing that Gusterin was unable to keep a tenant. "They soon move out; and, of the new ones that came in, some stayed a month, some two weeks, and some only one night." So before poor Weller moved his family in, several other families had attempted to live there, but their stays were invariably short-lived, due to the continuous strange sounds, like chains clanking and moans and groans.

They asked Gusterin about the supernatural activity, and for that they were ridiculed and insulted by the disbelieving German landlord. He told them they all had "chronic delirium tremens" and also "made sundry condemnatory remarks about the imaginary hobgoblins." Imagine his surprise when they turned on him and "almost demolished" him for his insinuations that they were crazy. After a period of vacancy, Gusterin was happy to have a new tenant in Mr. Weller. But Weller's stay would go the way of the rest of them, even though he had assured the landlord that he could "stand up" to the ghost, or even "all the ghosts in creation." In other words, he didn't have a clue what it's like to experience a genuine haunting, or he would have hesitated before making such assertions. Even his wife and daughter said they weren't afraid of a silly old ghost. By the next morning, however, all three of them were having second thoughts on the subject. Their first night—*first night*—"took all the courage out of Weller." He went to Gusterin at daybreak, prepared to cancel the lease on the spot because of the horrors the family had experienced. But the slick (and desperate) landlord offered to cut the rent by half if the family would stay. So they remained—one more "awful" sleepless night. Weller told the *Brooklyn Eagle,* which got to him before the *Times* at the train station, that he was "glad to get out with [his] life."

> . . . for if there was not a supernatural appearance, a ghost, a disturbed spirit or whatever it may be called, then my eyes and my ears deceive me, for I both saw and heard the uncanny visitor. The apparition had the appearance of an old man. I heard his moans and could clearly distinguish his footsteps as he walked about the empty rooms. Then came the sound as of a man tumbling down a flight of stairs, accompanied by shrieks that made my hair stand on end.

After less than forty-eight hours of living in the flat, the family hastily packed that second morning and fled. Weller returned to Gusterin and canceled his lease, and they headed straight to the train station with plans to return to Brooklyn. That was when the reporter from the *Times* caught up with them, and Weller bade him adieu. As for the landlord, even offering to rent the property for almost nothing, he couldn't get any takers (especially, I'm sure, once the *Times* and *Brooklyn Eagle* articles came out). He was "disgusted" by the whole ordeal. After all, he declared, everyone knows ghosts don't go near the ocean. (Tell that to the countless "ghost ships" and "ladies of the lake.")

Jackson Avenue

As with other such haunted abodes, the landlord of a tenement on Jackson Avenue, just off Dutch Kills Street in Long Island City, had been unable to rent his dwelling in 1874 for some time. Then along came the Daley family, who agreed to rent the building for "a nominal sum," according to a *New York Times* article dated January 29, 1874. The landlord dutifully told them that "there would be other occupants besides themselves in the house," meaning occupants of the spirit kind. Like the Wellers of Rockaway Beach, the Daley family was undeterred and insisted that they weren't afraid of ghosts, "or even the 'old boy' himself," apparently meaning Satan.

Everything went along fine—the ghosts being on their best behavior—for about a week. Then one night, shortly after the family went to bed, they heard what sounded like moans. Mr. Daley was concerned that somebody might be freezing to death in the bitter January cold, so he got up and stepped into the hall to get his bearings on where the sound was coming from. Just as he did so, the sound instantly moved to the kitchen, so he went in that direction. When he arrived in the kitchen, the sound suddenly appeared in the parlor, and the wild goose chase was on. Standing in the parlor, he could hear the sound in the basement. Realizing it was pointless to try to "catch it," he did a thorough search of the entire house but found nobody and nothing to suggest what the moaning sound was that he and his wife had heard. Defeated, and more than a little perplexed, he went back to bed. Just as his head hit the pillow, "a noise as if some heavy body were falling down stairs was heard." Back in the kitchen, he and Mrs. Daley found some of her crockery that had been in the closed cupboard lying broken across the floor. The supernatural ruckus was so traumatic for one of their young children that the boy suffered a fit of violent convulsions from which he never recovered. He died shortly after the family moved out.

The following night was even worse, if that were possible. "At midnight, cries of 'Murder! Murder!' rang through the house, creating confusion in the family." Neighbors came to the rescue of the terrified family, helping them scour the premises in search of the source of their troubles. Nothing was found. Just like their first week, all was quiet once again. But the family had experienced too much already—even before they knew that the fright their child had been subjected to would lead to his untimely death. They refused to admit that their original position on not being afraid of ghosts had changed, instead insisting that they were leaving, "not because they were afraid, but it was impossible to sleep in such racket."

Belasco Theatre

David Belasco—producer, playwright, actor, set designer, theater manager, proprietor, and impresario of the Belasco Theatre—is believed to have haunted the building since the day he died. A phantom bearing a striking resemblance to the jack-of-all-trades has often been seen sitting in the box that the living Belasco watched the shows from. Belasco was nicknamed the "Bishop of Broadway" for the dark suits with white collars that he wore; the apparition seen in his old box and elsewhere over the years has been dressed precisely in that same priestly manner. Some have seen the apparition with a frown on his face, both during and right after opening shows, as if he somehow disapproved of the performances. The occasional smell of cigar smoke, with no source, is also believed to be an indication of Belasco's presence.

The Belasco Theatre on Broadway at 111 West 44th Street opened the week of October 15, 1907, under David Belasco's capable management. Over the years, many of its shows, such as *All the Way Home, Hamlet,* and *The Doll House,* boasted Tony winners. Other notable shows included *Oh! Calcutta!* and *Follies.* The theater was originally called the Stuyvesant, but Belasco gave it his own name in 1910. Even though he died in the Hotel Gladstone in 1931 at the age of seventy-six following a heart attack, the theater, now owned by the Shubert Organization, still uses that famous name, so it makes sense that Belasco would be the one still lingering there to oversee the business he carefully nurtured.

The private elevator to Belasco's penthouse suite that once operated is backstage. It accommodated Belasco and his guests—including countless wannabe actresses hoping to make it to the "casting couch" with him to further their careers. A stagehand and several others have heard the rattling of the elevator's old chains, as if it were still in operation, even though it has been dismantled for some time now. The sounds of partying have reportedly emanated from within Belasco's suite when nobody is known to be inside. Stage curtains move on their own, and props sometimes vanish just before the show they are needed for and reappear immediately after the performance is over. And the list goes on. Is Belasco still presiding over productions at his theater? Most people who have experienced paranormal activity there believe he is. But he may not be alone.

A blue ghost has been seen in the balcony. It appears as either a blue orb that drifts up what would be the center aisle of the balcony (if there were one) or a fully manifested apparition of a woman wearing a blue gown. One performer saw such an apparition every night during her performance in a part of the show that required her to gaze in that direction for a few moments. And a stagehand saw the lady in blue walking across the back of the theater toward the stairs to the balcony after closing one night—when nobody was supposed to still be inside. As far as he knew, he and one other person were the only ones in the building at the time. Still another employee saw a blur of blue ascending the steps to Belasco's suite one night and simultaneously felt a strong chill go straight through him. It couldn't have been solid, because it didn't trip the motion-activated alarm system (or him, for that matter). The blue lady's identity may not be as obvious as Belasco's, but it seems that in death, Belasco still has at least one woman willing to do anything to get to his casting couch, even sticking with him to the very end.

Lake Ronkonkoma

At least three distinct legends are associated with Lake Ronkonkoma on Long Island. Though different, all share the same tragic outcome. Every summer, at least one young man or boy is said to drown under mysterious conditions in the lake. A kettle lake, Lake

Ronkonkoma is a massive, bowl-shaped impression in the earth caused by the melting of a glacier twenty thousand years ago. An old Native American tale of a scorned young Indian chief who dejectedly paddled to the middle of the lake, dove deep into the water, and never returned to the surface led to the misconception that the lake was bottomless. True, it is the largest lake on Long Island, but the myth that it was bottomless was put to rest in 1956 by a team of divers. In reality, its greatest depth is sixty-five feet. But the ominous designation that had been associated with it for hundreds of years undoubtedly spawned a series of legends. The Lady of Lake Ronkonkoma is an apparition said to brazenly lure young men to the depths of the so-called bottomless lake, never to return.

In the most popular version of that legend, an Indian princess named Ronkonkoma became acquainted with an Indian prince from a different tribe across the lake, and the two fell in love. But her parents did not share her enthusiasm for the young man. When they learned of the affair, they forbade their daughter to see the prince again, since he wasn't one of their own. In a story as old as time, nothing, especially not disapproving parents, could stop the young lovers from trying to meet—well, nothing but death. One night, the determined prince attempted to swim across the lake to see Ronkonkoma, but he somehow drowned. The Indian princess, who could hear his death cries, swam out to find him, but she met the same fate. Neither of their bodies was ever recovered. The story goes that each year, the princess returns to the surface to claim the life of at least one teenage boy that reminds her of her Indian prince, and that mysterious lights drifting by the shoreline also indicate her presence, although she fully manifests when she finds a worthy victim.

The same legend with a twist has the heartbroken Indian princess—after just being told she could not be with a prince from another tribe—rowing out to the middle of the lake, tying heavy rocks around her ankles, then slipping over the side. If the man she loved, regardless of his tribe, couldn't have her, she would make sure no other man ever would either. After that tragic event, her tribe believed that her restless spirit would forever haunt the lake, causing mysterious waves and unexplained whirlpools to form and crying out mournfully into the night for centuries. Indeed, an apparition allegedly appeared as a solid, beautiful young maiden near the shore, beckoning young men to follow her into the water, and ultimately leading them to their death. In this way, the loneliness her parents forced upon her—by refusing to let her be with the only man she loved—would not torment her in death.

But was the apparition even that of the Indian maiden? Could it be possible that the apparition many people have seen was that of another woman who met an untimely death? The *New York Times* of July 5, 1908, reported the following sad incident:

> Woman Dies Suddenly at a Hotel
>
> Sayville, L.I., July 4—Mrs. Lucy McKittrick of the Lake Front Hotel and Annex Cottage at Lake Ronkonkoma died suddenly today. She was the widow of Charles Brown, a New York broker.

A third legend tells of a curse one of the warring Native American tribes placed on the lake in which each year for all of eternity, a male child would drown in the lake. And yet another version has the Indian maiden's lover being murdered by a white man who wanted her, so she drowned herself, vowing that as revenge, she would claim the life of one white male a year.

In the 1970s, a *Newsday* reporter painstakingly researched old newspaper clippings from the area to see if there were any truth to the legend of young males drowning in Lake Ronkonkoma each year. Surprisingly, there was. For a lengthy stretch of consecutive years, at least one young male actually had drowned in the lake. Were the number of deaths by drowning statistically typical for a lake as popular and large as Ronkonkoma? Or was it something more sinister? Had the victims actually been lured by paranormal means to their demise, as the legends claim?

Unless there were witnesses, in many cases nobody will ever know. But boys, if you see a beautiful, dark-haired beauty by the side of the lake beckoning you—even though it goes against every ounce of your testosterone-ravaged being—whatever you do, don't follow her!

St. Mark's-in-the-Bowery

The ghost of Peter Stuyvesant, the last governor of New Amsterdam, has been seen, heard, or otherwise recognized since shortly after he died in 1672, making St. Mark's-in-the-Bowery—where Stuyvesant lived and died—one of New York City's most lasting and notorious haunted locales.

In 1651, Stuyvesant purchased a sizable tract of farmland in the East Village on which he built a family chapel in 1660. He was laid to rest in a vault of that chapel, but his remains were disturbed when St. Mark's-in-the-Bowery was built in 1799 on the site of that chapel at 10th Street and 2nd Avenue. Stuyvesant's tomb had to be integrated into the side of St. Mark's Church.

The Dutchman, known for being hotheaded and unyielding, had a wooden leg and used a walking stick after losing his right leg in battle, making his stride very noisy and distinctive. So when his servants saw a ghost hobbling around the Stuyvesant grounds just days after the governor's death, they knew old "Peg Leg" had returned. And in 1774, when the family mansion was heavily damaged by fire, Stuyvesant's ghost was seen again—this time shuffling through the rubble.

While there were many reports of people hearing Stuyvesant's unmistakable gait pacing up and down the aisles in the 1800s, the most memorable case occurred during the Civil War, when a sexton of St. Mark's was stalked by a ghost with a cane and wooden leg, who chased the poor man right off the property. But it wasn't just the screams of the terrified man that awakened the neighbors; it was also the church bell ringing in the midst of the ruckus, even though nobody they knew of was inside the locked church. A few brave souls volunteered to venture inside to see what was happening. Nobody was found inside the church or fleeing from it, yet someone had torn off a portion of the rope that was attached to the bell, leaving the other end too high for them to reach. The next day, the sexton went to Stuvyesant's crypt in the side of the church to see if Stuyvesant had somehow escaped his grave—as if a ghost couldn't have gone through a solid object without disturbing anything. Though the tomb was undisturbed on the outside, inside the protective gate, the other section of the rope from the church bell lay on the ground right beside Stuyvesant's grave. Well, that's what they say, anyway. The *New York Sun* told of a similar situation in a 2004 article by Jimmy Fragosa called "30 Years of Keeping Watch over Ghosts and Crypts at St. Mark's Church."

Reports of Stuyvesant's ghost were at their peak in the nineteenth century, but even though they have dwindled, the legends live on. And Stuyvesant may not be acting alone these days. A 1981 *New York Times* article said that A. T. Stewart, the department store magnate, and Washington Irving's "lost sweetheart," Matilda Hoffman, also haunt the grounds of St. Mark's-in-the-Bowery.

Regardless of its status as one of the city's most haunted sites, the community is obviously not afraid. To the contrary. Massive volunteer efforts to maintain and restore the church for future generations have been going on for decades. After a fire nearly gutted the church in 1978, the Citizens to Save St. Mark's raised funds for reconstruction, which was completed eight years later. Since 1979, St. Mark's Historic Landmark Fund has provided long-term care and preservation of the church and its grounds; and maybe that's all the reassurance it will take to finally quiet Stuyvesant's stick . . . that is, spirit.

Bridge Café

In a building such as the Bridge Café, which has seen sea captains, river pirates, prostitutes, murderers, gamblers, and aristocrats pass through its doors for more than two hundred years, one can only imagine the number of reasons a ghost might have to haunt it. Take, for example, the apparition of a sea captain that walked through the bar and sat at a stool in front of the speechless manager. Was he passing time until his ghost ship departed? Then there was the female ghost seen drifting across the room toward a window overlooking the East River. Was she waiting for a ship to come in, unaware that it had come and gone long ago? Is she looking for the captain who is as lost as she? Are they doomed to keep passing each other like two ships in the night, eternally searching but never finding? The possibilities are only as limited as one's imagination.

Adam Weprin's family has owned and operated the Bridge Café at 279 Water Street below the Brooklyn Bridge for nearly thirty years. Built in 1794 and later named for its obvious proximity to the Brooklyn Bridge, the Bridge Café holds a number of titles: the oldest eating and drinking establishment in New York; Manhattan's longest-running saloon, operating nonstop since 1847; the oldest wood-frame building in the city; and the oldest actual business in the city. Seriously, how could it not be haunted with credits like that to its name?

Herbert Asbury's 1928 book *The Gangs of New York: An Informal History of the Underworld* said a "vicious dive" called Hole-in-the-Wall, run by One-Armed Charley Monell, was situated at the southeast corner of Water and Dover Streets, which is very likely the same building now called the Bridge Café. Martin Scorsese's loose film adaptation of *Gangs of New York* re-created the Bridge Café as "Gallus Mag's Hole-in-the-Wall." According to Asbury, in its brothel days, a six-foot-tall barmaid at the Hole-in-the-Wall named Gallus Mag allegedly cut off the ears of rowdy patrons and kept them in a jar at the bar. Hmmm . . . reminds me of the "ear cutter" my grandmother used to tell me would get us if we went out in the hall of her tenth-floor apartment, an effective means of keeping rowdy—and gullible—youngsters like us inside and in line. Asbury said it was Mag's custom, after clubbing a quarrelsome customer to the ground, to "clutch his ear between her teeth and so drag him to the door." If the unfortunate victim protested, she bit his ear off, threw him out onto the street, and put the ear in a jar of alcohol at the bar, to join a whole morbid collection of such appendages. No wonder Gallus Mag was "one of the most feared denizens on the waterfront, and the police of the period shudderingly described her as the most savage female they'd ever encountered." How could that be good for business? Maybe One-Armed Charley Monell was too afraid to fire the mad Amazonian woman. At any rate, Gallus Mag is said to still haunt the building. So if you feel a little tug on your ear, I suggest you don't protest!

In a *New York Times* article from 1995 called "Streetscapes: The Bridge Café; On the Trail of New York's Oldest Surviving Bar," Christopher Gray details the meticulous research one Richard

McDermott has done on the café. He found that Henry Williams operated the building as a "porter house" in 1847, and the 1860 census showed six Irish prostitutes living there. A reference to the Bridge Café was also found in Frank Moss's *The American Metropolis* (1897), which said that the brothel at 279 Water Street was "filled with river pirates and Water Street hags" and operated by Tom Norton. Norton is believed to have run his business there from about 1861 to 1880. In 1888, Maurice Hyland purchased the building and turned it from a two-and-a-half-story structure with a peaked roof to a flat-topped, three-story one, but Hyland only owned it for two years. In 1892, Jeremiah Cronin took over until 1909. Peter J. Boyle then ran it as Boyle's Bar in 1910, and in 1922, the McCormacks took over. Adam Weprin's father, real estate broker Jack, purchased the bar from the McCormacks in 1979 on a whim—having never owned or operated a bar—and the family has owned it ever since. Before they purchased it, the building had not been renovated since 1888. Perhaps their renovations drew the curious spirits back to their former hangout.

Adam Weprin has twice heard the distinct sound of heavy footsteps overhead when only he and one other person were in the building. The incidents occurred ten years apart but were strikingly similar in nature. Staff and visitors have experienced other unexplained phenomena as well, such as equipment malfunctioning (more than the norm), cold drafts drifting past them, and keys vanishing but later being found in obvious places, and bent. What is it about ghosts and keys, anyway? It's as if they steal them per some *Ghostly Antics 101* manual or something.

The most bizarre—and dangerous—incident to date occurred when a former head chef, the son of an electrician, attempted to repair a broken refrigerator. He had unplugged the unit and turned off the breaker switch, but somehow the refrigerator sent a jolt of electricity through him as he began the repair work. Thankfully, it was only enough to stun him for a moment. It's possible that the unit had a capacitor (an electrical component used to store a high-voltage charge temporarily) that hadn't been discharged properly before the chef began the repair, but it's also believed to be possible for determined spirits to manipulate any form of energy, especially electrical. So the "shocking" incident was added to a long list of unexplained occurrences that have taken place at the Bridge Café.

Regardless of its token ghost or two, the Bridge Café is a must-visit place for tourists and New Yorkers alike. Serving up superb food in a truly authentic atmosphere of yesteryear, the Bridge Café has a historic past, a ghostly present, and a promising future. Just pray you don't encounter Old Mag, the ear cutter!

Manhattan Bistro

Both the manager and the owner of the Manhattan Bistro have agreed that strange things sometimes occur at the bar and restaurant, but the owner stops short of blaming it exclusively on the paranormal. Yet how else do you explain ashtrays flying off tables so forcefully that they crash into walls or bottles flying off shelves, plates falling off tables, and lights turning on and off without assistance? What else can you possibly blame full-blown apparitions of a woman with long hair on?

According to an article called "From Hamilton's Pen: The Mystery of Gulielma Sands," in the October 9, 1887, *Syracuse Herald*:

> Gulielma left the house alone about 8 o'clock on the evening of December 22, 1799, for the purpose, as she had previously told Mrs. Ring, of marrying Weekes. She left the house full of hope and spirits, but never returned alive. Inquiry was made, but no trace of the missing girl was discovered until the 21st of January following, when her dead body was found in a well in an open field . . . The well is now in the rear of a carpenter's shop at the end of an alley back of No. 59-1/2 Greene Street, about 100 feet north of Spring."

Gulielma, or Elma for short, was a beautiful, twenty-one-year-old hat maker who was murdered by her boyfriend, a shameless and spoiled player named Levi Weekes, who then stuffed her body into a well at the intersection of Greene and Spring Streets. The well-connected Weekes was arrested and accused after the body was discovered a month later, but his very rich uncle hired the best attorneys—none other than Alexander Hamilton and Aaron Burr.

Somehow the jury believed the young man's pathetic lies and his lawyers' claims that the woman had been suicidal and taken her own life, even though the badly bruised and beaten body that was recovered told a different story. But the guilty man was released, and the public was furious. They hounded and threatened Weekes until he finally fled from New York City. Still, he got off easy compared with his victim, and everyone knew it—including his attorneys.

According to news accounts, after the unfair verdict was read, the murdered girl's aunt put a curse on Hamilton, Burr, and the judge, Chief Justice Lansing, who had hinted strongly to the jury that they should find Weekes innocent. She said to Hamilton, "If thee dies a natural death, I shall think there is no justice in Heaven." Three years later, Burr killed Hamilton in a duel. The remainder of Burr's life was miserable and seemingly cursed. And Lansing disappeared from the face of the earth thirty years after the trial, after leaving the City Hotel, in a mystery that has never been solved.

For many years, the well in which the woman was found had disappeared, and everyone just assumed it had been moved to a dump or sunk to the bottom of the river. Nobody knew its final resting place, until the owner of the Manhattan Bistro had her basement dug up, since it had been filled in with dirt many years earlier, because she needed to expand her thriving business. That was when the unusual relic was discovered. Because her building was constructed in the 1800s, she sought the expertise of the Landmarks Conservancy and soon learned that her basement had been the final resting place of the infamous well into which Elma's brutalized body was stuffed in 1799. So it was the young woman's final resting place, which explains the apparitions and supernatural outbursts that sometimes occur in the building.

Elma's spirit has been seen where the actual murder is believed to have taken place on Spring Street, and witnesses say the apparition is covered with seaweed and goop. But other times, she has been seen in the middle of the night at people's bedsides in the vicinity wearing a long gown and looking as beautiful as she was in life. One artist who lived across the street from the crime scene, Vita Giorgi, became so mesmerized by the supernatural vision she saw outside her window that she painted a series of canvases depicting what she saw. She had never heard about the ghost of Spring Street or Gulielma Sands. In a news article in the February 5, 1975, *Amarillo Globe-Times* called "Artist Paints Image, Learns of Neighborhood Ghost," Giorgi told reporter Brent Bowers that the ghost she saw had a "solemn face, maybe even sad." But the apparition was gone in an instant, so the artist painted quickly from memory before she forgot the details . . . the red lips and almond-shaped eyes, the long brunette hair, and the flowing white robe.

Elma's spirit has been seen so often, in fact, that it's called the Spring Street Ghost. Although no full-blown apparition has ever been reported in the Manhattan Bistro, a visual phenomenon once was witnessed by a couple of workers in the basement, where the round, brick well that was Elma's grave still lies. They insisted they saw a spiraling mist emanating out of the well in a swirling pattern that calls to mind Jeannie in *I Dream of Jeannie* swirling out of her bottle. Elma is believed to be responsible for throwing the occasional harmless tantrum, as if to remind everyone she's there. Apparently she's still angry over what happened to her. And she's still unable to rest in peace.

St. Paul's Chapel

It is said that the decapitated ghost of Shakespearean actor George Frederick Cooke roams about the graveyard behind St. Paul's Chapel in Manhattan searching for his head. Cooke was a famous British actor hailed as the greatest early-nineteenth-century tragedian in both England and the States. Ironically, the end of his life read like one of the many tragic scripts he so convincingly performed onstage. Cooke made his American debut in 1810, but two years later, he died of alcoholism at the age of fifty-six in New York City. Knowing the end was near, he had made premortem arrangements to leave his head to science to help defray his outstanding medical bills. As directed, the decapitation was carried out, but before turning his skull over to science, it was used as a prop in a number of performances of Edwin Booth's production of *Hamlet*. Meanwhile, the headless body was buried in the graveyard behind

St. Paul's Chapel. There, a monument that still stands today was erected in Cooke's memory by a fellow British actor in 1821.

In *Haunted Places: The National Directory: Ghostly Abodes, Sacred Sites, UFO Landings and Other Supernatural Locations,* Dennis William Hauck describes another ghost believed to haunt St. Paul's Chapel: that of Civil War photographer Mathew Brady. In the mid-1800s, Brady operated photography studios (of the daguerreian type) at 161 Fulton Street, 187 Broadway, 205 Broadway, and 207 Broadway. The last was three doors down from St. Paul's Chapel, where Hauck said a ghost fitting Brady's description has approached people on the sidewalk in front of the chapel, as if to solicit their business, just as he did in the 1800s when he photographed people "dressed up for dinner, pushing baby carriages, or just strolling down Broadway." Aside from his pedestrian photography, Brady had become wealthy following a series of famous portraits he took of Abraham Lincoln and a book he published called *The Gallery of Illustrious Americans* (1850). But he lost his fortune during the Civil War after financing twenty apprentice photographers to spread out and cover all bases of the war. He believed his historic collection, which is invaluable today, would garner a pretty penny. But after the war, there wasn't the interest he thought there would be, perhaps because people didn't want to relive the war by seeing his photographs. Congress did acquire the negatives and prints that remained of his Civil War collection in 1875, although the purchase price did not cover Brady's debts. So he ended up dying penniless in 1896. Today the value of those photographs and the legacy Brady left in the fields of photography and photojournalism are finally recognized.

St. Paul's Chapel, a Georgian Classic Revival built in 1766, is New York City's oldest public building still in continual use. New York State's first governor, George Clinton, worshipped there, as did our country's first president, in the days when New York City was the nation's capital. It was built in a field five blocks from the bustling Wall Street, which graces the horizon today. Although it is right next door to Ground Zero, nestled between Vesey and Fulton Streets on Broadway, the chapel and its grounds were miraculously unscathed by the collapse of the World Trade Center towers on September 11, 2001. And because of that, the chapel offered a refuge for rescuers and relief workers in the immediate vicinity, opening its doors for the next eight months to provide firefighters, police officers, construction workers, and searchers a place to recoup, eat a warm meal, and pray. Today St. Paul's Chapel continues to provide a safe refuge for the weary . . . from the present and, apparently, the past.

Chumley's

Leland "Lee" Chumley's successful final venture was a speakeasy for the literary elite of New York City. As an artist, cartoonist, and editorial writer, he knew the importance of having a relaxing place where like minds could socialize and brainstorm over a drink or two. As the owner and operator of the oldest speakeasy in New York City, he obviously knew what he was doing. The Federal-style structure, built circa 1831, had been a home and a blacksmith shop before Chumley turned it into a legitimate printing office and prosperous speakeasy in 1922. It had a secret entrance, which continues the tradition of being unmarked today, around the corner and through a courtyard on Barrow Street. Though there has never been an actual sign to the entrance of Chumley's, it didn't stop an impressive list of famous literary and creative geniuses from finding their way to its hidden door during Prohibition.

If you could find it, it was well worth the effort. The atmosphere of Chumley's was always very friendly and relaxed. Much to an author's delight, hundreds of dust jackets and photographs of guests including F. Scott Fitzgerald, Norman Mailer, Edna St. Vincent Millay, Orson Welles, and Upton Sinclair graced the tavern's walls, reminding patrons of those who frequented the bar in its early covert days. The other, less tangible reminders of visitors who have passed through its doors—or walls, as it were—included Lee Chumley's wife, Henrietta, who nobody knew existed until shortly after her husband died of a heart attack in their upstairs apartment in 1935, when she showed up at the bar one day announcing that she was taking over.

Following the passing of her husband, she was at the speakeasy every single night, overseeing business from her table in front of the fireplace, where she inevitably drank until she passed out and then had to be carried home by the hired help. Henrietta died in 1960 in her usual seat in the bar, where she played solitaire and drank her Manhattans every night for twenty-five years. Some believe Henrietta continued watching over the business after she died, showing her disdain for renovations and updates by manipulating objects such as the jukebox and pinball machine. If so, I'd hate to see what she thought of the demolition of the building following a chimney collapse in April 2007. (Fear not, Chumley's is being rebuilt as I write.) During a tour of New York City's pubs, one tour group was treated to one of Henrietta's phantom tantrums when bottles and glasses started falling off the shelves of the bar when nobody was anywhere near them. The bartender continued about his business, casually telling the group that it was just Mrs. Chumley.

But Lee and Henrietta weren't the only people to die in the building. According to the June 2, 1960, *New York Times*, a forty-three-year-old writer named Clinton Curtis was murdered that year after defeating a seaman at a game of chess at Chumley's. The article, called "Slain over Chess Game," said a bitter argument led to a physical altercation between Curtis and a Florida man named Michael George. Curtis punched George, and George swung back at him with a beer glass, which broke as it connected with Curtis's neck, severing his jugular vein. Curtis died before help could arrive. So I would say Curtis has more reason to knock bottles and glasses off the shelves and throw tantrums than Mrs. Chumley. After all, it was one such glass that killed him.

According to Susan Smitten's *Ghost Stories of New York State*, owner Steve Shlopak admitted that he'd seen his share of unexplainable things at Chumley's, but he believed such incidents involved spirits of the recently deceased—such as firefighters he knew—rather than those from the distant past. Shlopak's close friend and firefighter Captain John Drennan, whose picture hung over the bar, died in a fire rescue attempt in 1994. Steve had just lost his business partner at the same time and was trying to decide what to do with Chumley's. As if someone had read his mind, seven firefighters from Engine 24, Ladder 5, showed up at his place shortly after to help him out. Steve ended up keeping them on as staff and eventually transitioned the pub into an all-firefighter crew. Some of those first firefighters have since passed away, including sixteen who died in the World Trade Center attack in 2001, but Steve believes they continued to visit Chumley's . . . in their own unique way.

When the employees are talking about a particular subject, they sometimes hear the jukebox start playing a song with lyrics relevant to their discussion. One time several of them were talking about the memorial services for one of their fallen comrades when the words "We're on the road again, we're on the way to paradise" came on. And the jukebox was not even plugged in at the time, they swore. It never got plugged in until just before 4 P.M., when Chumley's opened each day. The incident made three of the stunned employees "eighty-six it." That's a phrase that may have originated at Chumley's during Prohibition, when police would attempt a raid at the 86 Bedford address (the proper, though unused address), and someone would tell the patrons to "eighty-six it," or run for the secret rear exit. The phrase has since become synonymous with heading out, especially quickly. Incidents such as the jukebox knowing what to play and turning itself on at inappropriate times led Steve to believe that his historic bar was haunted by spirits of the dearly departed, rather than disgruntled ghosts with a bone to pick.

Merchant's House Museum

Imagine living and dying in the very same house you were born in, without ever having lived elsewhere in your entire ninety-three years. Pretty uncommon these days. But something happened the day Gertrude Tredwell's father told her she couldn't marry the only man she had ever loved: She made the conscious decision to stay in her childhood home for the rest of her life, avoiding Cupid's arrow and the searing pain it could inflict at all costs. If that decision meant shunning the public and refusing to move when the entire neighborhood was transforming before her eyes, then so be it. The only way to protect her heart was to never let love find her again, and the house now known as the Merchant's House Museum at 29 East Fourth Street offered plenty of room to hide.

Seabury Tredwell was a wealthy marine-hardware merchant who, upon retirement in 1835, moved his family to the exclusive Bond Street Area of "Old New York." The five-story, red brick and white marble row house he bought was only three years old when the Tredwells moved in, and he paid $18,000 for it. Today the house-museum is priceless. While the exterior is considered to be a fine example of a Federal-style home, the interior is Greek Revival at its best. Born in 1840, Gertrude was the youngest of the eight Tredwell children, and she was the only one born in the new house. She took her first steps in its stately double parlors with their thirteen-foot ceilings, mahogany pocket doors, breathtaking ornamental plasterwork, and black-and-gold marble mantelpieces. The family enjoyed the latest trends in fine home decor, and their house was equipped with what was then considered to be the most modern conveniences money could buy. Life was good.

Then, in her twenties, Gertrude met a doctor named Lewis Walton, and they fell in love. But the man she adored was a Catholic, and Gertrude's family was strictly Episcopalian, which presented the lovelorn couple with an insurmountable dilemma. The God-fearing Seabury Tredwell stood in their way. To her horror and deep sorrow, he forbade the marriage. Although her father passed away just a few years later, in 1865, she had promised him she wouldn't disobey him, and besides, the man she loved had already slipped away. Though the parlors held happy memories of two Tredwell daughters' wedding receptions, beginning with Seabury's passing, they also held funerals of several family members, as was often the case in those days.

Eliza, Gertrude's mother, died in 1882, leaving Phebe, Gertrude, and Julia to tend the house, as they were the only adult children still single and living at home. By this time, Gertrude was forty-two years old. The three daughters tended to their brother Horace when he returned home in 1885 to die. In 1906, Sarah died, followed by Phebe a year later, when she died from injuries suffered in a fall in the home. Gertrude's last surviving sibling, Julia, passed away in 1909, when Gertrude was sixty-nine years old. By then, she was considered an eccentric recluse whose only interest seemed to be keeping the house exactly as it was when her father was alive. Because of her determined efforts at preventing change, the house was practically in turnkey condition for its future as the Merchant's House Museum when she died in an upstairs bed in 1933.

Most of the Tredwells' personal possessions remained in the house upon Gertrude's death—the furnishings, vintage apparel that included an exquisite wedding gown and accessories, family photographs, and decorative objects—all in well-preserved condition. It was as if one was stepping through a door into another time period. Gertrude's cousin George Chapman, who saved the house from foreclosure or demolition upon hearing of her death, spent three years making necessary repairs and modernizing the property before opening it up as a museum in 1936. Today visitors can experience the typical life of upper-class, nineteenth-century city residents when they visit the museum, thanks to Gertrude's diligence and her cousin's tenacity. The house is rightfully on the National Register of Historic Places, and it's a member of the Historic House Trust and a national historic landmark. It is operated and maintained by the Old Merchant's House of New York and offers candlelight tours playing on the museum's status as "Manhattan's most haunted house," as dubbed by the *New York Times* in 2006. These include a video about its haunted history and a guided tour through the house, with actors playing the roles of past residents, such as Eliza, Gertrude, and an Irish maid.

There have been enough reports of paranormal phenomena at the Merchant's House Museum to fill an entire publication, and the museum is in the process of doing just that. *Some Say They Never Left: Spirited Tales and Ghostly Legends of the Merchant's House Museum* will likely be available by the time you read this. It is the museum's own story of the Tredwell family, and it "recounts numerous stories of unexplained happenings through the years, as told to museum staff by visitors, volunteers, and staff alike," according to its website. You can obtain your copy by emailing the museum at nyc1832@merchantshouse.org.

There have been many reports of an apparition believed to be Gertrude seen gliding up the stairs and around the house, and photographic anomalies depicting possible spirit energy may support those sightings. It's not hard to believe that even now, long after she died, she still stubbornly refuses to leave her beloved childhood haven, especially since it was the only place she ever knew. If it's true that ghosts like to linger in familiar surroundings, she certainly has it in Merchant's House Museum, because it remains remarkably unchanged today, long after her death.

Many sources report that the piano, which theoretically can't be played because it needs to be restored, has been heard playing by passersby on the street, and it's a well-known fact that playing the piano was one of Gertrude's pleasures in life. In the 1950s, two caretakers boarding at the house heard gentle tapping sounds on the wall behind their headboards, as if someone were tapping on the wall of the room adjacent to theirs, but they were the only ones there at the time. Teacups mysteriously move from one room to another, as if Gertrude or one of her sisters is going about her day as she once did, only from a different dimension. Visitors and staff, including the executive director (according to Newsday.com), have felt random cold spots and even a stiff breeze in the middle of the room in which Gertrude died, which could be indicative of the presence of her spirit . . . or that of another. Remember, Gertrude wasn't the only family member to pass away in the house, and she certainly wasn't the only family member who wanted to remain there.

Station House 2

In 1939, inside the New York Fire Patrol 2's headquarters at 84 West Third Street, forty-five-year-old fireman Alfred Stokes died of a heart attack. The Fire Department's rescue personnel and physician worked feverishly with inhalators to revive their fallen comrade, according to a *New York Times* article dated August 11, 1939, but their efforts were in vain. Today, seventy years later, the patrolmen who have been stationed at Station House 2 speak of seeing a ghost appearing and disappearing right in front of them in the building. Those who have gotten a pretty good look say he is dressed in a 1930s-style firefighting uniform. The rumor has long been that the resident ghost was a patrolman who hanged himself from a rafter in the building after learning about his wife's affair, but I found nothing to corroborate such a tragedy. Alfred Stokes's passing coincides with the time period from which the ghost allegedly hails, however. And he was not the only person to die tragically on the grounds.

Prior to the four-story structure currently standing at the same address, there had been a "disorderly resort." On July 10, 1887, the proprietress of the resort was arrested for abducting and prostituting a young black girl and for keeping a "house of ill repute." The building subsequently became a boardinghouse where, in 1888, a black cook named Alice Jackson was shot and killed by an angry drunk. Jackson had been seeing Lewis for a short time, but she left him when he began beating her. A *Times* article said that the scorned lover then went to 84 West Third Street, forcing his way past the servant at the door. "He met the Jackson woman in the hall, and after a few angry words, shot her in the breast." The woman fought back fiercely, trying to grab the gun away from him, but he shot her again, killing her. He was arrested and dragged off to "the Tombs"—the dreaded jail in lower Manhattan, where the Manhattan House of Detention now sits. Just over a year later, Lewis and four other "slayers of women" were hanged for their crimes in a quadruple execution in the Tombs yard.

Station House 2 moved to 84 West Third Street in 1907. The Fire Patrol was established in 1839 to complement the work of the New York City Fire Department by salvaging and protecting the property inside burning buildings from the effects of smoke, water, and fire damage for insurance companies. New York City was the first city in the nation to create a Fire Patrol and the last to still have one in operation—that is, until October 15, 2006, on which date the remaining Fire Patrol units were ordered to shut down operations. In spite of its history or necessity, the New York Board of Fire Underwriters, which created the Fire Patrol, stands to save approximately $8.5 million a year now.

Though the patrolmen once stationed at 84 West Third Street no longer work there, it doesn't necessarily mean they left the old building entirely unoccupied.

Conference House

The Conference House, named for a historic event that took place there in 1776, overlooks Raritan Bay on Staten Island in the Tottenville area. Built around 1680, when it was called the Manor of Bentley, it is also known as the Billopp House, after two of its illustrious owners: Captain Christopher Billopp, who built the house, and his great-grandson Colonel Christopher Billopp. When the Billopp men died, it seems they left behind more than the house and its legacy. Because of their alleged activities, they may have also left a spirit or two in their wake. But first a bit of history is in order.

Captain Billopp was in service to England when he sailed to America in 1674, at the time New York City was being settled. The governor of the New York colony, Thomas Dongan, recognized his efforts after Billopp—using his skillful seamanship—secured Staten Island for New York, beating New Jersey to the punch. Dongan rewarded Billopp with sixteen hundred acres of prime Staten Island real estate at the southernmost tip of New York, where, around 1680, Billopp built the stone house now called the Conference House. Modest by today's standards, the two-story house was nevertheless considered superior in its day, consisting of a basement kitchen, two floors of living quarters, and an attic with room enough for a number of servants to sleep.

Following Billopp's service to the British Navy, he ran a prosperous ferry service in the area, and his life seemed charmed. But there was a darker side to the captain. Those who knew him—family, servants, and acquaintances—were aware that he could be ruthless and unforgiving, according to Lynda Lee Macken's *Haunted History of Staten Island*. In fact, sometimes he could be downright frightening. The captain had been charged with assault at least twice that we know of—once in the colonies, and then later in England. Some sources say he killed a young female slave with a fireplace poker on the stairway landing in the Conference House after she rejected his advances—a story that was corroborated by a psychic who had no prior knowledge of the house's history but sensed a similar scenario.

Colonel Billopp, the great-grandson, was also known to exhibit the Billopp predisposition toward violence and callousness. Lucky for him, that's not what history remembers him for. He is most associated with the historic three-hour peace conference that was held at his house on September 11, 1776. The king of England had arranged the conference in an effort to thwart the likelihood of an all-out war for independence between England and the colonies, which had just penned the Declaration of Independence. The conference was to be hosted by Colonel Billopp. After all, his was the grandest house on Staten Island at the time, and the British royal family was well acquainted with the Billopps.

Lord Admiral Richard Howe was sent to speak on the king's behalf, with a warning that under no circumstances would the colonies actually be granted independence. In other words, it wasn't truly going to be a negotiation at all, but rather a meeting to relay the king's message to the colonies. Benjamin Franklin, John Adams, and Edward Rutledge attended on behalf of the colonies. Those three wise men had no illusions that England would bow to their demands, but Franklin wanted to hear what the king had to say. When it became obvious that neither side would give an inch, Franklin and company promptly left. The peace conference was over nearly as soon as it had begun, and war was inevitable. That's when things really got interesting.

Because of his well-known loyalty to the British throne, Colonel Billopp was targeted to be kidnapped and imprisoned several times by the colonists. He became understandably suspicious that someone within his own house was betraying him when he realized that the kidnappings always happened as soon as he returned home from his various travels. One day, when he saw a young servant girl place a lantern in an upstairs bedroom window that faced St. Peter's Church in Perth Amboy, where American troops were holed up, he believed his suspicions had been confirmed. Thinking the servant girl had been the one betraying him, he chased her to the stairs, where she either tripped and fell or was shoved all the way to the bottom, breaking her neck. When New York confiscated all property belonging to the British loyalists, Billopp was forced to move to Nova Scotia, where he was given property by the king of England. After nearly one hundred years of Billopp occupation, the famous Conference House became privately owned by various people until 1929, when it was acquired by a nonprofit organization called the Conference House Association, which saved it from being razed.

A tremendous amount of paranormal phenomena has been reported by people who have lived at, worked at, visited, or investigated the Conference House. Unexplainable shadows have been seen, along with apparitions of a young lady on the stair landing. Is it the rumored slave who was killed for rejecting Captain Billopp's advances? Or is it the young servant girl who died after breaking her neck in a fall on the stairs? Objects, especially old portraits, are found moved from their original location. Candles also get moved around and mysteriously snuffed out. Perhaps that too is the work of the servant girl's spirit, as she either signaled the troops of the colonel's return to his house or quickly snuffed out the evidence of her betrayal seconds before he confronted her about it. A feminine voice singing mournfully has been heard several times, as well as a woman's terrified scream. And a female apparition has been seen looking out of a second-floor window. A male apparition, believed to be a British soldier, has been seen, and people have felt someone tap them on the shoulder or tousle their hair.

The house seems to be haunted by several different ghosts, those of the young female slave girl who spurned the captain's advances or somehow provoked him to the point of murder by a hot poker, the servant girl the colonel believed had betrayed him, and at least one British soldier who was buried on the grounds when the basement kitchen was allegedly once used as a makeshift hospital and morgue. There are also stories of the child of a slave falling to her death long ago in a well on the property, and of a young boy who died of the plague and whose body was purportedly buried within the walls, out of necessity, to avoid detection of the family by British soldiers.

Rarely have I researched a historic house with so many legends associated with it. The problem with historical legends, however, is that they often consist of far less fact than fiction. Nevertheless, despite a lack of recorded history to substantiate many of the claims of murder and mayhem at the Conference House, the legends do provide as good an explanation as any for the paranormal activity so often reported there, and any house with such an extensive history has generally seen its share of tragedy and untimely deaths. Today the house and grounds are owned by the city of New York but operated and maintained by the Conference House Association, with the financial assistance of a number of public organizations interested in preserving the history and culture of Staten Island. The combined efforts of the community will ensure that the Conference House remains available for many future generations to appreciate.

Morris-Jumel Mansion

When Colonel Roger Morris, a retired British officer and loyalist, built what is now the two-story Morris-Jumel Mansion on the corner of West 160th Street and Edgecomb Avenue in 1765, it was a country house for him and his beautiful American wife, Mary Phillipse. The hilltop location at Washington Heights gave the couple an unencumbered view of the mainland, Long Island, Staten Island, and New Jersey. Mount Morris, as they called their property, was a prime location with a prime view, and it was those features that attracted General George Washington in 1776. It became a strategic military headquarters for Washington during the Revolutionary War, after the state of New York seized the estate of the general's old flame, who had rejected his advances twenty years earlier. It is rumored that Washington had fallen in love with Mary Phillipse two years before she married Colonel Morris, whose home the general subsequently commandeered. According to an 1897 *New York Times* article:

> Mary Phillipse was a great beauty, and her charming features, dark hair and eyes are said to have so impressed Washington, who met her at the house of Beverly Robinson, her brother-in-law, in this city in 1756, that it was difficult for him to leave her and return to

his home after he had transacted the business for which he came North. It is even said that she declined his suit, and, although his papers disprove the assertion, she no doubt will always be named among the women that Washington loved.

The Morrises moved to England, where they lived out the rest of their days after their property was confiscated. Washington lived at Mount Morris, which he called Fort Washington, in September and October 1776. He vacated the premises during the Battle of Harlem Heights, when his troops were forced to retreat from the British advance. After Washington's retreat from New York, British and Hessian commanders then occupied the house for a time. In 1790, when the mansion had become an inn and tavern for elite patrons, Washington—then president of the United States—returned for a visit with several esteemed guests and wrote in his diary, dated Saturday, July 10: "Having formed a party, consisting of the Vice President, his lady and son and Miss Smith, the Secretaries of State, Treasury, and War, and the ladies of the two latter, with all the gentlemen of my family, Mrs. Lear, and the two children, we visited the old position of Fort Washington, and afterward dined on a dinner provided by Mr. Marriner, at the house lately of Col. Roger Morris, but confiscated, and in the occupation of a common farmer."

The property changed hands several times, before John Jacob Astor acquired it from the Morris heirs in 1809 and subsequently sold it in 1810 to the wealthy French emigrant Stephen Jumel and his wife, Eliza. Jumel was a successful wine merchant and former Caribbean plantation owner. Eliza was a former prostitute, but she was described as "a beautiful blonde with a superb figure." The Jumels, along with eight male servants, returned the mansion to its original form—a stately, elegant private residence—and adorned it with French decor, including a couch bed that allegedly once belonged to Emperor Napoleon, who was a friend of theirs.

When Stephen Jumel died in 1832, under very suspicious circumstances, Eliza instantly became one of the richest women in New York. A year later, the fifty-eight-year-old widow married former vice president Aaron Burr, who was then seventy-seven years old, but that hasty union lasted only two years. The divorce actually became final on the very day that Burr died in 1836. Within a five-year span, she had lost two disillusioned husbands. Eliza never married again but remained on the estate, retaining ownership of the mansion until her death.

Eliza's life was fraught with mystery, rumors, and inconsistencies. A former curator of the Morris-Jumel Mansion, William Henry Shelton, attempted to set the record straight in his 1916 book, *The Jumel Mansion*. He said the accepted stories of Madam Jumel were untrue, "from the fantastic imaginings of a crazy woman who had sought all her life for social recognition." In truth, he said, she was not an heiress born at sea who was adopted after her mother died during childbirth, as she wanted people, including her first husband, to believe, so that she would be accepted into their social circle. In actuality, Shelton said Eliza's birth name was Betsy Bowen, and she was born in 1775, the daughter of Phebe Kelley Bowen, "a degraded and often vagrant woman, who, with her equally 'undesirable' husband—Betsy's father—had been expelled from the village of Providence." The curator said that Betsy and her sister left their mother "as they grew into womanhood, to vend their charms in another market, naturally drifting into the life in which they had been reared. Betsy Bowen had the reputation of being the handsomest girl in Providence." Because of her great beauty and charm, Betsy, who now went by Eliza, met "with many a social success" among French aristocrats when she visited her husband's native land. But in the States, she was frowned upon and not accepted by other socialites, yet seemingly adored by some of the most prominent and powerful men of the time. Such was the enigma of Eliza Jumel.

Court TV said that in her final years, "Eliza became reclusive, and she was a frightening sight to behold, with false teeth, unkempt hair, soiled clothing, and ungainly large feet. Finally, dementia took her and her babbling drove away even the staunchest relative." And an architectural historian who had studied the Morris-Jumel Mansion in 2002 said that there had been reports of an elderly, feeble-minded Eliza prancing around the grounds on horseback with a bunch of homeless men. She was ninety years old when she died in 1865, though a newspaper article the following year listed her age as ninety-six, because of inconsistencies in the stories she told of her life toward the end. After a lengthy litigation period, Eliza's estate, with bickering among heirs from both Stephen's and Eliza's families, was finally settled when a Judge Barrett, sitting in special term, ordered the property to be sold between October 1, 1891, and January 1, 1882, in parcels. To give you an idea of the widowed Eliza's wealth, her estate consisted of roughly 120 acres of land in Washington Heights, according to the *New York Times* in 1881. An article called "Fifteen Years in the Courts: The Jumel Estate to Be Sold and the Proceeds Divided" said the property included "1,400 city lots lying between 159th and 175th streets and the King's Bridge Road and Harlem River, and valuable water privileges in the Harlem River, and also of three lots and buildings at the northeast corner of Broadway and Liberty Streets." There was also prime real estate in Saratoga Springs.

In the late 1890s, after a series of careless tenants had inhabited the home, General Ferdinand P. and Lillie Earle purchased the house and called it Earle Cliff. General Earle, a proprietor of several well-known hotels, died at the mansion on January 2, 1902, at the age of sixty-three, following three years of declining health. His *New York Times* obituary said that "his death was due to heart disease. He became suddenly worse early yesterday morning and died after twelve hours of great suffering."

In 1903, the city of New York purchased the Morris-Jumel Mansion for about $200,000 and opened it as a museum the following year. Today the museum is owned by the New York City Department of Parks and Recreation. As the museum's website describes it:

> The first floor . . . features rooms for family and social gatherings, including the parlor in which Madame Eliza Jumel married Aaron Burr in 1833. Across the hall stands the dining room where George Washington entertained his guests in 1790. At the far end of the hall, the octagonal drawing room, or *with*drawing room, as it is properly known, provided a grand setting for social gatherings. Bedrooms on the second floor include those of George Washington, Eliza Jumel, and Aaron Burr. The basement houses the colonial-era kitchen and tells the story of domestic servitude at the Mansion.

Even if there were no ghost stories associated with the museum at all, it would still be an exciting place to visit. But there *are* ghost stories. According to the *New York Times*, "ghostly goings on" have been reported at the mansion since at least 1832, the year Jumel died. A 1981 article called "Belief in Ghost Haunts a Historic Mansion" said that even when the Jumels bought the mansion two hundred years ago, it was rumored to be haunted by a Hessian soldier. For that reason, Eliza persuaded Astor, from whom they purchased the house, to take $2,000 off the price of the mansion. Interestingly, in that same article, the museum director at the time denied the house was haunted, saying there were "simply troublesome people who think there are [ghosts]." Yet she inadvertently offered a telling thought. She said that she would occasionally have a "very unusual" phenomenon with four- and five-year-olds, with the children refusing to walk down the hall leading to the back room, insisting that "bad things" were down there. Children seem to be innately more open to sensing spirits than adults, so their fears shouldn't be automatically dismissed as silly or imaginary.

The museum's most famous ghost story occurred in January 1964, when a group of restless schoolchildren on the front lawn was told to shush by a blond woman on the second-floor balcony who was wearing a purple gown. She then turned and walked straight through the solid wood door—without ever opening it. On the outside chance that they were mistaken in what they thought they saw, they asked the curator about the strict woman, and they were told there was no such woman in the house. A current volunteer told me that some believe a former curator staged the appearance of the alleged spirit of Madame Jumel. If that's the case, how did she manage to walk straight through a closed door so effortlessly? Another time, a teacher hurried upstairs to the top floor, which is closed to the general public, and she was rewarded for her misdeed with a face-to-face encounter with a Revolutionary War soldier who seemed as though he stepped right out of a painting. Other ghosts have also been reported, such as Hessian soldiers and a maid who allegedly leaped to her death from the third-floor servants' quarters upon realizing her love affair with Stephen Jumel could go nowhere. But of all the spirits seen at the mansion, that of Aaron Burr is the hardest to pin down. It seems as if his ghost is all over New York state!

Stephen Jumel seems unable to rest in peace ever since he fell, or was pushed by Eliza, from a carriage and landed on a pitchfork, which gouged him. He may have survived had his bandages not somehow come undone during his sleep. Eliza may have allowed him to die so that she could enjoy the company of Aaron Burr, whom she married shortly after Jumel's tragic death. The 1964 *Times* article said Eliza had "become enamored of Aaron Burr" and somehow arranged for Stephen—twenty-five years her senior—to have an accident in a hay cart. The article said that according to some accounts, Eliza "stripped off [Stephen's] bandages and let him bleed to death." Besides Burr, she also purportedly enjoyed the company of Thomas Jefferson, Alexander Hamilton, and other rich and power political figures of the time. No wonder Stephen Jumel was turning over in his grave. The ghost that the schoolchildren saw is believed to have been Eliza. One news report had her telling the children to be quiet because her husband was "very ill." The female apparition people have reported wears a long purple gown or is dressed all in white. Footsteps also are heard going up and down the stairs when they appear to be empty.

In the great hall next to the museum's entrance is an old grandfather clock, and men of all ages have heard a female voice believed to be Eliza's telling them it's time to leave. Apparently the clock was one of Eliza's favorite pieces, and it still works. More than twenty men have reported hearing a woman's voice coming from somewhere near the clock, commanding them to leave or they will be harmed. Some have actually heeded the warning, but those who remained were not hurt. Those are the ones who sheepishly report such incidents to staff, worried that they'll be thought crazy.

To help determine who was haunting the house and why, in 1964, on the 132nd anniversary of Stephen Jumel's death, a séance was held at the Jumel House, presided over by the renowned paranormal author and investigator Hans Holzer. Holzer and the medium who accompanied him, Mrs. Myers, reportedly made contact with the spirits of Eliza and Stephen Jumel. According to the ghostbusting pair, Stephen was not happy about how his life had been prematurely terminated. He said that Eliza was responsible for his death and he had been buried alive. The spirit of Eliza was as obstinate as ever. Calling herself a lady, a point on which many would beg to differ, she said that if Holzer didn't go away, she would call the police.

As I finish writing this lengthier-than-usual ghost story, I just had something happen—twice—that has never occurred before while typing a story. The following three lines regarding Stephen Jumel's carriage accident appeared on my screen, repeating over and over, with none of the rest of the story anywhere to be seen:

"Stephen Jumel seems unable to rest in peace ever since he fell, or was pushed by Eliza, from a carriage and landed on a pitchfork, which gouged him. He may have survived had his bandages not somehow come undone during his sleep. Eliza may have allowed him to die so"

I leaned forward to be sure of what I was seeing, fearing that all my hard work was lost . . . or that I had somehow upset Eliza's ghost, but a moment later the same thing happened again with the following lines from above:

"how his life had been prematurely terminated. He said that Eliza was responsible for his death and he had been buried alive. The spirit of Eliza was as obstinate as ever. Calling herself a lady, a point on which many would beg to differ, she said that if Holzer didn't go away, she"

I'm sure it's nothing, but still, I can't help but wonder . . . so I think I'll wrap up this story quickly! In 1881, a *New York Times* article that was written while the Jumel property was still in litigation said, "It is to be feared that when the case is once settled . . . the beautiful acres may go into strange hands, and the fine old mansion go the way that so many mansions hereabout have gone, and fade away." As a member of the Historic House Trust, and under the watchful eye of Morris-Jumel Mansion, Inc., which maintains it, it's unlikely anyone has to worry about Manhattan's oldest house fading away anytime soon. And as far as its status as one of New York City's most haunted places, the volunteer I spoke with said that although she has never experienced anything paranormal at the museum, she did feel that the very fact that it has historically been known as a haunted house, even if it's not, is still an important part of its history. Well said. The museum is part of the Jumel Terrace Historic District and is open to the public Wednesdays through Sundays from 10 A.M. to 4 P.M.

Bowne House

In 1661, John Bowne built what has become the oldest house in Queens. In 1947, the New York City landmark opened to the public as a museum aptly called the Bowne House, where thousands of objects once owned by the John Bowne family and his descendants are on display. John Bowne immigrated to Boston in 1648, marrying into the affluent Feake family in 1656. He and his new wife, Hannah, converted to Quakerism—choosing a religion they felt most aligned with—but they were met with hostility in New England, finding that their spiritual beliefs were not popular there. So the determined young couple moved to Flushing, New York, where other Quakers had settled before them, hoping to find greater acceptance of their religious preferences.

Peter Stuyvesant, the Dutch governor of New Netherland when New York was under Dutch rule, was extremely intolerant of what he considered "objectionable minority religions." In 1656, he passed an ordinance stating that anyone providing a meeting house for Quakers for even one night was to be fined. It was clearly an infringement on the people's rights as set forth in the town charter, which guaranteed "liberty of conscience," so the citizens penned the historic Flushing Remonstrance—a declaration of religious freedom signed by the settlers—and sent it to the governor in protest. Their gesture had no effect on the pretentious governor, at least at that time. And when Stuyvesant found out that John Bowne was using his home as an actual Quaker meeting place in Flushing in 1662, he had Bowne picked up for "aiding and abetting" Quakerism. Bowne held fast to his principles and refused to pay the fine, keeping the remonstrance in the back of his mind.

In September that year, the governor dispatched his men to the Bowne residence, where John was tending to the ill and pregnant Hannah and their infant child. The men snatched the baby from his arms and dragged Bowne off and away from his family, "banishing" him to Holland for a trial before the Dutch West India Company, which ruled the colony of New Netherland. During his eighteen months of imprisonment, Bowne had plenty of time to think about what he would say to the judge at trial. So when his big chance finally came in 1664, he invoked the Flushing Remonstrance. A precursor to the Bill of Rights, the remonstrance was the major catalyst of religious tolerance in America, and because of it, Bowne was required to be set free and returned to his homestead in Flushing. Furthermore, the governor was ordered to cease all harassment of religious minorities in New Netherland. Bowne, by standing up for what he believed in, inadvertently paved the way for religious tolerance for all in our fledgling nation.

So the Bowne House at 37–01 Bowne Street is historic not only because it's the oldest house in Queens, but also because it is often considered the birthplace of religious freedom and tolerance in America. And just as Bowne refused to budge on his religious beliefs, he apparently refuses to budge from the old homestead he lived and died in as well. According to the Halloween 2000 issue of the *Southeast Queens Press*, a "Colonial-era spirit" has been seen and felt in the house, especially roaming the halls. In the 1997 Halloween issue of the *Daily News*, reporter Lorraine Diehl said, "A few years ago, a couple of tourists saw a ghost in what they described as an aura of 'miasmic' light, dressed in Colonial clothes and smiling at them" while visiting the Bowne House. Well, if we've learned anything about John Bowne, it's that he's never been one to be pushed around, even when it's his time to go. Perhaps he is as determined today as he was in 1662 not to be forced from his home and family.

Hannah died at home in 1678; the couple had been married for thirty years and had eight children in the home together. John Bowne remarried and had eight more children before he died in 1695, seventeen years after his beloved Hannah. After that, the Bowne Homestead remained in the Bowne and Parsons families for nine generations, until the Parsons family sold it to the Bowne House Historical Society, whose mission, according to the Bowne House website, "includes the preservation of the house, its contents and grounds for its historical and educational interest, for its significance to the history of New York and for its importance in the establishment in this country of the fundamental principles of freedom of conscience and religious liberty." Though the society continues to operate the museum as it has for more than sixty years, it transferred ownership to the New York State Department of Parks, Recreation and Historic Preservation to comply with Historic House Trust guidelines, paving the way for additional funding for continuing renovations. Interestingly, the president of the historical society is a twelfth-generation Bowne, Rosemary Veitor. So in a sense, the house is still in the family . . . and the original family perhaps is still in the house in the form of the ghost of John Bowne.

McCarren Park Pool

McCarren Park was chosen in 1936 by the Works Progress Administration as one of eleven sites citywide that would host an Olympic-size public swimming pool large enough to accommodate a whopping sixty-eight hundred bathers. The entrance to the site is on Lorimer, between Driggs Avenue and Bayard Street. During its forty-eight years of being open, at least three tragedies occurred, either in the pool or in the surrounding area, in three consecutive decades: the fifties, sixties, and the seventies. Then in 1984, the pool closed in anticipation of a foiled plan to restore it—along with the other ten such pools in the city—in time for their fiftieth anniversary. But the community voiced such opposition, over concerns that the restoration would bring undesirable traffic and crime into the Greenpoint district, that the plans were axed altogether, and the pool, by then surrounded by razor wire fencing, remained closed and neglected for more than twenty years.

Around 1992, rumors of the pool being haunted began to surface. Perhaps it's because it looked the part—so foreboding and desolate in its abandoned state. The most common rumor circulating is that a little girl drowned in the pool years ago, according to Jeff Belanger's 2005 *Encyclopedia of Haunted Places: Ghostly Locales from Around the World.* Though the entry, which was submitted by Dominick Villella of Paranormal Investigation of NYC, states that there "are no public records of deaths at McCarren Park pool," I did find several archived newspaper articles about two drownings and a murder that occurred many years ago. None of the three victims was a young girl, so claims of the girl ghost can't be substantiated. But that's not to say that there weren't other deaths that didn't make the news, or that there aren't other restless spirits floating around.

The June 28, 1952, *New York Times* ran an article called "Student Shot Dead in a Park Mystery," regarding a young man named Samuel Bernard London whose murderers ended up being a couple young hoodlums trying to impress each other. London was a twenty-three-year-old graduate rabbinical student who was returning home through McCarren Park after praying in memory of his mother. It was around 10 P.M. on the "hottest night of the year." When London was about "200 feet south of the corner of the park at Lorimer Street," a bullet from a .22-caliber rifle was fired and "passed into the victim's head from a point about two inches behind his right ear." He never saw it coming.

On September 2, 1969, Robert Mason, also twenty-three years old, climbed over the fence that surrounded McCarren Park Pool and "failed to reappear, according to his friends." At 2:30 A.M., his friends notified the police, who recovered the body in sixteen feet of water at the bottom of the pool.

And exactly twenty-five years after the first tragic death, that of Samuel London, the *Times* ran an article titled "Boy Dies in Brooklyn Pool." On June 28, 1977, a fourteen-year-old boy named Vernon Weiderhold climbed over the fence and into McCarren Park to go for a swim in the public pool with two friends. At 3:30 A.M., it was reported that he had drowned.

Along with numerous eyewitness claims that a child has been seen or heard calling for help—perhaps the young boy who drowned?—scientific findings of paranormal investigators have revealed drastic temperature drops, erratic electromagnetic field readings, and evidence of spirit energy in photographs.

In 2006, Clear Channel Entertainment and Live Nation joined forces to refurbish McCarren Park Pool as an outdoor concert venue, a popular attraction today. And Mayor Michael Bloomberg recently announced plans to restore and reopen the pool, considered a historic cultural landmark, within the next couple years as a functioning public pool once again, as part of his twenty-five-year plan for a "greener New York."

Danforth House

A woman going by the assumed name of Mrs. Dartway Crawley visited the police station the day before her own murder, distraught at having seen a seedy woman from her past named Estelle Ridley at the foot of her bed the night before. She became even more distraught after the police informed her that Ridley had hanged herself in her jail cell years earlier, so it wasn't possible that she had been seen at the foot of anyone's bed. But there was no doubt in Mrs. Crawley's mind that it was Ridley she saw, which meant that she was being stalked by an angry spirit. Mrs. Crawley decided then and there that she would leave town the next morning and return to England to escape the vengeful ghost. But the next morning never came for her. The legend is that Ridley returned from the dead and stuffed a phantom doll's head down Crawley's throat, killing her and ensuring that she would never again open her big mouth, getting someone into trouble like she'd done to Ridley.

It began in the mid-1860s, when Mrs. Ada Danforth and the young "Fanchon Moncare" made regular trips between Paris and their "summer home" on Staten Island, a mansion overlooking the Kill Van Kull channel near the Bayonne Bridge and the site of the Old Bergen Point Ferry. To customs personnel and passengers, the two seemed agreeable enough—a well-dressed nanny with her courteous little charge. But it was all an act. The "child" was well spoken for her age—perhaps too well spoken, in hindsight—but though she seemed wise beyond her years, she held her china doll clutched tightly to her chest at all times, as little girls do. Hence, to outward appearances, the doll was nothing more than her security blanket. Customs officials and neighbors in Port Richmond wouldn't learn for some time that the little girl was actually a notorious forty-year-old former sideshow midget with a penchant for stealing jewels. Her real name was Estelle Ridley, and Ada Danforth was her accomplice in crime. The two were jewel thieves who smuggled jewels and stolen cash between Paris and New York City by hiding them inside the doll's head. Customs officials never considered that the innocent, childlike "Fanchon" could actually be a hardened criminal, so it hadn't crossed their minds to search the doll's head.

Once back in the States, the women could relax as long as they were paying their dues to members of the corrupt Tweed Ring, which consisted of influential city officials who pilfered more than $200 million from the city coffers between 1865 and 1871. Besides city officials, the ring also included city news media, court officials, judges, and district attorneys. William Marcy "Boss" Tweed was at the helm of Tammany Hall—the smooth-running Democratic political engine that was so instrumental at the time in controlling New York City politics, even if it was through criminal means. Like other New York City criminals at the time, Ada Danforth and Estelle Ridley simply paid the Tweed Ring a fee to look the other way, allowing them to continue their illegal activities while living lavishly on Staten Island.

Most New Yorkers were unaware of Tweed's activities or the fact that his ring was effectively bankrupting the city's treasury. The public was smitten by Tweed's lofty status, and for a time, he could do no wrong. Before the ring was busted and dissolved, a *New York Times* article dated December 28, 1870, described a large diamond pin valued at $15,500 that Tweed's "friends" had given him, saying, "It will no doubt cast a reflection of light upon the Tammany Party that will dazzle the eyes of the Young Democracy, and blind the Republicans by a Democratic victory in 1872." One can't help but wonder if the so-called "friends" who gave the Boss the pin could have been Ridley and Danforth.

When she wasn't disguised as Fanchon Moncare, Estelle Ridley had no scruples. She was said to be promiscuous, wicked, and hot-tempered, and she often drank or gambled her wealth away at the racetrack, with the attitude that she could easily get more where that came from. Ridley met a woman named Magda Hamilton at the racetrack, and the two hit it off immediately, realizing their shared interests. Both had ties to the Tweed Ring, Hamilton on a more intimate level than Ridley, and both were open to a new unlawful venture. Against the wishes of Ada Danforth, who tried to tell Ridley she would regret the unfamiliar partnership with Hamilton, the new crime pair left for Illinois, where they easily robbed a wealthy, widowed old man. But when they returned to Staten Island, the arrogant Ridley was willing to give Hamilton only $5,000 out of the $350,000 they had stolen. Ridley justified her actions by claiming the burglary had been her idea, so she should get most of it. It was a mistake that would seal her fate—and ultimately that of Hamilton, who stormed out of the Staten Island mansion swearing that Ridley hadn't seen the last of her.

At the end of summer that year, Danforth and Ridley returned once again to France. Growing increasingly brazen by the day, the pair hired a man to rob the very rich Vicomte de Point Talbiere at an opera house in Marseilles. When the botched robbery led to the man's beating death, Ridley and Danforth knew the investigation would eventually point to them, as they had been seen in public with the murdered man shortly before his untimely death. With blood on their hands—and a doll's head brimming with stolen jewels—the two quickly departed for New York, certain that Tweed's Ring would help them avoid capture.

But this time, as the ferry docked and the women, playing their usual roles of nanny and child, disembarked, they were taken into custody by several policemen who had been tipped off by Magda Hamilton. At their trial, in exchange for a leaner sentence, Ada Danforth offered information about the inner workings of the Tweed Ring and the money bribes they were forced to pay to continue their illicit activities. It had recently been revealed that the ring had nearly bankrupted the city, and Danforth's insights and accusations were simply more icing on the cake. Eventually Tweed was sentenced to prison, where he died in 1876.

Ada Danforth was initially sentenced to twenty years, and Ridley was sentenced to life in prison for being the mastermind. But Danforth's cooperation at the trial led to her early release on parole after just three years. With a small fortune the bank somehow had not confiscated from her account, she was able to live well for the rest of her life. On the other hand, Estelle Ridley heard through the prison grapevine that her archenemy, Magda Hamilton, had bought her house on Staten Island. And what's worse, Hamilton had changed her name to Mrs. Dartway Crawley, the local gambler whose affection both women had sought. Hamilton hadn't really married him, but taking his name was another jab to an already fuming Ridley. For a number of years, Crawley enjoyed the sweet revenge she had inflicted on Ridley, just as she'd promised she would when she told Ridley the woman hadn't seen the last of her.

But then came the night of her mysterious murder. There had been no signs of forced entry into the house. There *were* signs, however, of an object being forced down her throat. When police found Mrs. Crawley's body, her jaw was locked open. A look of unspeakable terror was frozen on her face, and she had choked on her own blood, caused by a violent trauma to her throat from a large object. Though no sign of a murder weapon was ever found, several pieces of doll's hair were said to be in her mouth—the only clue to a brutal, baffling murder. With that, the evil Ridley got the last laugh after all.

New York University

Washington Square Park is smack in the center of the New York University (NYU) campus. Seeing it today, with students and staff strolling about the grounds, it's hard to imagine the thousands of remains buried underfoot. Most were victims of the deadly cholera epidemic of the 1800s, which necessitated mass burials, but others were hanged there before being buried in what was New York City's central potter's field until 1819. Because of its morbid history, the *New York Times* said in 1981 that Washington Square Park is inhabited by ghosts. But there's another place on campus with an equally tragic past. A horrific disaster occurred in NYU's Brown Building on March 25, 1911.

The Triangle Shirtwaist Factory Fire claimed the lives of 146 mostly female employees between the ages of thirteen and twenty-three. The Brown Building, on the northwest corner of Washington Place and Greene Street, was known then as the Asch Building, and it had been designed as an example of "modern" fireproof construction when it was built in 1901. But on the day of the fire, the building became a colossal brick oven when, as on every other day, the exit doors were bolted shut to prevent workers from leaving early. Management exclusively had the keys to open them, but they escaped at the first sign of smoke, with complete disregard for their employees. The Shirtwaist Factory was located on the top three floors of the ten-story building. When panicking workers realized the doors were locked, they headed for the fire escape, but it collapsed under the weight of too many, sending countless young women hurtling to the pavement far below. And when the elevator seized up, others, in desperation, tried to climb down the cables, plunging to their death in the elevator shaft, crushing each other as they landed in heaps below. Within fifteen minutes, fire had consumed all three floors.

Seven years after the tragedy, NYU leased and remodeled the ninth floor, where most of the victims had been trapped. A year later, the university leased the tenth floor, and in 1929, it acquired the entire building, renaming it the Frederick Brown Building. Today a memorial plaque marks the corner of the building at 23–29 Washington Place, where so many young people perished. Students who have had classes in the building report the occasional muted sense of desperation, like a desire to escape and get outdoors quickly to take a deep breath.

NYU was founded in 1831, and the earliest classes were held in Clinton Hall. The land on the east side of Washington Square was purchased in 1833 for the university, and the Old University Building was built. But when the Washington Square campus became congested, a larger campus, University Heights, was opened in the Bronx. For some time, it was the base of NYU operations. In the 1970s, NYU was forced to sell University Heights as a result of financial hardship, but the Washington Square campus was spared. A period of revitalization and rising popularity followed the merging of University College with the Washington Square College to form NYU as we know it today. Ranked "America's #1 dream school" by *Princeton Review*, NYU is one of the premier research universities in the country. It is also the country's largest private university and one of the largest landholders in New York City. The campus encompasses Washington Square Park, as well as Union Square Park in the trendy Greenwich Village. With the magnitude of people passing through—sixteen thousand employees and roughly fifty-one thousand students annually—is it any wonder there are ghost stories on this campus?

The Old University Building was allegedly haunted by a young artist whose spirit was heard pacing through the hallways. And the *San Francisco Chronicle* in 1880 said the building had "an evil repute with the servant girls of the neighborhood . . . [who] have a notion that deep in the sub cellars be corpses, skeletons, and other dreadful things." Not such a far stretch to fathom, considering that the nearby potter's field in Washington Square Park was filled with just such skeletons and undoubtedly dreadful things.

The NYU Library at Washington Square South is a stop on the "Ghosts of Greenwich Village" tour, and though the building isn't nearly as old as many other buildings on campus, it has suffered several fairly recent student suicides, which tend to spur rumors of hauntings on campuses across the country. Brittany Residence Hall at 55 East Tenth Street is one of the university's better-known haunted buildings. Built in 1929 as the Brittany Hotel, it had a penthouse that served as a speakeasy during Prohibition. Today that area is the student lounge. Before it became a dorm, guests at the Brittany Hotel included the late Jerry Garcia of the Grateful Dead. Besides the common subtle signs of a haunting, such as feeling as if they are being watched, residents of Brittany Hall report hearing unexplainable footsteps and music that has no traceable source. Finally, there's the Third Avenue North Residence Hall, with its doors that rattle and shake or slam shut—all of which could be brushed off as wind or subways or other environmental factors. But what about the doors that lock themselves, or the objects that levitate or move by themselves?

The bottom line is, regardless of NYU's current glory days, the campus and surrounds have witnessed some very dark times in its history, and if ever a place has reason to be haunted, it's this one.

Dakota Apartment Building

Time magazine in 1979 reported that the Dakota, a well-known upscale apartment building on the northwest corner of 72nd Street and Central Park West, had several purported ghosts. Indeed, John Lennon and Yoko Ono—both known for their open-mindedness regarding such things—are reported to have held a séance in their apartment at the Dakota to contact deceased tenants. According to *Mersey Beat*'s Bill Harry, Lennon once claimed to have seen the ghost of a woman crying as she walked down the hallway. Later Lennon—the dreamer and the peacemaker—was assassinated by a deranged fan as he entered the Dakota on December 8, 1980. The John sightings began almost immediately. Some people claimed to have seen his spirit at the building's front entrance, where in one case it looked so alive that the couple who saw it almost approached it. Others said they saw him inside the building, including one source that said Yoko Ono allegedly saw him sitting at his piano in their apartment, as if to comfort her.

Though the building has always been well known in celebrity circles, the general public became aware of it following the release of Roman Polanski's hit horror flick *Rosemary's Baby*. Polanski filmed the outdoor scenes in front of the Dakota, but interior footage, contrary to popular belief, was filmed on a stage in Hollywood. According to wikipedia.com, filming inside the building is prohibited. But the cult classic instantly altered the public perception of the Dakota. What had always been considered a lavish and awe-inspiring structure suddenly was recognized as a backdrop of horror—at least on film. So when reports of the spirit of a little girl emerged, it seemed quite believable that such a historic old place was haunted. The girl, wearing nineteenth-century clothing, reportedly said, "Today is my birthday," to a Dakota employee. It seems that ghosts often return on important occasions, such as birthdays, anniversaries, and dates of death.

The Upper West Side was sparsely populated when construction of the lavish tenement began in 1880. Nevertheless, Singer Sewing Machine mogul Edward Clark went out on a limb to finance the project. He named his crown jewel the Dakota because it reminded him of the Dakota Territory of the time, being in a remote area away from the mainstream population. Of course, all of that changed quickly. But luckily for Clark, instead of the isolated location scaring off potential renters, the 1880s view of his apartments rising over Central Park West attracted enough wealthy tenants who reserved apartments during construction that the Dakota was filled to capacity before it ever opened.

Since that day long ago, celebrities including Judy Garland, Lauren Bacall, Gilda Radner, U2's Bono, Paul Simon, Maury Povich, and John Lennon and Yoko Ono have resided at the Dakota. In fact, you can take in the grandeur of the Dakota—and walk in the footsteps of the late John Lennon—directly across the street at Strawberry Fields, a poignant garden memorial in Central Park dedicated to him.

Ear Inn

The Ear Inn at 326 Spring Street was built in 1817, making it among the oldest bars in Manhattan, although it didn't actually start serving beer until the 1890s. The three-story building that now houses the Ear Inn bar and restaurant is also known as the James Brown House, for its original owner. Brown was a man of color who fought in the American Revolution, before settling in at the house and selling tobacco. Legend has it that Brown is the black man depicted in Leutze's painting "Washington Crossing the Delaware," and that he served under Washington. In 1833, Brown sold his house to a couple pharmaceuticals merchants.

In 1888, grocer William Hays sold the building to George Vestner, who rented its rooms out to local craftsmen and their families. Then, shortly after, it was bought by Thomas Cloke, who, along with his brother, turned it into a "watering hole" for longshoremen. They also made whiskey and beer and sold it to ships on the Hudson waterfront, before the waterfront was moved westward by the massive amounts of landfill that have reshaped the topography of New York City. During Prohibition, the building again changed hands, becoming a speakeasy and a dive called the Green Door. It was also during that time that the Holland Tunnel was built, running directly under the Brown House. In 1969 the Landmarks Preservation Commission designated the house a historic landmark.

In 1973, R. I. P. Hayman and another student who were renting rooms on the upper floor of the house found out the place was going up for sale and bought it. They fixed it up on a limited income, as both were of modest means at the time, and they probably weren't altogether sure the building could withstand major structural changes to its ancient frame. One of the first things they did was to slap some black paint over the right half of the letter "B" on their neon "Bar" sign, making it look like "Ear"— a simple, ingenious way of changing the name of their place without buying a whole new sign. Business was once again booming at the old James Brown House, thanks in no small part to visits from John Lennon and Salvador Dali. Hayman still owns the Ear Inn today.

The reputation of being haunted hasn't slowed business down any at the Ear Inn. Mickey the sailor is the ghost of a former regular. He apparently loves the ladies and has been known to pinch an occasional female derriere in the bar—so ladies, please refrain from slapping the face of the hapless guy passing by, who's probably innocent. Mickey also is accused of shaking the beds of female boarders in the rooms upstairs. It's all harmless stuff—more humorous than frightening. Camera and cell phone batteries draining quickly and electrical equipment malfunctioning are the most common phenomena. Such paranormal activity may be annoying at times, but it's well tolerated by staff and customers. After all, every respectable New York City pub from that era is expected to have a resident ghost of Mickey's caliber.

Most Holy Trinity Church

Father John Stephen Raffeiner was born in Austria in 1785 and practiced medicine in the Napoleonic Wars of the early 1800s before realizing his true calling in 1825, when he became an ordained priest. At the prime of his life, he received word from the States that priests were sorely needed to minister the growing German immigrant population in the Brooklyn area. In 1836, Father Raffeiner, having made a small fortune as a physician, used his wealth to establish the oldest German church in the New York diocese, St. Nicholas Parish. Then, in 1841, he established the Most Holy Trinity Roman Catholic Church, a simple frame building on Montrose Avenue in which he lived in the basement.

In 1850, after the Reverend John Raufeisen succeeded him, a larger church was built on a parochial burial ground at the corner of Montrose and Graham Avenues to accommodate the growing congregation. The remains of *most* of those buried there were transferred to a lot adjacent to the Evergreen Cemetery, where today stands a parish school building that was built in 1877. The legend is that though all of the existing tombstones were transferred, not necessarily all of the remains were moved from the original burial ground, leaving some restless souls behind searching for their grave markers. The lights in the school are said to go on and off, unexplained voices and footsteps are heard by janitorial staff when they're alone in the building, and so on.

The Holy Trinity Church that you see today—the one the church itself says is haunted—is the third and final one, which held its first service in 1882. The church's website states that because of so many inquiries regarding their alleged ghosts, they decided to share the most popular legends "solely for entertainment purposes." Their website tells of secret passageways, false closets, and tunnels on the triforium level, which were used for runaway Southern slaves escaping to the North via the Underground Railroad. Beneath the church is the crypt housing both Raffeiner and Father May, a pastor who died in his sleep in his bedroom on the second floor in 1895. That room, now a guest room, is believed by those who have slept in it to be haunted. Guests say they hear the sound of someone pacing the floor beside them in the middle of the night. Others have heard loud, very distinctive footsteps in the rectory's staircase, and dogs react to something unseen on the stairs leading to the basement.

In 1897, the cold, calculated murder of sexton George Stelz took place at Holy Trinity Church. He was slaughtered in the church vestibule as he descended the stairs after ringing the church bell one late-summer evening. The poor boxes had been emptied, and Stelz's personally engraved watch was missing. Though he had been struck viciously in the head seven times in the struggle, the cause of death was determined to be strangulation. Three days before Halloween, police arrested Constantine Steiger for killing a police officer during a botched robbery attempt in another city church. He had in his possession Stelz's watch. Steiger was convicted of murder for the killing of the police officer but refused to admit that he had killed Stelz several months earlier, despite overwhelming evidence suggesting that he had. As a result, nobody was ever held accountable in Stelz's slaying. Stelz's blood, the legend goes, now continues to appear on the wall in the stairway to the bell tower, and his spirit is believed to roam the building, occasionally ringing the bell as if to remind people he's still here, waiting for a justice that can never come.

Vanderbilt Mausoleum

Who wants to live and die an inordinately rich man when even his remains have to be protected by such extraordinary expedients as this: Every fifteen minutes each clock placed in the Vanderbilt tomb is visited by a Pinkerton detective, two of whom are constantly on guard. One of these detectives patrols outside the tomb, while the other is locked *in and behind the bars* with a loaded repeating rifle across his knee ready for instant use. It would be next to impossible for any robber to get away with the remains of William H. Vanderbilt so long as the tomb is protected as it is now. The Pinkerton men are hired by the year, and there is quite a little colony of them established on Staten Island very near the mausoleum.

—*Iowa State Reporter*, May 28, 1891

Such is the life—and death—of the exceedingly rich and famous, and it all began with one man. Cornelius Vanderbilt was born in 1794 and married Sophia Johnson, his cousin, when he was only nineteen. Thirteen children were born to the couple, including William Henry, who built the famous mausoleum at Staten Island's largest burial ground, Moravian Cemetery, at 2205 Richmond Road. Shortly before Sophia died, Cornelius met a beautiful clairvoyant named Tennessee Claflin, who offered him "magnetic healing" and otherworldly insight. Christine Wicker, author of *Lily Dale: The True*

Story of the Town That Talks to the Dead, speculated that Vanderbilt had become so trusting of clairvoyants like Claflin that he may have based some of his business decisions on their advice—*may* being the key word.

Vanderbilt built his empire on the shipping and railroad industries, through old-fashioned hard work and persistence, but he did allegedly trust divine insight and guidance. And he had always believed that portraits provided an ethereal connection to the dead, so he carried a diminutive portrait of his deceased mother at all times in his pocket, according to Wicker. Because of that belief, some say the commodore proved his theory by manipulating photographs from beyond the dead that visitors took at the family mausoleum.

After his wife passed on, Cornelius purportedly proposed to Claflin, whom some sources refer to as his mistress. When she rejected him, he married instead his distant cousin, the thirty-two-year-old Ms. Crawford, in 1869. Eight years later, Cornelius Vanderbilt died, leaving more than nine-tenths of his $100 million fortune to his son William Henry, whom he believed to be best suited to protect and maintain the family fortune. The other tenth was divided among his daughters, his wife, the Church of the Strangers, and Vanderbilt University. His other sons were left out of the will, allegedly prompting one to commit suicide. But William Henry, as expected, doubled the Vanderbilt family fortune.

Still, when he hired the famous architect Richard Morris to design the mausoleum in 1885, he insisted on making the design large but simple. In fact, he rejected Morris's first attempt at a design, saying the Vanderbilts were "plain, quiet, unostentatious people" who wouldn't want to be buried in anything as "showy" as Morris's initial design, according to *The Vanderbilts and the Story of Their Fortune,* by William Augustus Croffut. At the time Vanderbilt made that statement in 1885, he was the richest man in the United States, but tragically, he ended up dying the same year, before the mausoleum was ever finished. Two years after his death, the mausoleum was nearly completed, and you can see from the following description in the September 22, 1887, Statesville, North Carolina, *Landmark* the scope of the project:

For some months—in fact since May—very extensive improvements have been going on at the approaches to the Vanderbilt mausoleum on Staten Island. That tomb is going to be one of the sights
of the country. Several hundred Italians and twenty-five teams have
been at work leveling five acres of land. Hundreds of trees, which
have heretofore obstructed the view, have been cut down. Around
the mausoleum they are building a handsome stone wall. The space
within the wall is to be turned into a beautiful garden. It will be some
time yet before these improvements will be completed; but the great
monument can now be seen from the decks of vessels miles out at
sea. Pinkerton's detectives watch the place continually to see that
no one steals the body of William H. Vanderbilt.

The Vanderbilt contribution to the Moravian Cemetery goes far
beyond their impressive family mausoleum, though. Between the
commodore and William Henry, the Vanderbilt men donated
twelve and a half acres of land to the cemetery, as well as the cemetery's superintendent's house. The mausoleum, which replicates a
French Romanesque church, is said to be the largest private family tomb in the nation, but it's a fitting memorial for a family of such
stature. When it was built, it was designed to hold seventy-two
coffins in its vaults and even more under the floor. But regardless
of its expansiveness, there were strict guidelines as to who could
be buried in the tomb. Admittance was limited, per William Henry,
to male Vanderbilts, their wives, and only the unmarried daughters. Married daughters and their husbands and children, who did
not share the Vanderbilt name, could be buried on the family's
grounds, but not actually in the mausoleum. The remains of Cornelius, the family patriarch, were transplanted to the tomb upon
its completion.

On June 11, 1967, a twenty-four-year-old woman was crushed
to death as she attempted to close the fifteen-foot-tall iron gate at
the tomb, and—probably as a result of aging and weathering—it
came off its old hinges, falling on top of her. At the time, the tomb
was a popular attraction, and the woman and her sisters had just
visited their own relative's grave nearby. Because of that tragic incident, coupled with intentional vandalism, the Vanderbilt plot has
been closed to the public since the 1970s. But before it was closed,

the tomb was said to be haunted. Many people reported taking photographs that had people in them, even though nobody had been seen in the viewfinder when the pictures were taken, and vice versa—people who *were* standing in front of the tomb when the pictures were taken were *not* in the developed film, or so they say. The fact that the commodore believed photographs provided a bridge to communicate with the dead made some wonder if he were somehow responsible for the frequently reported photographic anomalies.

Flushing Town Hall

For its first three years, the Flushing Town Hall, built in downtown Flushing in 1862, served as an assembly point for Union recruits during the Civil War. In the late 1800s, the building was expanded to accommodate the Flushing Opera House and Theatre, where such names as Tom Thumb and P. T. Barnum took to the great stage of the grand ballroom. Not only was it a hub of community activity, but it then became a venue for artistic expression and the performing arts as well. In the same time period, the end of the nineteenth century, the town hall and opera house were being converted into a municipal courthouse, which opened in 1902, with a jail following in 1904.

In 1898, when Flushing ceased being a town (since Queens County, where Flushing was located, became part of the borough of Queens), a town hall, per se, was no longer needed. But the handsome two-story Romanesque Revival building at the corner of Linden Place and Northern Boulevard continued serving its community in other capacities: as a courthouse until the early 1960s, a venue for community events, a bank (in the lobby), and the headquarters of Flushing's Department of Sanitation. In 1967, the Landmarks Preservation Commission declared the Flushing Town Hall to be an official landmark, thus sparing it from being turned into a parking lot. But by 1972, when the unoccupied building was placed on the National Register of Historic Places, it had fallen into a state of disrepair and neglect and was invaded by homeless people. Then in 1976, it was saved by a local resident who acquired a thirty-year lease from the city to restore the building and convert it into a dinner theater. That was when the first ghost sightings were reported.

Periods of renovation and remodeling often seem to increase paranormal activity in places already prone to unexplained phenomena. So it's not surprising that work crews actually saw a radio on the other side of a room they were plastering turn itself on—not once, but twice, according to a 2006 *Queens Gazette* article by reporter Liz Goff, called "Settling Queens." Reports soon followed of unexplained music emanating from the empty ballroom and an apparition of a Civil War soldier whom several construction workers saw climb onstage in the seventies. They subsequently refused to stay in the building alone after that incident. The rumor mill says that it's the impresario—the head honcho—of the Flushing Opera House, who was allegedly pulled from his duties when he was called off to war. Although he vowed to return after the Civil War to take up his duties, he was killed in action. And though he never returned physically to his beloved opera hall, many believe that his spirit has returned, taking its rightful place near the stage in the concert hall.

At any rate, several years and half a million dollars later, when the restaurateur's venture failed, the lease was transferred to a businessman who used part of the building for his insurance business and leased the remainder for office space. When he died in 1988, the city sought to break the thirty-year lease because of the vacant building's deteriorating condition. In 1990, their wish was granted, and the Flushing Council on Culture and the Arts was tasked with the job of creating and managing a community center for visual and performing arts there. Thanks to the ensuing multimillion-dollar renovation, the building reopened to the public in 1993 and now houses a spacious concert hall and theater, art galleries featuring the works of local artists, a visitors center with a classroom, office space, and a large garden that doubles as an outdoor venue. In other words, the Flushing Town Hall is once again a hub of community activity and artistic expression, just as it was in days of old. The impresario should be quite happy with the changes.

New Amsterdam Theatre

Olive Thomas was a beauty queen, having won a contest as the "Most Beautiful Girl in New York City," and a former Ziegfeld Follies girl who went on to become a silent film star. She died of mysterious causes in 1920 and was found holding a blue medicine bottle in her hand. According to Robert Viagas's article "The Ghosts of Broadway," in the June 10, 2005, *New York Times*, her last words may have been, "My God, what have I done?" He said she was celebrating a second honeymoon in a Paris hotel with her husband, Jack Pickford, and after partying late into the night, she swallowed the mercury bichloride pills that her husband used to treat his syphilis. The question, of course, was why would she swallow a whole blue bottle of coffin-shaped pills if she only intended to take her usual dosage of sleeping pills? Newspaper articles at the time of her death offer a different version of events. According to an article titled "Olive Thomas near Death," in the September 9, 1920, *New York Times*:

> At the American Hospital at Neuilly-sur-Seine, where she is a patient, only the slightest hopes are entertained for the recovery of Olive Thomas, the American motion-picture actress, who in private life is Mrs. Jack Pickford. As a result of a dose of poisonous medicine which she drank on last Sunday morning, she has lost the power of speech and sight and the doctors are fighting a stern battle for her life . . . As she has been unable to talk since she took the poison, Miss Thomas has not been able to explain how she came to make the mistake of drinking from the bottle, which was plainly marked . . . Jack Pickford was at the hospital all day and most of the night, and in his distress at the tragic accident, declines to give any particulars.

So, although some more modern accounts have her swallowing a bottle of pills, articles written at the time of her demise—which are probably more accurate—have her drinking a bottle of clearly marked poison. A September 10 "Special Cable to the *New York Times*" said: "Olive Thomas died at 10:15 o'clock this morning . . . She had been in a state of coma since yesterday evening and the end was without pain. The medical report of the doctor in charge of the case ascribes death to acute nephritic inflammation.

Miss Thomas was certified as perfectly well a few weeks ago for a heavy insurance policy by the same doctor who later attended her to the end." A "heavy insurance policy"? Interesting. On September 11, 1920, a *Times* article titled "Investigate Death of Olive Thomas" told of "cocaine orgies" and "champagne dinners" that may have played a role in the death.

Investigators interviewed a number of people, but they were up against a brick wall trying to get information out of Olive's husband. He repeatedly refused to speak to them or even provide his account of the events leading up to her death, which was very frustrating—and very suspicious—to the investigators. Another article on September 12, 1920, titled "Miss Thomas' Death Found Accidental," said that contrary to some theories, no evidence of depression was found, "but how she took [the] poison remains unexplained." After five days of "excruciating torture," during which she was left speechless and blind, "she seemed to be warding off with her hands the spectre of death which haunted her bedside. The fatal bottle from which she had drunk became a nightmare to her." Then, saying it was still unknown how she had come to drink from the bottle of poison, the reporter offered that it "may have been that she was seeking some sleeping draught and by a mistake not easy to explain and of which she was never able to furnish an explanation, she picked up the bottle which contained a preparation of mercury bichloride. Her screams when it burned her roused her husband, and it was not long before medical attention was summoned. The mouth burns prevented her giving a full explanation of how she came to make the mistake." But the amount of poison she drank was lethal. "Until unconsciousness came in the last hours, she suffered untold agony, made worse by her mental anguish."

The mystery surrounding the moments leading up to her death has never been satisfactorily solved. Had she committed suicide? Had it been an accident that occurred in a drunken state? Or had someone poured the poison down the sleeping woman's throat? Why hadn't her husband wanted to share "any particulars" of the events of that night with authorities? For fear that they might suspect him, even if he had nothing to feel guilty about? Had he pushed her over the edge? All that is known for certain about her death is that she died far too young, and at the height of her career, under very mysterious, unsolved conditions—and she was buried in a white gown with silver trim.

In 1995, Walt Disney and Company took over a number of theaters on Broadway, including the New Amsterdam Theatre on West 42nd Street. The New Amsterdam was built in 1903 and was once owned by Florez Ziegfeld, creator of the famed Ziegfeld Follies. It seems that Ziegfeld's onetime mistress, Olive Thomas, began haunting the theater even before Disney's renovation. But her style of haunting was far more spectacular than the simple closing and opening of doors and such. With a flair for drama, she made her presence known in an unmistakable way. Employees—especially janitors, security guards, and projectionists—and audience members alike were graced by her spectral presence. She was often reported as a woman in a white gown with silver trim, like the one Olive was buried in, in the balcony late at night, holding a medicine bottle in her hand. At least one person saw her on the stage; another watched her apparition glide right through a window and out onto 42nd Street.

During renovations, construction workers often reported seeing a beautiful woman wandering about the theater, wearing a sash that said "Olive" and a beaded, green Follies dress and headpiece. You can't get more direct than that. They said the woman appeared so solid that they had no idea she was a ghost. They were also unaware that the costume they described the apparition as wearing was easily identified, by those in the know, as a Follies costume. And what of the large, blue bottle they saw her holding? That made more sense to them, once they were told what she was holding when her body was found in her Paris hotel room. A security guard once spotted what he called "a beautiful young woman" in the theater at 2:30 A.M. She was dressed just like the woman the construction workers saw—the green, beaded dress; the sash; the Follies headband—and carried a blue medicine bottle. When he yelled to her, because obviously nobody was supposed to be in the building at that hour, he watched in horror as she walked straight through the solid wall onto 41st Street. He called his supervisor and resigned.

Olive seems to be having fun in her current form, at least. In 1997, men who encountered the ghost said she actually flirted with them, saying, "Hi, fella!" Those who work there believe Olive still watches over her old domain, where she was the sweetheart of the stage. She makes her presence known on a regular basis, but mostly after-hours . . . and mostly to the boys, who seem to appreciate her unusual good looks, even if they aren't entirely solid.

Fordham University

Fordham University's Queen's Court consists of three buildings—St. John's Hall, St. Robert's Hall, and Bishop's Hall—which are among the most haunted on this Bronx campus. St. John's Hall is the earliest part of the university, built in 1844 as the Archdiocese of New York, and it became part of St. John's College (later named Fordham University) in 1860, when it was combined with other early structures on the campus. During construction of St. John's Hall, a private burial ground was discovered on farmland that had belonged to the Corsa family and is now occupied by the university. Andrew Corsa, for whom Corsa Avenue was named, was the same age as freshman and sophomore university students when he volunteered to guide George Washington, the Comte de Rochambeau, and the allied U.S.-France army of five thousand troops to survey British defenses around Manhattan just prior to the Grand Reconnaissance on July 21, 1781. The circular garden behind St. John's Hall marks the Corsa family's burial grounds.

In the summer of 2003, the only people occupying Queen's Court, the university's first-year residential college, were five resident assistants (RAs) and one residence hall director for each hall. Their task was to complete reports on the condition of each outgoing freshman's room and prepare the rooms for incoming students. The first floor of St. Robert's Hall, built in 1940, was experiencing a strange phenomenon with the mattresses in one particular room. Every time the RAs entered the room in question, they found the mattresses of both beds leaning upright against the wall, instead of on the box springs where they should have been.

At first they thought someone must be playing a practical joke on them. After all, college campuses are rife with tales of the unexplained. But nobody would admit to it. So a determined RA went to extremes to make sure nobody could get into the room again, locking the door after placing the mattresses where they belonged. An hour later, just to make sure his plan worked, he returned to the room, only to find the mattresses once again leaning up against the wall. But that was nothing compared with what happened next. The same RA was awakened that night by a knock on his door. It was a Jesuit priest (the order that runs Fordham University), who told the RA apologetically that a mischievous ghost that usually stayed in a room at the end of the hall had gotten out, but there was nothing to worry about, because he had "taken care of it." The next morning, the story goes, the RA went to the head nun's office to thank her for sending in a helpful priest, assuming she had told one about the mattress mystery. But the nun insisted that as far as she knew, nobody had asked a priest for assistance in the matter; and furthermore, the description the RA gave of the Jesuit priest didn't fit anyone she had ever seen before. Is a Jesuit priest who's unaware that he's a ghost trying to rid the campus of another ghost?

Another popular ghost story that the RAs like to share with incoming freshmen is about a Jesuit priest who allegedly hanged himself in a wing in St. John's Hall. They say that long ago, one was found hanging, still swaying back and forth as his feet repeatedly bumped against the radiator in the hall. That's why, they explain, the radiator makes a repetitive thumping noise to this day. Finlay Hall has reports of doors slamming inexplicably shut, furniture being moved about, and the sound of children's laughter where no children are present. In fact, apparitions of children have been seen by students at both Hughes Hall and Martyr's Court. At the latter, a terrified upperclassman once caught a fleeting glimpse of a young girl standing silently in a shower, staring blankly straight ahead before vanishing.

Who the child was is anyone's guess. She was too young to be a former university student. But she might be a deceased descendant of the Corsa family. The subtitle of a *New York Times* article dated June 9, 1899, said a "Descendant of Andrew Corsa Claims

Some of the Property on Which St. John's, Fordham, Stands."
According to the article, a Mrs. Davensport Bolsbridge claimed that
her first husband, John H. Corsa, the grandnephew of Andrew
Corsa, had refused to sign a release for a man who had purchased
the property from Andrew's widow, Ann. Because of financial dif-
ficulties, she was seeking the property on behalf of her children,
who, she said, were "in sore need of any property which may be
rightfully theirs." Do her children, the direct descendants of Andrew
Corsa, now inhabit the Fordham grounds?

St. Patrick's Old Cathedral

A candidate for sainthood who helped raise money for construction of St. Patrick's Old Cathedral is said to be the most famous person buried in the church's cemetery . . . and the most publicized
ghost haunting its grounds. Pierre Toussaint was a Haitian slave
who became a free man when his master died in 1807. Because his
master had taught him to read and write, he was well equipped to
apprentice under one of New York City's leading hairdressers of the
time when he arrived from Haiti. Branching out on his own, he
became a popular and wealthy hairdresser in his own right. But he
was a born philanthropist, and he and his young wife opted to use
their considerable wealth to help those less fortunate. As parish-
ioners of St. Patrick's Old Cathedral in the heart of "Old New York"
for sixty-six years, they took in orphans and opened their home to
the poor, sick, and weary seeking refuge.

The defining legacy Toussaint left, however, was his financial
contribution in fund-raising efforts for the construction of St.
Patrick's Old Cathedral at 263 Mulberry Street in Little Italy, built in
1809 and dedicated in 1815. In 1866, a fire gutted Old St. Patrick's,
but it was quickly restored and remained the seat of the Roman
Catholic Archdiocese of New York until 1879, when it was usurped
by the new St. Patrick's Cathedral at 50th Street and Fifth Avenue. St.
Patrick's Old Cathedral, with its mortuary vaults beneath the
church and an ancient cemetery outside, is where New York's first
bishops, including "Dagger John" (Bishop Hughes), are buried,

along with other persons of note, such as the founders of the Emigrant Savings Bank, a ratifier of the Constitution named Dominic Lynch, and the first American papal countess, Annie Leary.

In 1981, the *New York Times* said that Toussaint was a "hairdresser and probably spy for George Washington," whose ghost now wanders around the grounds of the city's second-oldest Catholic site. While I'm dubious about the spy part (after all, who ever heard of a canonized spy?), who am I to say that Toussaint's spirit doesn't haunt Old St. Patrick's? When Cardinal John O'Connor began the cause-for-canonization process for Toussaint, in honor of his charity and piousness, he had the Haitian's grave, which had been discovered on Mott Street by Reverend Charles McTague, moved from the graveyard at St. Patrick's Old Cathedral to the crypt below the main altar at the new St. Patrick's Cathedral, right beside two other candidates for sainthood: Fulton Sheen and Terrance Cook. And moving remains around does seem to have the effect of disrupting a person's eternal rest, at least in literature.

But Toussaint's ghost isn't the only one said to be roaming the sacred grounds. Bishop John Dubois served the diocese as the third bishop of New York from 1826 until his death in 1842. He is remembered for his famous response to the trustees of St. Patrick's Old Cathedral, who once threatened to withhold his salary during a period of financial woes. Being the first presiding bishop to actually live at the diocese, Dubois said, "I am an old man and do not need much. I can live in a basement or in a garret. But whether I come up from the basement or down from the garret, I shall still be your bishop." His request to be buried under the sidewalk at the entrance to St. Patrick's Old Cathedral, where a slab of granite bears his name, was granted. His spirit has reportedly been seen wandering inside of the church since then. That may be so. He wasn't about to be forced out then, and perhaps he isn't about to be forced out now. At least, not until he is given the respect he deserves. After all, they say that the reason he wanted to be buried under the sidewalk is because he felt had been "walked all over" for years, and why should that change after he died?

Fort Totten

More than half of Fort Totten's 147 acres, which includes several hundred-year-old buildings, are occupied by the 77th Regional Readiness Command of the U.S. Army and the EMS Academy (Battalion 53) of the Fire Department of the City of New York (FDNY). But they're not the only ones occupying the fort, according to witnesses who claim that a number of buildings are still inhabited by the dearly departed.

According to a fireman with Battalion 53, nearly everybody who works at Fort Totten has heard unexplainable voices in Building 305 when they are alone. Sometimes the voices sound as if they're right beside them; other times they seem to emanate from behind closed doors in bathrooms and classrooms of the EMS training academy. When those doors are opened, the rooms are found to be vacant. Lights and bathroom fixtures turn on and off, television sets change channels . . . the usual paranormal phenomena. Shadows seen under doors would appear to be a sign of someone walking by on the other side, but such rooms in question are invariably empty when checked. And an apparition of a woman in white has been seen floating across the grounds. She is, according to legend, a general's wife who hanged herself after learning of her husband's affairs. Although Building 323 is boarded up, anomalous photographs and aberrant temperature readings taken by paranormal investigators there indicate that it too may be among Fort Totten's haunted buildings. There seems no doubt that the fort is haunted. The question, then, is by whom?

In 1857, the U.S. government purchased the peninsula at Willets Point near Bayside in Queens from heirs of the Willet family for the purpose of constructing a fort, which initially was called Camp Morgan. The fort played a major role in protecting the entrance to the East River during times of war. In 1898, it was renamed for Brevet Major General Joseph Totten, a distinguished military officer who had fought and served as chief engineer in several conflicts, including the Civil War. Totten was instrumental in the construction of at least three forts that would secure San Francisco and New York before he died in 1864. Some theorize that the indefatigable general doesn't rest, even in death—that perhaps instead he has returned from beyond periodically to inspect the fort named in his honor. And if that's the case, then he has certainly witnessed a lot of changes in occupation and utilization of the fort over the years.

Among its many tenants were the Engineer School of Application and the Electric Mines and Army School of Submarine Defense. In 1941, the sprawling coastal military complex became headquarters for the Eastern Defense Command's Anti-Aircraft Command. A few years later, it was the headquarters for the Air Transport Command's North Atlantic region, and a few years after that, the headquarters for more than half of the NIKI missile sites in the nation. When the air defense command moved out in 1967, the hundred plus buildings on base were mostly converted into military housing for Army families, or leased out as administrative offices for nonprofit and governmental agencies such as Job Corps, the Coast Guard, and the YMCA.

Fort Totten Park opened on June 13, 2005, after the city of New York Parks and Recreation Department acquired nearly fifty acres of Fort Totten from the government. The Fort Totten Historical District inside the park consists of eleven historic buildings, and other areas of the park include a pre–Civil War battery, a thirteen-acre parade ground that also serves as soccer fields, and an outdoor sporting and concert venue. Today, besides the Army Reserve and New York City Fire Department, the Bayside Historical Society and the Northeastern Queens Nature and Historical Preserve Commission call Fort Totten home, and the Parks Department has big plans for the fort's continued development. For example, a new fire marshal base just opened, the renovations to the museum and visitors center are complete, and the Fort Totten pool is now open to the public, as is the historic battery. Although there are plans to demolish a number of unsalvageable old buildings, consideration is being given to creating new paths, recreation areas, a tram and other handicap-friendly features, a veterans garden, and a performance area. It will be interesting to see, with the continuing renovations and changes being made at Fort Totten, how the restless spirits that may still linger there will respond. Typically, in a property prone to hauntings, paranormal activity seems to increase when renovations are being done.

One if by Land, Two if by Sea

In 2004, I included One if by Land, Two if by Sea in *Haunted New York*, and the first sentence I wrote was "It seems appropriate that I'm writing this story about One if by Land, Two if by Sea on Valentine's Day." So what are the odds that I would sit down to write an updated version about the same place on Valentine's Day exactly four years later? I didn't do it on purpose. Out of the 130 files I have yet to work on for this book, I grabbed my file about what is considered to be New York City's "most romantic restaurant" simply because it was next in the heap.

One if by Land, Two if by Sea is located at 17 Barrow Street in Greenwich Village. It's a gorgeous restaurant that many believe was built in 1767 as the carriage house of the Richmond Hill estate that Aaron Burr leased from Trinity Church from 1797 until his infamous duel with Alexander Hamilton in 1804. After that fatal duel, Burr transferred his lease to John Jacob Astor, who allegedly had the carriage house gutted and relocated to 17 Barrow Street. In reality, the house in which Burr lived on Richmond Hill was built in 1750 by Andrew Mortier, the commissary and paymaster of the British Army, and it was leveled in 1849, when Richmond Hill was razed to accommodate street improvements. Whether the accompanying carriage house was also leveled or was relocated is lost to history. Barrow Street's oldest house, No. 25, according to a 1998 *New York Times* article, was built in 1826, and by 1850, the rest of the houses lining the street had been built, including, presumably, 17 Barrow Street. That's not to say that One if by Land, Two if by Sea is not Burr's onetime carriage house—maybe Astor really did have the structure relocated to Barrow Street—but I was unable to substantiate that legend with historical documentation.

Because of the claim that the building was once his carriage house, Burr is said to now haunt the restaurant, smashing dishes, moving chairs, clinking glasses, and so on. The general manager, Roseanne Martino, said she has heard heavy footfalls that sound like a man walking up the stairs to the third floor. Also from the third floor, she has heard the sound of glasses clinking together, as if in a toast. Another unexplained sound comes in the form of a cat that has been heard meowing, even though there are no cats in the restaurant (it wouldn't sit well with the health inspectors).

I do believe the restaurant is haunted, based on the many varied reports of paranormal phenomena occurring there, but I don't believe Burr is our man. After all, of all the glorious homes the former vice president is known to have lived in, why would he choose to haunt the one he was in for only seven of his eighty years? And why haunt a carriage house—an outbuilding that held horse-drawn carriages—instead of one of his stately mansions? No, I don't believe it's Burr who haunts One if by Land, Two if by Sea. And I also don't think, as some have speculated, that it's the enchanting Theodosia Burr Alston, his thirty-year-old daughter, who was lost at sea on her way to New York City to visit him from her home in South Carolina. But there are other possibilities . . .

Roseanne Martino told the *New York Post* in 2006 that several years earlier, the owners came upon a pair of headstones during excavation in the backyard, prompting them to stop their work. The name on one of the headstones was Elizabeth Seaman, and sure enough, a psychic later claimed that she could hear the voice of a young girl named Elizabeth telling her that the death had been an accident. A team of parapsychologists who were brought in to investigate also captured an EVP recording of a girl calling herself Elizabeth, adding credence to the psychic's impressions. The legend, according to Martino, is that a young girl who once lived at that address had a suspicious death, and her loved ones didn't know whether it had been suicide or an accident. If true, it would certainly make sense that her spirit would haunt the place. And perhaps it's this girl, now dubbed Lizzie, who is responsible for tugging on female patrons' earrings as they sit at the bar.

I was unable, however, to find an old obituary of an Elizabeth Seaman in the *New York Times* archives. Interestingly, however, I did find an article dated August 6, 1940, called "Drowned in a Prank," about a *seaman* named Manuel Perry who was pushed "playfully" off Pier 43 at the bottom of Barrow Street into the North River by an eleven-year-old girl named *Elizabeth* Hass. After hitting his head on the pier, he drowned in what was called "a freak accident."

What I do know for certain about 17 Barrow Street that could account for the paranormal phenomena so often experienced there today is that a number of people died or were laid out for a funeral in the building before it became the glamorous restaurant that it is today, according to many old newspaper articles. In 1872, for example, "Mr. James Emergy, sixty years old and an invalid, residing at No. 17 Barrow Street, New York, hanged himself on Saturday morning," according to the February 26 *Brooklyn Eagle* of that year.

On February 7, 1884, it was reported in the *New York Times* that after Charlotte Heaselden Reed died, funeral services were held at "her late residence, 17 Barrow Street." In 1897, blacksmith Michael Hallanan, "the father of Sheridan Square," moved his prosperous horseshoeing business to the first floor of 17 Barrow Street, giving the front of the building a makeover, which it still retains today. And one of Hallanan's sons was still living in an apartment over the shop as late as 1959. On April 22, 1902, that same paper reported that two-year-old Reginald Norris died at 17 Barrow Street, and the following year, seventy-three-year-old Abraham Norris also died at the same residence, as listed in the *Times'* July 4 obituaries. Fast-forward to April 20, 1932, when the *Times* reported that Katherine A. Conway died "at her residence, 17 Barrow Street, New York City." That's at least four individuals—a toddler, two older gentlemen, and one woman—who all died at 17 Barrow Street. Any one of them may be responsible for various ghostly antics reported today. The apparition of a woman has been seen floating around after-hours, passing through one level of the building. And the silhouette of a woman in a long gown appeared on a tablecloth one evening, baffling both staff and customers, who couldn't make it go away even by adjusting the lighting.

In 1938, the estate of Katherine Conway leased the two-story building to R. Bayron and M. Navas, who intended to turn it into a cabaret. In 1943, the building became a bar and restaurant operated by Miss Mayme Kaye. In the sixties, the bar was abandoned, awaiting its final transformation, which occurred in 1969 when Armand Braiger and Mario DeMartini began renovating the legend-laden structure into what would open as One if by Land, Two if by Sea in 1972. During renovations, elements of the blacksmith shop were exposed, such as the original bricks and the hitching posts Hallanan used to tether horses at his shop. According to folklore, tunnels that were revealed in the basement during excavation may have been used as part of the Underground Railroad, if they lead to where the Hudson River's edge once was, as is believed. When DeMartini passed away, Braiger partnered with Noury Gourjjane. Today the restaurant is owned by Gourjjane, managed by Roseanne Martino, and has a new executive chef, Craig Hopson. Reporter Kathleen Squires, from the New York City blog "Bottomless Dish" on citysearch.com, asked if he had witnessed anything paranormal since he has been there; Hopson said, "All of the time." For example, a batch of food he made and placed in the walk-in cooler to set overnight came up missing the next day. Apparently, everybody helped him look for it, to no avail. It resurfaced the next day, none the worse for wear.

The ghosts at One if by Sea, Two if by Land are harmless, by all accounts. In fact, a love-struck couple experiencing an awkward lull in conversation during an intimate candlelight dinner might find the history and hauntings of the restaurant to be a good conversation starter. Whatever you do, don't call the ghost stories nonsense. One former employee, admittedly a nonbeliever, said he was sick and tired of hearing about the ghosts. His careless words were rewarded with a paranormal encounter of his own a short time later. He was working alone one night when the copier started running on its own, going through the sort function. The employee quit the next day.

Raynham Hall

One of the most famous ghost photographs ever taken was at the Townshend (aka Townsend) family's ancestral country estate in Norfolk, England. The stately mansion is called Raynham Hall for the area where it's located, the Raynhams. The apparition descending the main staircase is called the Brown Lady of Raynham Hall, who some believe is Lady Dorothy Walpole, wife of Second Viscount

Townshend, who died of smallpox in 1726. Although Lady Dorothy was captured on film only once, her spirit was allegedly encountered many times at England's Raynham Hall, making the Townshend estate one of England's most well-known haunted places.

The United States also has a very haunted Raynham Hall, which is located in Oyster Bay, Long Island. It started out as just a simple four-room frame house in 1738, when Samuel Townsend—a descendant of the aforementioned English Townshends—purchased the house on a six-acre plot. Within two years, he had enlarged it to eight rooms by adding a lean-to addition onto the north side, giving it a peculiar saltbox design. The Townsends called their house the Homestead, but it was more than that to them. True, Samuel and Sarah raised their eight children there: Solomon, who later became a captain, as well as Samuel Jr., William, Robert, Audrey, David, Sally, and Phebe. But they also operated a general store from the house as a natural extension of Samuel Sr.'s prosperous mercantile business. He owned several ships, which brought back such necessities as lumber, fabric, and spices, as well as rum and wine, from South America, Europe, and the West Indies. Besides his success as a merchant, Samuel was also active in local government and the community. He served as justice of the peace and town clerk and was a member of the New York Provincial Congress when the Declaration of Independence was ratified.

Obviously, Samuel sided with the colonists during the Revolution, rather than the British loyalists, whom the majority of his Oyster Bay neighbors tended to favor. But when the colonists were defeated at the Battle of Long Island in 1776, the law of the American colonies required that the British be quartered in any house they chose to occupy until the end of the Revolutionary War, which was not until seven years later. The Townsend home was occupied by Lieutenant Colonel John Graves Simcoe and served as British headquarters for a six-month period between 1778 and 1779—but it proved to be a pivotal, albeit brief, stay. British Major John André often visited Simcoe at the Homestead, and during one such visit, the two discussed Benedict Arnold's plot to surrender the fort at West Point to the British. As fate would have it, Townsend's daughter Sally overheard the conversation, and she quickly told her brother Robert, who belonged to the patriots' Culper Spy Ring and was nicknamed "Culper Junior." Thanks to the Townsend daughter's quick thinking and the spy ring's quick actions, the plot was foiled. Arnold escaped to the British, and Major André was caught and hanged.

André's ghost was one of the first reportedly seen at Raynham, riding on horseback. And Sally's tragic story may be reason for her to haunt the place as well. According to *Ghost Stories of New York State*, by Susan Smitten, Sally died in an upstairs bedroom as an elderly spinster, having never dared to love again after John Simcoe—who gave her the first valentine ever given in America—left after the war and never returned to her. Some believe she still waits for him, in a story as old as time. The room in which she died is said to remain persistently cold, even when the rest of the house is warm, and several people have seen an apparition of a woman dressed in a dark, hooded cloak passing fluidly through the rooms of the first floor, especially the kitchen, dining room, parlor, and pantry. One witness said the vague figure, whose face could not be discerned, approached the sink and then simply vanished. And a person on the 2003 ghost tour of the house described seeing a hooded female figure wearing black, passing from the kitchen to the parlor. She thought this was perhaps an actual person dressed up as a former servant, but it wasn't. Also during that tour, several people captured orbs on film, cameras malfunctioned, and lights sometimes turned off unexpectedly. The same year, a volunteer saw an apparition of a beautiful woman with her hair pulled up in a bun, wearing a long, dark dress, who was standing at the top of the stairs when he arrived one morning. She looked straight at him, then turned and disappeared through a door. Nobody else had arrived to work yet that day, and if it was an intruder, she hadn't set off the house alarm. He encountered the same woman later that day at the bottom of the main staircase. As he watched her ascend the stairs, she faded and disappeared on the fourth step.

The Homestead eventually passed into the hands of daughter Phebe Townsend and her husband Ebenezer Seeley, and in 1851, their son Solomon Townsend II purchased it and made significant changes to its appearance. By adding a rear wing and tower, he doubled the size, while at the same time transforming it from an old Colonial into an elegant Victorian. He also changed the name from the Homestead to Raynham Hall, after his ancestral home in Norfolk, England. Just like his grandfather, Solomon II was a wealthy merchant and one of the most respected men in the community, serving as president of the Oyster Bay Board of Education and as a member of the state legislature. He and his wife, Helene, raised six children at the familial Raynham Hall. In 1914, one of Helene's nieces, Julia Weeks Coles, and her sister Sallie Townsend Coles purchased the house for just $100 to keep it preserved and in the family. The Oyster Bay Historical and Genealogical Society then used it as a meeting place and tearoom, and Townsend family relics throughout the house gave it a museumlike quality.

Julia Coles moved out in 1933 later and wrote the first documented ghost story about Raynham Hall in an article in the *Glen Cove Record* in 1938. This was the report of John André's ghost. She said a guest who had stayed with her overnight one time awakened during the night to the sound of a horse galloping by outside her window. When the woman got up to look, she allegedly saw an apparition of a white horse and white rider that Julia believes was André. In 1941, Julia gave the house to the Daughters of the American Revolution—an appropriate gesture, considering the house's history—and that organization maintained it until 1947, when they offered it to the town of Oyster Bay. The town restored the house to its Colonial appearance, that of the original Homestead circa 1740. While the town owns it, a group called the Friends of Raynham Hall has continued operating it as a museum, focusing on its important role in history, but staff are always happy to share their ghost stories, especially in the fall during their annual ghost tours.

The director of the museum told Smitten that sometimes things are quiet paranormally, but other times it's unbelievable the number of unexplained incidents taking place. She said one of the more common phenomena they experience is out-of-place odors that can't be traced to a source, including the fleeting scents of roses and candle, fireplace, and tobacco smoke. Several people at the same time have also heard footsteps in the bedrooms below them, when they were in the attic, and went downstairs to find the smell of candle smoke on the first floor. Sometimes they will arrive in the morning to find a triple-locked window open or lights on that were off when they left the night before. During one tour, as a former director talked about servants from long ago who might still be haunting the house, the door behind him slowly opened, then closed just as carefully. Again, there was no explanation for it.

A investigation by Long Island Paranormal Investigators (LIPI) in January 2006 revealed evidence of two or three spirits. The group experienced an olfactory phenomenon when they smelled apple pie. They took numerous photographs of orbs and captured several convincing EVPs of both male and female entities that seem to indicate the presence of both residual spirit energy and interacting spirits. The New York Ghost Chapter has also investigated the house and, based on its investigation, deemed Raynham Hall to be perhaps the most haunted house on Long Island, just as England's Raynham Hall has been called the most haunted house in Norfolk.

Snug Harbor

A sudden roll of the ship on a deep swell churned the water between decks, and the bloated body of a dead sailor was thrown up the ladder and so wedged in the passageway that the face stared straight up at us. The flesh was soft and white, as if ready to drop from the bones, and the eyes had already fallen out. The hideous face seemed to mock at us with a ghastly leer.

That was the climax of a terrifying ordeal told by a veteran "sea dog." He lived at the Sailors' Snug Harbor at 1000 Richmond Terrace on Staten Island and shared the story with his fellow "inmates," as the old sailors there used to be called. But relax, the story took place far from here, on the Sargasso Sea, in the heart of the feared Bermuda Triangle. It was reported in full in the *Spirit Lake Beacon* on August 25, 1899. Every sailor had his story to tell, and what better way to pass away his well-deserved retirement days?

When Sailors' Snug Harbor, the 140-acre property along the Kill van Kull Waterway, was developed in 1833 as a residential compound and medical center for retired seamen, it was the only such facility in the United States. Robert Randall, the son of a wealthy sea merchant, who dreamed up and funded the institution, died thirty-some years before it came to fruition. He had left the majority of his inherited fortune and a large tract of land to the Trustees of Sailors' Snug Harbor in a will dated in 1801 to fund the construction of a "marine hospital" to maintain and support "aged, decrepit, and worn-out sailors," be they naval seamen or merchant marines, from all nations. But in exchange for room and board and the comforts of home, the old sailors were required to attend regular prayer services, say grace before meals, stay sober, and go to bed by 9 P.M. In other words, they had to convert to gentlemanly behavior.

Many who had lived rough, unstructured lives on the seas for too many years believed it was a good trade-off. But for those who couldn't handle it, the grass wasn't necessarily greener on the other side. The *Sioux County Herald* on July 21, 1881, reported what could happen to a sailor unable to clean up his ways. Richard Rosseau, it said, "was picked up near the track of the Main Central Railroad, near Topsham . . . drunk and severely injured. He was a tramp, and apparently had been struck by an engine. He was taken to the county poorhouse, where he soon afterward died. He stated before his death that he had formerly been an inmate of Sailors' Snug Harbor . . . He was drunk when he died and seemed to be from all appearances a wreck."

In 1900, in the days before other retirement options, Snug Harbor housed about a thousand seamen. A newspaper clipping from the *Freeborn County Standard* two years earlier said, "At Sailors' Snug Harbor, on Staten Island, are eight hundred aged but for the most part hearty sailors. Most of these are between seventy and eighty: active old fellows they are, with clear minds and good appetites." By the mid-1950s, however, that number had dwindled to roughly two hundred. To reduce the cost of maintaining unnecessary buildings for the decreasing numbers, several structures were razed. In 1976, the city of New York took possession of the property, after moving the remaining sailors to Sea Level, North Carolina, making way for the old Sailors' Snug Harbor to become the new Snug Harbor Cultural Center. Today the eighty-three-acre center has a children's museum, botanical garden, maritime collection, music hall, offices, classrooms, and more. According to its website, it has become "one of the largest adaptive reuse sites in the country." The renovated buildings are as diverse, in purpose, as the ghosts that apparently haunt them.

Resident artists from around the world can set up their studios in the Governor's House and Victorian Cottages, which are thought to be especially haunted. In *Haunted Staten Island*, Lynda Lee Macken reported that a weeping woman dressed in white has been seen vanishing into thin air near Cottage No. 3. Spirit presence is felt so often by staff that they even have names for some of the more active spirits, according to Macken. There's the Older Matron, as well as the Music Hall Ghost, which is seen in the balcony of that building. And then there's Old Salt. According to a snippet in the *Indiana Progress* dating from 1877, "An old salt, named Webster, who claims to be 105 years of age, is an inmate of Sailors' Snug Harbor at Staten Island, and has been there for more than twenty years." Mysterious footsteps have been heard in the Matron's House, and a female apparition has been seen looking out of the second-floor window from the bedroom in which a young woman gave birth to a stillborn baby and, they say, never recovered from the shock.

Robert Randall, Snug Harbor's founder, never saw the dream he had envisioned become a reality in his lifetime, and he has good reason to haunt the grounds as well. First his grave was moved from its original resting place at Trinity Church Cemetery in Manhattan to Sailors' Snug Harbor. Then a bronze statue in his likeness, which had been unveiled at Snug Harbor in 1881, was moved in 1976, along with the remaining old sailors, to Sea Level, North Carolina, when New York City acquired the property. Though Randall's physical body and statue have both been moved, his spirit may still remain at Sailors' Snug Harbor, along with those of any number of old inmates who died there or just passed through.

Old Bermuda Inn

Besides being one of the most romantic facilities on Staten Island, the restaurant at the Old Bermuda Inn, built in the 1830s, is also one of its most haunted establishments—according to legend— and it harbors one of the area's most famous ghosts. This is the tragic tale of Martha Mesereau.

William and Martha Mesereau were living in the two-story Greek Revival Cortelyou-Mesereau mansion at 2512 Arthur Kill Road, when William was called off to war in 1861. Like many other wives during the Civil War, twenty-seven-year-old Martha watched out her bedroom window overlooking the water day and night, wringing her hands nervously, awaiting her husband's safe return. She made sure to keep a candle burning all night in the window, to help guide him back to their house, in case he returned in the dark. But all her efforts were for naught. Her worst nightmare came true the day she received news that her beloved William was missing in action. It is said that she retreated to her room, refusing to believe the horrible news. He would return, she was sure. And when that time came, she would be waiting for him, even if it took forever. After all, they said he was missing, not dead. And that gave hope to Martha, as it would to any loved one. In the end, her physical body eventually yielded to death, regardless of how it happened. But she apparently continues her vigil in spirit to this day.

Some sources say the bereaved young widow refused to eat and starved in the very room in which she held her futile vigil. Others say she died of a broken heart not long after receiving the dreaded word of William's disappearance. But for all the conflicting reports of how she died, most agree that her spirit remains in the house, refusing to give up hope for her husband's return. Over the years, the Old Bermuda Inn has expanded into what the *Staten Island Advance* called a two-acre "intriguing hospitality complex," with a fine seafood restaurant in the original mansion, an impressive catering hall, and a bed-and-breakfast called the Wedding Cottage, which is a beautifully restored 1840s parsonage. Martha reputedly haunts the mansion at the historic Old Bermuda Inn— in the first-floor hallway, where a painting of her hangs; on the main staircase; in the dining area; and in the second-floor rooms and restrooms.

In the first-floor hallway, while construction was going on during expansion, a worker happened to notice that a portrait of Martha that was hanging on the wall was on fire. He quickly put it out, according to Jeff Belanger's *Encyclopedia of Haunted Places*, taking note that nobody was anywhere in sight who could have caused it. Was Martha displeased with the changes to her home, thinking that perhaps William wouldn't recognize the place when he returned? Also in the first-floor hallway is a chandelier that had one stubborn light that refused to turn off. Even when all the other lights around it went off, and even when the switch to the chandelier was flipped off, that one single light—much like the single candle Martha kept lit in the window—refused to go out. Other lights in the mansion turn themselves on after everyone has left. So even now, a century and a half since William disappeared, a light still shines in the night for him.

Many people claim to have seen a woman's silhouette in the windows at the inn, which they attribute to an apparition of Martha. Her misty form has also been seen breezing through several of the dining areas and ascending the main staircase to the second floor, where a woman of her likeness has been seen wandering between rooms. What is believed to be her restless spirit has been heard crying, and diners occasionally report the feeling that something icy has brushed past them. In fact, some say they feel someone softly touch their arm or hair. One young person said it felt as if someone were trying to tenderly pull her hair back, as if to put it in a bun or ponytail. A former manager admitted to seeing or hearing a woman crying at least once a week, usually after closing.

A group of paranormal investigators known as Real Hauntings has found further evidence that the Old Bermuda Inn is haunted, with their findings published in the *Encyclopedia of Haunted Places*. Their investigation revealed cold spots, high EMF readings, a woman's voice captured on EVP, multiple photographs of a single orb, and equipment malfunctioning or draining—all indicative of possible paranormal activity. In other words, there's a good chance that Martha's ghost really does continue to haunt the Old Bermuda Inn.

Garibaldi–Meucci Museum

Staffers at the Garibaldi-Meucci Museum have accumulated enough paranormal experiences under their collective belts to warrant a haunted tour at the museum. The most commonly reported activity involves witnessing shadows moving, hearing unexplained footsteps and unaccountable bumps, seeing doors move with no help, and feeling intense sadness for no known reason. Paranormal investigators have corroborated the personal experiences by gathering both visual and audio evidence representative of an authentic haunting. According to the museum's official website, the Staten Island Paranormal Society has captured spirit energy in digital photographs and spirit communication in the form of EVPs on digital voice recorders, and the crew of *Scared!* has even paid an overnight visit to the museum.

The Gothic Revival house-museum smack in the middle of Rosebank was once home to two very important individuals: Guiseppe Garibaldi and Antonio Meucci. The two died many years ago, but their legacy—and some say their essence—survives at the Garibaldi-Meucci Museum at 420 Tompkins Avenue on Staten Island. The house was built in 1840, but Meucci, the *true* inventor of the first telephone, and his wife, Ester, didn't move in as tenants until 1850. At the same time, their good friend Garibaldi was in exile from Italy and arrived in New York City seeking refuge, so the Meuccis opened their home to him, and he ended up staying with them for a brief time, working at Meucci's candle factory. Garibaldi returned to Italy in 1854 and became an Italian revolutionary war champion for leading victories that unified the country. When he died thirty years later, a marble plaque commemorating his valor was secured over the front door of the house he had shared with Meucci. Garibaldi died a hero in 1882, whereas Meucci, by contrast, died impoverished, long before his significant contribution to society was recognized.

On June 16, 2002, the U.S. House of Representatives credited Meucci, and not Alexander Graham Bell, with being the inventor of the first telephone. While working with patients using therapeutic electrical shock therapy, Meucci had inadvertently discovered that sounds travel through copper wires by electrical impulses. Armed with that knowledge, he then created a device several years later to facilitate communication with his bedridden wife while she was in her room and he was in his workshop. Several years later, in 1860, he demonstrated this "talking telegraph," or "teletrefono," as he called it, in New York City. But he couldn't afford the $250 for the patent on his device.

Alexander Graham Bell, as the cruel hand of fate would have it, was sharing a lab with Meucci at the time, and Bell *did* have enough money for a patent on the device. But instead of lending it to Meucci, it is now believed that Bell tweaked Meucci's prototype, to which only Bell had access in the lab, and submitted his slightly revamped version for a patent in his own name in 1876. Bell rose to instant fame and fortune for inventing the first telephone, while Meucci struggled vainly just to keep himself and his paralyzed wife out of poverty. In 1899, the Supreme Court agreed to hear the case of fraud against Bell, but it was too little, too late, as they say. The charges were dropped when Meucci died that same year, never having earned the respect he so deserved for his invention, at least not in his lifetime.

After Meucci's death, the Italian community acquired the house to preserve as a memorial to Garibaldi. In 1907, it was moved to its current location, and in 1919, it was turned over to the Order Sons of Italy in America, who continue to own and operate it. Before opening to the public as the Garibaldi-Meucci Museum in 1956, the house was restored and filled with Italian artifacts.

In the summer of 2007, the Eastern Paranormal Investigation Center (EPIC) investigated the site and gathered some very interesting evidence of paranormal activity and experienced firsthand what staffers had been reporting: strange sounds and unexplained shadows. A number of EVPs captured the sound of groans and coughing, perhaps the bedridden Mrs. Meucci, or the discouraged Mr. Meucci upon learning that his invention had been patented by Bell. Even more interesting was the distinct sound of a sigh, or someone exhaling loudly into the mike, that was caught on a camcorder left alone on the second-floor landing. Seconds before the exhalation, the sound of something touching the camera is heard.

Was Meucci testing the device, as he had his teletrefono a hundred years ago? Imagine how intrigued he must be with today's technology if, in fact, he is still around.

The museum now offers historical, educational, *and* paranormal programs and is part of the Ghost Hunter's University, sponsored by *Haunted Times* magazine. This unique traveling university visits locations that are recognized as being haunted, and the museum joins such paranormal elite as Eastern State Penitentiary and the Lizzie Borden Bed and Breakfast on the university's roster. The annual "Haunted Tour at the Garibaldi-Meucci Museum" is a program created in response to an ever-increasing interest in the ghostly inhabitants thought to dwell within the museum. During the ninety-minute candlelit tours, the staff share their own and others' experiences, as well as theories as to who haunts the museum and why.

Kingsland Homestead

"For God's sake, let me in!" Those were the words a Mrs. Ford heard coming from the front door of the Kingsland House in the late 1800s, according to legend. Nervously checking the door, she found nobody there, so she frantically hunted down the owner, Mr. H. G. Murray, and told him what she had heard. He agreed to stand by her front door the following night—not because he believed the hysterical woman, but because he looked forward to proving to her that it was just her overactive imagination. But to his surprise, the next night at exactly midnight—the same time as the incident the night before—he too heard someone demanding to be let in. Immediately opening the door, he found nobody there. If there had been a real live human at the door, the person wouldn't have had time to get out of sight in the millisecond it took Murray to open the door, as he was standing right by it when he heard the voice. The house has never lost its status as one of Queens' most haunted places since then.

The historic Kingsland Estate is a two-and-a-half-story Dutch-English Colonial built by a Quaker farmer named Charles Doughty around 1785, making the house the oldest and only remaining eighteenth-century house in Flushing. It was named Kingsland when Doughty's son-in-law Joseph King, a British sea captain who made his fortune trading agricultural commodities, bought the house in 1801. Today personal items such as notebooks and diaries of both the Doughty and King families are available to view on the premises, which the Queens Historical Society acquired in the 1970s and now uses as its headquarters. The Historical Society opened Kingsland Homestead in 1973 as a museum, hosting exhibitions and lectures regarding the history of Queens—as the borough's primary repository of local history—on the first floor. The second-floor parlor replicates that of a typical middle-class family in Victorian-era Flushing and includes personal objects that once belonged to members of the Doughty and King families. A permanent exhibit about Kingsland's history and previous owners is maintained there.

Originally built at what would now be 40–25 155th Street, the house has been moved twice: in the 1920s, when it was threatened by a proposed subway that would have run through the property, and in the 1960s, when the owner agreed to raze it to make way for the Murray Hill Plaza at Northern Boulevard and 155th Street. Thankfully, a group of concerned citizens calling themselves the Kingsland Preservation Committee stepped in, arranging to have the house designated as a historic landmark. The house was then moved to its current location at 143–35 37th Avenue in Flushing in the Weeping Beech Park, where it shared the yard with the nation's first weeping beech tree, which was delivered from Belgium in 1847. Until it died in 1998, the tree was one of two New York City living landmarks, because all of the country's weeping beech trees are believed to be direct descendants of this one. Like the old beech tree, the homestead was uprooted and transplanted onto the same property, and time will tell if it has finally reached its final resting place as well.

But there are rumors that previous inhabitants of the old homestead may still be searching for theirs. According to a number of sources, Kingsland Homestead is still haunted. The *New York Times* once mentioned that unexplainable sounds of infants crying have been reported in the building. There's nothing like a good ghost story to really bring history to life.

Houdini's Grave

In the early 1900s, Harry Houdini was the world's greatest magician, a legendary escape artist who died at age fifty-two under suspicious circumstances on Halloween in 1926. He is buried at Machpelah Cemetery in Flushing, and it is rumored that his spirit lingers, not only at his gravesite, but also at his former Hollywood home, where his apparition has allegedly been seen. A *New York Times* article called "Is New York Too Scary Even for Its Ghosts?" lists the magician's home at 278 West 113th Street, where he lived for twenty-two years, as perhaps being haunted by a handcuff-rattling Houdini. He was living there when he died, and when he walked out the door for the last time, prior to his final show in Detroit, he had a premonition of his own death and began to cry. Does Harry Houdini haunt three different locations? He certainly has good reason to. With the truth surrounding his death still unsettled after all this time, and especially if his murderer got away with it, would it be any wonder if his spirit is not able to rest in peace?

Houdini's grave has been vandalized a number of times, and the bust of his likeness stolen or even destroyed by disrespectful thugs. Even though he had suffered a blow to his abdomen and received numerous death threats shortly before he died, his death was nonetheless ruled natural, a result of intestinal injury resulting in appendicitis and peritonitis. That official explanation might have been easier to swallow if he hadn't been a middle-aged man in otherwise excellent health . . . and if he hadn't died on Halloween. That's a little too appropriate for a man of his mystique. The fact that Houdini was buried in the last casket in which he ever performed an escape stunt, because the casket had somehow been the only prop, of many, left behind prior to his next scheduled show, adds even more to the list of curiosities surrounding his untimely death. Even the *New York Times* expressed incredulity in an article dated November 2, 1920, called "Houdini's Body Gets Here Today":

> Houdini, a staunch believer in mental telepathy, placed much faith in coincidence. This was born out in the fact that the coffin in which he wished to be buried was in Detroit when [and where] he died.

When Houdini's show disbanded last week, all the stage equipment was shipped to New York, but by a queer trick of fate, or coincidence, this coffin was left behind . . . coming to light a few days after the other baggage had been shipped.

If all that weren't enough, Houdini's beloved wife, Beatrice, called "Bess" for short, wasn't allowed to be buried next to him when she died, because she was Catholic but the cemetery where he was buried is strictly for Jewish interments. His remains are in the Weiss-Houdini plot at the entrance to Machpelah Cemetery at 8230 Cypress Hills Street. To prevent vandalism, the cemetery closes on Halloween, the anniversary of his death. But a ceremony to celebrate the life and legacy of Houdini is held by the Society of American Magicians at the gravesite every November 16, the anniversary of Houdini's death on the Jewish calendar. Houdini had been very vocal in his crusade to expose phony mediums and spirit rappers, popular at the time, yet he was always a strong believer in the supernatural and the afterlife, and he allegedly made pacts with others to try to make contact from the beyond. He promised Bess that if it were at all possible, he would contact her after death, using a secret message known only to the two of them at the time to prove that it really was him.

Unfortunately, Bess accidentally revealed some of the contents of that secret message—*"Rosabelle, believe"*—to reporters, making it impossible to know whether any séance since then held to elicit his spirit has been successful, and there have been many. On the tenth anniversary of Houdini's death, Bess held a well-publicized séance on the roof of the Knickerbocker Hotel in Hollywood, but her husband didn't show any sign of being present, even though a number of props had been prepared for him to manipulate, such as a trumpet, locked handcuffs, and a bell. When it ended more than an hour later, however, just as the participants got up to leave, it began to thunder and pour, drenching everyone. The skies, according to a 1985 *New York Times* article, then cleared. From a mighty magician like the Great Houdini, would we expect any less of show? They wanted a sign from above, and perhaps they got just that, in a dramatic way.

Though Houdini took his magic secrets to the grave with him, even keeping them from his wife and assistant, we may one day solve another secret he took with him—the true cause of his death. On March 23, 2007, the Associated Press reported that Houdini's kin had requested an exhumation of his remains to prove their suspicion that he had been poisoned to death. After all, there were a lot of cunning spiritualists of the day that Houdini had upset by exposing them for what they really were—fraudulent opportunists preying on the vulnerabilities of their customers, who were deep in mourning and would pay anything just to believe the spiritualist had truly made contact with their deceased loved ones. And the alleged peritonitis and/or appendicitis could have been triggered by poison, which would mean that the death wasn't natural after all. It may have been murder. Maybe one day we'll know.

Whether any answers are ever found to the questions still surrounding Houdini's premature death, one thing seems certain: Houdini lives on. And it may be just a matter of time until he proves it. To the celebrated magician and escape artist, breaching the thin veil that separates the physical world from the spirit world may not be an impossibility.

Gay Street Phantom

On Tuesday afternoon, as Mrs. Patton was getting out of one of the cars of the Eighth-Avenue Line at the corner of Christopher and Hudson Streets, having at the time an infant in her arms, she was knocked down and run over by a heavy express wagon; with great presence of mind, she threw the child from her and thus put it beyond the reach of the wheels, two of which however passed completely over her own body [which was then] conveyed in a coach to the residence of her sister, No. 12 Gay Street, by policeman Carpenter of the Ninth District. During the excitement, the driver of the wagon made his escape.

—*New York Times*, August 30, 1855

That's one spirit with a reason to linger—a young mother who threw her infant to safety while she was run over and killed by a reckless driver who got away. Imagine her sister's horror when the policeman showed up at her apartment at 12 Gay Street with the body. There are probably dozens of lingering spirits on Gay Street, as a morgue from the Revolutionary War was once located there, but only one is truly deserving of the moniker the Gay Street Phantom.

Manhattan's tiny Gay Street, named in 1833 for abolitionist and editor Sidney Howard Gay, is one of the oldest streets in the city. It started out as an alley entrance to stables, and the first row of houses was built on the east side of the street in 1827. The earliest residents of Gay Street were mostly black servants who worked for wealthy families of the Washington Square neighborhood. But the street eventually attracted musicians, aspiring artists, and writers, giving it a distinct Bohemian flavor. New York mayor Jimmy Walker once owned the four-story townhouse at 12 Gay Street during a scandalous affair with his mistress, actress Betty Compton, for whom he purchased the tenement. They were married in 1936 but divorced five years later. Another famous tenant was puppeteer Frank Paris, who designed the original Howdy Doody in a puppet shop in the basement. A 1995 *New York Times* guide to "City Haunts" said that Paris claimed to have seen three ghosts while living there, including a man wearing a top hat, vest, and black cape. He also smelled violets and fried onions when there seemed to be no source for those particular scents, so the famous puppeteer definitely believed 12 Gay Street was haunted.

It seems there has never been a dull moment at 12 Gay Street. On December 16, 1933, a stunning young former Ziegfeld Follies showgirl named Edith Birney fell, jumped, or was pushed to her death off the roof of the building next door, 10 Gay Street, where she lived with her mother. The twenty-five-year-old had been working as a model but had been recently beset by a series of misfortunes. After a brief stint as a speakeasy called the Pirate's Den, the building became a private residence, and then was converted into apartments. Many types of paranormal activity have been experienced by previous owners, houseguests, and tenants. Unexplained footsteps have been heard going up and down the stairs in the middle of the night, while shadows were seen gliding up and down those same stairways. Three psychic mediums who were consulted individually all sensed that someone had died violently on the grounds before the house was even built, possibly, they said, being tortured for withholding information—maybe during the Revolutionary War, when the morgue was nearby.

The most persistent ghost is the Gay Street Phantom, a dapper apparition that is sometimes seen, even today, standing on the front steps before vanishing into thin air. The same apparition has allegedly appeared throughout the apartment building, but it is most often seen on the interior stairs and front steps. Wearing a top hat and tails, the phantom always smiles just before vanishing into thin air. Some say he looks like an alter ego of Walter B. Gibson's "the Shadow." Perhaps the friendly Gay Street Phantom is there to comfort or free the tortured spirits the psychics sensed, or that of the beautiful showgirl who fell to her death next door.

Historic Richmond Town

One of Staten Island's most well-known haunted places, Historic Richmond Town, has hosted many paranormal investigations, including one with the crew from the *Scared!* television show. The crew experienced paranormal phenomena firsthand at the Parsonage Restaurant, which has long been said to be haunted. Originally the home of a Dutch Reformed Church minister, the building first became a private residence in 1875 and was sold in 1885 when the Richmond congregation was dissolved. According to *Haunted History of Staten Island*, by Lynda Lee Macken, ghostly moans have been heard in the building, lights malfunction with no reasonable explanation, and orbs are seen drifting from room to room after-hours. In fact, on one occasion, police were called to investigate because the orbs caused concern that an intruder with a flashlight had entered the building. Of course, nobody was found inside. With more than two dozen early buildings grouped together in one historic village—all decked out in authentic period furnishings and occupied by staff wearing original articles of clothing—no wonder Historic Richmond Town is believed to be haunted. If ever a ghost could feel at home somewhere, it would be in a place such as this, where everything is just as it was up to three hundred years ago.

The village's Guyon-Lake-Tysen House, built by Joseph Guyon in 1740 on his farm in New Dorp, is believed to be haunted. The farmhouse, which still amazingly has most of its original woodwork inside, may still also have a few of its original occupants as well. Childlike apparitions have been seen inside when the house was inaccessible to the public. And objects such as toys and bedspreads are often found moved or disturbed. People have seen many things that can't be explained, including cupboard doors opening on their own and doors that had been working fine one moment suddenly refusing to budge the next. Although photographic anomalies may offer tangible evidence of paranormal phenomena, people have more commonly experienced the intangible sensation of someone brushing up against them or watching them when they knew they were alone in the house. Staffers have heard what sounds like someone walking upstairs in the empty house and wonder if it might be the spirits of the Lake family's slaves, who were housed in the rooms above the kitchen, a room that was added in the 1820s. Faint, unaccountable odors that can't be traced to an obvious source have also been detected.

Historic Richmond Town's website proclaims that it is a place "where the past can still be experienced with all your senses." Certainly, in the Guyon-Lake-Tysen House, all of the senses—including the sixth sense—have experienced what appear to be manifestations of unseen inhabitants from the past, even if that's not exactly what was meant by that statement.

Another house that appears to be haunted is the Stephens-Black House, where people have heard unexplainable knocks at the doors. Stephen D. Stephens built the house in 1838 and lived there with his family until 1870, after which the Joseph Black family lived there until 1926. Three of the Blacks—Sarah, Mary, and Josephine—owned and operated the family's general store (also built by Stephens) from 1880 to 1918. Apparitions also have been seen at the Rezeau-Van Pelt Cemetery, where the earliest occupants of the Voorlezers' House were interred between 1780 and 1860.

Historic Richmond Town is one of only three living-history museums in New York State, and the only such village in New York City. Visitors taking in the many historic old buildings and sites step back in time, greeted by hosts dressed in period garb and strolling through homes and businesses depicting life from the period in which they originated. The Staten Island Historical Society and the city of New York strive to keep the hundred-acre living museum as true to the past as possible. The fact that some of the early inhabitants of the structures may haunt it today is the icing on the cake, adding to the already authentic atmosphere and giving visitors the opportunity to actually mingle—if only subliminally—with yesteryear's residents. And after all, that's one of the primary goals of a book like this: to show people where the ghosts are.

Happy Hauntings!

Bibliography

Books

Asbury, Herbert. *The Gangs of New York: An Informal History of the Underworld.* New York: Alfred A. Knopf, 1928.

Belanger, Jeff. *Encyclopedia of Haunted Places: Ghostly Locales from Around the World.* Franklin Lakes, NJ: New Page Books, 2005.

Brady, Mathew. *The Gallery of Illustrious Americans.* New York: Self-published, 1850.

Brown, John M. *A Brief Sketch of the First Settlement of the County of Schoharie by the Germans.* Cobleskill, NY: Self-published, 1823.

Buffum, Herbert Edward. *The Household Physician, A Twentieth Century Medica: A Practical Description in Plain Language of all the Diseases.* Boston, Physicians' Pub. Co., 1905.

Chernow, Barbara Ann, and George A. Vallasi. *The Columbia Encyclopedia.* New York: Columbia University Press, 1993.

Croffut, William Augustus. *The Vanderbilts and the Story of Their Fortune.* Chicago: Belford, Clarke and Company, 1886.

Curtis, Gates, ed. *History of St. Lawrence County, New York.* Syracuse, NY: D. Mason and Company, 1894.

Fowler, Barney. *Adirondack Album—Volume Two.* Schenectady, NY: Outdoor Associates, 1974.

Hauck, Dennis William. *Haunted Places: The National Directory: Ghostly Abodes, Sacred Sites, UFO Landings and Other Supernatural Locations.* New York: Penguin-Putnam, 2002.

Hough, Franklin Benjamin. "War of 1812." *History of St. Lawrence and Franklin Counties.* Albany, NY: Little & Co., 1853.

Macken, Lynda Lee. *Empire Ghosts*. Forked River, NJ: Black Cat Press, 2004.

———. *Haunted History of Staten Island*. Forked River, NJ: Black Cat Press, 2000.

Meyers, Arthur. *The Ghostly Register*. New York: McGraw-Hill/Contemporary Books, 1986.

Moss, Frank. *The American Metropolis*. New York: P. F. Collier, 1897.

Revai, Cheri. *Haunted New York: Ghosts and Strange Phenomena of the Empire State*. Mechanicsburg, PA: Stackpole Books, 2005.

———. *Haunted New York City: Ghosts and Strange Phenomena of the Big Apple*. Mechanicsburg, PA: Stackpole Books, 2008.

———. *Haunted Northern New York*. Utica, NY: North Country Books, 2002.

———. *More Haunted Northern New York*. Utica, NY: North Country Books, 2003.

———. *Still More Haunted Northern New York*. Utica, NY: North Country Books, 2004.

Schlosser, S. E. *Spooky New York*. Guilford, CT: Globe Pequot, 2005.

Shelton, William Henry. *The Jumel Mansion*. New York: Houghton Mifflin Company, 1916.

Smitten, Susan. *Ghost Stories of New York State*. Auburn, WA: Ghost House Books, 2004.

Taylor, Troy. "Revenge from Beyond the Grave." *No Rest for the Wicked*. Decatur, IL: Whitechapel Press, 2001.

Wicker, Christine. *Lily Dale: The True Story of the Town That Talks to the Dead*. New York: HarperCollins, 2004.

Online Sources
(in order by story)

"Ghost on the Hill." *Greeneyezz Reflections: 2006*. Retrieved 6 February 2008. http://greeneyezz-reflections.blogspot.com/2006_10_01_archive.html.

Walters, Sally. "From My Window." *Fulton History*. Retrieved 6 February 2008. http://fultonhistory.com.

DoggyDew. "Phantom Sightings on 13 Curves." *Strange CNY – Syracuse.com*. Retrieved 6 February 2008. http://blog.syracuse.com/strangecny/2007/10/phantom_sightings_on_13_curves/html.

"Ghostly Theater in Oswego." *5WTVH*. Retrieved 19 March 2008. www.wtvh.com/news/local/10933201.html.

Place, Erin. "Hauntings." *Palltimes.com*. Retrieved 10 November 2007. http://pall-times.com/articles/2007/10/30/news/news3.prt.

"Oswego Players." *Discover Oswego*. Retrieved 20 March 2008. http:// discoveroswego.com/content/view/66/35/.

"Oswego Players Theater." *The Ultimate Collection of the Strange*. Retrieved 20 March 2008. www.strangeusa.com/ViewLocation/aspx?locationid =6925.

"Hypothermia: First Aid." *Mayo Clinic*. Retrieved 20 March 2008. www .mayoclinic.com/health/first-aid-hypothermia/FA00017.

Bramlett, Chuck. "Cold Weather Camping and Hypothermia." *US Scouting Service Project*. Retrieved 20 March 2008. http://usscouts.org/us scouts/safety/safe-cold.asp.

"The LeRay Mansion Historic District." *Public Works Division—Fort Drum, NY—Cultural Resources*. Retrieved 22 February 2008. www.drum .army.mil/garrison/pw/PWCulturalResources.html.

Burnham, Spec. Travis. "News Crew Spends Night in Basement of LeRay Mansion." *Fort Drum Blizzard Online*. Retrieved 22 February 2008.

Anne. "The Slightly Haunted LeRay Mansion at Fort Drum." *Other Ghost Stories*. Retrieved 22 February 2008. http://home.jps.net/~chthonic/ ringwood/other.html.

"2002—An Ongoing Investigation at The Harrison-Morley Grist Mill in Morley, New York." *Ghost Seekers of Central New York*. Retrieved 5 March 2008. www.cnyghost.com/investigations.php.

"Press Release—August 20, 2002." *Morley Grist Mill*. Retrieved 28 February 2008. www.morleygristmill.com/release.htm.

McFarland, George F. "The Old Stone Mill at Morley." *Morley Grist Mill*. Retrieved 22 February 2008. www.morleygristmill.com/mcfarland .htm.

"Empire State Paranormal" *Empire State Paranormal*. Retrieved 28 September 2008. www.empirestateparanormal.com.

"Burrville Cider Mill." *Syracuse Ghost Hunters*. Retrieved 10 January 2008. www.syracuseghosthunters.com/investigations/burrvillecidermill .html.

Ohler, Amy. "Hauntings at Cider Mill?" *News 10 Now*. Retrieved 11 January 2007. http://news10now.com/shared/print/default.asp?ArID= 84619.

"Ameriga Vespucci." *The Lady Who Sailed the Soul and the First Solar Sail*. Retrieved 7 April 2008. www.fouth-millennium.net/cordwainer-vr/ lady-who-sailed-the-soul.html.

Ohler, Amy. "New Burial Law." *News 10 Now*. Retrieved 9 April 2008. http://news10now.com/printarticle.aspx?ArID=23924.

"History of Massena—Raquette River." *Rays Place*. Retrieved 11 March 2008. http://history.rays-place.com/ny/massena-ny.htm.

PAO. "News Release: WWII German and Italian POW's to Be Honored Nov. 19." *Fort Drum Public Affairs Office – News Releases/Advisories*.

Retrieved 22 February 2008. www.drum.army.mil/sites/installation/pao/releases/newsItem.asp?id=2006/0611-24.

"Cemeteries." *Public Works Division—Fort Drum, NY—Cultural Resources.* Retrieved 22 February 2008. www.drum.army.mil/garrison/pw/PW CulturalResources.html.

"History of Russell, NY." *Rays Place.* Retrieved 26 February 2008. http://history.rays-place.com/ny/russell-ny.htm.

"Paul Smith's College." *Answers.com.* Retrieved 22 April 2008. www.answers.com/topic/paul-smith-s-college-1.

"Paul Smith's Hotel." *Answers.com.* Retrieved 22 April 2008. www.answers.com/topic/paul-smith-s-hotel?cat=travel.

"Paul Smith's, New York." *Answers.com.* Retrieved 22 April 2008. www.answers.com/topic/paul-smiths-new-york?cat=travel.

"Welcome to the Plattsburgh Air Base Redevelopment Corporation PARC Web Site." *Parc-USA.* Retrieved 26 February 2008. www.parc-usa.com/Introduction/Old%20Base%20Virtual%Tour%20Intro.htm.

"Plattsburgh Air Force Base." *Wikipedia.* Retrieved 26 February 2008. http://en.wikipedia.org/wiki/Plattsburgh_Air_Force_Base.

"History of Parishville, NY." *Rays Place.* Retrieved 14 December 2007. http://history.rays-place.com/ny/parishville-ny.htm.

"Lyonsdale, New York." *Answers.com.* Retrieved 16 April 2008. www.answers.com/topic/lyonsdale-new-york?cat=travel.

"Hand, Marcia." *Roots Web.* Retrieved 4 March 2008. www.rootsweb.com/~nyessex/extract.htm.

"Beware, the Brightside Is Haunted!" *Brightside on Raquette.* Retrieved 4 December 2007. http://brightsideonraquette.com/hauntings.html.

"Tanya—Origin and Meaning of the Name Tanya at BabyNamesWorld." *Baby Names World.* Retrieved 18 February 2008. www.babynamesworld.com/meaning_of_Tanya.html.

"Elected to US House of Representatives 1833–35." *Buffalo 1832–1840.* Retrieved 18 February 2008. www4.bfn.org/bah/h/1840.html.

"Holiday Inn Grand Island Ghost Story." *Holiday Inn Grand Island, Grand Island Haunted Hotels, AllStays Ghost Hotel Guide.* Retrieved 10 February 2008. www.allstays.com/Haunted/ny_buffalo_holidayinn.htm.

"Durand Eastman Park." *City of Rochester.* Retrieved 15 November 2007. http://cityofrochester.gov/prhs/index.cfm?action=showvenuandid=70andtype=playground.

"Durand-Eastman Park." *Monroe County.* Retrieved 16 March 2008. www.monroecounty.gov/parks-durandeastman.php.

"Alphabet Murders." *Rochester Wiki.* Retrieved 10 April 2008. http://rocwiki.org/Alphabet_Murders.

"Durand-Eastman Park." *Wikipedia.* Retrieved 10 April 2008. http://en.wikipedia.org/wiki/Durand-Eastman_Park.

"Fort Niagara." *Wikipedia.* Retrieved 24 November 2007. http://en .wikipedia.org/wiki/Fort_Niagara.

"Old Fort Niagara." *Paranormal & Ghost Society.* Retrieved 9 February 2008. www.paranormalghostsociety.org/Old%20Fort%20Niagara.htm.

"Ghostly Sightings and Spirit Experiences." *EagleSoars.* Retrieved 9 February 2008. http://eaglesoars.homestead.com/Spirits.html.

"Old Fort Niagara: Western New York's Most Popular State Historic Site." *Old Fort Niagara.* Retrieved 4 April 2008. https://oldfortniagara.org/.

Nickell, Joe. "Investigative Files—Headless Ghosts I Have Known." Retrieved 4 April 2008. www.csicop.org/sb/2006-12/i-files.html.

Mendola, Nicholas. "One Reporter, One Haunted Castle, One Night." *Tonawanda News.* Retrieved 24 November 2007. www.tonawanda-news.com/nightandday/gnnnightandday_story_305115907.html.

"The Friends of Mount Hope Cemetery." *Mount Hope Cemetery.* Retrieved 19 March 2008. www.fomh.org/about.php.

"Rochester's History." *Mt. Hope Cemetery.* Retrieved 19 March 2008. www.vintageviews.org/vv-tl/pages/Mt_Hope.html.

"Mount Hope Cemetery, Rochester." *Wikipedia.* Retrieved 19 March 2008. http://en.wikipedia.org/wiki/Mount_Hope_Cemetery,_Rochester.

"The Van Horn Mansion." *The Van Horn Mansion.* Retrieved 12 December 2007. www.angelfire.com/ny4/miaja38/vanhorn.html.

"Welcome to My Page." (Bruce Ludemann) *Welcome to Our Page.* Retrieved 12 December 2007. www.angelfire.com/ny3/arsonk9/.

"The Van Horn Mansion." *Town of Newfane Historical Society.* Retrieved 12 December 2007. www.niagaracounty.org/town_of_newfane_hs .htm.

"The Van Horn Mansion in Burt . . ." *Olcott Beach and Newfane.* Retrieved 12 December 2007. http://olcott-newfane.com/html/van_horn _mansion.html.

Horton, Victoria. "Legends and Myths of SBU." *St. Bonaventure University.* Retrieved 26 November 2007. http://web.sbu.edu/friedsam/ archives/studentpages/ghost/index.html.

———. "Devereaux." *St. Bonaventure University.* Retrieved 26 November 2007. http://web.sbu.edu/friedsam/archives/studentpages/buildings/ Devereux.htm.

———. "Fr. Alphonsus Trabold." *St. Bonaventure University.* Retrieved 26 November 2007. http://web.sbu.edu/friedsman/archives/student pages/ghost/new_page_6.htm.

———. "3rd Floor Legends." *St. Bonaventure University.* Retrieved 26 November 2007. http://web.sbu.edu/friedsam/archives/student pages/ghost/3rd_floor_legends.htm.

Zaniello, James. "Paranormal Rumors Lurk in the Shadows of St. Bonaventure." *St. Bonaventure University.* Retrieved 26 November 2007. http://

web.sbu.edu/friedsam/archives/studentpages/ghost/paranormal_
rumors_lurk_in_the_shadows_of_st_bonaventure.htm.

Pavia, Joyce. "Fifth Dev—A Lounge May End Mystery." *St. Bonaventure
University*. Retrieved 26 November 2007. http://web.sbu.edu/
friedsam/archives/studentpages/ghost/fifth_dev_a_ounge_may_end
_mystery.htm.

Sexton, Jen. "Spectral Visits inside Devereux Hall." *St. Bonaventure University*. Retrieved 26 November 2007. http://web.sbu.edu/friedsam/
archives/studentpages/ghost/new_page_8.htm.

Bowers, Kristin. "Spooky Ghost Stories Haunt Students, Halls of Devereux." *St. Bonaventure University*. Retrieved 26 November 2007.
http://web.sbu.edu/friedsam/archives/studentpages/ghost/spooky_
ghost_stories_haunt_students,_halls_of_devereux.htm.

"St. Bonaventure University." *Answers.com*. Retrieved 1 May 2008. www
.answers.com/%22st.%20bonaventure%20university%22.

"Black Hand." *Answers.com*. Retrieved 2 May 2008. www.answers.com/
black%20hand.

"The Ghosts of Devereux Hall." *Chautauqua Ghosts*. Retrieved 25
November 2007. www.chautauquaghosts.com/stories/devereux.htm.

"The Incomplete Paper of De La Roche Hall." *Chautauqua Ghosts*.
Retrieved 25 November 2007. www.chautauquaghosts.com/stories/
de_la_roche.htm.

"A Brief History of Saint Bonaventure University." *Chautauqua Ghosts*.
Retrieved 25 November 2007. www.chautauquaghosts.com/stories/
st_bonaventure.htm.

"De La Roche Hall." *St. Bonaventure University*. Retrieved 26 November
2007. http://web.sbu.edu/friedsam/archives/studentpages/ghost/
delaroche.htm.

"Nicholas Devereux." *Catholic Encyclopedia*. Retrieved 2 May 2008. www
.newadvent.org/cathen/16033b.htm.

"About SBU—History." *St. Bonaventure University*. Retrieved 2 May 2008.
www.sbu.edu/about_sbu.aspx?id=1758.

"John Timon." *Wikipedia*. Retrieved 2 May 2008. http://en.wikipedia.org/
wiki/John_Timon.

"We Stick Together." *Sixth Scale Battle*. Retrieved 30 January 2008. www
.sixthscalebattle.com/contact.html.

"USS *Juneau*." *Answers.com*. Retrieved 30 January 2008. www.answers
.com/topic/USS-juneau-cl-52.

"Ghost Hunters Investigate Strange Happenings at Valentown Museum."
Victor Historical Society – Valentown Museum. Retrieved 4 April 2008.
http://valentown.org/taps_investigation.

"Ghost City of Valentown Ghost Hunts." *Victor Historical Society—Valentown
Museum*. Retrieved 4 April 2008. http://valentown.org/ghost _tours.

"Valentown Museum." *Victor Historical Society—Valentown Museum.* Retrieved 4 April 2008. http://valentown.org/about_the_museum.

"Mr. Sheldon Fisher." *Victor Historical Society—Valentown Museum.* Retrieved 4 April 2008. http://valentown.org/j__sheldon_fisher.

"Walking Ghost Caught on Tape?" *WUSA9 News Now.* Retrieved 4 April 2008. www.wusa9.com/news/news_article.aspx?storyid=50214.

"Valentown." *Wikipedia.* Retrieved 9 April 2008. http://en.wikipedia.org/wiki/Valentown.

"Villa Serendip Bed and Breakfast." *The B and B Registry.* Retrieved 11 December 2007. www.the-b-and-b-registry.com/usa/new-york/villa-serendip.bnb.

Ambroselli, Fran. "Genealogy and History of the Woodworth Homestead: Ambroselli's Villa Serendip Bed and Breakfast." *Villa Serendip.* Retrieved 2 December 2007. http://villaserendip.com/Genealogy%20 and%20History%20of%20Woodworth%20House.html

"Library History." *University of Rochester—River Campus Libraries.* Retrieved 6 February 2008. www.library.rochester.edu/index.cfm ?PAGE=745.

"Haunted Inns: Investigative Files." *Skeptical Inquirer—September 2000.* Retrieved 5 January 2008. http://csicop.org/si/2000-09/i-files.html.

"Market Hall." *Syracuse Then and Now.* Retrieved 26 March 2008. http:// syracusethenandnow.org/Dwntwn/MontgmrySt/CityHall/MarketHall .htm.

Pierce, Frederic. "Charlie the Ghost Haunts Historic Syracuse City Hall." *Strange CNY – The Post Standard.* Posted 7 February 2008. Retrieved 26 March 2008. http://blog.syracuse.com/strangecny/2008/02/charlie_ the_ghost_histo.html.

"Historical Marker Unveiled." *Craig Brandon—News.* Retrieved 7 March 2008. www.craigbrandon.com/MITAnews.html.

"Herkimer County 1834 Jail Named to Seven to Save List." *PLNYS: Preservation League Programs.* Retrieved 7 March 2008. www.preservenys .org/7S05_herkimer.html.

"Chester Gillette." *Wikipedia.* Retrieved 14 March 2008. http://en.wikipedia .org/wiki/Chester_Gillette.

"Grace Brown." *Wikipedia.* Retrieved 14 March 2008. http://en.wikipedia .org/wiki/Grace_Brown.

Gelb, Steven A. "Sentenced in Sorrow: The Role of Asylum in the Jean Gianini Murder Defence." *Science Direct.* Retrieved 14 March 2008. www.sciencedirect.com/science?_ob=ArticleURLand_udi=B6VH5-3SWY0CD-6and_u

Simonson, Mark. "A True Tale of Horror Found in Herkimer County." *The Daily Star.* Retrieved 8 November 2007. www.thedailystar.com/ columns/local_story_300081638.html/resources_printstory

"Forest Park Cemetery—Pinewood 2001—Brunswick (Troy), NY." *IMOVES*. Retrieved 28 March 2008. www.imoves.net/ForestPark2001Doc.html.

"Forest Park Cemetery—Pinewood 2002—Brunswick (Troy), NY." *IMOVES*. Retrieved 28 March 2008. www.imoves.net/ForestPark2002Doc.html.

"Forest Park Cemetery, Brunswick." *Wikipedia*. Retrieved 28 March 2008. http://en.wikipedia.org/wiki/Forest_Park_Cemetery%2C_Brunswick.

"Factual Information about Forest Park Cemetery." *Long Island Genealogy*. Retrieved 28 March 2008. www.longislandgenealogy.com/forest park.html.

"Forest Park Cemetery." *I Spy My Hometown—Brunswick, NY*. Retrieved 28 March 2008. www.uhls.org/ISpy/brun/brun-forest.html.

Morrow, Ann. "What Was That?" *Online Metroland*. Retrieved 28 March 2008. www.metroland.net/back_issues/vol_26_no44/halloween.html.

"The College of Saint Rose." *Wikipedia*. Retrieved 14 March 2008. http://en.wikipedia.org/wiki/the_College_of_Saint_Rose.

"History." *Saint Rose*. Retrieved 1 December 2007. www.strose.edu/Visitors/About_Saint_Rose/history_mission.asp.

Szubielski, Jola. "Real Haunted Houses in Albany?" *Capital News 9*. Retrieved 1 December 2007. www.capitalnews9.com/shared/print/default.asp?ArID=102153.

Melsert, Ashley. "Saint Rose Students Are Not Alone . . ." *The Saint Rose Chronicle*. Retrieved 1 December 2007. www.strosechronicle.com/home/index.cfm.

Senecal, Meg A. "Albany Hauntings: Fact or Fiction?" *The College of Saint Rose Communications Department*. Retrieved 14 March 2008. http://communications.strose.edu/Pring-JournalismF07-MegSenecal.htm.

"The Spirits of Beardslee Castle." *Beardslee Castle*. Retrieved 28 November 2007.

"The Cohoes Music Hall." *Cohoes Caretakers*. Retrieved 28 March 2008. www.cohoescaretakers.com/music%20hall.htm.

"The Hall." *C-R Productions at Cohoes Music Hall*. Retrieved 28 March 2008.

"Cohoes Music Hall and Visitors Center, NY." *Byways*. Retrieved 28 March 2008. www.byways.org/explore/byways/57185/places62386/.

"Split Rock." *Split Rock*. Retrieved 6 December 2007. http://home.twcny.rr.com/splitrock/splitrock.html.

"Split Rock, New York." *Answers.com*. Retrieved 6 December 2007. www.answers.com/topic/split-rock-new-york.

"Nitric Acid." *NIOSH Document: Pocket Guide to Chemical Hazards (2005-149)*. Retrieved 7 December 2007. www.cdc.gov/niosh/npg/npgd0447.html.

"The Man Who Froze to Death." *Elpis History*. Retrieved 21 April 2008. www.rootsweb.ancestry.com/~nyoneida/towns/vienna/elpis2.html.

"The Pierce Murder." *Elpis History*. Retrieved 15 April 2008. www.roots
web.ancestry.com/~nyoneida/towns/vienna/elpis2.html.

"New York State Capitol." *Wikipedia*. Retrieved 8 April 2008. http://en
.wikipedia.org/wiki/New_York_State_Capitol.

"Troy Hospital, 8th Street at Fulton Street." *1880 Federal Census, Troy*.
Retrieved 10 December 2007. www.connorsgenealogy.com/troy/Troy
Hospital.htm.

"A Brief History of West Hall." *Rensselaer Polytechnic Institute Department
of Earth & Environmental Sciences*. Retrieved 10 December 2007.
http://ees2.geo.rpi.edu/History/westhall.html.

"Rensselaer's History." *RPI: Rensselaer's History*. Retrieved 10 December
2007. www.rpi.edu/about/history.html.

"City of Troy." *Rensselaer County, NY GenWeb Site—History of City of Troy*.
Retrieved 10 December 2007. www.rootsweb.com/~nyrensse/troy
.htm.

"Landmark Theatre (Syracuse, New York)." *Wikipedia*. Retrieved 31 March
2008. http://en.wikipedia.org/wiki/Landmark_Theatre_(Syracuse,
_New_York).

"Ancestors Inn at the Bassett House—A Bed and Breakfast Experience."
Ancestors Inn. Retrieved 20 March 2008. www.ancestorsinn.com.

"Welcome to the Shanley Hotel." *Shanley Hotel*. Retrieved 19 March 2008.
http://shanleyhotel.com/index.html.

"The Historic Shanley Hotel." *Shanley Hotel*. Retrieved 19 March 2008.
http://shanleyhotel.com/History.html.

"Evidence." *Shanley Hotel*. Retrieved 19 March 2008. http://shanleyhotel
.com/evidence.html.

Hart, Doug (posted by). "Faughnan—Shanley Connection (forum)." *Faughnan Genealogy Discussion Board*. Retrieved 19 March 2008. http://
publ.bravenet.com/forum/8032291/fetch/594194/.

"The Lady Who Loathed Liquor—and They Built a Bar in Her Bedroom."
Metalgrrlism. Retrieved 15 January 2008. www.geocities.com/iron
maiden28/ghostsny.html?200815.

Scharling, Cheryl J. "Will the Real Mrs. Stacy Please Step Forward?" *Cheryl
Scharling.com*. Retrieved 16 January 2008. http://cherylscharling
.com/.

"Early History." *Woman's Christian Temperance Union*. Retrieved 16 January 2008. www.wctu.org/earlyhistory.html.

"I Spy in Cobleskill." *Mohawk Valley Library Association*. Retrieved 16 January 2008. www.mvls.info/ispy/cobleskill/cobl_05.html.

"Charles Courter." *Schoharie County NYGenWeb Site*. Retrieved 16 January 2008. www.rootsweb.com/~nyschoha/rospix16.html.

"Giving & Membership—Campaign for the New Century." *Bardavon*.
Retrieved 24 January 2008. www.bardavon.org/gi_capital2.php.

"Esplanade Walk of Fame." *Bardavon*. Retrieved 24 January 2008. www
.bardavon.org/gi_esplanade.htm.

"Architectural History." *Bardavon*. Retrieved 24 January 2008. www
.bardavon.org/ab_to_arch.htm.

"A Man's Vision Created the Bardavon." *Poughkeepsie Journal.com*.
Retrieved 23 January 2008. http://cityguide.pogonews.com/fe/Arts/
stories/art_bardavon_collingwood.asp.

Adams, Annon. "History of 35 Market Street." *CGR Law*. Retrieved 23 January 2008. www.cgrlaw.com/history35market.htm.

"Bardavon 1869 Opera House—Entertaining the Hudson Valley!" *Bardavon*. Retrieved 14 January 2008. www.bardavon.org.

"Smalley's Inn & Restaurant." *Wikipedia*. Retrieved 20 March 2008.
http://en.wikipedia.org/wiki/Smalley's_Inn_&_Restaurant.

Moirastyx. "Christ Episcopal Church—Part of the Haunted Tour." *Off the
Beaten Path*. Retrieved 13 February 2008. http://members.virtual
tourist.com/m/b6528/cd92f/6/.

"History of Kings Park Psychiatric Center." *Main*. Retrieved 18 March
2008. http://s.albalux.com/webpage/history.html.

"Kings Park." *Long Island Oddities*. Retrieved 18 March 2008. www
.lioddities.com/ghost/kingspark.htm

"Kings Park Psychiatric Center." *Long Island Ghost Hunters*. Retrieved 9
February 2008. www.longislandghosthunters.com/kings_park.htm.

Bleyer, Bill. "Kings Park—A Beacon for Those in Need." *Kings Farm*.
Retrieved 18 March 2008. www.geocities.com/KINGS_FARM/.

"Dylan Marlais Thomas." *Neurotic Poets*. Retrieved 4 April 2008. www
.neuroticpoets.com.

"White Horse Tavern." *New York Magazine Bar Guide*. Retrieved 4 April
2008. http://nymag.com/listings/bar/white_horse_tavern/.

"White Horse Tavern (New York City)." *Wikipedia*. Retrieved 4 April 2008.
http://en.wikipedia.org/wiki/White_Horse_Tavern_(New_York_City).

"NYC Post #9: Brooklyn, Downtown Brooklyn, Fort Greene/Clinton Hill,
the Brooklyn Navy Yard." *Blue Skies Falling*. Retrieved 17 April 2008.
www.hereisnowwhy.com/blog/2005/10/nyc-post-9-brooklyn-down
town-brooklyn.html.

"Lefferts-Laidlaw House." *Archiplanet*. Retrieved 17 April 2008. www
.archiplanet.org/wiki/Lefferts-Laidlaw_House.

"Neighborhood at Risk: Wallabout." *Historic Districts Council*. Retrieved
17 April 2008. www.hdc.org/neighborhoodatriskwallabout.htm.

"Landmark Permit Issued for 136 Clinton Avenue, Brooklyn." *Landmark
Building Permits*. Retrieved 17 April 2008. http://nyc.everyblock.com/
landmark-building-permits/by-date/2007/5/9/563820/.

"Blissville." *Joey in Astoria: April 2007*. Retrieved 17 April 2008. http://
astoriannyc.blogspot.com/2007_04_01_archive.html.

"Blissville, Queens." *Wikipedia.* Retrieved 17 April 2008. http://en
.wikipedia.org/wiki/Blissville%2C_Queens.

"History of Flushing Meeting." *NYYM (New York Yearly Meeting).* Retrieved
17 April 2008. www.nyym.org/flushing/history.html.

"Neighborhoods: Dutch Kills." *Greater Astoria Historical Society.* Retrieved
17 April 2008. www.astorialic.org/neighborhoods/dk_p.php.

"Dutch Kills, Queens." *Wikipedia.* Retrieved 17 April 2008. http://en
.wikipedia.org/wiki/Dutch_Kills.

"Gallus Mag." *Wikipedia.* Retrieved 4 April 2008. http://en.wikipedia
.org/wiki/Gallus_Mag.

Thompson, Andrea. "Bridge Café." *New Yorker.* Retrieved 4 April 2008.
www.newyorker.com/archive/2006/11/27/061127gota_GOAT_tables.

"Exploring Old Haunts (and a Few Hauntings)." *New York Times Archives
Online.* Retrieved 26 January 2008. www.nytimes.com/2006/10/27/
arts/27fami.ART.html.

"Ghost Hunters Episode 207." *SCIFIPEDIA.* Retrieved 29 January 2008.
http://scifipedia.scifi.com/index.php/Ghost_Hunters_Episode_207.

Haller, Vera. "A Haunted Tale of Broken Love." *NYNewsday.com.* Retrieved
29 January 2008. www.newsday.com/news/local/newyork/nyc-haunted
,0,3227569.story.

Bellow, Anthony. "Old Merchant's House." *The Tredwell Family.* Retrieved
25 January 2008. http://freepages.genealogy.rootsweb.com/~treadwell/
merchant.html.

"Merchant's House Museum." *New York Architecture Images.* Retrieved 25
January 2008. www.nyc-architecture.com/LES/LES017.htm.

"Home (in Old New York)." *Merchants House.* Retrieved 15 November
2007. www.merchantshouse.com/.

"Haunted Mansion: The Morris-Jumel House Ghost." *Essortment.* Retrieved
3 March 2008. www.essortment.com/all/hauntedmansion_rund.htm.

"Morris-Jumel Mansion Museum." *The Historic House Trust of New York
City.* Retrieved 3 March 2008. www.historichousetrust.org/item.php?i
_id=20.

"Morris-Jumel Mansion: History." *Morris Jumel.* Retrieved 13 March 2008.
www.morrisjumel.org/history/index.php?sec=hist.

"Morris-Jumel Mansion." *Places Where Women Made History.* Retrieved 3
March 2008. www.nps.gov/history/nr/travel/pwwmh/ny23.htm.

"McCarren Park Pool to Become a Functioning Swimming Pool Again . . ."
FREE Williamsburg. Retrieved 22 January 2008. www.freewilliamsburg
.com/archives/2007/04/mccarren_park_p_3.html.

Dwyer, Kevin. "Blasts from the Past." *NY Magazine.* Retrieved 2 April 2008.
http://nymag.com/nymetro/nightlife/barbuzz/11924/.

"Welcome to the Ear Inn." *Ear Inn.* Retrieved 15 November 2007. http://
earinn.com/?page_id=2.

"Andrew Corsa." *Bronx County Clerks Office*. Retrieved 21 January 2008. www.bronxcountyclerksoffice.com/en/notable.htm.

Rutkoff, Aaron, Angela Montefinise and Myles Gordon. "The Afterlife of Fort Totten: From Platoons to Playgrounds." *Queens Tribune Online*. Retrieved 29 January 2008. www.queenstribune.com/anniversary 2003/fortotten.htm.

"Historical Timeline." *Fort Totten*. Retrieved 29 January 2008. www.fort totten.org/Timeline.shtml.

Squires, Kathleen. "Chef Talk: Craig Hopson of One if by Land, Two if by Sea." *New York City Bottomless Dish Blog*. Retrieved 14 February 2008.

D'Alessandro, Dina R. "Birthday Dinner." *Daily Dish*. Retrieved 20 February 2008. http://dishwithdina.blogspot.com/2007/02/birthday-dinner.html.

"One if by Land, Two if by Sea Restaurant." *Long Island Paranormal Investigators*. Retrieved 14 February 2008. www.liparanormalinvestigators.com/nyc.shtml.

"Theodosia Burr Alston." *Wikipedia*. Retrieved 14 February 2008. http://en.wikipedia.org/wiki/Theodosia_Burr_Alston.

"Greenwich Village—The Story of Richmond Hill." *Old and Sold*. Retrieved 14 February 2008. www.oldandsold.com/articles13/greenwich-village-4.shtml.

"Raynham Hall, Oyster Bay." *Long Island Paranormal Investigators*. Retrieved 20 March 2008. www.liparanormalinvestigators.com/raynham.shtml.

"Raynham Hall." *Wikipedia*. Retrieved 20 March 2008. http://en.wikipedia.org/wiki/Raynham_Hall.

"History—The Townsend Family and Raynham Hall." *Raynham Hall Museum*. Retrieved 20 March 2008. www.raynhamhallmuseum.org/history.asp.

"A Country Bed & Breakfast." *Wedding Cottage*. Retrieved 13 February 2008. www.weddingcottage.com/.

Untitled, story about Old Bermuda Inn. *Hells Hounds Lair*. Retrieved 13 February 2008. www.hellhoundslair.com/returnofdead.html.

"The Old Bermuda Inn." *Real Haunted Houses*. Retrieved 14 February 2008. www.realhaunts.com/united-states/new-york/staten-island/the-old-bermuda-inn/.

"Meucci Museum—Staten Island, NY." *Eastern Paranormal Investigation Center*. Retrieved 2 April 2008. www.epicparanormal.com/gmm_6_23_07.htm.

Untitled. *Garibaldi Meucci Museum*. Retrieved 2 April 2008. www.garibaldimeuccimuseum.org/Resources/haunte1b.gif.

"Queens Historical Society." *Queens Historical Society*. Retrieved 30 January 2008. www.queenshistoricalsociety.org/about.html.

"Kingsland Homestead." *Queens Historical Society.* Retrieved 30 January 2008. www.queenshistoricalsociety.org/kingsland.html.

Roleke, John. "Haunted Queens." *John Roleke's Queens, NY, Blog.* Retrieved 30 January 2008. http://queens.about.com/b/2005/10/31/haunted -queens.htm.

"History of Richmond Town, Staten Island and Development of the Museum." *Historic Richmond Town.* Retrieved 1 February 2008. http:// historicrichmondtown.org/about.html.

Newspaper and Periodical Articles

(in order by story)

"Killed by a Train near Oswego." *New York Times.* 2 August 1897.

"Triple Murder at Oswego." *New York Times.* 25 June 1898.

"Miscellaneous." *New York Times.* 18 July 1859.

"No Evidence to Prove Murder." *New York Times.* 23 October 1885.

"Children Drown in Oswego River." *New York Times.* 18 June 1900.

"Mrs. Ledyard P. Hale Critically Ill, Dies." *Commercial Advertiser* (Canton). 20 August 1935.

"Betsey Russell Hale." *Commercial Advertiser* (Canton). 23 July 1907.

"U.S. Mail Box Broken Letters Scattered." *Commercial Advertiser* (Canton). 13 October 1936.

"Notes." *Commercial Advertiser* (Canton). 9 October 1951.

"Horace C. Hale Will Practice Law in Canton." *Commercial Advertiser* (Canton). 28 October 1919.

"Major Horace C. Hale Dies in Fort Devens Hospital." *Commercial Advertiser* (Canton). 2 March 1948.

"Kappa Deltas Occupy New Chapter Home." *Commercial Advertiser* (Canton). Date illegible, 1942.

"Contractors Working on New Kappa Delta House." *Commercial Advertiser* (Canton). 14 October 1941.

"Engagement of Miss Margaret Currie and Clyde Thompson Announced." *Commercial Advertiser* (Canton). 8 March 1938.

"Leo Ward Killed in Car Crash." *Ogdensburg Advance-News.* 7 October 1956.

"Heuvelton Searchers Mystified." *Ogdensburg Advance-News.* Date unknown, 1951.

Crawford, Lyle. "Frogman Joins in the Search for Youth Missing since Kendrew Bridge Fatality. 2,000 People Gather to Watch Operations." *Ogdensburg Advance-News.* 9 December 1951.

"Missing Boy Found Drowned." *Ogdensburg Advance-News.* 6 April 1952.

"Wife Murders Her Husband Then Turns Gun on Herself." *Journal and Republican* (Lowville). 24 August 1922.

Barber, Peter R. "In Chaumont, a Favorite Haunt, Full of Spirit." *Watertown Daily Times.* 31 October 1999.

"Burlingame's Relatives to Inherit His Estate." *Journal and Republican* (Lowville). 26 October 1922.

"Court Orders Estate Split." *Journal and Republican* (Lowville). 25 September 1924.

"Local Hunter Shot Monday; Dies Instantly." *Massena Observer.* 24 November 1949.

Untitled, notes about Julia Phelps. *Watertown Herald.* 6 July 1912.

Untitled, notes about LeRay Mansion. *Tribune-Press* (Gouverneur). 2 March 1983.

"Mrs. Sisson of Potsdam Dead at 84." *Ogdensburg Advance-News.* 28 June 1953.

"George W. Sisson, Ex-Farm Official." *New York Times.* 8 February 1954.

Untitled, notes. *St. Lawrence Herald* (Potsdam). 24 October 1902.

Anderson, Jeannine. "Costanzo's Old Grist Mill May Go on Federal Register." *Courier & Freeman* (Potsdam). 19 January 1982.

"William Newby Passes Away at Morley." *Commercial Advertiser* (Canton). 3 January 1933.

Ellen, Martha. "Ghost Seekers Investigate Signs of Haunting at Old Morley Mill." *Watertown Daily Times.* 2 February 2002.

———. "Ghost Seekers Say They Sensed Spirits Milling About at 160-Year-Old Site in Morley." *Watertown Daily Times.* 3 March 2002.

Untitled, notes about William Newby. *Ogdensburg Advance.* 28 August 1913.

Untitled, notes about Leland Freeman. *Commercial Advertiser* (Canton). 12 August 1919.

Untitled, notes about Morley Grist Mill. *Commercial Advertiser* (Canton). 17 May 1927.

"Barnes Corners." *Journal and Republican* (Lowville). 21 December 1922.

Untitled, notes about Homer Rebb, asthma. *Journal and Republican* (Lowville). 10 January 1924.

Untitled, notes about Homer Rebb, bronchial trouble. *Journal and Republican* (Lowville). 7 February 1924.

Untitled, notes about Homer Rebb, violin. *Journal and Republican* (Lowville). 14 August 1924.

Untitled, notes about Homer Rebb, new Studebaker. *Journal and Republican* (Lowville). 27 January 1924.

Untitled, notes about Homer Rebb, trip to Florida. *Journal and Republican* (Lowville). 27 November 1924.

Untitled, notes about Girl Scout visit to Cider Mill. *Gouverneur Tribune-Press.* 21 October 1980.

Untitled, notes about visit to Cider Mill. *Courier & Freeman* (Potsdam). 7 October 1975.

Pominville, Karen. "Cider Mill Spooked by Ghost of Capt. Burr." *Watertown Daily Times*. 30 October 1997.

Untitled, notes about Fort Ontario. *Malone Farmer*. 23 January 1907.

"Ghosts of Old Fort Ontario Program Set." *Valley News*. 19 October 2002.

Prince, Leonard H. "Massena's Oldest House Was Built from Grasse River Stone by Lemuel Haskell in 1826." *Courier & Freeman* (Potsdam). 10 July 1975.

"Story of Buried Treasure in Historic Haskell Homestead Often Stirs Search among Walls." *Post-Standard*. 29 August 1926 (date illegible).

"Madam Vespucci—Story of Her Alliance with George Parish—First Met at Evans Mills." *Sunday Herald* (Syracuse). 8 August 1897.

"Patrick Cummings." *Watertown Herald*. 19 March 1910.

Hornak, Paul. "Hoover Inn's New Operator Inherits 174 Years of History—and a Ghost." *Watertown Daily Times*. 8 December 2002.

Untitled, notes about Spanky's. *Potsdam Herald-Recorder*. 13 March 1942.

"Massena to Have Private Hospital." *Advance News*. 19 May 1940.

"Massena Man Died from Bullet Wound." *Courier & Freeman* (Potsdam). August 1940.

Hornak, Paul. "Drum Plans Observance for German POWs Who Died While Imprisoned." *Watertown Daily Times*. 4 November 2002.

Moffat, George J. "And All for the Love of a Maiden!" *Journal*. 30 August 1973.

"Haunted Plum Brook Mill." *Ogdensburg Advance*. Illegible date, 1905.

"Area Briefs—Student Dies." *Adirondack Daily Enterprise*. 4 February 1963.

Cobb, Stephen. "Believe It or Not—The Ghosts of Paul Smith's College." *Sequel* (Paul Smith's College newsletter) Fall 2004.

"Another Suicide." *Malone Farmer*. 15 November 1905.

"100 Flee Fire Razing Paul Smith's Hotel." *New York Times*. 6 September 1930.

"Elizabeth Meron "Betty" Bergman." *Press-Republican* (Plattsburgh). 10 September 2007.

"Restaurateur Meron Dies." *Press-Republican* (Plattsburgh). 25 October 1984.

"Plattsburgh State Normal School Destroyed by Fire Saturday." *Plattsburgh Sentinel*. 29 January 1929.

"Blanchard a Suicide—Janitor of Normal Takes His Own Life—Body Found by His Assistant." *Plattsburgh Sentinel*. 16 March 1917.

Untitled, notes about John Blanchard. *Plattsburgh Sentinel*. 24 November 1916.

"Restive Spirits." *Watertown Herald*. 26 November 1887.

"Port Leyden" (notes). *Journal & Republican* (Lowville). 20 October 1898.

Untitled, notes about McKims. *Democrat* (Lowville). 19 November 1898.

Untitled, notes about McKims. *Democrat* (Lowville). 8 May 1901.

"Triple Drowning at Elizabethtown." *Ticonderoga Sentinel.* 8 September 1921.

"ACT and Bruce L. Crary Foundation Merge into $22 Million Foundation." *ACT Adirondack Community Trust* (newsletter). Summer 2007.

"50 Years Ago." *Courier & Freeman* (Potsdam). 15 October 1947.

"Malone's Mystery." *Plattsburgh Sentinel.* 12 November 1897.

"Letter to the Editor." *St. Lawrence Herald.* 15 October 1897.

"Mystery in Malone House." *New York Times.* 8 October 1897.

"Personal." *New York Times.* 9 October 1897.

"Kills Daughter, Shoots 2 Escorts." *New York Times.* 30 March 1936.

"Boy Scout Drowned in Demonstration." *Evening Tribune* (Albert Lea, Minnesota). 3 April 1944.

"Missing Rochester Child Slain." *Post-Standard* (Syracuse). 4 April 1973.

"The Niagara Tragedy." *New York Times.* 6 May 1871.

"The Drowning of Capt. Dove." *New York Times.* 8 June 1884.

"Think Ruins Old Chapel—Historians Believe Masonry at Fort Niagara Relic of 1759." *New York Times.* 3 May 1931.

Ballingrud, David. "Phantom or Phenomenon?" *St. Petersburg Times.* 20 October 2002.

Powell, Alvin. "How Oliver Wendell Holmes Helped Conquer the 'Black Death of Childbed.'" *Harvard University Gazette.* 18 September 1997.

"Buffalo Priest Found Shot Dead." *New York Times.* 2 January 1960.

"Statue Will Be Memorial for Three Students." *Olean Times Herald.* 11 April 1946.

"Firemen Injured Fighting Lynch Hall Blaze Tuesday Night." *Olean Times-Herald.* 19 April 1933.

"Death of Nicholas Devereux." *Utica Observer.* 29 December 1855.

"Father Leo Laid to Rest." *Marshfield Times* (Marshfield, Wisconsin). 4 March 1908.

"Incendiary Fire—St. Bonaventure College Building Burned." *Syracuse Herald.* 30 June 1908.

Maloney, George. "Concerning Pete Nicosia." *Soap-Box* (Rochester University newsletter). March 1934.

Weiss, Bob. "Hark! Pete Nicosia's Back—And Rush Rhees Has Him." *Campus* (University of Rochester newsletter). 21 May 1948.

"Mystery of Pete Nicosia Probed by Faculty, Students, 'Campus.'" *Campus* (University of Rochester newsletter). 16 march 1934.

University of Rochester Library Bulletin. 25, no. 3 (Spring 1970).

"19-Story Tower to House Rochester University Books." *New York Times.* 21 March 1930.

"Library near Completion." *New York Times*. 28 January 1929.

"More Library Units Open at Rochester." *New York Times*. 15 December 1940.

Loudon, Bennett J. "Local Haunts." *Rochester Democrat & Chronicle*. 29 October 2003.

"Auburn Italians Scared by Haunted House Story." *Syracuse Herald*. 28 March 1915.

"Murderer Wilson Executed." *New York Times*. 15 May 1894.

"No Belief in Electrocution—Dr. Gibbon's Request to Experiment on Murderer Charles F. Wilson." *New York Times*. 14 November 1894.

"Wilson Must Remain Dead." *New York Times*. 22 November 1894.

"C. F. Wilson Sentenced to Death." *New York Times*. 9 May 1895.

"Wilson's Sentence Commuted." *New York Times*. 12 June 1895.

"Roxie Druse's Last Sunday." *New York Times*. 28 February 1887.

Untitled, notes about Herkimer Jail ghost. *Sun* (Fort Covington). 7 July 1887.

"Twenty-Five Years Ago." *Journal and Republican* (Lowville). 8 October 1885.

Ackerman, Bryon. "Horror Fills Historic Herkimer Jail." *Mid-York Weekly & Pennysaver*. 27 October 2005.

"Teacher Boy Killed Had Befriended Him." *New York Times*. 1 April 1914.

"Bares Chum's Plot to Kill Teacher." *New York Times*. 30 March 1914.

"Jurymen Failed to Do Duty." *Journal and Republican* (Lowville). 11 June 1914.

Untitled. *Troy Record*. 27 October 1996.

Stickel, Julie. "Spirits Roam Beardslee Castle." *Rome Observer*. 23 October 2006.

Baber, Cassaundra. "A Haunting Good Time." *Observer-Dispatch* (Utica). 25 October 2007.

"Eva Tanguay Dies in Hollywood, 68." *New York Times*. 12 January 1947.

"Eva Tanguay Left $500." *New York Times*. 24 January 1947.

"Eva Tanguay's Funeral." *New York Times*. 15 January 1947.

"60 Killed by Blast in Syracuse Plant." *New York Times*. 4 July 1918.

"So-Called Haunted Farm." *Watertown Herald*. 29 January 1910.

"Caught after Twelve Years." *New York Times*. 15 November 1885.

"By Mail and Telegraph." *New York Times*. 24 September 1874.

"Arrested and Discharged." *Journal and Republican*. 23 April 1873.

"Terrible Murder near Camden." *Journal and Republican*. 16 April 1873.

"Pierce, the Camden Murder." *New York Times*. 15 April 1873.

"Albany Capitol Ruined by Fire." *Warren Evening Mirror*. 29 March 1911.

"Capitol Fire-Swept; Pride of the State Is Quickly a Wreck." *Post-Standard*. 30 March 1911.

"Many Millions Loss in New York Capitol Fire." *Daily Review* (Decatur, IL). 29 March 1911.

"Fire Does $10,000,000 Damage to New York's Great State Capital." *San Antonio Light.* 29 March 1911.

"Body Recovered—Samuel Abbott, Victim of Capitol Fire in Albany." *Lowell Sun.* 31 March 1911.

Agosta, Brian, Christina Goldschmidt, Rob Sable. "If There's Something Strange in the Neighborhood." *Poly Features.* 27 October 1999.

Marquis, Robyn. "Ghost Hunters Search West Hall for Spirits." *Poly Features.* 20 September 2006.

Brownstein, Andrew. "Ghost Talk Won't R.I.P. at RPI." *Times Union* (Albany). October 1997.

Ackerman, Jodi. "Ghost Seekers Come to Rensselaer." *Union Speakers Forum—Rensselaer newsletter.* Date unknown, 1999.

"West Hall Revival." *Rensselaer Magazine.* Winter 2004.

Kirst, Sean. "Ghost Hunt Raises Spirits at Landmark Theatre." *Post-Standard.* 31 October 2005.

"Loew's State, Syracuse." *Fulton Patriot.* 8 August 1928.

"Loew's State Theater Is Grateful." *Syracuse Herald.* Date unknown, 1928.

Tomcho, Sandy. "Ghost Hunting at the Shanley Hotel." *Times Herald-Record.* 19 October 2007.

"Little Girl Is Drowned in a Farm Well." *Middletown Daily Times.* 31 May 1911.

"Firemen Combat Napanoch Blaze in Easter Suits." *Middletown Times Herald.* 14 April 1941.

Untitled, notes regarding Shanley infant. *Middletown Daily Times-Press.* 9 January 1912.

"Napanoch Man Dies on Tuesday." *Kingston Daily Freeman.* 25 August 1937.

"Charles Courter." *New York Times.* 2 January 1879.

"Lillian Graham's Recovery Doubtful." *New York Times.* 26 March 1895.

"Poughkeepsie's Pest House—Where Poor Little Lillian Graham, the Child Actress, Is Confined with Diphtheria." *New York Times.* 31 March 1895.

"The Sad Plight of a Youthful Actress." *New York Times.* 19 March 1895.

Hunt, Alice. "Hudson Valley Hauntings." *Poughkeepsie Journal.* 31 October 2005.

Thomas, Robert McG., Jr. "Center of Carmel Destroyed in Fire." *New York Times.* 23 October 1974.

"Joseph Brooks Smalley." *New York Times.* 6 July 1942.

"Historic Court House at Carmel Is Burned: Fire, in High Wind, Razes Bank, Newspaper Plant, Hotel and Two Stables." *New York Times.* 18 November 1924.

Hanley-Goff, M. J. "Ghost Encounters with the Hudson Valley Paranormal Investigations." *Times Herald-Record.* 19 October 2007.

"Ghosts in Smalley's Inn in Carmel and Putnam Execution Are Part of New Book." *Journal News.* 27 October 2007.

"Ends Life in Leap under Truck." *New York Times.* 22 January 1933.

"Held in Patient's Death." *New York Times.* 14 June 1928.

"Asylum Keepers Discharged." *New York Times.* 25 November 1899.

"Sisters Describe 10 Years in Asylum." *New York Times.* 20 March 1920.

"Woman Sues Brothers—Charges She Was Placed in Insane Asylum without Cause." *New York Times.* 8 August 1923.

"Reilly Is Found Sane; Freed from Hospital." *New York Times.* 24 March 1938.

"Two Insane Sisters Roam Long Island." *New York Times.* 16 May 1915.

"Brush Sisters Lose Suit." *New York Times.* 5 February 1927.

"Brush Sisters Get Verdict of $10,000 Each Against Doctors Who Sent Them to Asylum." *New York Times.* 29 November 1924.

"Jury Awards $15,000 for Term in Asylum." *New York Times.* 29 January 1938.

"Love Wrecks Girl's Mind—Musician Insane After Suppressing Affection for a Married Man." *New York Times.* 19 August 1922.

"Roosevelt Orders Hospital Inquiry—Governor Will Sift Charges That Insane Patients Are Abused at Kings Park." *New York Times.* 2 April 1929.

"The New Kings County Farm." *New York Times.* 5 December 1884.

"Dylan Thomas, Poet, Very Ill." *New York Times.* 6 November 1953.

"City Haunts: A Ghostly Guide." *New York Times.* 29 October 1995.

Finn, Robin. "Public Lives; Fame and Fingernails as a TV Mobster's Wife." *New York Times.* 24 April 2001.

Bird, David and David W. Dunlap. "New York Day by Day; Welsh Honor Thomas at the White Horse." *New York Times.* 4 April 2008.

"Mysterious—Spiritual Phenomena on Clinton Avenue." *Brooklyn Eagle.* 20 December 1878.

"The Brooklyn Ghost." *New York Times.* 21 December 1878.

"For Sale—Houses." *Brooklyn Eagle.* 31 March 1876.

"Long Island (re Blissville)." *New York Times.* 1 July 1875.

"George Reinhardt's Death." *New York Times.* 25 February 1878.

"George Reinhardt's Death—Indication that he was not murdered." *New York Times.* 21 December 1879.

"Killed on the Track." *New York Times.* 21 June 1882.

"A Deputy Collector Murdered." *New York Times.* 14 February 1883.

"Ghost-Hunting in Blissville." *New York Times.* 9 March 1884.

"A Red-Haired, Blue-Eyed Ghost." *New York Times.* 10 March 1884.

"The Blissville Ghost Treed." *New York Times.* 12 March 1884.

"The Banshee of Blissville." *New York Times.* 17 March 1884.

Untitled, notes about Blissville ghost. *New York Times.* 11 February 1885.

Onishi, Norimitsu. "Neighborhood Report: Blissville/Long Island City; Don't Blink, or You Might Miss the bliss." *New York Times.* 17 July 1994.

"Quaker Ghosts." *New York Times*. 22 April 1884.

"Flushing's Ghostly Visitor." *New York Times*. 20 April 1884.

"Quakers Unmoved by Ghosts." *New York Times*. 21 April 1884.

Lippincott, E. E. "Neighborhood Report: Flushing; Theft of a Quaker Tombstone Provokes Scholarly Sleuthing." *New York Times*. 29 October 2000.

"Will Celebrate Its Birthday - Flushing's Two Hundred and Fiftieth Anniversary." *New York Times*. 10 June 1894.

"Latest Long Island News—A Brooklyn Family's Experience with a Rockaway Spook." *Brooklyn Eagle*. 8 January 1896.

"A Ghost in Gusterin's Flat." *New York Times*. 9 January 1896.

"A Ghost in Long Island City." *New York Times*. 29 January 1874.

"Woman Dies Suddenly at a Hotel." *New York Times*. 5 July 1908.

Dunning, Jennifer. "A Skeleton Key to Halloween Tricks and Treats." *New York Times*. 30 October 1981.

Gray, Christopher. "Streetscapes: The Bridge Café; On the Trail of New York's Oldest Surviving Bar." *New York Times*. 19 November 1995.

"From Hamilton's Pen: The Mystery of Gulielma Sands." *Herald* (Syracuse). 9 October 1887.

"Downtown Bar and Grill Held Up." *New York Times*. 10 February 1937.

Bowers, Brent. "Artist Paints Image, Learns of Neighborhood Ghost." *Amarillo Globe-Times*. 5 February 1975.

Mooney, Jake. "Beer-Soaked Myths, Boarded Up for Now." *New York Times*. 6 May 2007.

"Slain Over Chess Game." *New York Times*. 2 June 1960.

"Lieut. Alfred A. Stokes." *New York Times*. 11 August 1939.

"Four Murderers Hanged." *New York Times*. 24 August 1889.

"Charged with Abduction." *New York Times*. 10 July 1887.

"He Killed Her." *New York Times*. 18 July 1888.

"About New York; Belief in Ghost Haunts a Historic Mansion." *New York Times*. 31 October 1981.

Glueck, Grace. "2 Uptown 'Ghosts' Get Eviction Call." *New York Times*. 23 May 1964.

"Fighting for Millions." *New York Times*. 29 March 1877.

"Death of Gen. F. P. Earle—Was a Noted Hotel Man and Owner of the Jumel Mansion." *New York Times*. 3 January 1903.

"The Jumel Mansion." *New York Times*. 10 January 1897.

"Fifteen Years in the Courts." *New York Times*. 1 July 1881.

Gray, Christopher. "Streetscapes/The Morris-Jumel Mansion, 160th Street and Edgecombe Avenue; 1760's House Filled with History." *New York Times*. 24 March 2002.

"The Contest About the Alleged Will of the Late Widow of Aaron Burr—Motion to Settle the Issue—Over $1,000,000 of Property Involved." *New York Times*. 8 February 1866.

"City to Buy Jumel Mansion." *New York Times.* 7 March 1901.

"The Jumel Mansion in Fact and Legend." *New York Times.* 29 April 1917.

Goff, Liz. "Queens' Ghosts Are Here All Year Round." *Queens Gazette.* 1 November 2006.

"Student Shot Dead in a Park Mystery." *New York Times.* 28 June 1952.

"Boy Dies in Brooklyn Pool." *New York Times.* 29 June 1977.

"Man Drowns in Park Pool." *New York Times.* 3 September 1969.

Anderson, Susan Heller, and David W. Dunlap. "New York Day by Day; From Home to Speakeasy to Bar to Landmark." *New York Times.* 17 June 1986.

"In and About the City." *New York Times.* 7 July 1888.

"Woman Is Crushed by Gate at Vanderbilt Tomb on S.I." *New York Times.* 12 June 1967.

Untitled, notes about Vanderbilt Tomb. *Iowa State Reporter.* 28 May 1891.

Untitled, notes about Vanderbilt Tomb. *Landmark* (Statesville, NC). 22 September 1887.

Fried, Joseph P. "A Clash over Revival of a Queens Landmark." *New York Times.* 19 February 1989.

"Miss Thomas' Death Found Accidental." *New York Times.* 12 September 1920.

Viagas, Robert. "The Ghosts of Broadway." *New York Times.* 10 June 2005.

"Paris Authorities Investigate Death of Olive Thomas." *New York Times.* 11 September 1920.

Bertrand, Donald. "Fort Totten Development Marches On." *Daily News—Queens.* 15 January 2008.

"Boo York City." *New York Post.* 28 October 2006.

"Apartments Pass to New Ownership." *New York Times.* 24 February 1938.

Gray, Christopher. "Streetscapes/Barrow Street: A Block That Reflects Greenwich Village's History." *New York Times.* 1 November 1998.

"Michael Hallanan's Will." *New York Times.* 13 April 1926.

"Sheridan Square Loses Its Father." *New York Times.* 5 April 1926.

"Died." *New York Times.* 7 February 1884.

"In the Real Estate Field." *New York Times.* 18 January 1899.

"Deaths Reported April 21." *New York Times.* 22 April 1902.

"Deaths Reported July 3." *New York Times.* 4 July 1903.

"News Summary." *Brooklyn Eagle.* 26 February 1872.

"Drowned in Prank: Seaman, Pushed off Pier by Girl, Strikes His Head." *New York Times.* 6 August 1940.

"Where Aaron Burr Used to Live." *New York Times.* 19 January 1913.

Untitled, notes about Snug Harbor. *Sioux County Herald.* 21 July 1881.

"A Ship—That Rose from the Sea. A Sailor's Yarn." *Spirit Lake Beacon* (Spirit Lake, IA). 25 August 1899.

Untitled, notes about Snug Harbor. *Freeborn County Standard* (Albert, MN). 24 October 1888.

Untitled, notes about Snug Harbor. *Indiana Progress* (Indiana, PA). 4 October 1877.

"Kingsland Homestead Now a Museum." *New York Times.* 25 March 1973.

Dowd, Maureen. "Is New York Too Scary Even for Its Ghosts?" *New York Times.* 31 October 1985.

"Houdini's Body Gets Here Today." *New York Times.* 2 November 1920.

Martin, Douglas. "Resting in Comparative Peace; to Keep Vandals Away, Houdini's Grave is Closed for Halloween." *New York Times.* 30 October 1995.

"Serious Accident—A Mother's Care." *New York Times.* 30 August 1855.

"City Haunts: A Ghostly Guide." *New York Times.* 29 March 1995.

"Life Style: Sunday Outing; Ghoulies and Ghosties with Senses of History." *New York Times.* 22 October 1989.

Acknowledgments

I thank Kyle Weaver, my editor, for his friendship and expertise; Brett Keener, assistant editor, for his patience and keen eye; and all of the others at Stackpole Books who work their magic. It's always a pleasure to work with you.

Many, many thanks to the following individuals who have shared their ghostly encounters, passed on legends regarding properties they have been associated with, given a nod of approval to the stories I've written about them, or otherwise assisted me in my remarkable six-year quest to compile the New York State ghost stories in this book: Megan Crowley of Kappa Delta Sigma, Macreena Doyle of St. Lawrence University, Ron and Diane Kines, Joan Szarka, Phillip Creighton and Kate Heuser of the Shadow Chasers, Fred and Diane Murphy, Nili Gold of the Tau Epsilon Phi fraternity house, Charlie LaShombe of the Harison-Morley Grist Mill, Greg Sr. and Cindy Steiner, Greg Jr. and Tina Steiner of the Burrville Cider Mill, Craig and Laurie of Empire State Paranormal, Greather Ithaca Paranormal Society, Gerry Coleman, Julie Weston, and the rest of the WPBS crew, Barry and Allison Verville, Stephanie Comini of John Hoover Inn, Bud and Bev Perry, Alex Krywanszyk, Valerie LeValley, Ronnie Guindon, Marjorie Thorpe, Joanne Derouchia, Jeff Clark, Margaret M., Denise L., Paraphysical Scientific Investigations (PSI), Margaret Gibbs of the Adirondack History Center Museum, Jessie Olcott, Jerimy, Grace Bergman of Meron's Restaurant, Barb Beamish, Mitchel C. Koen, Connie Repas, Laura Whalen, Jared and Maureen McCargar, Marc and Sarah Spicer,

Belle and Gary Salisbury, Hannelore Kissam, Linda and Randolph Stanley of Wellscroft Lodge, the Light Connection, Daniel R. Gilliland of Holiday Inn Grand Island Resort and Conference Center, Christie, Pam Wilkins, Rick (Angel of Thy Night) of Paranormal and Ghost Society, Dorothy Ludemann, Dennis Frank, Fran Ambroselli of the Villa Serendip Bed and Breakfast, Nancy Martin and Sally Roche of the University of Rochester, Ghost Seekers of Central New York, Frances T. Barbieri of the Seneca Falls Historical Society, IMOVES, Randall Brown of Beardslee Castle, Tracey Leibach of *Rensselaer* alumni magazine, Charles A. Pemburn of Professor Java's Coffee Sanctuary, the Landmark Theatre Board of Trustees, Mary and Dan Weidman, Sal and Cindy Nicosia of the Shanley Hotel, Jason Adams of the Bardavon 1869 Opera House, Tony Porto of Smalley's Inn, Adam Weprin of the Bridge Café, Maria DaGrossa of the Manhattan Bistro, Chumley's, Rip Haymen of the Ear Inn, Rosanne Manetta of One if by Land, Two if by Sea, and C. Brennan of Old Bermuda Inn.

As always, I give the most thanks to my family: my wonderful husband and greatest fan, Leland Farnsworth II, whose wisdom, love, and support are invaluable; my beautiful daughters—Michelle, Jamie, Katie, and Nicole—who are hands-down the finest works I'll ever create in my lifetime; my parents, Tom and Jean Dishaw, who taught me the power of the written word, the importance of an open mind, and the value of persistence; and my wonderful siblings—Tom Dishaw, Christina Walker, and Cindy "C. J." Barry—all of whom are driven by the Dishaw family trait (or, I daresay, obsession) of creativity, whether in ink, on canvas, or in the recording studio. Thank you all for continually inspiring me.

About the Author

*U*nder the name of Cheri Revai (aka "the Ghost Author"), Cheri Farnsworth has written the best-selling, three-book *Haunted Northern New York* series, as well as *Haunted Connecticut, Haunted Massachusetts, Haunted New York,* and *Haunted New York City.* She is a North Country native, mother of four, secretary, parahistorian, and author with a penchant for research and history who lives in Northern New York with her husband and daughters. She has been extensively interviewed by the media—print, radio, and television—for her expertise in the field.

You may write to the author at Cheri Revai, P.O. Box 295, Massena, NY 13662 or email her at hauntedny@yahoo.com. Her website is www.theghostauthor.com.